Lincolnites and Rebels

LINCOLNITES AND REBELS

A Divided Town in the American Civil War

ROBERT TRACY McKENZIE

OXFORD
UNIVERSITY PRESS

2006

OXFORD
UNIVERSITY PRESS

Oxford University Press, Inc., publishes works that further
Oxford University's objective of excellence
in research, scholarship, and education.

Oxford   New York
Auckland   Cape Town   Dar es Salaam   Hong Kong   Karachi
Kuala Lumpur   Madrid   Melbourne   Mexico City   Nairobi
New Delhi   Shanghai   Taipei   Toronto

With offices in
Argentina   Austria   Brazil   Chile   Czech Republic   France   Greece
Guatemala   Hungary   Italy   Japan   Poland   Portugal   Singapore
South Korea   Switzerland   Thailand   Turkey   Ukraine   Vietnam

Copyright © 2006 by Oxford University Press, Inc.

Published by Oxford University Press, Inc.
198 Madison Avenue, New York, New York 10016

Oxford is a registered trademark of Oxford University Press

ISBN-13 978-0-19-518294-1
ISBN 0-19-518294-4

Printed in the United States of America

In honor of my parents,
EDWIN AND MARGARET MCKENZIE

ACKNOWLEDGMENTS

OF THE MAKING OF BOOKS "there is no end," the author of *Ecclesiastes* observed thousands of years ago. I used to think he was writing prophetically about the American Civil War in general—Americans have churned out nearly a book or pamphlet a day on the subject since Lee surrendered to Grant—but after spending more years on this project than I had ever anticipated, I began to fear that the ancient sage had *Lincolnites and Rebels* specifically in mind. Suffice it to say that I have been looking forward to writing these acknowledgments for a long time. Countless individuals have assisted me along the way, and I am grateful, finally, to be able to thank them in print.

At the earliest stages of my research, I benefited enormously from financial support from the University of Washington Graduate School Research Fund and from a pair of grants from the U.W. Department of History's Howard and Frances Keller Fund, the latter named in honor of two gracious supporters of the university whom I am privileged to call friends. While such financial assistance made research at distant repositories possible, the assistance of countless librarians and archivists made such research profitable. In addition to the staffs at the National Archives and Library of Congress, I would like to thank in particular Nick Wyman and Bill Eigelsbach of the University of Tennessee Special Collections Library, Steve Cotham and Sally Polhemus of the McClung Historical Collection of the Knox County Public Library, and Marilyn Bell and Vince McGrath of the Tennessee State Library and Archives. Here in Seattle, the staff in the Interlibrary Borrowing Office of the University of Washington, Cynthia Blanding in particular, greatly reduced the difficulty of studying southern history from the Pacific Northwest.

Once I began to put thoughts on paper, numerous scholars generously shared their time and expertise to help me in sharpening my argument. Stephen Ash, Jonathan Atkins, Paul Bergeron, Daniel Crofts, Durwood Dunn, Thomas Dyer, Todd Groce, John Inscoe, Richard Johnson, Gordon McKinney, Thomas Pressly, and Bill Rorabaugh all read conference papers or drafts of chapters and offered constructive and encouraging feedback. At a crucial stage, Susan Ferber of Oxford University Press showed an encouraging interest in the story I wanted to tell, and the quality of the final product owes much to her input, to the careful editing of production editor Stacey Hamilton, and to the helpful critiques of two anonymous referees.

My greatest debts, though, are personal rather than professional. My wife, Robyn—my best friend and companion these past twenty years—has been unfailingly encouraging and steadfast. My children—Callie, Margaret, and Robert—have had to listen to their dad talk way too much about the Civil War around the dinner table, but they have endured it graciously, and each day they warm my heart and make me smile. Robyn's parents, Hunter and Brenda Searcy, have helped to lighten my load in countless ways. And although we are separated by far too many miles, my own mother and father, Edwin and Margaret McKenzie, will always be a vital part of anything I accomplish. No son ever had more supportive parents; what a joy it is to dedicate this book to them.

CONTENTS

Lincolnites and Rebels

INTRODUCTION

I WAS BORN AND RAISED in Athens, Tennessee, a quiet southern town of some ten to twelve thousand inhabitants. Like most schoolboys in "the Friendly City"—as the chamber of commerce styled the small, traditionally segregated community—I was enthralled with the American Civil War from an early age. The Halloween that I was eight, my grandmother dyed my old Sunday suit gray, and I went trick-or-treating as a Confederate officer. I wore a yellow sash and a plumed hat, carried a plastic sword, and was the envy of the entire third grade. I wore my Confederate "uniform" as long as it would fit and then carefully preserved it in my closet. (I have since passed it on to my son.) The uniform was great for backyard play, as I repeatedly defended the sacred soil of my homeland from the dastardly feet of imaginary Yankee invaders. It also came in quite handy when my older sister had the audacity to bring home a Yankee invader of a different sort, a boyfriend from New York State. As my future brother-in-law pulled up the driveway to meet us for the first time, I was waiting in the front yard to "welcome" him, wearing my uniform, plastic sword drawn and at the ready. Neither of us has forgotten that first encounter.

My desire for a Civil War uniform that Halloween was unexceptional. A fascination with the "War between the States" was widespread among my playmates and still common among white southerners of all ages as I was growing up during the 1960s. The impact of the war somehow still seemed palpable, which meant that "history" was not just "something unpleasant that happens to other people," to borrow a phrase from Arnold Toynbee.[1] We were viscerally connected to and shaped by the past—as we remembered it.

3

My determination to dye the uniform gray—rather than blue—was also understandable for that time and place, yet it deserves more comment. To begin with, it was an unthinking decision. As best I can recall, it never entered my mind that the color could be otherwise. I was "southern," and even an eight-year-old boy knew that southerners wore gray between 1861 and 1865. Like most unthinking decisions, though, mine was also ignorant. I grew up in *East* Tennessee. When Middle and West Tennesseans voted overwhelmingly in favor of separation after the attack on Fort Sumter, East Tennesseans opposed secession by more than two to one. Nor did their opposition wilt thereafter, for the region stubbornly persisted as an island of Unionism within the Confederacy for the next four years. In much of the area the pro-Confederate minority was quite large, however, and East Tennesseans manifested divided loyalties to an extent rarely equaled elsewhere, North or South.

I remained largely unaware of this more complicated past throughout my youth, a fact that now—as a historian—I find embarrassing but not remarkable. The late David Potter, an eminent American historian and a Georgian by birth, once remarked that the South was a land that remembered the past "very vividly [but] somewhat inaccurately, because the present had nothing exciting to offer, and accuracy about either the past or the present was psychologically not very rewarding."[2] Potter penned those words the year I donned my Confederate uniform, and although he was writing about an earlier period (the 1910s and 1920s), I suspect that his description still applied. The adults I knew while I was growing up varied in their political philosophies and racial attitudes, but all associated the North with a sort of self-righteous Pharisaism, and they particularly resented what they perceived as a collective effort to make the South a scapegoat for a national race problem. This mind-set of resentment promoted southern solidarity, and it left little room in the region's history for whites who had apparently sided with the North during the "War between the States." In my hometown at least (which was itself badly divided during the Civil War), there was simply no room for a more complex past.

Unfortunately, there was nothing in the local library to complicate my understanding, though not because the relevant books had been purged from the shelves. I did not know it then, but for more than a century southern Appalachia had been marginalized, if not completely ignored, in the grand narrative histories of the South during the Civil War. The pattern actually dates back to the war itself. Historian Mark Neely has characterized East Tennessee as the "Confederacy's madman in the attic," the embarrassing secret that the family hides from the prying eyes of the neighborhood. It was the location for the largest civilian uprising of the entire war, and preserving order in the region ultimately required some ten thousand Confederate troops. Even so, Confederate president Jefferson Davis never once mentioned the area in his messages to the Confederate Congress, and for much of the war he and other high-ranking officials in Richmond seemed to pretend that East Tennessee did not exist.[3]

Modern-day historians have largely followed suit. Although a handful of scholars have begun to pay serious attention to the Civil War in southern Appalachia, the region still commands little more than a footnote in most general histories of the Confederacy.[4] To cite a few examples, the volume on the Confederacy in the New American Nation series devotes but two sentences to East Tennessee; a recent survey of Confederate politics allocates the same number; a major study of "the failure of Confederate nationalism" allots three sentences; a new investigation of "anti-Confederate Southerners" devotes all of two paragraphs.[5] Why studies of the Civil War have paid so little attention to the region can only be guessed. The answer may lie partly in scholars' long-standing fascination with the Black Belt and their corresponding disinterest in the Appalachian South. I suspect that there is more to it than that, however. My sense is that historians just don't know what to do with this peripheral, perverse region. The cultural bonds that scholars have cited to explain southern white unity at the outset of the Civil War—commitment to slavery and white supremacy, evangelical religion, and republican political values, to name three of the most prominent—all characterized East Tennessee, but there they did not lead reliably to support for the Confederacy. On the other hand, those factors historians have typically mentioned in explaining the onset of dissent within the Confederacy—including a commitment to state rights, war weariness stemming from economic hardship, and the resentment of conscription, taxation, and impressment—were all lacking when East Tennesseans first manifested a staunch opposition to the Confederacy. In short, the area is a maddening riddle. It has a way of frustrating the tidy generalizations we would like to make about the Civil War South, and most scholars—like Jefferson Davis before them—refer to it as little as possible.

Lincolnites and Rebels goes right into the heart of this contrary region, focusing on the Civil War in Knoxville, Tennessee. By northern standards Knoxville was barely a decent-sized village, but with a population in 1860 of roughly forty-four hundred (almost a tenth of whom were slaves), it was actually the largest town within a radius of 150 miles and the chief commercial hub of a vast area encompassing portions of northeastern Tennessee, western North Carolina, northern Georgia, and southwestern Virginia. I vividly recall the moment that I first became really intrigued by Knoxville's Civil War. Although I had grown up only an hour's drive from Knoxville, my "epiphany" came nearly two decades later and 2,500 miles away, years after I had left the South for the Pacific Northwest. As I was perusing a book by a twentieth-century Knoxville surgeon and Civil War buff, I came across a pencil sketch of the town's main business street not long after the fall of Fort Sumter.[6] The Knoxville resident who drew the sketch from memory was not particularly skilled, but the scene that he depicted (and which I later found corroborated in numerous contemporary sources) has captivated my imagination ever since. The drawing shows a large gathering at the foot of a U.S. flag on the near end of the street. Except for a few bystanders on the fringe of the crowd, most appear to be listening intently to a gesticulating orator (who I now suspect was supposed to be Andrew Johnson, then U.S. senator from Tennessee). At the far end of the street is another throng of men at the foot of a Confederate flag. Although the detail is fuzzy, they appear to be watching a sort of military parade headed straight for the other public meeting a block away.

One small-town street, simultaneous Union and Confederate rallies. I couldn't forget this image, nor could I shake the questions that it raised. Historians often use pictures to illustrate their books. I began this book because I wanted to understand a picture. Not knowing what I would find, as I delved into the community's past I became increasingly fascinated by the extraordinary story that unfolded there. Four factors particularly intrigued me. To begin with, as the drawing suggested, Knoxville was a *divided* town. Although the surrounding countryside was predominantly Unionist, Knoxville itself was split down the middle by the momentous issues rending North and South. When the town's voters cast their ballots on the question of secession—roughly a month after the street scene depicted in the sketch—49 percent supported the drastic step and 51 percent opposed it. What followed was a conflict among neighbors—a civil war within the Civil War.

Knoxville was also a continuously *occupied* town. After Tennessee seceded, officials in both Washington and Richmond immediately recognized Knoxville's strategic significance. It not only was the commercial center of one of the leading food-producing regions in the South but also sat astride the main railroad line linking the eastern and western theaters of the war, and was surrounded by a population of Unionists who constituted a potential "fifth column" within the heart of the Confederacy. No wonder that nearly forty thousand soldiers fought over the town in the fall of 1863, culminating in the bloody but little-studied Battle of Fort Sanders, or that the townspeople endured perpetual military occupation, hosting Confederate troops during the first half of the conflict and Union forces throughout the remainder. This constant military presence, perhaps more than any other factor, shaped the contours of the local conflict that occurred there. Without it, the town might have experienced the guerrilla violence that often scarred the more remote recesses of upper East Tennessee, a land of hills and hollows rarely penetrated by troops of either army. But there were no grizzled mountaineers with long rifles in Knoxville's civil war, no tyrannical Home Guards terrorizing barefoot women and children. Instead, its chief characters were ordinary townspeople—doctors, lawyers, shopkeepers, clerks, and their families.

Surprisingly, little Knoxville also became a *famous* town, especially in the wartime North. In large part because of the active labors of Knoxville refugees, who fled or were banished northward during the period of Confederate ascendancy, this bitterly divided community eventually became synonymous in the northern mind with southern Unionism. When Union General Ambrose Burnside and the Army of the Ohio occupied the town in the summer of 1863, northern newspapers rejoiced in the liberation of the "downtrodden" residents of the "renowned Union stronghold" and lauded their matchless courage and fidelity. When Burnside subsequently repulsed an effort by Confederate General James Longstreet to reclaim the town, Abraham Lincoln issued a proclamation calling for a national day of thanksgiving, one of only a handful of such decrees that he made during the war's four long years.[7]

Finally, Civil War Knoxville was a *historically persistent* town, in that countless traces of the community's civil war still survive, preserved in an extraordinarily rich historical record. There were always at least one and sometimes two functioning newspapers in Knoxville during the war. In keeping with the customs of antebellum journalism, they were openly (and often viciously) partisan. Americans in the mid–nineteenth century did not expect objective journalism from their newspaper of choice. They subscribed to a paper for the same reason that they hired lawyers—to abuse the other side—and Knoxville readers generally got their money's worth. Given the small size of the town, a remarkable wealth of other kinds of traditional evidence was also left behind: extensive correspondence, several personal diaries, and even four book-length memoirs. In them I read of a Confederate mother who had just lost her youngest child on a battlefield in Virginia, of a physician who attributed the outbreak of war to God's judgment against widespread violation of the Sabbath, and of a court clerk who blamed not God but the politicians, North and South. In them I happened upon a recent college graduate arrested for reading "incendiary" abolitionist literature, a secessionist postmaster who tried to impersonate Andrew Johnson, a Swiss family that hid foodstuffs from both armies, a teenage girl who boasted of her Confederate boyfriends, and a young Union soldier incensed by the treatment of his aged parents.

As is typically true of historical evidence, many of these sources are frustratingly incomplete, offering tantalizing clues while raising as many questions as they answer. Nearly a dozen provide unusually detailed insights, however. On the Confederate side, for example, I have come to know remarkable individuals such as J. G. M. Ramsey and Ellen House. James Gettys McGready Ramsey was a 110-pound renaissance man, a physician, slaveholding farmer, banker, railroad speculator, and historian whose slight frame housed a zealous commitment to the South and to southern independence. Long before the election of Abraham Lincoln, the elderly Ramsey was telling correspondents that the days of the Union were numbered; the North and South must eventually separate because they were inhabited by two distinct peoples. The typical southerner was characterized by "high-souled honor" and a "strict regard to truth," Ramsey concluded, whereas these traits were "wanting in the Yankee and [made] him offensive and hateful to a Southern freeman." Ellen House would have agreed. This nineteen-year-old daughter of a Knoxville bookkeeper began a diary when the Army of the Ohio marched into town, and from the first page she revealed herself to be a "very violent rebel." House reveled in displaying her contempt for Union soldiers and boasted of countless personal acts of petty defiance, from visiting Confederate prisoners in local hospitals, to insulting the wives of Union officers, to stepping off of the sidewalk into the street to avoid walking underneath a U.S. flag. Her diary does not disclose why she so passionately sided with the Confederacy, only the depth of that passion. "I believe I would kill a Yankee and not a muscle quiver," the teenager noted in early 1864. "Oh! The intensity with which I hate them."[8]

On the Unionist side were individuals such as Horace Maynard, a Massachusetts-born lawyer who campaigned against secession and then represented East Tennessee in the *United States* Congress during the first two years of the war, as well as the Reverend Thomas Humes, an Episcopal minister who refused to pray for Jefferson Davis and was ultimately driven from his pulpit. Towering above them all, however, was William G. "Parson" Brownlow. Few Americans are familiar with his name these days, but in the middle decades of the nineteenth century the "Fighting Parson" was a figure first of regional and then of national distinction, his reputation based on equal parts fame and notoriety. Before the Civil War he was best known within southern Appalachia as a combative Methodist minister and an outspoken newspaper editor with a gift for "vituperation," a nineteenth-century euphemism for blistering personal attacks on religious and political opponents. During the Civil War he became a national celebrity when he emerged as one of the most famous of all southern Unionists, condemning secession as a "diabolical revolution" and "vile heresy" until he was finally arrested and banished to the North.[9]

Most Knoxville residents failed to leave such paper trails, however, and those who did came disproportionately from middle- and upper-class households, hindering efforts to recover the sympathies and experiences of men and women, both free and enslaved, who earned their livings by the sweat of their brows. To a considerable extent this problem is unavoidable, and the following narrative necessarily gives greater voice to the town's more educated and influential white inhabitants. And yet a variety of military and civil records survive that offer clues concerning the sympathies and experiences of the town's less articulate residents. Confederate and Union court records list individuals charged with "treason."

Regimental rosters, although short on biographical information, help to identify Knoxville men who served in either army. The staff of the Union provost marshal general for East Tennessee—headquartered in Knoxville for the last twenty months of the war—kept detailed registers of local civilians filing claims against the U.S. government for food and forage confiscated by Federal soldiers, and the postwar records of a variety of claims commissions yield helpful information as well. Cumulatively, these sources provide information concerning the individual loyalties of 483 Knoxville adults residing in some 323 households, or just over one out of every two white households in town on the eve of the war.[10] In proportional terms, the population of no other town during the Civil War has been documented more extensively.

To make maximum use of these records requires taking a running start at the events of 1861–65; it is impossible to understand the dynamic unleashed by the war without first getting to know the community in peacetime. Consequently, chapter 1 provides an overview of Knoxville's settlement and a snapshot of the town around midcentury, while chapters 2 and 3 chronicle the gradual erosion of community consensus during the presidential election of 1860 and the secession crisis, respectively. The next two chapters carry the narrative through the twenty-seven months during which Knoxville was under Confederate occupation. Chapter 4 documents the increasing repression that had come to characterize Confederate policy by the winter of 1862, and chapter 5 explores the resulting patterns of resistance and accommodation among Knoxville Unionists, juxtaposing their behavior with the glowing portrayal of Knoxville's loyalists advanced by Parson Brownlow, by this time the Confederacy's most famous exile and a wildly popular speaker across the North. The book's final three chapters cover the period from the Federal army's "liberation" of Knoxville in September 1863 through the end of the war and several months beyond. Chapter 6 focuses on the arrival of the Union Army of the Ohio, the subsequent siege of Knoxville, and the climactic Battle of Fort Sanders. Chapter 7 surveys the range of responses among Confederate civilians to Union military occupation and traces the growing schism among local Unionists over the issue of emancipation. Chapter 8 concludes by examining the war's culmination and the troubled "peace" that followed, paying special attention to divisions among Unionists concerning the proper policy toward their disloyal neighbors.

Throughout *Lincolnites and Rebels* I have asked many of the questions that historians now commonly ask about Civil War communities: What did the war reveal about the values of those who lived there? How did the conflict affect the lives of the townspeople? What impact did it have on patterns of status and influence in the community? How did racial attitudes change, if at all? Yet because I have sensed a rare opportunity to explore the nature of loyalty in the presence of the enemy, I have given extra weight to those questions that cut to the heart of Knoxville's internal divisions. Along what lines did the town's residents divide in the first place? How did Unionists define the minimum obligations of authentic loyalty when the town was under Confederate occupation? How did Confederates answer the same question after the Union army had arrived? At bottom, how did patterns of allegiance inform the daily routine of a small town caught in the upheaval of an internal civil war? In the pages that follow I try to breathe life into that two-dimensional pencil sketch.

CHAPTER ONE

The "Metropolis" of East Tennessee

> We are fast approaching that bright destiny which has heretofore lived only
> in the vision of an inflated imagination. May we not soon expect to realize the
> fact that ours is the great central metropolis of this once remote and mountain
> bound region known as the "Switzerland of America."
> —*Knoxville Whig*, 17 April 1858

I T WAS FEBRUARY 1849 when William Brownlow, the editor of the *Jonesborough Whig and Independent Journal*, informed his readers that he planned to leave the tiny village that had been his home for the past nine years. Curiously—given the editor's healthy ego—he buried the announcement on the back page, where it competed for attention with advertisements for "Wright's Vegetable Pills" (unusually effective against "bilious disorders"), "House's Indian Tonic," and *The Goldometer* or *Gold Seeker's Guide*," a miraculous invention now available for the "remarkably low price of THREE DOLLARS."[1] Amid such marvels the editor gave notice that he would soon begin publication in Knoxville, a larger town some ninety miles to the southwest. He offered but the briefest of explanations: Knoxville offered superior mail facilities for distributing his paper, the move "might advance his own pecuniary interests," and he was confident that he could serve his party more effectively there.[2]

The final factor was likely paramount. In 1849 most East Tennesseans, like most Americans generally, were zealously committed to either the Democratic or the Whig Party. Voter turnout was enormous by today's standards—typically between 80 and 90 percent—and "independent" voters were almost nonexistent. Employing a tried-and-true strategy, politicians warned the citizenry that their freedom was in jeopardy and pointed to the other party as the greatest source of danger. Whigs and Democrats regularly damned one another as "potential conspirators" who would subvert the interests of the masses to serve their own agendas. In the 1830s and 1840s their competing "crusades for liberty" had centered on issues such as banking and tariffs and railroads, but since the war with Mexico the focus had begun to shift toward the issues of slavery and territorial expansion. Given all that was ostensibly at stake during the Second Party System, as it is called, it is not surprising that popular involvement was extensive, nor that party loyalty was pronounced and partisan rhetoric overheated.[3]

This last was where men like William Brownlow came in. Democrats and Whigs both relied on partisan newspapers to catechize the faithful, and as a polemicist the Jonesborough journalist was unsurpassed. The forty-four-year-old editor had spent most of his adult life embroiled in controversy; it was his "natural element," a political ally recalled. Along the way he had developed, by his own admission, a unique talent for "piling up epithets." He had first honed this skill in the pulpit. Throughout his twenties Brownlow preached across the southern highlands as a Methodist circuit rider, waging war against Baptists and Presbyterians all the while.[4] Although he ridiculed their doctrines, he focused more on the character of his rivals than on the fine points of their theology. His strategy for dealing with an opponent was simple and consistent: "Lather him with aqua fortis [nitric acid] and shave him with a handsaw." Thus he blistered a Presbyterian enemy as "low-bred, false-hearted, adulterous, and unprincipled." A Baptist minister he excoriated as "destitute of feeling . . . blind to the beauties of religion . . . hackneyed in crime, and . . . lost to all sense of honor and shame." A third antagonist he lambasted, more creatively, as "an inflated *gasometer* whose brain I believe to be a mass of living, creeping, crawling, writhing, twisting, turning, loathsome vermin." Although such a colorful vocabulary soon earned him the title of the "Fighting Parson," Brownlow always insisted that he fought only in self-defense, responding to assaults from the "obdurate sinners and unprincipled scoundrels" who surrounded him. He took solace in the cautioning words of Jesus, "Woe to you when all men think well of you," and he averred bluntly that he hoped "always . . . to make a certain class of human beings hate me."[5]

Brownlow's shift from the ministry to journalism in the late 1830s served to further this ambition. Tired of circuit riding and ready to settle down and marry, he dabbled briefly in iron manufacturing and then switched to the newspaper business. Although he would answer to the title of "Parson" Brownlow for the rest of his life, he now redirected his scorching prose away from Presbyterians and Baptists and began to specialize in assaults on Democrats. When, for example, voters in nearby Greene County first elected future president Andrew Johnson to the House of Representatives, the Whig editor flew into a rage: "God of compassion! What could the people have been thinking of when they elected this huge mass of corruption to Congress!—this beast in human form, whose violence and rule of passion, vicious life and unprovided death, alone qualify him to serve as one of the body guards of Belzebub! [*sic*]" He similarly blasted Andrew Jackson—another Tennessee Democrat—in the former president's obituary, of all places: "After a life of eighty long years, spent in the indulgence of the most bitter and vindictive passions, which disgrace human nature, and distract the human mind, the existence of Andrew Jackson terminated, at his residence near Nashville, on Sabbath the 8th inst., at 6 o'clock P.M.," Brownlow informed his readers. "He is 'gone to a land of deepest shades,'" the editor proceeded. "He has passed out of our hands, into the hands of a just God, who will deal with him and by him 'according to his works.' We would not, if even we could, turn aside the veil of the future, to show his deluded followers, and blind admirers, what awaits him!"[6]

If such language was in bad taste, it was also popular among his Whig readers. The editor dipped his pen in gall not to persuade the undecided but to encourage the faithful—common folk like E. G. Caren, who thanked Brownlow for having "constantly, perseveringly and boldly fought both the Devil & Democracy [i.e., the Democratic Party] for lo these many years," or James Clift, who praised him for meting out justice "to the low flung and Hell deserving" Democrats. Not everyone had such a high opinion of the Parson's prose, of course, and those who were on the receiving end of the editor's invective sometimes answered him with more than words. Antebellum newspapermen often came to blows with those whom they assailed in print, and Brownlow arguably got off lightly, all things considered. In 1840 he was shot in the leg during a brawl with a rival editor; in 1842 he was attacked and beaten outside a Methodist camp meeting; and in 1849, only days before he was scheduled to leave Jonesborough for Knoxville, he was clubbed over the head from behind by an unknown assailant, presumably a low-flung and hell-deserving Democrat. The attack cracked his skull, left him bedridden for two weeks, and temporarily delayed his departure for the town he liked to call the "metropolis of East Tennessee."[7]

IN 1849 PROBABLY FEWER than 2,000 souls inhabited that "metropolis." According to the federal census taken the year after Brownlow's arrival, the town's population in 1850 consisted of 1,478 whites, 136 "free colored" residents, and 462 slaves, although many of the latter actually may have lived and worked outside of town. Despite its small size the community was still the largest population center in East Tennessee—an area encompassing some thirteen thousand square miles—a fact that speaks volumes concerning the overwhelmingly rural nature of the region.[8] But there was more to Knoxville's claim to regional prominence than mere size. Knoxville residents were understandably proud of their past: the town was one of the oldest in the trans-Appalachian South, and up to the War of 1812 at least, it had been an important seat of government. Settlers from Virginia and the Carolinas had begun to migrate into the vicinity toward the end of the American Revolution, and in 1786 a veteran named James White had staked out the future site of the town, laying claim to a large tract of land on a ridge overlooking the north bank of the Tennessee River (then called the Holston) and framed by two parallel creeks emptying into it.[9] There, according to tradition, he built his cabin and planted a turnip patch on the future site of the First

Presbyterian Church of Knoxville. Within five years some forty houses dotted the hillside, and the settlement, which according to an early history "possessed an air of unusual refinement," was chosen as the state's first capital when Tennessee was admitted to the Union in 1796.[10]

The honor was only temporary, however, for in 1812 the state legislature voted to leave Knoxville in favor of the Middle Tennessee boomtown of Nashville. Mirroring the trend in the state's population, the legislators abandoned East Tennessee and headed west, leaving in their wake an abundance of hurt pride and the beginnings of a regional inferiority complex. In hindsight, East Tennesseans would remember the removal of the capital as a watershed event that symbolized their eclipse in state politics. Although they were inclined to exaggerate the extent of their fall from power, a recurring theme in their political rhetoric thereafter portrayed the section as an outlying "province," as one congressman from the region put it. Once, they had lived at the center of political power in the state. Now they feared becoming a political backwater, "passed over and left behind" with nothing to look forward to but demeaning domination by the rest of the state.[11]

In truth, East Tennessee's declining political influence accurately reflected the area's dwindling share of the state's population and wealth. In 1795, five-sixths of the state's non-Indian population had resided in East Tennessee. Within twenty-five years the proportion had dropped below one-third; after another generation it was barely one-quarter. The reason was quite simple: economic opportunities were dramatically greater in the western two-thirds of the state. Middle Tennessee, in particular its lush Central Basin, was characterized by slightly rolling terrain, extremely fertile soil, and a navigable river (the Cumberland) that offered relatively cheap transportation to markets at Cincinnati, St. Louis, Memphis, and New Orleans. By the 1830s the area was developing into one of the leading food-producing regions in the country, widely famous for its superior horses, sheep, and mules. West Tennessee, in contrast, closely resembled northern Mississippi in landscape and environment, and featured a flat, well-watered plain that sloped gently toward the alluvial lands along the Mississippi River. The soil and climate were ideal for the cultivation of cotton, and after the area was opened to white settlement during the 1820s, large plantations rapidly filled the countryside and Memphis quickly emerged as the leading internal cotton market in the entire South.[12]

Conditions in East Tennessee differed greatly. Knoxville lies almost exactly in the center of the Valley of East Tennessee, part of the Great Appalachian Valley that runs northeast to southwest all the way from western Pennsylvania to northern Alabama. In East Tennessee this valley is framed on the southeast by the Smoky Mountains—with an average elevation of around five thousand feet—and on the northwest by the Cumberland Plateau, which rises abruptly, almost resembling a cliff on its eastern border, to a height of between two thousand and twenty-five hundred feet. Despite its name, the area lying between the

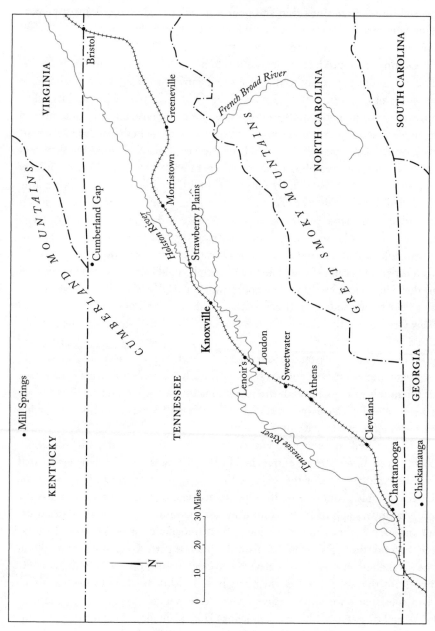

East Tennessee in 1860.

KENTUCKY

VIRGINIA

• Mill Springs

• Cumberland Gap

CUMBERLAND MOUNTAINS

TENNESSEE

Bristol

Greeneville

Morristown

Holston River

Strawberry Plains

French Broad River

GREAT SMOKY MOUNTAINS

NORTH CAROLINA

Knoxville

Lenoir's

Loudon

Sweetwater

Athens

Tennessee River

Cleveland

Chattanooga

Chickamauga

GEORGIA

SOUTH CAROLINA

—N—

0   10   20   30 Miles

two mountain ranges consists of not a single, broad valley but a succession of parallel, narrow valleys separated by heavily wooded mountain ridges. Although the soil on the ridges was thin and poor, the valley lands, which constitute perhaps four-fifths of the region as a whole, were generally quite fertile and well suited to produce corn, wheat, hay, cattle, and hogs.[13]

Getting these products to market could be prohibitively expensive, however. The mountains to the east and west formed barriers to profitable overland trade that were nearly, if not totally, impenetrable. The Tennessee River and its tributaries offered a potential north-south avenue for commerce, but they were marred by numerous obstructions and were excessively shallow in dry weather. At best, they were reliably navigable for half of the year, and then only for rafts and keelboats, or light steamboats that could operate in water sometimes as shallow as eighteen inches. Even under optimum conditions, the river system primarily facilitated trade *within* East Tennessee, thanks to a serious of treacherous shoals in northern Alabama, not far below Chattanooga. All this meant that East Tennessee farmers who wished to produce for export had severely limited options. They could ship their produce to New Orleans by carrying it overland across the Cumberland Plateau to Nashville, from which it could be transported by riverboat to the Gulf. More cheaply, they could wait for a "tide" (unusually high water) and float their goods by raft across the shoals and then onward all the way to New Orleans, via the Tennessee, the Ohio, and the Mississippi, after which they could walk home with their earnings. Probably most commonly they shipped their goods overland to coastal markets such as Charleston or Savannah, sometimes by wagon but as often as not "on the hoof." Each November, drovers herded tens of thousands of hogs through the mountains by way of the French Broad River gorge, following that river on to Asheville, North Carolina, and points farther east at the breakneck pace of eight miles a day.[14]

Two related consequences ensued from the region's comparative isolation. First, slavery never became entrenched in East Tennessee to the same extent that characterized the rest of the state or the South as a whole. On the eve of the Civil War only about one-tenth of white households owned slaves, whereas the proportion was approximately one-third for the future Confederate states overall and even higher still for the lower South, including parts of West Tennessee. Second, the region would remain the poorest part of Tennessee throughout the antebellum era. As late as 1860 the average wealth per free family was only two-fifths that for the rest of the state. In sum, while the land yielded an abundant subsistence for white yeomen, the terrain tended to prevent a handsome profit and discouraged the development of large plantations. Capturing this combination of opportunity and limitation, a census official later in the century would christen the region the "poor man's rich land."[15]

East Tennesseans responded to their relative poverty in a variety of overlapping and sometimes contradictory ways. Many pulled up stakes and sought better opportunities farther west. In 1829 David Deaderick, a future Knoxville resident, complained in his diary about the widespread "disposition to remove to the fertile countries West and North of us," where "the enterprise, prospect of wealth, and comparative ease of living in those countries, seem inviting to us of poor East Tennessee." Concerning the same period, Knoxville's J. G. M. Ramsey recalled that "the non-remunerative character of East Tennessee farming" was prompting "a constant emigration of the industrious and enterprising . . . to sections of the country having greater commercial facilities."[16]

Those who stayed behind often claimed that the natural environment brought other benefits that made up for their lack of wealth. Boosters regularly described their home land as the "Switzerland of America," stressing the healthfulness of the climate and the rugged beauty of the landscape. "There is probably no healthier climate in the world than this," Knoxville attorney Horace Maynard boasted to his father in Massachusetts. It was subject to no extremes, and there was plenty of running water and "pure mountain air." Similarly, an East Tennessee congressman declared to a northern audience that the southern Switzerland was "unsurpassed for loveliness and beauty on the American continent," a land "that God made for man to love and enjoy." Others found moral benefits in the region's comparative isolation. A Knoxville physician concluded that the area had been spared much of "the vices & the crimes of the world," in part because the love of luxury, a constant temptation in more economically developed areas, had had no chance to take root there. Another local champion agreed, noting that "where there are temptations and opportunity to get wealth men are less apt to be virtuous and happy."[17]

Even so, by the early 1830s a majority of East Tennesseans clearly favored a variety of transportation improvements aimed at reducing the section's isolation. In the best-case scenario, a viable transportation network would increase commercial opportunities, narrow the wealth gap between East Tennessee and the rest of the state, reduce migration from the region, and halt the section's political decline. Although there was considerable support for projects that would improve river navigation, the key to realizing this grand vision was extensive railroad construction, and that, all agreed, would be impossible without state subsidies. There was the rub. To increase the section's political influence, East Tennesseans needed state funds; to procure the funds, they needed political influence. It was not readily forthcoming. As if to tease them, the state General Assembly passed a measure in 1838 allocating up to $4 million for the promotion of internal improvements, but it repealed the act only two years later, thanks largely to the unified action of Middle Tennessee legislators.[18]

The repeal of the 1838 internal improvements act generated enormous resentment in much of East Tennessee, and more than any other political event prior to the secession crisis, it prompted East Tennesseans to question their attachment to the rest of the state. Three times between 1840 and 1843, East Tennessee politicians introduced resolutions to the state legislature calling for independent statehood, and popular support for the idea appears to have been widespread east of the Cumberland Plateau. A delegate to an internal improvements convention held in Knoxville in December 1841 wrote to a correspondent in New York that the idea of separate statehood "is now popular in all parts of E Ten. While here I have not heard an individual opinion against it." William Brownlow certainly championed the prospect enthusiastically from his newspaper desk in Jonesborough. He denounced Nashville as the "*seat of Dictation*" and declared that "we have long enough been 'hewers of wood and drawers of water,' in the hands of Middle Tennesseans." Independent statehood would liberate those east of the Cumberland Plateau from subservience to the "lordly inhabitants" of "the Nashville Temple" and lead to a glorious economic future.[19]

Realistically, the proposal for independent statehood was doomed from the beginning. The idea came closest to securing the approval of the state legislature early in 1842, when both houses of the General Assembly actually passed different versions of an enabling bill but could not agree on how to reconcile the conflicting details. Even if the legislature had approved it, it still required the consent of the U.S. Congress, and northern congressmen undoubtedly would have opposed the creation of an additional slave state from an existing one. Even the staunchest supporters of statehood must have realized that their chances were slim, and one suspects that the movement represented part frustration, part protest, and part political posturing with an eye toward exacting future concessions. If the last, it may have had some effect, for the Assembly was noticeably more supportive of both river and railroad improvements by the late 1840s. In particular, a generous state appropriation in 1848 resurrected the hope of a rail connection between Knoxville and the lower South. Although no longer at the center of political power in the state, East Tennesseans once more became optimistic that their region would grow and flourish. Even though the "political sceptre [had] departed from Knoxville," as *Harper's New Monthly Magazine* observed a decade later, the town might yet serve as the "great centre of commerce, learning, and the arts" in an economically dynamic and prosperous region.[20]

THIS VISION WAS STILL more "bright destiny" than present reality when William Brownlow settled in Knoxville in 1849. In 1844 a British visitor had passed through the town and declared it "a poor neglected-looking place," despite "some tolerable dwelling-houses."[21] He would have been little more impressed five years later. Most of the town's two thousand inhabitants were scattered across an area resembling an irregular rectangle three-quarters of a mile by one-half mile. Most families had vegetable gardens, and many kept a cow and a few chickens. They built their stables and garden houses right on the street fronts, interspersed side by side with their residences, so that apart from a few square blocks constituting the "business district," the town had a decidedly rural

The "metropolis of East Tennessee" at the close of the 1850s.
Photograph courtesy of McClung Historical Collection, Knox County Public Library.

air. Only one street had been paved, and even Gay Street, where farmers from the countryside congregated to sell fresh produce from their wagons, was as yet a dirt thoroughfare. In one of the first issues of the *Knoxville Whig*, Knoxville's newest resident complained of the streets in "this otherwise comfortable and pleasant town." In the summer, except immediately after a heavy rain, they were so dusty that the merchants all closed their doors to protect their wares, and townspeople who ventured outdoors for a breath of "fresh air" returned to their homes "having the lungs loaded with fine particles of sand." During the winter, on the other hand, "these streets are so loaded with mud, manure and filth, that they are quite impassible on foot, except at a few crossings usually called '*shallow fords*.'"[22]

Nor was there any industry in the town to speak of. Apart from the Holston Manufacturing Company—which employed forty-five hands and boasted of being the largest producer of window glass in the South—there was not a single business in Knoxville with as many as ten employees. Most of the "industry" in town consisted of sawmills, tanneries, and the workshops of saddlers and boot and shoe makers—all small-scale establishments that typically employed a half dozen hands or fewer and yielded an annual product valued at $3,000 to $4,000, if that much. With few exceptions they catered to a farming clientele, underscoring Knoxville's ties with the agricultural economy of the surrounding countryside and its identity as a country town.[23]

And yet Knoxville was already the commercial hub of a region that included not only East Tennessee but also portions of western North Carolina, northern

Georgia, northern Alabama, and southwestern Virginia. It had long been a concentration point for the livestock trade with the Carolinas and Georgia. Furthermore, its advantageous position near the fork of the Holston and French Broad
rivers, enhanced by the institution during the 1830s of regular steamboat traffic
between Knoxville and northern Alabama, had made the town a natural entrepôt
for a small but significant trade in foodstuffs between the small farms of the East
Tennessee Valley and the plantations of the cotton frontier. Perhaps as many as
eighteen steamboats simultaneously worked the run between Decatur, Alabama,
and Knoxville, and warehouses dotted the riverbanks along Front Street as a testimony to the traffic. Two full blocks of Gay Street were similarly lined on either side with the stores of retail and wholesale merchants. Many of the retailers
were very small operators (often specializing in "spirituous and vinous liquors"),
but a handful of mercantile houses were already doing an extensive retail and
wholesale business. Chief among these was James Williams and Company, which
owned several of its own steamboats and specialized in the river trade, and the
firm of Cowan and Dickinson, which led all merchants with more than $54,000
in inventory expenses in 1850.[24]

In addition to the bustle of commercial activity, the town also offered some
evidence of future potential as a center of "learning and the arts." The town
boasted *four* newspapers—two Whig papers, a Democratic sheet, and a religious
weekly—suggesting an educated populace, or at the very least widespread literacy.
It was also home to both the Hampden-Sydney Academy (a sort of college pre-
paratory school) and East Tennessee College (the future University of Tennessee). In 1850 the latter boasted five faculty members, seventy students (all male),
a library of nearly three thousand volumes, and an endowment of $2,400. For
the young ladies of the town there was the East Tennessee Female Institute,
which had been chartered in 1846 and graduated its first class in 1850, when it
conferred on four Knoxville belles the degree of "Mistress of Polite Literature."
The Female Institute apparently had difficulty attracting students from elsewhere
in East Tennessee because of "the supposed extravagance of dress . . . to which
they are subjected in Knoxville." In 1849 the board of trustees addressed this
insidious rumor head-on, assuring the parents of prospective students from across
the region that "our citizens are perhaps less obnoxious to the charge of extravagance in dress or other unnecessary and imprudent expenditures than those of
any other town of its population in the state."[25]

Knoxville's population and economy both boomed during the next decade,
although not without interruption. A severe outbreak of cholera struck in the
summer of 1854, prompting a temporary exodus and ultimately claiming the lives
of one hundred townspeople. Three years later the effects of the panic of 1857
also touched the town, briefly retarding expansion. Such momentary pauses aside,
Knoxville's free population more than doubled during the 1850s, reaching the
neighborhood of four thousand by 1860, to which should be added nearly four

hundred slaves, down slightly from ten years earlier.[26] In every direction there were signs of vitality, prosperity, and civic improvement. The town's first bookstore opened for business in 1851. The following year the board of aldermen prohibited the emptying of slop buckets on the public streets, and by 1854 the town's principal business avenue, Gay Street, had been paved with cobblestones. That same year the Knoxville Market House was opened to accommodate trade from the countryside, meaning that farmers no longer had to sell their wares from the back of a wagon. Farm wives tended to dominate the stalls on the market's east side, selling butter, eggs, chickens, and fresh fruit in season. In the stalls on the opposite side—the "spitting side"—their husbands marketed corn, beans, cabbages, and potatoes by the lot to the town's boardinghouses and hotels. The following year the Knoxville Gas Light Company began to bring artificial illumination to both businesses and homes. Around the same time the Knoxville Manufacturing Company commenced production of steam engines and boilers, the first steam flouring mill was erected, and the firm of Shepard, Leeds and Hoyt began manufacturing railroad cars, car wheels, and agricultural implements. The town built a new jail in 1857—at a cost of $10,000 to the taxpayers—and in 1859 it organized volunteer fire companies and purchased from a Baltimore manufacturer its first hand-powered fire engines. As a final indication of the town's increased opulence, in 1860 the congregation of the Second Presbyterian Church dedicated its new meeting house. The structure, which cost an estimated $16,000 to build, measured sixty-two feet by forty-six feet and featured seventy-two mahogany-top pews with seat cushions, chandeliers, stained-glass windows, and gas lighting. Even an obviously envious Parson Brownlow could proclaim it "the finest church we have ever entered the walls of in this State."[27]

Fueling this undeniable vitality was the arrival of not one but two railroads during the decade. In the summer of 1855 the East Tennessee and Georgia Railroad was completed to Knoxville. The first train puffed into town on 23 June—having averaged fourteen miles an hour on its inaugural trek from northern Georgia. "A new era had arrived," according to the editor of the *Knoxville Register*, who along with a large crowd gathered to watch "the swift passenger train dart up to our very city." A generous state subsidy had facilitated construction, but so had the investments of numerous Knoxville citizens, whose names dominate a list of company stockholders from the early 1850s. Their money was well spent. When finished, the line stretched roughly one hundred miles to Dalton, Georgia, where it intersected with the Western and Atlantic Railroad, effectively connecting Knoxville with Atlanta, Charleston, Savannah, and Montgomery; the completion of a spur from Cleveland to Chattanooga three years later also allowed direct rail traffic with Nashville and Memphis.[28] On the very same day that the townspeople turned out to celebrate the completion of the East Tennessee and Georgia, railroad crews began laying track from Knoxville toward the Virginia state line. They were laboring to finish the last uncompleted stretch of the East Tennessee and Virginia Railroad, a line chartered in 1848 to run from Knoxville to Bristol, where it would in turn link with the Virginia and Tennessee Railroad, 130 miles to the northeast. When the East Tennessee and Virginia was completed in the spring of 1858, it connected Knoxville with Richmond, Washington, D.C., Philadelphia, and New York City. Travelers could now get from New York to Memphis in only three days and nine hours, but to do so they had to pass through the metropolis of East Tennessee. "We are fast approaching that bright destiny which has heretofore lived only in the vision of an inflated imagination," Brownlow rhapsodized. "May we not soon expect to realize the fact that ours is the great central metropolis of this once remote and mountain bound region known as the 'Switzerland of America.'"[29]

Brownlow overstated the case in predicting that Knoxville would one day be "the most important point on the continent of America," but he was on the mark in observing that the railroads "infuse[d] new life into every grade of business." Farmers in the surrounding countryside felt the impact first. Far more fully than the establishment of steamboat service, the advent of the railroads served to integrate much of the Valley of East Tennessee into broader regional and national markets. As late as 1850, corn sold in Knoxville at more than 40 percent below prices quoted in national market centers such as Charleston or Philadelphia. Prohibitive transportation costs discouraged the sale of East Tennessee corn in those and other distant markets, resulting in local surpluses and depressed prices. By the end of the 1850s, however, the price differential had decreased by nearly three-quarters, and the railroads were largely responsible. East Tennessee farmers also shifted heavily into the production of wheat to take advantage of the new commercial opportunities. The amount of wheat produced annually in East Tennessee tripled during the 1850s. Much of it was shipped south, but by 1858 East Tennessee wheat was also commanding a premium in the New York market. As a result of these trends the value of farmland in the area also rose considerably; in Knox County the average value per acre more than doubled.[30]

The agricultural boom in the countryside sparked a major expansion of the wholesale trade in Knoxville, intensifying the town's role as the commercial center of the region. Whereas in 1850 there had been only four wholesale firms in Knoxville, by 1860 there were fourteen, two of which—Cowan, McClung, and Company, and Cowan and Dickinson—had annual sales close to $200,000. In 1857 a New York credit-rating agency described the latter firm as "doing the largest business in E[ast] Tenn[essee]" and estimated that "if their bus[iness] was wound up to day, they could show a bal[ance] of over a ¼ of a million after paying all liabilities."[31] The retail trade also grew apace. A city directory from 1859 lists two businesses specializing in agricultural implements, one book and stationery store, four confectioners, a cigar and tobacco shop, twenty-one firms dealing in groceries, and another twelve stores specializing in dry goods. Small-scale industry (usually "manufacturing" in the literal sense of the word) had increased as well.

In the same year there were three boot and shoe makers, two cabinet manufac-
turers, two carriage makers, two furniture makers, three flour and grist mills, an
iron foundry, two machine shops, three stove makers, and an assortment of saddlers, tanners, and tinners. As testimony to the town's increasing commercial
sophistication, there were three tailors, three undertakers (two of whom also made
cabinets), a telegraph line, a stagecoach line, two druggists, a pair of insurance
agents, one restaurant, five "coffee houses," six hotels, two taverns, and a "bowl-
ing saloon." Finally, there were a whopping thirty attorneys, roughly one for every
twenty-two households in the community. By the end of the 1850s, Knoxville had
earned its title as East Tennessee's metropolis.[32]

With such dynamic growth came a variety of social strains, however. For one,
the arrival of the railroads resurrected age-old concerns about the implications
of economic development for the moral values of the community. Although a
railroad enthusiast from way back, Parson Brownlow complained in 1856 that
"railroading is not doing much for the morals of men." On a recent journey by
rail to Washington, D.C., he had been repulsed by the behavior of supposed
gentlemen who "swear profanely, smoke cigars and openly drink liquor upon
the cars." Because the trains also passed through town on Sundays, some of
Knoxville's Presbyterians feared that the railroads were working to undermine the
sanctity of the Sabbath. This was a touchy point, for the town council had traditionally looked askance on even the slightest hint of business activity on Sunday.
A municipal ordinance in effect since 1838 prohibited any grocery, confectionary,
or other place of business from opening on the Sabbath, and even steamboats
were required to obtain special permission to unload their cargoes on that day.
Other kinds of business were unwelcome on any day of the week, at least among
the "respectable" sort who attended one of the community's seven churches. Most
noticeable in this objectionable category were the town's twenty-six "liquor shops"
and seven "houses of ill fame."[33]

By facilitating rapid population growth, the advent of the railroads also contributed to a sizable increase in population turnover. Knoxville during the 1850s
was not a stable community. To be sure, what passed for "society" was impres-
sively stationary. A list of the wealthiest families in town would have overlapped
extensively with a list of the oldest, including a large number of Whites (descendants of the town's founder), McClungs (descendants of the man who had sur-
veyed and laid out the town), and Cowans (heirs of the town's first merchant),
not to mention Ramseys, Armstrongs, Parks, and Boyds, all of whom could trace
their roots to the earliest years of settlement. The longevity of these families
contrasted starkly with the swirl of in- and out-migration permeating the ranks
of the common folk "beneath" them. Of the free adult males living in Knoxville
in 1850, only 29 percent remained in town ten years later. This low rate of persistence, combined with the town's rapid population growth during the same
period, meant that in 1860 the vast majority of the townspeople were relative new-

Knoxville's business district shortly after the Civil War.
Photograph courtesy of McClung Historical Collection, Knox County Public Library.

comers. A mere 23 percent of all heads of free households had lived in town for at least a decade; among the wealthiest tenth, on the other hand, fully 71 percent were longtime residents.

The 1850s had also been marked by an increase in ethnic diversity that many older townspeople found disturbing. When local writers first began to define "Appalachia" to national readers after the Civil War, they regularly portrayed the "typical" inhabitant of the region as a white, Anglo-Saxon Protestant. For much of antebellum East Tennessee this stereotype was not far off the mark, with the obvious exception of the black slaves who constituted nearly one-tenth of the population of the region. In rural Knox County in 1860, for example, Tennessee-born whites accounted for three-quarters of all free adult males, and only one in every twenty had been born outside of the United States. Knoxville closely approximated this broader regional pattern as late as 1850, when fewer than 6 percent of its free adult male population was born outside of the United States. By 1860, however, the foreign-born made up almost one-fourth (22 percent) of Knoxville's free adult male population. Among these, Irish immigrants were by far the most numerous. Overwhelmingly poor and unskilled, most had come to Knoxville during the previous decade to work on the railroads, and their numbers were already large enough by 1851 to justify the establishment of Knoxville's first Roman Catholic church. Behind the Irish in size were the town's German, English, and Swiss immigrants, followed by a sprinkling of French, Scots, Italians, and Canadians. This upsurge in ethnic diversity figured prominently in local politics during the 1850s, as most of Knoxville's Whig majority moved into the anti-immigrant Know-Nothing Party when the Whig Party collapsed nationally around middecade. The foreign-born newcomers voted disproportionately Democratic, and Brownlow and other longtime Whigs attacked the rival party by attributing its strength to the support of "drunken, red-mouthed Irishmen" and "lousy Germans."[34]

The widespread poverty among the newcomers also served to underscore the disparity between rich and poor among the free population that was growing noticeably along with the town's overall prosperity. The distribution of wealth was generally quite skewed in America's urban areas before the Civil War, and Knoxville was no exception. The rapid commercial development of the 1850s did not initiate this pattern, but it certainly rendered it more visible. At one extreme, the Irishmen who arrived with the railroad were almost invariably poor; more than nine-tenths did not own their own home, and almost none possessed more than a few hundred dollars' worth of property. At the end of each workday they congregated in dingy taverns (the *Knoxville Whig* labeled them "breathing holes of hell") and then staggered wearily home to one of the cheap boardinghouses or worker's hotels that sprang up overnight around the depot. At the other extreme—and yet only a few blocks away—lived the town's increasingly affluent business and professional elite. After earning their bread by the sweat of other men's brows, these merchants and attorneys were wont to gather at the Lamar House Hotel for imported wines, fine cigars, and fresh oysters in season, and then to stroll home to comfortable dwellings adorned with all the trappings of wealth: libraries, carriages, pianos, mahogany staircases, silver serving platters—and slaves.[35]

Although the security of this last form of property was already dividing the country, the people of Knoxville did not know that a great civil war loomed on the horizon. Through the summer of 1860 at least, life went on pretty much as usual, and the distant rumblings of sectional crisis had to compete for the townspeople's attention with the more urgent demands of daily existence. As 1860 opened, both farmers and merchants worried over the damage to the wheat crop from an unusually severe winter. A shortage of vacant dwellings and business houses was also driving rents up to a level as much as 25 percent higher than in any other town in the region, which threatened to discourage continued growth.[36] Even more serious was the recent closure of the Bank of East Tennessee, which had suspended its operations with outstanding debts of $625,000. A series of reckless speculations had forced the president, William M. Churchwell, to declare bankruptcy, leaving depositors with a bunch of worthless paper currency. A perusal of the pages of the *Knoxville Whig* also reveals complaints about the numerous dogs running loose in town, about sleeping in church, about "idlers and loafers" on public corners, and about "the furious rate at which hacks are driven through our streets . . . to the imminent danger of human life."[37]

There was also a fair share of scandal in this little town. The *Whig* reported on a number of unwanted babies and implied that one young unwed mother had contemplated murdering her newborn. Another had apparently been seduced by a married man, prompting the accusation that "too many married gentlemen here keep late hours." There were also sensational charges against J. C. Ramsey, the U.S. district attorney for East Tennessee, who was accused by James Newman, a former editor of the *Knoxville Register*, of helping clients procure fraudulent pensions; the conflict reached a head when Newman entered Ramsey's office and attacked him with a hickory stick, breaking the arm of the DA, who in turn emptied the contents of a derringer into his assailant's arm. Even more shocking was the news that William Brownlow's son John had been charged with the murder of a fellow student at Emory and Henry College, a Methodist institution in southwestern Virginia. The 107-pound Brownlow pleaded self-defense and was ultimately found "not guilty," but for nearly two months his combative father had almost no time for politics.[38]

The point is not that folks in Knoxville found national political currents irrelevant—far from it—but rather that their passionate interest in the controversial political developments of the day existed against a backdrop of mundane challenges and commonplace concerns. And even when they did evaluate and respond to national events, they did so first and foremost through the medium of local institutions and in a manner shaped by local circumstances. History was about to happen to the people of Knoxville—huge developments far beyond their control were about to shake the community to its very foundations—and when the calamity finally occurred, it would test not only the townspeople's loyalty to the Union but their fidelity to each other as well.

CHAPTER TWO

Contemplating Calamity

This is not a contest, as to who shall be President the next four years. But shall there any longer be a *United States*. . . . Lincoln is the representative of the sectional party, and Breckinridge of the Constitution. . . . The great conservative masses must arise in their majesty and strength and sustain the constitutional representatives and defenders, or we shall have to meet the dangers of sectional strife and disunion.

—*Knoxville Daily Register*, 27 September 1860

The true national men will regret to see Lincoln elected to the Presidency, because he is the candidate of a sectional party. Indeed his election, which we hope never to witness, will be the greatest calamity that ever befell our country.

—*Knoxville Whig*, 6 October 1860

B Y THE FALL of 1860 the country's political party system was visibly in shambles. The old Whig Party had disappeared, the Democratic Party had divided into hostile northern and southern wings, and a wholly sectional Republican Party had emerged to contend for preeminence. Voters in the upcoming presidential election had not two choices but four: the Republican Abraham Lincoln, the northern Democrat Stephen Douglas, the southern Democrat John Breckinridge, and the Constitutional Unionist John Bell. And yet for all the upheaval nationally, within Tennessee the old Jacksonian parties still stood firm. Admittedly, the Whigs had gone through a number of incarnations since 1854: most East Tennessee Whigs had become Know-Nothings in the mid-1850s, called themselves the "Opposition" toward the end of the decade, and assumed the label of the Constitutional Union Party in 1860. Such name changes aside, however, both major parties commanded stable and highly loyal followings of voters who trusted them to defend their freedom from attack. Only the details of the seemingly perpetual danger had changed. By 1860 the two parties had long since shifted their focus from issues of banking and internal improvements and were targeting new threats to popular liberty. To the Democrats, the great danger lay in the subjugation that would follow the election of an abolitionist Black Republican president. Whigs, in contrast, feared the consolidation of power sure to eventuate in a southern confederacy established by disunionist Fire-Eaters. The stakes were high, but in the minds of voters, they always had been.[1]

This helps to explain why some four hundred men—nearly half of the adult white males in Knoxville—would gather at noon on a weekday in September 1860 to listen to a speech by a famous visitor. The presidential campaign of that year had been well under way for several months, but in hindsight the townspeople would see this afternoon as a defining moment in the contest. The crowd had turned out to hear William L. Yancey, U.S. senator from Alabama and one of the primary architects of the fissure in the Democratic Party at its national convention in Charleston the preceding April.[2] In the public mind, Yancey had personified the secessionist movement at least since 1858, when in a letter to a South Carolina journalist he had declared that the time had come to "fire the Southern heart—instruct the Southern mind—give courage to each other, and at the proper moment, . . . precipitate the cotton States into a revolution."[3] Yancey had stopped in Knoxville to deliver a speech in support of southern Democratic nominee John C. Breckinridge of Kentucky. For the most part local Democrats shared his enthusiasm for Breckinridge and, like him, they heartily detested the northern Democratic candidate Stephen Douglas of Illinois. The Breckinridge faction escorted their illustrious guest from the Lamar House Hotel to a grove in northwest Knoxville, where a speaker's stand had been erected for the occasion under a large oak tree. A number of Knoxville's leading Democrats joined him on the platform, including John H. Crozier, a former U.S. congressman who had crossed over from the Whig Party in the mid-1850s; J. G. M. Ramsey, a prominent physician, banker, and director of the East Tennessee and Georgia Railroad; and Isaac Lewis, a licensed Methodist minister and currently the local pension agent, thanks to an appointment from President James Buchanan. Local Whigs (now known as Constitutional Unionists), who backed Tennessean John Bell for president, marched as a group to the same location, having canceled the regular meeting of the Bell and Everett Club in order to see the devil incarnate in person.

For the next three and one half hours the fire-eating Democrat explained to the assembled throng why Breckinridge was the only candidate truly acceptable to the South. "He is a fluent speaker, with a good voice," Parson Brownlow conceded the next day in the *Whig*, but he also exhibits "an excess of vanity, and a large sprinkle of the demagogue. He makes an ingenious speech, interspersed with a good degree of recklessness, but by no means meets the expectations of strangers."[4] The cheering Democrats in the audience likely disagreed. Yancey's strategy throughout the speech was straightforward. First, he argued forcefully for the constitutionality of slavery. Then he sought to demonstrate that every other candidate in the upcoming election was either hostile to the institution or less than determined to protect it. Finally, to drive home just how much was at stake, he reminded his audience of the crucial importance of slavery to white southerners. Realizing that only a tiny percentage of his audience actually owned slaves, the senator tried to build a case designed specifically for nonslaveholding whites, following the lead of other proslavery radicals across the South such as Governor Joe Brown of Georgia, Senator James Henry Hammond of South Carolina, and journalist J. D. B. DeBow of Louisiana. The gist of their argument was that slavery guaranteed a superior social status for all whites. Every society required a "mudsill," as Hammond put it, a class of menial workers "to perform the drudgery of life." Because slaves fulfilled this function in the South, even the poorest white laborer need never worry about falling to the lowest rung of the southern social ladder. Indeed, as Brown asserted, the latter "belongs to the only true aristocracy, the race of *white men*."[5] Yancey developed this theme for his East Tennessee listeners by emphasizing the degradation of whites in the North, where white women "stand over the tub and cook," and white men "black boots and drive carriages."[6]

As Yancey began to wind down, the Bell and Everett men realized that the senator had not yet defined his position on the appropriate southern response to a Republican victory in November. Accordingly, they sent a note up to the speaker's platform. The question it contained was blunt: Should Abraham Lincoln be elected, would the senator advocate the immediate dissolution of the Union, even in the absence of any overt action against slavery by the new president? The query was signed by a number of Knoxville's leading Bell supporters, namely, Brownlow, Dr. William Rodgers, and attorneys Samuel Rodgers, Oliver Temple, and John Fleming. Upon receiving the message, Yancey called the five up to the front. Rather than responding to their question, he asked each a series of questions of his own, including whether they would favor the use of force against southern states that might choose to secede. Caught off guard, four of the five equivocated. Temple, for example, declared that he opposed federal coercion against a state but also denied the right of a state to use force in defying federal authority. In contrast, Brownlow responded forcefully, although he, too, did not answer Yancey's question directly. "I am of a numerous party in the South," he declared, "who will, if even Lincoln shall be elected under the forms of our Constitution, and by the authority of law, *without committing any other offense than being elected*, force the vile Disunionists and Secessionists of the South TO PASS OVER OUR DEAD BODIES ON THEIR MARCH TO WASHINGTON, TO BREAK UP THE GOVERNMENT!"[7]

This created something of a stir, to put it mildly. An account of the affair recorded long afterward recalled that the crowd pressed close around the platform, and that a number of the more "imprudent" partisans on both sides could be seen reaching discreetly for their revolvers. Yancey resumed his speech and,

William G. Brownlow—minister,
editor, and outspoken Unionist—as
he appeared in his wartime memoir
Sketches of the Rise, Progress, and
Decline of Secession.

Photograph courtesy of Special Collections,
University of Tennessee Libraries.

singling out Brownlow in particular, expressed his astonishment at meeting even "one Southern man, a *native* of the South, who was willing to plunge a *Northern Bayonet* into a Southern brother!" Should his state determine to resist the election of a Black Republican, Yancey vowed to go with her, "and if I meet this gentlemen . . . marshaled with his bayonet to oppose us," he thundered, pointing to Brownlow, "I'll plunge my bayonet to the hilt through and through his heart, and feel no compunction for the act, and thank my God my country has been freed from such a foe."[8] Before concluding, he took pains also to lecture the Parson on the responsibility of ministers of the gospel to preach peace rather than to stir up strife, and then, having by this time spoken for four hours, he sat down. The Bell and Everett men called for their champion to respond, and Brownlow, who had been suffering from a throat infection off and on for nearly two years, offered only a few brief, but pungent, remarks. Pointedly observing that Yancey still had not answered the question directed to him and objecting to his patronizing advice concerning the proper role of the clergy, the Parson confessed that he could think of only one verse of scripture throughout Yancey's diatribe: "Get thee behind me SATAN!"[9]

ON THE SURFACE, the Yancey-Brownlow exchange has all the ingredients necessary for a great drama. A poor white minister from Appalachia and a powerful politician from the Cotton Kingdom literally mount a stage and debate the future of the country. The mouthpiece of the master class professes his commitment to the South and the perpetuation of slavery, while the champion of the hill-country yeomen declares his undying commitment to the Union of his forefathers. Looking more deeply, the encounter between the senator and the Parson offers a valuable window into the history of Knoxville's Civil War, for it reveals that things are not always what they seem. Many of Knoxville's Demo-

crats, although they would overwhelmingly support the same presidential candidate as William Yancey, were far less prepared than he was to dissolve the
Union until Republicans had proved their foul intentions more concretely. On
the other hand, William Brownlow had long ago expressed a willingness to accept the breakup of the Union over the issue of slavery, and only two years earlier he had proclaimed to a Philadelphia audience that the right of "Hamitic
servitude" was guaranteed by the Constitution and the laws of God, "and these
rights we intend to enjoy, or to a man we will die, strung along Mason and
Dixon's line, with our faces looking north!"[10]

The Yancey-Brownlow encounter underscored the continued importance of
partisan attachments as the town contemplated the possibility of a Republican
victory in November. Brownlow never let his readers forget that Yancey was a
Democrat, and Democratic politicians, by definition, were ambitious and corrupt. (The rank and file were merely stupid.) Although the election of Abraham
Lincoln would constitute "the most dire calamity that has ever befallen us in the
way of a presidential election," the election of Breckinridge would be "as great a
calamity." Indeed, four years of Republican rule would probably be no worse,
Brownlow offered, and perhaps a good deal better, than the preceding four years
of "the thieving, lying, all-pervading corruptions, and wasteful extravagance of
the Buchanan wing of Democracy."[11]

Yancey's tactical response to Brownlow's bravado was also telling. In declaring his disbelief that a "Southern man" would stand against a "Southern brother,"
the Alabamian vividly foreshadowed a strategy that secessionists would employ
to good effect in marshaling support for separation. The day would come when
to be labeled "antisecession" was to be condemned as "antisouthern," a linguis-
tic victory for secessionists that put southern Unionists in a very difficult position. This is one reason Brownlow so frequently emphasized his Virginia
nativity—to deflect recurring accusations that he was a "Yankee."[12]

In addition to the ties of party and region, the Yancey-Brownlow confrontation also highlighted the importance of long-standing personal animosities. The
Parson made much of the fact that the man who introduced Yancey was John
H. Crozier, the former Whig congressman turned Democrat. When Brownlow
arrived in town in 1849, Crozier had been one of the principal stockholders of
the *Knoxville Register*, at the time a Whig newspaper, and he had not appreciated
the extra competition for readers. Indeed, Crozier and his business partners—
especially brothers Bill and Jim Williams and Judge William G. Swan—had done
everything in their power to drive the Parson out of business, including extensive litigation and, according to a number of credible sources, threats of physical
violence. Although Brownlow openly warred with Crozier and his allies throughout the 1850s, the latter's defection to the Democrats in 1856 freed Brownlow to
voice his animosity with more venom. In the aftermath of Yancey's Knoxville
address, the *Whig* editor was pleased to remind his readers that the man who

introduced him was "notoriously a little, a pitiful, a sordid, and a wretched apology for a man." In the weeks that followed, Brownlow repeatedly linked Yancey with Crozier, that "disappointed office-seeker, apostate Whig, liar and scoundrel."[13]

Two other issues would have been in the minds of the townspeople as they contemplated not only the election of 1860 but also the possibility of secession in the event of a Republican victory and, beyond that, the unnerving likelihood of civil war. The first involved the fate of slavery. The second, always related to the first, involved the fate of white men. Long after the war, prominent Knoxville Unionists sometimes tried to claim that slavery had been largely irrelevant to East Tennesseans. Episcopal minister Thomas Humes, for instance, maintained that most "felt no concern about the institution," and attorney Oliver Temple insisted that "the question of slavery did not enter largely into their minds."[14] The rhetoric in the Knoxville oak grove demonstrated otherwise. Granted, Humes and Temple were correct to point out that slavery was less deeply entrenched in East Tennessee than almost anywhere else in the future Confederacy. Enslaved African Americans constituted only 9 percent of the total population of Knoxville in 1860, average for the region as a whole, and barely 10 percent of white households actually owned slaves. Large slaveholders were almost nonexistent. Only one resident owned as many as twenty, and one-half of Knoxville's masters owned four slaves or fewer. Nevertheless, in this overwhelmingly white, nonslaveholding community, the debate over slavery and its implications for whites was still central to the presidential campaign.

William L. Yancey set the tone by underscoring the importance of slavery to nonslaveholders and by accusing both John Bell and Stephen Douglas of being "soft" on slavery and secretly supported by abolitionists. A week after the Fire-Eater's visit, the pro-Breckinridge *Knoxville Daily Register* (which had been bought out by Democratic ownership in 1859) picked up the refrain. "The contest is emphatically between Breckinridge and Lincoln," the newspaper declared, between "Northern Abolitionism and the friends of the Constitution." An anonymous correspondent to the paper later predicted that Lincoln would replace the "glorious old Constitution" with the "inglorious platform of the black republican party, [which] places the African negro on an equality with you and every white man." Throughout the campaign, local Breckinridge Democrats claimed that their candidate was the only one with a chance of preventing a Republican victory in November. The implications of this were clear: those who cast their ballots for Bell or Douglas were effectively voting for Abraham Lincoln and, by definition, for abolition and black equality.[15]

White East Tennesseans were vulnerable to such explosive accusations for one simple reason: the region had something of an antislavery heritage in its not-too-distant past. One can build a persuasive case for East Tennessee as the leading center of antislavery agitation in the entire United States between the War of

1812 and the early 1830s. The Tennessee Manumission Society, founded in 1815 in Jefferson County, eventually had sixteen chapters in East Tennessee (although none in the rest of the state), and by one estimate the region contained one-fifth of all the antislavery societies in the country in the 1820s. One of the first abolitionist newspapers in the United States was published in 1819 by Elihu Embree in Jonesborough, while Benjamin Lundy edited the *Genius of Universal Emancipation* in nearby Greeneville in the early 1820s before relocating to Baltimore. When a state constitutional convention was held in 1834, eleven East Tennessee counties (including Knox) submitted petitions advocating some form of gradual emancipation, and two-thirds of East Tennessee's convention delegates supported consideration of the idea. (The convention tabled a motion to consider the issue, citing the degraded status of Tennessee's free blacks and the relatively benign character of bondage in the state.)[16]

Much of this antislavery sentiment breathed moral condemnation of human bondage. A member of the Manumission Society of Knox County declared that slavery promoted "outrages on the laws of nature and nature's God." Elihu Embree denounced slavery as a sin and slaveholders as "monsters in human form." Citizens from Blount County (adjacent to Knox) condemned the institution as "a dishonor to the Christian religion" and "repugnant to the spirit of our Republican government." Petitioners from nearby Washington County criticized it as "contrary to the law of God and the principles of our far-famed declaration of independence." Other petitions affirmed that slavery was "morally wrong" and maintained that both "justice and sound policy require its speedy abolition." As late as the 1830s East Tennessee was a place where men could—and frequently did—openly castigate slavery as immoral.[17]

It would be easy to make too much of this. For one thing, such antislavery convictions were always held by a tiny minority. Both Embree and Lundy had small followings, and the proportion of individuals signing antislavery petitions likely never exceeded 5 percent of the adult male population. Second, even antislavery East Tennesseans shared in the predominant cultural commitment to white supremacy. Even at the close of the Civil War, after thousands of young men in the region had donned blue uniforms and actively supported emancipation, visitors to East Tennessee commented regularly on the pervasive racism in the area. A Union officer, for example, testified before Congress in 1865 that "among the bitterest opponents of the negro in Tennessee are the intensely radical loyalists of the mountain districts." Thus there was a noticeable lack of sympathy for the slaves themselves in much of the "antislavery" sentiment of the 1820s and 1830s. Even those who condemned slavery on moral grounds regularly coupled their opposition to involuntary servitude with support for mandatory colonization. The antislavery petitions to the 1834 constitutional convention regularly favored provisions that would also require all emancipated slaves either to leave the state on their own—"and never return to reside

therein"—or to be forcibly removed to Liberia. The free society that would
result was to be exclusively white.[18]

The logical result was that much of the opposition to slavery in East Tennessee did not focus on the slaves at all but emphasized nonslaveholding whites
as the primary victims of the institution. When future Knoxville resident David
Deaderick visited West Tennessee in 1826, for example, he concluded that slavery "vitiated" whites wherever it took hold. Because slaves did almost all of the
manual labor in the plantation districts, the "great evil" of slavery was that it
promoted "inaction and idleness" among whites. Whig congressman Horace
Maynard reached the same conclusion not long after he moved to Knoxville from
Massachusetts in 1838. Slavery "tends to make labor a disgrace," he wrote to his
father, "and consequently there is just as little done as possible, and there is everywhere observable a degree of slackness and unthriftiness of which you can have
but a dim conception. Nothing can exceed the sluggishness and inefficiency of
the negroes, except that of the white laborers, which is tenfold worse." Objecting to the political power of slaveholders, a Jefferson County petition in 1834—
signed by then circuit rider Brownlow—claimed that because of slavery
Tennesseans were to be "cursed with some of the most odious features of aristocracy." In ominous and remarkably prescient wording, the petition predicted
that "the very toleration of slavery . . . will ultimately end in anarchy, ruin, &
bloodshed."[19]

Such overt assaults on the South's defining institution became increasingly
unpopular after the emergence of a radical abolitionist movement in the North
during the early 1830s. Antislavery petitions to the state legislature dwindled to
insignificance after 1837, and open condemnation of slavery in any form almost
entirely vanished, silenced by the "omnipotent despotism of public opinion," as
Oliver Temple remembered. Discreet discussion of the subject was still possible,
as long as it was out of the public eye, but East Tennesseans who maintained
antislavery convictions—their number is impossible to determine—mostly kept
their views to themselves. A Knoxville Baptist minister, for example, ended an
1846 report to the American Baptist Home Missionary Society by confiding that
he was teaching slaves to read and was also endeavoring to influence the views
of other local ministers on slavery. His closing sentence was revealing: "These
last remarks I wish sacredly kept from the public."[20]

At the close of the 1840s there was a brief resurgence of interest in colonization, but this time it was couched in a way that few slaveholders could have found
threatening. In 1849 Knox Countians formed a chapter of the American Colonization Society, whose members met at least annually into the early 1850s. Some
of those involved may have sincerely advocated colonization as a way to encourage voluntary manumission among masters, but many more likely viewed the
undertaking as a means of strengthening slavery by eliminating troublesome free
blacks. One member conceded that many free blacks were "respectable and

inoffensive" but observed that "too large a portion of them are proverbially idle and vicious and as a general rule to which there are exceptions, they are looked upon by the whites as a sore upon the social body, which would be a matter of congratulation to see removed." The main speakers at the annual meetings in 1849 and 1852—Episcopalian rector Humes and Presbyterian minister Joseph Martin— were both slaveholders. Both explicitly stressed that they had no desire to inter- fere with slavery per se, and each emphatically endorsed one of the cardinal tenets of the southern defense of slavery: the axiom that slaves were actually better off than free blacks.[21]

Free blacks constituted nearly half of Knoxville's small African American population in 1860, and of these, 20 percent were engaged in skilled occupations and 28 percent owned their own homes. By way of comparison, among Irish households in the same year, 24 percent were headed by skilled laborers or pro- fessionals, but only 8 percent owned real estate. Nevertheless, it was an unassail- able dogma among whites that emancipation was a curse rather than a blessing. The most zealous defenders of slavery attributed this to slavery's "civilizing" influence on an inferior race. A Knoxville physician, for instance, wrote to a South Carolina newspaperman about how slavery spared enslaved Africans from their natural tendencies to barbarism and even cannibalism. In a similar tone, a Knox- ville writer (in a published review of *Uncle Tom's Cabin*) observed that Knoxville's slaves "looked fat, saucy, happy and contented, while the free blacks, with a few exceptions, had a miserable and dejected appearance. When slaves are liberated in the South," he concluded, "they immediately become stupid, indolent, and improvident." Humes and Martin, on the other hand, blamed the condition of free blacks on the ubiquitous racism of whites, which ensured that they would never escape the stigma of their color. Even when legally emancipated, free people of color remained virtually enslaved, so what was the point?[22]

For at least a generation before the Civil War, then, this small town that would ultimately divide so bitterly over secession was essentially unified in de- fense of slavery. As sectional tensions mounted, the range of opinion on the topic became minuscule. Some individuals, like J. G. M. Ramsey, had always been proslavery. The future staunch secessionist, who owned eight slaves in 1860, likely held the most extreme proslavery convictions in town. In addition to being a doctor, banker, farmer, railroad entrepreneur, and historian, Ramsey also fancied himself something of an economic theorist. The South's greatest handicap was its inadequate supply of labor, the doctor explained to one of his many corre- spondents, and this made slavery utterly essential to the region's prosperity. Even when white immigrants were induced to come south, they too often found the patterns of cultivation unfamiliar and the climate dangerous, ultimately render- ing them ineffective and discontent. In contrast, because of his inferior "physi- cal, moral and intellectual nature," the African was "at home and happy in the field." Because the rate of natural increase among slaves was inadequate to meet the South's labor needs, however, the doctor determined that a revival of the African slave trade was imperative. This "gainful commerce" would not only energize the southern economy but also rescue the African from paganism and idolatry. As such, he concluded, it was to be considered "promotive . . . of the great cause of humanity, and essential to the paramount object of civilization and Christianity."[23]

Others had converted to support for the institution. Horace Maynard, who owned four slaves by 1860, went through an evolution of opinion reflected in his regular correspondence with his father. Maynard came to Knoxville from Massachusetts in 1838 to accept a position at East Tennessee College. Fresh from earning his bachelor degree at Amherst, he was underwhelmed by the sophistication of the Appalachian metropolis and particularly repulsed by the adverse effects of slavery on the local culture and economy. "As for Slavery I do not hesitate to think it a curse to the country," he wrote in early 1839. Because the pay for a college professor was poor, Maynard soon began to contemplate a change of career and in 1841 informed his father that he would likely be leaving Tennessee, given that "slavery is an important objection to the South." In the meantime, he would continue reading law and hoped to apply for admission to the bar before the beginning of the next school session.[24]

Within a few years changes in Maynard's convictions began to appear. Although he had regularly contemplated moving to the Midwest or back to New England, Maynard explained to his father in February 1844 that he had determined for the present to stay in East Tennessee, where, for the moment at least, his career opportunities had taken a turn for the better. "As to keeping slaves," he went on to note, "I do not think it absolutely necessary to own them; at least I own none. I hire one who helps Laura [his wife] do all her work. Most families think it necessary to have four or five about the house but we have always made one suffice." ("Most" white families, of course, had no slaves at all in their households.) A year and a half later he was still debating the wisdom of his decision not to move. "There are serious objections to living in a slaveholding country," he explained, "especially to those who have been brought up in a free state & are determined not to traffic in that kind of property. As a lawyer a great deal of my business relates to slaves."[25]

Ephraim Maynard's letters to his son have not survived, but he seems to have touched a nerve in a letter written sometime in the summer of 1850. Although Horace Maynard did not yet own slaves in his own right, he apparently continued to hire slaves as household servants. "You suggest that you & mother can do very well without any servants," Horace Maynard responded to his father. "So I have no doubt you can. Still a faithful man & woman would much enhance your comforts. There is a bright as well as a dark side to the picture of slavery," the son explained to the father. "The old family servants, who so completely identify themselves with the interests of the Family, as even to speak of the children as 'ours,' to say nothing of the property, are not the least intelligent, interesting, & agreeable portion of the human race. Their servitude is no more a burden to them, than is the service of our children until they arrive at twenty one years of age."[26]

Mentally, Maynard's conversion to proslavery was complete at this point, a process made official the same year by the purchase of his first slave. "Since I wrote you last, I bought a man by name Abram," the new master reported in December 1850. "Abe" formerly belonged to a member of Congress, who had been forced to sell him to satisfy a debt. "I bought him at his own urgent insistence to save him from being taken out of the country," Maynard stressed to his father. Ephraim Maynard must have found this less than assuring, for he evidently wrote back to express the concern that his son might become a large slaveholder. "You need have no fear of that," Horace reassured him. "I only want such as will be sufficient for my servants and that [many?] it is almost necessary to have." The younger Maynard went on to note that since his last letter he had also bought a ten-year-old girl named Caroline. "I had a debt to collect from a broken merchant of between $1000.00 and $1100.00," he explained. "He had nothing but two young negroes[,] a boy 13 years old and this girl & I took them for the debts. Laura wanted a house girl . . . & after a trial she consented to keep Caroline. The boy I shall have to sell." Six years later he took his proslavery opinions with him to Washington when he was elected as a Whig congressman from Tennessee's second district. One of his first acts was to support the admission of Kansas as a slave state; three years later, in the midst of the secession crisis, he would denounce abolitionism in Congress as a popular delusion threatening to destroy the Union.[27]

Massachusetts-born attorney Horace Maynard. Although he converted to support of slavery after relocating to Knoxville, Maynard staunchly opposed secession and represented East Tennessee in the U.S. Congress during the first half of the war.
Photograph courtesy of Special Collections, University of Tennessee Libraries.

Maynard was far from the only Knoxville resident to change his mind about slavery during the years before the Civil War. David Deaderick, who before moving to Knoxville in the 1830s had maintained that the presence of slavery "vitiated" whites, owned a half dozen in 1860. By that time Judge Robert McKinney, who had supported gradual emancipation at the 1834 constitutional convention, owned six slaves as well. Joseph Mabry, whose father had also favored emancipation at the same convention as a representative of Knox County, owned seventeen slaves and was one of Knoxville's largest slaveholders by the close of the 1850s. There were likely numerous others. Oliver Temple—who owned seven slaves in 1860 and had no qualms of conscience about it—remembered that such conversions were commonplace after the early 1830s, when "the antislavery current . . . turned back in its course, and was lost in the maelstrom of slavery propagandism." According to Temple, "many men who had denounced slavery, away back in emancipation days, now hastened to set themselves right with their neighbors by purchasing slaves."[28]

The most dramatic transformation was William Brownlow's, even though it is doubtful that the Parson actually ever owned slaves himself.[29] In the early 1830s he had described slavery as a "great evil . . . condemned by the law of God." Brownlow expressed an occasional reservation about the economic effects of slavery into the 1840s, and he could never go as far as J. G. M. Ramsey in endorsing the reopening of the slave trade, but by the 1850s he had clearly emerged as a vociferous champion of slavery within the South.[30] Why his views changed so radically is a matter of conjecture. It is doubtful that a man who so thrived on controversy would have altered his opinions merely to "set himself right with his neighbors." It is far more likely that he was responding to the escalating moral condemnation of slavery from outside the South. In 1835, for example, northern abolitionists embarked upon an aggressive strategy to use the mails to flood the South with abolitionist propaganda. As William Lloyd Garrison, Wendell Phillips, and other New England abolitionists began to damn slavery as a sin and slaveholders as sinners, southern clergy—many of whom had been somewhat ambivalent in their views on slavery—began to formulate a systematic vindication of slavery as an institution ordained by God and a blessing to both slave and master.[31]

Brownlow's resentment of abolitionists was intense and long-standing. Even back in 1834, when he had professed to "lament the evils of slavery as much as any other man," he had stood firmly opposed to immediate emancipation on the grounds that it would lead both to "the murder and robbery of thousands of the slave holders, and the absolute starvation of even a greater number of the emancipated slaves." To figure out how to remedy "the evil" without injuring both white and blacks "will require a better head and heart than mine," he wrote, "or those possessed by these emancipating preachers, who are continually bawling out *set your negroes free!*" His dislike of abolitionists mounted in the 1840s when northern antislavery zealots pushed through a resolution at the General Conference of the Methodist Church demanding the resignation of a bishop from Georgia who had recently acquired slaves by marriage. "The vile spirit of *Abolition* has been at work in the Conference," Brownlow reported in the *Whig*. Engaged in an "unholy crusade," New England abolitionists had accomplished their insidious purposes under "the pretended sanctity of religion." Brownlow was further outraged when Harriet Beecher Stowe's *Uncle Tom's Cabin* was so enthusiastically received across the North. Picking up on a threatening quotation attributed to Stowe's abolitionist husband, Brownlow concluded bitterly that "'a bloody revolution' is the only alternative the Abolitionists of the North intend to present to the South. If so, then so be it. As a Southern man, we accept the proposition for 'a bloody revolution,' and we are ready to go into it, when ever the ball opens."[32]

Brownlow's transformation into a proslavery apologist reached its apogee in 1858, when he offered to go north to debate any abolitionist who was brave enough to face him on the question "ought American slavery to be perpetuated?" A Congregational minister from New York named Abram Pryne accepted his challenge, and in September the two met in Philadelphia, where they debated for five successive evenings before crowds of between four and seven hundred. The Parson left no doubt now about his view of slavery as a Christian institution. Opening the scriptures, he found no biblical grounds whatsoever for arguing that slavery per se was inherently immoral. On the contrary, it had expanded across the globe "by and with the consent, knowledge, and approbation of Almighty God."[33]

Brownlow defended *southern* slavery specifically by emphasizing the innate racial inferiority of Africans, which uniquely suited them for enslavement by their superiors. "I repudiate, as ridiculously absurd, that much lauded, but nowhere accredited dogma of THOMAS JEFFERSON'S, that 'all men are born equal,'" the Parson thundered in the very first debate. "God never intended to make the negro the equal of the white man, either morally, mentally, or physically." And yet, happily, slavery "elevate[d] the negro race from their state of pristine barbarism." They were "comfortable and prosperous beyond any peasantry in the world," and abolitionists only showed their utter disregard for the slaves by advocating their emancipation. The slaves need not worry, however, for southern whites were determined to protect them from their so-called friends. Indeed, Brownlow assured his audience, "Before we will have them seized and carried off by Abolitionists, we will pour out our blood as freely as we would water." He preferred to fight the abolitionists *in* the Union, not out of it, Brownlow stressed on the final night of the debates. Either way, however, southerners would defend their right to "Hamitic servitude," and slavery would survive. "When the angel Gabriel sounds the last trump of God," the Parson prophesied, "and calls the nations of the earth to judgment—then, and not before, will slavery be abolished south of Mason and Dixon's line." William Yancey could not have said it better.[34]

AND YET TWO YEARS later Yancey offended Brownlow deeply in the way that he defended slavery before the townspeople of Knoxville. It was all right as long as the Alabamian had upheld the institution on constitutional grounds. When he sought to appeal to the self-interest of nonslaveholders, Yancey miscalculated badly. The argument that slavery spared whites from the most "menial" tasks may have worked well in the Cotton Belt, where one-third to two-thirds of adult males were masters, and a clear majority either owned slaves or had a reasonable chance of acquiring them in the future. Linking manual labor with slavery before an East Tennessee audience, on the other hand, could be disastrous. Brownlow noted this immediately in his account of Yancey's speech, observing that the Fire-Eater's remarks were a direct affront to the vast majority of his audience. All but "every tenth man he was speaking to did not own a negro," Brownlow observed, "while the wives and daughters of nine-tenths of all who heard him, wash, cook, and milk cows, without ever suspecting that they were performing menial services!"[35]

Brownlow was dead-on in his estimate of the proportion of the audience who were not slave owners, and he was undoubtedly correct as well in emphasizing that they were no strangers to arduous manual labor. According to the 1860 federal census, nearly three-quarters (73 percent) of Knoxville's adult males held blue-collar jobs. What Brownlow did not point out was that, for a sizable proportion of the town, manual labor was also a sign of dependence. It was one thing to milk your *own* cow or black your *own* boots, but quite another thing to perform these tasks for others. On the eve of the war nearly 22 percent of the town's adult white males were unskilled manual laborers, who worked primarily as gardeners, woodcutters, railroad hands, or generic "day laborers." Another 6 percent held low-paying semiskilled jobs, laboring as cooks, waiters, meat cutters, teamsters, or night watchmen. Even skilled workers primarily labored for others, if not necessarily in "menial" tasks. Nearly 45 percent of the town's adult white males reported skilled occupations—blacksmiths, masons, carpenters, printers, mechanics, and shoemakers were the most common. Almost two-thirds of these did not own their own shops, however, so the chances are good that a large proportion were not self-employed. Most females in blue-collar families also were accustomed to grueling labor. Probably nine-tenths of adult females performed household work exclusively. Except for a handful of schoolteachers, those who worked outside the home were seamstresses, cooks, or maids. In addition, girls in their middle to late teens frequently worked as household servants in the homes of Knoxville's more privileged property-owning families. Although Horace Maynard had implied that the family in need of domestic help was practically forced to buy or hire slaves, about one-tenth of home-owning families in 1860 employed a white housekeeper or "housegirl."[36]

An analogous pattern could be found in the countryside. Until quite recently, historians believed that adult white farm laborers were extremely scarce in the southern countryside before the Civil War; teenage boys might hire themselves out to neighbors occasionally, according to the received wisdom, but by the time a man was the head of his own household he typically owned, or at least operated, his own piece of land.[37] Tennessee Civil War veterans interviewed in their old age frequently suggested otherwise, however. One East Tennessee veteran, for example, recalled that his father "always had hired hands," while another remembered that in his community "the non–land owners hired as farm laborers." Corroborating these anecdotal reports, a study of three counties in upper East Tennessee estimates that perhaps one-fourth of all farm households in 1860 were headed by agricultural laborers who worked on farms owned and operated by others. When tenants are added to the mix—that is, farm operators who rented their acreage—the proportion of farm households that were landless in these counties climbs above two-fifths. In Knox County the situation was comparable—fully 44 percent of farm households did not own their own land. Although scholars have traditionally maintained that landownership was extremely widespread in southern Appalachia, landlessness appears to have been greater in East Tennessee than almost anywhere else in the antebellum South.[38]

The same holds true for the overall concentration of wealth. During and after the Civil War, Unionists from East Tennessee regularly claimed otherwise. "There are fewer slaves in East Tennessee than in any other portion of the State of equal extent," William Brownlow told northern audiences in 1862, "and, as a general thing, the people are very much upon an equality as to their possessions." Oliver Temple later affirmed his friend's assessment, maintaining that the minimal importance of slavery in the area precluded the growth of a class of "great lordly proprietors," with the result that "all were equals."[39] In reality, in rural Knox County the top 5 percent of free households in 1860 owned nearly half (49 percent) of all real and personal property, while the bottom half of households owned less than 3 percent. Studies of other agricultural regions for the same year indicate that wealth was at least as highly concentrated in the countryside surrounding Knoxville as it was in the wealthiest plantation regions of the Cotton Belt, and considerably more concentrated than in much of the rural Northeast and Midwest.[40]

The distribution of wealth was even more skewed in Knoxville itself. In this small Appalachian town the top 5 percent of free households owned nearly two-thirds of the total wealth held by the community; at the same time, the bottom half controlled proportionally almost nothing—only 1 percent of the total. Indeed, the distribution of wealth in Knoxville was almost indistinguishable from that in major northern urban centers such as New York and Boston.[41] The concentration of wealth in Knoxville was almost as great as in Charleston, South Carolina, the second-largest city in the future Confederacy and the very embodiment of Old South wealth and aristocratic privilege.[42] The absolute range between the richest and poorest households was not nearly as great, of course, but it would be absurd to argue that economic distinctions were insignificant. The bottom half of Knoxville's free households owned real and personal property valued at $500 or less in 1860, whereas the richest 5 percent reported an average wealth of nearly $84,000, an amount that would make them millionaires in today's dollars.

In contrast to most of the folks in town, these thirty-three individuals (thirty men and three women) most definitely did not earn their bread by working with their hands. With the exception of one miller and a retired farmer who moved into town, Knoxville's economic elite were merchants, bankers, and lawyers. They stood apart from the rank and file in several respects. Perhaps as many as two-thirds were college educated, with East Tennessee College being their most common alma mater.[43] Their aspirations for the rising generation were more ambitious. Two of the elite—merchants John Williams and Abner Jackson—sent their teenage sons to the Edgehill Academy, a boarding school in Princeton, New Jersey. Others made sure that their daughters learned the finer points of gracious living by enrolling them at the East Tennessee Female Institute. Their wealth and superior education also translated into political and social, as well as economic, influence. They held most of the political offices above the level of alderman and dominated the boards of Knoxville's leading businesses, educational institutions, and charitable organizations. Merchant Columbus Powell, for example, was on the board of directors of the Union Bank, the Knoxville Gas Light Company, and the Knoxville and Kentucky Railroad. Merchant and stock breeder Joseph A. Mabry was the president of that railroad, as well as a director of the East Tennessee and Georgia Railroad, a director of the Knoxville branch of the Bank of Tennessee, and a trustee of East Tennessee University. Businessman Campbell Wallace was president of the East Tennessee and Georgia, trustee of East Tennessee University, and a director of the Deaf and Dumb Asylum.[44]

Many also exhibited the more visible trappings of wealth. Even his enemies admitted that John H. Crozier had a "magnificent" library. Attorney William H. Sneed enjoyed being driven through town in an open barouche, at a time when most townspeople either walked or rode on horseback. Horace Maynard's wife raised flowers in a glass-covered greenhouse, situated immediately behind the Maynard residence, which was easily recognizable by its ornate facade and elaborate "gingerbread" latticework. Banker and former congressman William Churchwell may have been the most ostentatious. A local attorney derided him in his diary as "Louis Napoleon Churchwell, Emperor of Knoxville," and noted regrettably that with some creative financiering he would probably survive the collapse of the bank that he headed as president, thus allowing him to maintain "his traveling, his drunk-up wine, pleasures, etc. etc." (Although not widely known at the time, the "etc. etc." also included $9,000 he spent on a hideaway for his New York City mistress, actress "Mademoiselle Minnie Montez.")[45] Finally, and perhaps most significant, three-quarters of the wealthiest households owned slaves. Knoxville's enslaved persons were not field hands, as was the case with nine-tenths of the slaves across the South, but were disproportionately domestic servants—cooks, maids, gardeners, and laundresses—who worked with their hands so their masters and mistresses would not have to.

This is all necessary context for understanding the potential explosiveness of the way that editor Brownlow responded to William Yancey's clumsy defense of slavery before the nonslaveholders of Knoxville. Brownlow's reaction introduced a populist theme to the campaign that had been heretofore lacking. It centered on the use of one pejorative adjective: aristocratic. "Verily," the Parson declared in the first issue of the *Whig* after Yancey's speech, "if this Aristocratic Southern party desire no votes from that class who black their own boots, and drive their own carriages and wagons, their share in East Tennessee will be small." Continuing to harp upon the theme, the October 13 issue included a drawing of a woman standing over a washtub, with the comment that, according to Senator Yancey, the "poor white woman" was "degrading" herself by "menial service." "That sort of slur upon honest labor may do in South Alabama, among purse-proud aristocratic Democrats," Brownlow sneered to his readers, but it would not go over well with the hardy laborers of East Tennessee. Political campaigns are always in some measure centered on symbols, and Brownlow was doing his level best to make William Yancey a symbol to the Whig faithful of their worst fears. The typical Breckinridge Democrat, he wanted his audience to conclude, represented the plantation South, not the South as a whole, and spoke for "aristocrats," not for common whites.[46]

There was nothing particularly new about Brownlow's use of populist rhetoric. Over the years he had often disavowed any intention "to array the poor against the rich," but the context was usually an editorial in which he was arraying the poor against the rich.[47] In reality, from the moment Brownlow arrived in Knoxville in 1849, he was emphasizing his own humble beginnings and ridiculing the "scrub aristocracy" that ruled over the town. Identifying himself as a "House-Carpenter, by trade, and a poor man by birth and raising," the editor promised that his sympathies would be "with the Mechanics, Farmers, and laboring classes." He denounced the "clique" that controlled the rival *Knoxville Register* and protested that "the vanity, aristocracy, *fictitious* capital, and *pretended* decency of Knoxville is against us." Later, he complained that "a life of patient industry and honest toil, has been too long requited by contempt, on the part of a self-styled aristocracy," and went on to assert that "in no town in all the South-west is this more true, than in the town of *Knoxville*." He ridiculed Horace Maynard for his supposed contempt for the masses, and he attributed the rapid growth of his subscription list during the early 1850s to the support of "the People," who sympathized with his "struggle against Merchants, Banks, Universities, Cliques, and corrupt money-holders."[48]

The list is revealing for what it does not include. Although Brownlow had often employed class-based appeals since arriving in Knoxville, especially during the early 1850s, he had always been careful to avoid pitting slaveholders against nonslaveholders, a tactic he derided as "abolitionist."[49] In the aftermath of Yancey's visit to Knoxville his resolve was weakening. He actually crossed over the line only once prior to election day. The week after Yancey's speech he again reminded readers of the Fire-Eater's disparaging remarks about the dignity of labor and then argued that this was merely a foreshadowing of what they could expect if a southern Confederacy was ever created. Only slaveholders would be allowed to vote in this new "Slave Oligarchy," he warned, while the poor would be excluded. Significantly, Brownlow did not repeat the argument again until well after the election.[50]

Perhaps such a tack was as yet too controversial. Perhaps the editor simply deemed it unnecessary, given that John Bell's chances of winning Tennessee looked good. Although it is tempting to speculate, it is more crucial to note the tensions inherent in Brownlow's customary restraint. In terms both of political strategy and personal philosophy, he might best be described as adhering to a *proslavery populism*—he endorsed slavery unqualifiedly while portraying most political conflict as a struggle between the masses and a corrupt, powerful minority. Proslavery populism may have made long-term political sense in the Deep South, given the social reality there, but the situation in East Tennessee was markedly different. White East Tennesseans, too, were nearly unanimous in their support of slavery—in the abstract. They were self-conscious, however, of their more humble economic circumstances compared with other southern regions, and they lived in an area characterized by an extremely pronounced stratification of wealth in which only the very richest households owned slaves. Slave owners there were disproportionately merchants, bankers, and professionals—precisely the kind of "aristocrats" that the Parson had usually singled out for abuse. In such a milieu, the logic of populist appeals tended inevitably toward the identification of slaveholders as enemies, a tendency constrained primarily by the dictates of white supremacy and sectional loyalty, both of which traditionally had required that masters be viewed as allies.

IN THE END, neither loyalty to the South nor allegiance to slavery and the white race was severely tested among Knoxville's white voters during the 1860 presidential campaign. Nor was the contest a clear referendum on their commitment to the Union. All three issues thoroughly pervaded the rhetoric leading up to the election, and yet the election presented clear-cut choices on none of them.

As the campaign played out in Knoxville, it was never a battle between North and South but rather a struggle within the South between Constitutional Unionists and Democrats. The Jacksonian party system had fragmented nationally but not locally. Abraham Lincoln was not even on the ballot, and Stephen Douglas might as well not have been. Except for the 5 percent of voters who cast their ballots for the "Little Giant," the men in town evidently believed that they had only two choices—Breckinridge or Bell. The two-party system was still alive and well in Knoxville—as across much of the upper South—and it continued to do what it had long done effectively: defuse divisive questions and maintain conflict within manageable bounds.[51]

Both sides affirmed their most basic commitments according to the time-honored strategy of American politics—by attacking their rivals for allegedly different values. Breckinridge men damned the supporters of John Bell (a large slave owner) as closet abolitionists. Bell had, after all, voted against the Kansas-Nebraska Act of 1854, and four years later he had opposed the admission of Kansas as a slave state because he believed this violated the will of the majority of whites in the territory.[52] The *Knoxville Register* asserted that the Constitutional Union Party was merely one element in a monstrous coalition with "Abolitionists" and "Douglasites" aimed at thwarting the "great conservative masses" who supported Breckinridge. A Democrat debating Oliver Temple claimed that Bell supported the abolition of slavery in the District of Columbia, while John H. Crozier told a gathering at Walker's School House that Bell opposed the Dred Scott decision.[53] Shortly before the election Crozier aimed his charges a little closer to home. At a rally for Breckinridge in front of the Lamar House Hotel, he fired off a few shots at Oliver Temple and then took aim at William Brownlow. The Parson was a coward, Crozier told the crowd of Democrats, and he had never earned an honest dollar in his life. Worst of all, he was guilty of "going over to the Abolitionists."[54]

When the Parson learned of Crozier's attack, he immediately printed a stack of handbills, grabbed a bucket of glue and a brush, and posted the following all over town:

TAKE NOTICE!

That after speaking by Mr. [Thomas A. R.] Nelson tonight, in front of the Court House, I WILL REPLY TO THE ASSAULT UPON ME, last evening by that CONTEMPTIBLE PUPPY, INFAMOUS LIAR, and, WHITE LIVERED SCOUNDREL, *John H. Crozier.*

October 17, 1860   W. G. Brownlow

That evening he delivered a forty-minute harangue that focused primarily on the despicable character of his accuser, "one of the most unmitigated scoundrels, cold-blooded hypocrites, insincere and selfish villains who walks the streets of Knoxville." The address was 90 percent ad hominem attack. Crozier was politically and personally corrupt, Brownlow insisted, an unbelievably stingy man who starved his slaves and made his wife take in sewing. For those who could not hear the Parson's response in person, he printed the entire text of the diatribe— five full columns—across the front page of the *Whig*.[55]

The attack on Crozier was only the most extreme example of a more general Constitutional Unionist offensive against local Democrats. To begin with, they asserted that it was the Democrats, not themselves, who were really soft on slavery. They called attention to the large number of former Democrats in the North who had become Republicans (disregarding the even larger number of former Whigs in the party), and they underscored the Democratic Party's traditional support for "squatter sovereignty," a position now clearly associated in the southern mind with antislavery northerners. They maintained, furthermore, that it was southern Democrats' irresponsible agitation of the slavery issue that had actually given rise to the Republican Party in the first place. Building on this point, they argued—not without cause—that if Abraham Lincoln should claim the presidency in November, he would owe his election directly to the breakup of the Democratic Party.[56]

Continuing a theme as old as the party system itself, Constitutional Unionists also regularly blasted the Breckinridge faction as a gang of hypocritical opportunists. The Breckinridge men, they claimed, were cynically manipulating popular fears to advance their own selfish ends. In support of their allegations, they noted that several of Knoxville's leading Democrats, notably Crozier and William G. Swan, were former Whigs who had supposedly left that party because of frustrated political ambitions. In a similar manner, the Breckinridge wing had now split from the national Democratic Party because they could no longer rule it. Patronage, not principle, guided them. To drive home the point, only days before the election the *Whig* published a wholly unfounded allegation that the southern Democrats were preparing to sell out to the Republicans and that Lincoln and Breckinridge aides were meeting to divide the spoils.[57]

Finally, Bell men repeatedly charged that the Breckinridge Democrats were bent on destroying the Union. The Breckinridge ticket was "the disunion ticket," William Brownlow informed his readers. The Kentuckian had been nominated by "a set of men, who have uttered sentiments the most vile and treasonable." The party as a whole had become dominated by sectional wings aimed at wrecking the Union, and as such, the Parson concluded, it "deserves the scorn, contempt, and hatred of every patriot in the land." He called on supporters of the Constitutional Union Party to win the state for John Bell and "rebuke the disunionists."[58]

Despite such rhetoric, the issue of union or disunion was muddled in the local campaign. For one thing, most local Democrats were unwilling to go on record as advocating secession as an immediate and justifiable response to the mere election of a Republican president. John Breckinridge had not been their first choice as Democratic standard-bearer. A large proportion had hoped instead to see the nomination go to Senator Andrew Johnson, an East Tennessean from nearby Greene County who would emerge in a few months as one of the most stalwart of all southern Unionists. Although the *Knoxville Register* (whose editor was a Breckinridge man from the beginning) declared that the election was "not a contest, as to who shall be President the next four years," but rather "shall there any longer be a United States," more often the paper stressed that southern Democrats desired to preserve the Union even more than the Constitutional Unionists. Ignoring the regional basis of Breckinridge's support, the *Register* characterized every other party in the field as "sectional" and called on those who "really desire the perpetuity of the Union" to give "their earnest support to Breckinridge and Lane [the vice presidential nominee], as the only parties that can defeat the sectional nominees, and thereby save the Union." J. D. Thomas, a Democratic candidate for presidential elector in Tennessee's second district, explicitly avowed on the stump that his party would submit should Lincoln be elected.[59]

If most Democrats stopped short of calling for immediate secession in the event of a Republican victory, most Constitutional Unionists stopped short of declaring an absolute loyalty to the Union. Long after the secession crisis, Knoxville Unionists like William Brownlow, Oliver Temple, and Thomas Humes were fond of claiming that their commitment to the Union in 1860–61 had been "unconditional." If so, they never let on at the time. Granted, Constitutional Union leaders seemed less willing than their Democratic counterparts to contemplate secession, and Brownlow, at least, publicly denied that there was a constitutional right of secession. But a denial of the constitutional right of secession was not equivalent to "unconditional" Unionism for a very simple reason: Americans in the mid–nineteenth century still widely acknowledged a natural right of revolution. Abraham Lincoln expressed this belief as well as any of his contemporaries in a speech before Congress in 1848:

> Any people anywhere, being inclined and having the power, have the right to rise up and shake off the existing government, and form a new one that suits them better. This is a most valuable, a most sacred right—a right which, we hope and believe, is to liberate the world. Nor is this right confined to cases in which the whole people of an existing government may choose to exercise it. Any portion of such people that *can may* revolutionize, and make their *own* of so much of the territory as they inhabit.[60]

Admittedly, *white* southerners in 1860 were sometimes a bit uneasy about justifying disunion on these grounds, inasmuch as they lived side by side with some four million slaves who might find the same doctrine appealing. Nevertheless, they often did so.[61] In Tennessee the future debate over disunion would be framed explicitly in these terms. Advocates of disunion appealed to the Tennessee state constitution of 1834, which opened with the declaration that the people possess "at all times, an inalienable and indefeasible right to alter, reform, or abolish the government in such manner as they may think proper." Alone among the future states of the Confederacy, Tennessee never formally "seceded" from the Union. When the state legislature voted in 1861 to sunder its tie with the Union, it explicitly "waiv[ed] any expression of opinion as to the abstract doctrine of secession" and passed instead a "declaration of independence."[62]

For Knoxville's Constitutional Unionists to have declared an "unconditional" Unionism would have been politically disastrous on two grounds. It not only would have obliged them to repudiate a natural right that white Americans almost universally venerated. Even more unthinkable, it would have required them publicly to declare their willingness to submit to possible northern aggression against slavery rather than jeopardize the Union. Intricacies of constitutional interpretation aside, this is what "unconditional" Unionism meant in the minds of white southerners by the fall of 1860. To endorse such a position meant political suicide, and no Constitutional Union leader was willing to do so openly, although some later insisted that they had done so. Instead, they emphasized their zealous commitment to moderation. This came naturally, for the former Whigs who dominated the party had long since come to think of themselves as the great conservative bulwark against political extremism, North and South. In coming out for the Constitutional Union ticket, for example, the *Whig* had promised to fight to the bitter end against the "fire-eating, Union-dissolving, political charlatanism, truculence, imprudence, unsoundness, and unfaithfulness of the Southern extremists," as well as against the "*sectionalism* of the Northern Republicans, as a band of outlaws, menacing the integrity of the Union."[63]

The middle ground between Fire-Eaters and abolitionists was vast, however, and Constitutional Unionists' position on the sectional crisis was ambiguous. When they denounced the secret disunionist designs of the Breckinridge Democrats, they appeared in the light of stalwart champions of the Union. But when they defined their response to antislavery aggression, their commitment to the Union looked rather different. This became most evident toward the end of the campaign, when the election of Abraham Lincoln began to look more and more likely. Beginning with the 20 October issue of the *Whig*, William Brownlow evidently felt compelled to clarify his position should Lincoln be elected. He had long maintained that the mere election of a Republican president ("which may God in His mercy prevent") would not be grounds for disunion, but during the last two weeks of the campaign he made clear that there were limits to his allegiance to the federal government. His position was undeniably conservative, and his commitment to the Union was strong—but it was not unconditional. Should the new president personally advocate "unfriendly legislation toward any one section of the country," Brownlow explained, he would first wait to see whether Congress would sustain the executive. If the legislative branch should endorse the hostile measure, he allowed that he would then look to the Supreme Court as the "last resort for justice." If the judiciary also sustained the president, Brownlow declared, "I shall consider that the *time for Revolution has come*—that the sixteen Southern States should go into it—AND I WILL GO WITH THEM, AND FIGHT THE ENEMY TO THE DEATH!"[64]

For all their differences, Knoxville's Constitutional Unionists and Democrats agreed about a great deal in the fall of 1860. With few exceptions, the followers of both John Bell and John Breckinridge were staunchly committed to the defense of slavery. They took white supremacy for granted and abhorred abolitionist efforts to interfere with southern institutions. They preferred to remain within the Union, at least as long as southern rights were secure, and they agreed that the election of Abraham Lincoln would constitute a tragedy of unprecedented proportions. Perhaps it is not surprising, then, that the momentous issues of the election seem to have had little effect on traditional partisan alliances. As was widely true across the border states, local party loyalties held firm in the midst of the most emotionally charged and nationally divisive campaign in American history. The returns from the polling places showed that Bell had won in Knoxville quite handily. The Constitutional Union nominee had received 737 votes, compared with 303 for Breckinridge and 52 for Stephen Douglas, who likely did well only among the town's Irish voters. Bell's proportion of the total vote, 67.5 percent, was remarkably close to that for previous Whig (or Opposition) candidates. The most recent election for national office had occurred in the summer of 1859, when two Knoxville attorneys—Horace Maynard and J. Crozier Ramsey—had squared off against one another in a race for the U.S. congressional seat for Tennessee's second district. Campaigning under the Opposition label, Maynard had earned 67.1 percent of the Knoxville vote en route to victory over his Democratic opponent. This time around, the candidates were not local, but the outcome was almost identical. Party ties were unshaken.[65]

Bell's success in Knoxville was duplicated in much of the upper South. The Tennessean took 74 percent of the vote in rural Knox County, won East Tennessee by about a thousand votes, and received a plurality in the state as a whole. Thanks to the division within the Democratic Party, he claimed Tennessee's twelve electoral votes. Virginia and Kentucky also went for Bell, but the lower South went solidly for Breckinridge. Neither party had much to celebrate, however. Abraham Lincoln had swept across the North, and although the Republican candidate had received less than 40 percent of the popular vote nationally, his 180 electoral votes were more than enough to send him to the White House.[66] The long-dreaded calamity had finally occurred.

CHAPTER THREE

A Town Dividing

In December, 1860, the question was whether there was a sufficient cause for dissolving the Union. In February following, the question was, shall Tennessee secede? In May, it was, what shall I, as an individual, do? Shall I go with my state into secession, or shall I remain true to the old government? So, with each stage of the great revolution, new questions arose for the solution of each individual.   —Knoxville attorney Oliver P. Temple[1]

F OR WILLIAM MCADOO, the final days preceding the election of 6 November were filled with frenetic activity. On Friday the second the forty-year-old lawyer delivered a speech in Knoxville in support of John Bell. On Saturday he spoke on the Tennessean's behalf at a smaller meeting outside of town, accompanied at the gathering by the fittingly named John Bell Brownlow, the Parson's oldest son. Sunday was a day of rest, but on Monday he presided at a Constitutional Union rally near the courthouse, and on election day he cast his ballot and then campaigned around the polls, doing all that he could to encourage the party faithful. After that, along with everyone else in town, he waited to learn the outcome.[2]

There were no exit surveys or Gallup polls in 1860. The process by which the country's thirty-three states elected their chief executive was cumbersome and decentralized, and a wait was to be expected. On Wednesday evening McAdoo and Parson Brownlow had dinner in the home of Oliver P. Temple, and the three prominent Constitutional Unionists discussed the early election returns, but it was still too soon to expect a definite resolution. On Thursday the situation began to come clear. McAdoo spent most of the morning on Gay Street, soaking up election news and sifting through rumors. Much of the news was bad. Lincoln's victory looked pretty firm. On the other hand, Bell appeared to have done extremely well, even better than expected. Reliable information indicated that he had made a strong showing in Knoxville and throughout East Tennessee, and a telegram arrived from Nashville during the day declaring that he had carried the state as a whole. Early reports even suggested (incorrectly, as it turned out) that Bell had also swept the remainder of the border states, claiming the electoral votes of Kentucky, Virginia, North Carolina, Delaware, Missouri, and Maryland.[3]

If there was a silver lining it was that Knoxville Democrats felt even more dejected than local Constitutional Unionists in the election's aftermath. In a letter written the same day, McAdoo reported to an associate in nearby Kingston that "the Brecks are badly used up here." Some of them were already calling for secession, he acknowledged, but an unnamed prankster had ridiculed the idea by tying to a dog's tail a tin bucket marked "Going Out of the Union" and then turning the poor creature loose. The bewildered canine had gone clattering down Gay Street, much to the amusement of a crowd of bystanders. McAdoo closed his letter with the "hope that the vicarious secession of the animal will answer all the purposes of his friends and 'save the union.'"[4]

The time for treating secession lightly was fleeting. Two days later the South Carolina legislature called for the election of a special convention to consider secession. Within three weeks the entire lower South seemed to be rushing headlong toward the precipice. By the time McAdoo joined Brownlow and Temple for Thanksgiving dinner on 29 November, Alabama, Mississippi, Georgia, and Florida had all imitated South Carolina in calling for state secession conventions, and the governor of Louisiana had called for a special session of the state legislature to do the same. The mood around the Parson's table was somber, and the holiday became an occasion more for supplication than for giving thanks. The following evening McAdoo meditated on the November sky and revealed an anxiety that must have been common that Thanksgiving. The heavens were "gloomy, dark, cloudy, [and] boisterous," he recorded in his diary. "How emblematic of the portentous state of public affairs, threatening the integrity of the Government and the infliction of civil war on its citizens!"[5]

McAdoo feared for the fate of the Union, but he also agonized over the difficult personal decision that the momentum of events was thrusting upon him. Immediately after Lincoln's election, when the key question was whether the South should leave the Union in response to the election of a Republican president, McAdoo's answer had been a resounding no. He sincerely desired to preserve the Union; furthermore, he was convinced that the South could secure redress of all its legitimate grievances without disrupting it. Thus, when the rumor reached Knoxville on 8 November that South Carolina was contemplating secession, the lawyer had condemned such a unilateral course as criminally reckless. "God speed her," he had written sarcastically in his diary that night. "I am willing to go with spade and pick axe and work a month to ditch around her and float her out into the Atlantic a thousand miles." Only three weeks later, though, developments in the lower South had transformed the situation. It now appeared certain that many of the southern states were on their way out, which meant that the question of the hour had become, "Shall we Tennesseans go with the South or with the North?" By the middle of December, McAdoo knew how he must answer. "I deplore South Carolina's 'hot haste,'" he confided to his diary, "and the precipitate and uncompromising withdrawal of other Cotton States. But my position is if they will go, now or at any time, I go with them." He would do so with "the darkest forebodings," however. The possibility of a peaceful dissolution of the Union seemed remote. "Soon comes the effusion of blood," he predicted, "soon the Lexington of this revolutionary struggle. With that effusion of blood the maddened masses of both extremes of sectional feeling will rush into a general and bloody war. Such seems the future to me."[6]

Few Knoxvillians saw the future so clearly, and only a small proportion followed the prescient attorney into open support for secession prior to the attack on Fort Sumter. Even so, McAdoo's agonizing reflections highlight two key features of the town's postelection crisis. Like him, most in the community felt an overwhelming sense of powerlessness. They were being swept up by events beyond their control, forced by the distant decisions of extremists—Fire-Eaters and Black Republicans—to struggle with heartrending choices they would rather not face. The Knoxville attorney's experience also underscores the temporal dynamic of the secession crisis. The momentum of events repeatedly altered the exact nature of the dilemma the townspeople confronted. As his former political ally Oliver Temple later recalled, "With each stage of the great revolution, new questions arose for the solution of each individual."[7] Invariably, these questions demanded consideration of multiple and sometimes competing loyalties: most obviously to the Union and to the South, which is how William McAdoo understood the crisis, but also to Tennessee as a whole, to East Tennessee more particularly, and always to the compelling obligations of class, of race, and of party.

ALTHOUGH THEIR WORST FEARS had been realized, on 9 November the people of Knoxville still typically denied that the mere election of Abraham Lincoln required an immediate reaction on the part of the South. They conceded the natural right of revolution and agreed that Tennesseans were free to leave the Union whenever the federal Constitution could no longer protect their safety and happiness from Republican aggression.[8] But the right of revolution was a *moral* right, they believed, only when employed as a last resort to defend a morally justifiable cause.[9] Although subsequent generations of southerners would conspire to remember it differently, white East Tennesseans understood that the cause at stake was the defense of slavery and white supremacy. They agreed with the cotton states that the cause was morally justifiable, but they were far less certain that slavery was seriously in danger. The issue, then, boiled down to whether revolution was called for in the present circumstances. Posed most starkly, was slavery sufficiently in jeopardy to warrant a revolutionary response— a response that might itself further jeopardize slavery? For the moment, caution and prudence seemed to rule the day. When news first arrived of the Republican victory, the overwhelming majority of the town's white population agreed with Parson Brownlow when he asserted that the South had "no right to judge of Lincoln by any thing but his *acts*, and these can only be appreciated *after* his inauguration."[10]

Support for such "masterly inactivity" was not unanimous.[11] A small minority of townspeople maintained that the very election of a Republican president signaled the end of southern security within the Union. According to George Bradfield, the pro-secession editor of the *Knoxville Register*, the election's outcome testified to the ascendancy of the "dangerous *leprosy of Abolitionism*." "*We are a divided people*," he proclaimed not long after the election. "*The last link is broken.*" From the beginning a small group of leading citizens who shared this view did all that they could to promote immediate secession. Their influence far exceeded their numbers, so much so that a visitor in the fall of 1860 concluded that they were "easily in control" of the town. This "little squad of infernal disunionists," as a local confectioner described them, consisted primarily of slaveholding professionals, wealthy men in their thirties and forties drawn disproportionately from Knoxville's oldest and "best" families. They were extensively interrelated by marriage and almost invariably Democrats.[12]

In terms of political influence, perhaps the leading figure among them was attorney John H. Crozier. Crozier had served two terms in Congress during the 1840s as a Whig, but he had converted to the Democratic Party in the mid-1850s, about the time that the Whig Party was collapsing nationally. Shortly after the presidential race, a Knoxville attorney recorded in his diary that Crozier was "bent on dissolution of the Union *now*, in spite of the world, the flesh, and the devil."[13] Also "exceedingly ultra" was William G. Swan, another former Whig politician who had served as state attorney general in the early 1850s before leaving the party. Since then he had focused more on his legal practice and on a variety of business ventures, including the Knoxville Gas and Light Company and a proposed railroad that would connect Knoxville with Charleston, South Carolina.[14] The wealthiest of the group was Swan's brother-in-law, Joseph A. Mabry, an ambitious entrepreneur and incurable speculator. Worth nearly $100,000, the thirty-five-year-old "stock raiser," as he was identified in the 1860 census, was also actively involved in a number of merchandising, banking, and railroad ventures. A credit reporting service described him as "ready for a trade of any kind," and his early support for secession may have had as much to do with an eye for profit as anything else.[15] Likely less opportunistic was another of Mabry's brothers-in-law, C. W. Charlton, postmaster of Knoxville and sometime Methodist minister and journalist. By December he was openly denouncing Democratic leader

Andrew Johnson for his persistent Unionism, and in a subsequent public announcement in the *Whig* he confessed that "his opposition to Black Republicanism has been relentless and uncompromising, as I trust, before high heaven, it may ever be."[16]

For pure ideological zeal, however, none could rival Dr. J. G. M. Ramsey. Sixty-three years young, the energetic physician, banker, railroad director, and historian was a generation older than Knoxville's other leading secessionists. He had cast his first Democratic ballot before either Charlton or Mabry was born, and nearly three decades before either Crozier (his brother-in-law) or Swan (his nephew) joined the party. From the beginning he had gravitated to the Democratic Party's states' rights wing, styling himself a Democrat "of the Jeffersonian school—a believer in that theory of government which makes the states really sovereigns." As early as the 1830s, extensive travel in the North had convinced the doctor that the North and South were really two peoples, "as different in their civilization as the people of France and England." This Appalachian aristocrat had found the people of New England to be "less intelligent, less virtuous, less sensible of their personal rights and liberty, than even our unlettered and uncultivated common people." During his travels Ramsey had discovered that the typical Yankee lacked the "strict regard to truth, probity, virtue, jealousy of liberty and personal self-respect, that constitute the character of a Southern man."[17]

The chasm between the regions could be traced to their labor systems, the physician explained to the editor of the *Charleston Courier* in a letter in 1858. "The free soil and equality notions of the North" were leading predictably to materialism and licentiousness, whereas the South benefited from slavery's "tendency

J. G. M. Ramsey, doctor, banker, farmer, historian. The doctor was correct in his conviction that the days of the Union were numbered, mistaken in his optimism that the separation would be peaceful.

Photograph courtesy of McClung Historical Collection, Knox County Public Library.

not only to improve but to elevate, refine, and ennoble society." The differences between North and South were insuperable. "I conceal from no one my deep conviction that the days of the present Union are nearly numbered," Ramsey wrote some three years before the attack on Fort Sumter. "We are destined to a separation. . . . It is inevitable." Unlike William McAdoo, Ramsey anticipated the prospect with equanimity. "Shall the separation be peaceful?" he asked rhetorically in closing his correspondence. "I hope it may. I almost think it will."[18]

For immediate secessionists like Crozier and Ramsey, the certain secession of the lower South presented an opportunity rather than a dilemma. Building a convincing case for secession solely on a supposedly imminent threat to slavery had always been a tall order in East Tennessee. To begin with the obvious, nine-tenths of the white population did not own slaves. Although the region's white majority had been outspoken in support of the institution for at least a generation, the anxiety over the security of slavery was quite naturally less pronounced there than in plantation regions to the south and west. Beyond this, opponents of separation were quick to point out that the slave states still effectively controlled the Senate and the Supreme Court. Thus even if the president-elect wished to strike a blow at slavery in the states (and they denied that he did), his hands would be effectively tied. With equal validity, they ridiculed Dr. Ramsey's hopes for peaceable secession. ("Only a mad man or a fool" could hold to such a view, according to Brownlow.) Secession would likely lead to war, they predicted, and the attendant turmoil would render slavery very insecure. As Oliver Temple declared at a public rally the Sunday before Thanksgiving, they believed that "the only safety for Slavery is in the Union under the Constitution."[19]

The impending departure of the cotton states threatened to change this. It altered the terms of the debate by introducing a new and difficult question: Even if separation was adjudged rash or premature, didn't deep and long-standing ties with her sister slave states dictate that Tennessee stand with the lower South? Several prominent Knoxvillians thought so. The clerk of the federal district court recalled long afterward that "he never was dissatisfied with the Government of the United States" and "regretted the prospect of its disruption." Even so, when it became evident that the two sections could no longer coexist peacefully within the Union, "he decided to go with the South and accept her destiny." A profit-minded Knoxville professional who had originally opposed secession reversed his course in December, citing Tennessee's greater commercial connections with the lower South. "The laws of trade compel us. Every mans [sic] pocket binds him there." The best-known convert was former congressman William H. Sneed, a prominent Whig leader who had slowly gravitated to the Democratic Party at the very close of the 1850s. "I am for the South," he declared in a public statement after New Year's, and "I shall lend my aid to place Tennessee . . . for weal or woe, with her 'Sister Southern States.'"[20]

Immediate secessionists altered their strategy in order to exploit such sympathies and draw more of their reluctant neighbors into the fold. They now couched efforts to promote secession in passionate declarations that the South must stand united in its time of trial. The Ramsey-Crozier faction unveiled this approach at a meeting in Knoxville called for the Monday evening before Thanksgiving. Although the expressed goal of the gathering was merely to provide a forum in which to discuss the current crisis, it is clear that the immediate secessionists hoped to dominate the meeting and use it to bolster support for disunion. The chair was a secessionist, Knoxville grocer Joseph Walker, and eight of the ten men on the resolutions committee were future Confederates. They submitted a series of resolutions that, if implemented, would have ensured Tennessee's secession. Granted, the resolutions began with a condemnation of the unilateral secession of individual states as likely to "imperil the peace, safety, and happiness" of the others. But they then called for a convention of all the slave states that would propose an ultimatum to the new Republican administration. The convention should call for the immediate repeal of northern "liberty laws" (state acts aimed at interfering with the return of fugitive slaves), as well as ironclad guarantees to the South of "her rights in the Territories of our common government." Should these "reasonable demands" be disregarded, the resolutions concluded, the southern states should secede en masse.[21]

By condemning unilateral secession and concentrating on "reasonable demands," this "cooperationist" strategy smacked just enough of moderation to attract a number of sincere opponents of disunion. Seventy-five-year-old Frederick Heiskell, a Constitutional Unionist who would remain staunchly loyal to the Union throughout the war, wrote to John Bell only days after Lincoln's election with a series of very similar proposals. Heiskell recommended that Bell call for a convention of all the states in which the South, "in a mild and dignified manner," might "make known her requirements." Simply calling the conference would "induce the people to pause and reflect." And when the North conceded all that the South had any right to ask, which Heiskell fully expected, their response would "stay the torrent of southern fanaticism." William J. Baker, a local physician, concurred with Heiskell's proposal, believing that it would "result in much good, & possibly save the Constitution & the Union." William McAdoo believed that all of the North except perhaps for New England would readily accede to southern demands. "The temperate action of all the slave states in conference," he noted in his diary, "could *preserve the union*."[22] John Baxter, a wealthy Knoxville attorney and banker who waffled repeatedly after the Fort Sumter crisis, emerged in late November as a strong advocate of a southern convention, and those who knew him best insisted that he did so to undermine the building momentum for secession across the cotton states. Even Parson Brownlow flirted with the idea, allowing Baxter to write an unsigned editorial endorsing such a convention in the 24 November issue of the *Whig*. In a piece entitled "What Shall the South Do?" Baxter contended that a southern convention would enable the upper South to exert a calming influence on the lower South. "Possibly such a conference may save the Union," Baxter later averred.[23]

Other Unionists disagreed. At the meeting on 26 November, Horace Maynard, Oliver Temple, and attorney John Fleming led the effort to derail the support for a cooperationist strategy. Maynard, the U.S. representative for Tennessee's second district, opposed the resolutions on the grounds that Congress (due shortly to convene) was likely to produce some sort of compromise legislation that would assuage southern concerns. Temple and Fleming concentrated on persuading the gathering to postpone a vote on the resolutions until 8 December, and in the interim they went to work to convince Brownlow that extremists would inevitably dominate a slave-state convention and force Tennessee into support for secession. They also put the word out in the surrounding countryside, alerting those "as yet untainted with disloyalty" to the danger of endorsing a southern convention. The result, as William McAdoo ruefully recorded, was that "large numbers flocked in from the County, all possessed of the one idea that the former meeting was a disunion concern, and that the perpetuity of our Government depended on their putting down every thing the town people proposed." With a far larger number in attendance, the meeting of 8 December voted down the cooperationist resolutions and passed instead a declaration that Tennessee was "loyal and devoted to the union of these states" and "recognized no constitutional right in any state, or combination of states, to *force her into an attitude of hostility to the Union.*" McAdoo berated the decision as ignorant and unwise, and lawyer W. B. Reese, another recent advocate of southern independence, claimed that the people did not understand what they had done.[24]

In reality they probably did. By demanding recognition of the right to take slaves anywhere into the territories, the defeated resolutions had effectively required the Republican president-elect to repudiate the platform on which he had been elected. The resolutions committee might have considered their demands "reasonable," but the prospect of their being accepted by the North was negligible. And regardless of which politicians ultimately dominated the proposed southern convention, no ultimatum would carry any weight at all unless its proponents really were prepared to act if the ultimatum was rejected. What would upper South "Union men" do, John Baxter asked, should the delegates to the southern conference determine to secede if their demands were not met? "Go with them," was the answer, "and go all together, at once and at the same time, although we deny the right of secession." In the lower South the cooperationist position could rightly be viewed as a moderate alternative to Fire-Eaters' demands for immediate, unilateral secession. In East Tennessee, on the other hand, as in much of the upper South, a large majority already opposed a precipitate response. No matter how it was presented, the most likely effect of a southern ultimatum would be to increase support for secession in the name of southern unity. With a few exceptions, supporters on both sides of the issue recognized this, and the vote on 8 December was effectively the town's first referendum on secession. The secessionists lost badly.[25]

TWO MONTHS LATER THEY lost badly again, this time when the overwhelming opposition of East Tennessee voters derailed a statewide movement to consider the possibility of secession. South Carolina formally seceded on 20 December, and thereafter the cooperationist strategy as a cover for out-and-out secessionism no longer made sense. Now to cooperate with the cotton states simply meant following them out of the Union. In Tennessee the issue was explicitly broached in early January when the state legislature convened in special session at the behest of Democratic governor Isham G. Harris. In his opening address, Harris castigated the North for its "long, systematic, and wanton agitation of the slavery question." He intimated that the preservation of the Union required at least five constitutional amendments, including the permanent resurrection of the Missouri Compromise line all the way to the Pacific Ocean and a provision that would require northern states to pay southern slave owners double the value of all fugitive slaves harbored within their borders. Should the North reject these "just and reasonable" demands, the governor suggested that secession would be an appropriate recourse.[26]

Acting on the governor's recommendation, the General Assembly passed an act on 19 January calling for a general referendum to be held across the state a mere three weeks later. According to the act, when voters went to the polls they were to fulfill two tasks. First, they were to vote on whether to hold a special convention to consider the desirability of secession or any other measures necessary to vindicate the sovereignty of the state. Second, they were to elect delegates to attend such a convention should it be approved. Within days, separate meetings of Unionists and secessionists had been held in Knoxville to nominate slates of three candidates to represent Knox County in the proposed convention. The Union men of Knox County nominated three well-known Unionists: Temple, Baxter, and Connally F. Trigg, a prominent Knoxville lawyer and later U.S. district judge. All were wealthy and politically active Constitutional Unionists, and Temple and Baxter were also slaveholders. The pro-secession meeting seems to have consciously avoided candidates identified in the public mind as "original secessionists," individuals such as John Crozier and J. G. M. Ramsey who had advocated separation immediately after Lincoln's election. Two of their three nominees, dry-goods merchant Wilburn Walker and physician James W. Paxton, had little if any experience in politics. The third, former congressman William H. Sneed (the only slaveholder in the group), was at the time widely seen as a moderate, having arrived at a pro-secession stance only after the secession of the lower South appeared inevitable.[27]

Leading up to the referendum, Sneed issued a lengthy campaign circular that neatly encapsulated the secessionist argument not only in Knoxville but also all across the upper South. Sneed's statement appeared in its entirety in the *Whig*, accompanied by a rare personal tribute from the editor, who was not in the habit of praising political opponents. "Our relations with those of Col. Sneed are those of sincere friendship," the Parson observed, and we have been accustomed to vote for him, and regret that we are now on different sides." But his former ally was now in the wrong, Brownlow stated matter-of-factly, and it would be his duty to work to defeat him. There was only one question before the voters: "whether we shall break up this Government and plunge our country into anarchy and civil war, or whether we shall stay *in* the Union, and demand our rights *under* the Constitution and Laws of our country."[28]

Not so, Sneed argued. At the outset he stressed that the real question before the voters concerned the division of the South, not of the Union. The division of the Union—however regrettable—was an accomplished fact, and the voters of Tennessee could do nothing to undo it. They did, however, have it within their power to forestall the division of the South, a catastrophe of immense proportions. If the South was unified, even the Black Republicans were not foolhardy enough to attempt their subjugation. But if the southern states did not stand united in this hour of crisis, then "northern Abolitionists" would most certainly attempt by force of arms to coerce them into submission. The result would not only be war against the North, Sneed warned ominously, but also civil war within the South. "Are you prepared, my countrymen, to see your fields desolated, your habitations destroyed, your fellow citizens, your wives and children slaughtered, either by abolitionism from abroad, or by discordant, conflicting, divided and phrensied [*sic*] passion of brothers and neighbors at home?" It was all so unnecessary, the congressman argued, given that white southerners all agreed about the North's grievous offenses. True, they differed concerning the appropriate response to northern aggression, but was this really a sufficient reason to instigate a "fratricidal war"?

Sneed then proceeded to defend the cotton states' assessment of the South's imminent peril. The incoming Republican president had openly admitted his desire for the destruction of slavery. Lincoln had also designated as his "premier" William H. Seward, an antislavery zealot who had declared that the slave and free states were locked in an "irrepressible conflict." The future secretary of state had even claimed that a "higher law" than the Constitution should govern national policy toward slavery. In the hope of saving the Union, southerners had offered "proposition after proposition for conciliation," but each offer had been spurned by the Republican fanatics. "Can we hope for justice from Abolitionism and its rulers?" Sneed asked. The past offenses of "Abolitionism" (i.e., the Republican Party) dictated the unavoidable conclusion. Abolitionism had sought restrictions on slavery in the territories and had denounced the decision of the

Supreme Court when it had asserted slaveholders' lawful interests there. Abolitionism had interfered with the constitutional protections of the fugitive slave
clause, promoted the Underground Railroad, and canonized the murderer John
Brown as a saint and martyr. Finally, "in the person of the president-elect," abolitionism had "asserted the equality of the *black* with the *white* race."[29]

The entire white South was endangered by this fanatical course, Sneed maintained, but nonslaveholders—poor whites especially—had the most to fear.
Emancipation would remove slaves from the taxable property of the state and lead
necessarily to higher taxes on all other forms of property. It would also force
working-class whites to compete for jobs with rude and unskilled Africans, inevitably resulting in lower wage rates for manual labor. Worst of all, the resulting racial equality would create an intolerable social climate, and whereas the
wealthy would have the resources to leave the South, the poor would remain
behind to face ignominy and shame.

Sneed's circular foreshadowed every major argument employed by local secessionists during the remainder of the secession crisis: (1) loyalty to the Union
per se was a moot point, because the Union handed down by the Founding
Fathers no longer existed; (2) given the Union's regrettable collapse, the loyalty
of Tennessee properly belonged with the South; (3) a divided South would lead
to civil war within the region and the lamentable prospect of white southerners
assisting in the coercion of the seceding states; (4) both slavery and white supremacy were in imminent danger, and the only hope for their preservation lay
in southern unity; and (5) the demise of slavery would harm nonslaveholding
whites most of all.

The readers of the *Whig* were unconvinced. Local secessionists suffered a
lopsided defeat when voters went to the polls on 9 February, the very day after
a convention meeting in Montgomery, Alabama, finished drafting a provisional
constitution for the Confederate States of America. West Tennessee voters
strongly favored holding a convention, while voters in Middle Tennessee were
pretty evenly divided. East Tennesseans, by contrast, made it clear that they
wanted no part of this new confederacy. Fully 81 percent opposed holding a convention even to consider such a course, and the resulting twenty-five-thousand-
vote margin determined the outcome of the convention proposal statewide.[30] The
returns from Knox County showed that 89 percent of voters had opposed a convention. There, as elsewhere in East Tennessee, support for secession was apparently greater in urban areas than in the countryside, prompting one Unionist
to crow that "when we go out of the town into the country, Secessionists are as
scarce as *hen's teeth*." They were far from plentiful in town, however, even though
the local secessionist leadership was centered there. The proportion favoring a
convention was 23 percent, but roughly half of those voting "yea" also voted for
Unionist delegates to attend it and presumably expected the convention to exert
a conservative influence. In short, as late as the second week in February, nearly

nine-tenths of Knoxville's voters still opposed immediate secession. "The city of Knoxville has covered herself all over with glory," Parson Brownlow exulted, "by her vindication of the Union, her devotion to the Constitution, and her crushing repudiation of the Hell-born monster Secession!"[31]

BROWNLOW CAN BE FORGIVEN for gloating, but his jubilant rhetoric oversimplified a complex reality. Yes, the majority of Knoxville voters had repudiated secession, but did they necessarily do so primarily to vindicate the Union and express their devotion to the Constitution? It is crucial at this point to distinguish between two related but distinct dimensions of "Unionism."[32] On the one hand, the term speaks to the *behavior* of an individual. A "Unionist," either by word or by deed, supported the preservation of the Union rather than the cause of secession. On the other hand, the label can refer to the emotional and ideological commitments that underlie behavior, meaning the individual's *state of mind*. Here things get complicated.

During and after the Civil War, leading East Tennessee loyalists sought to educate northern audiences with regard to both facets of southern Unionism. They stressed the widespread opposition to the Confederacy in their homeland and recounted innumerable individual acts of daring and sacrifice for the cause of Union victory. At the same time—often in the same breath—they ascribed such behavior to an unalloyed patriotism that placed fidelity to the nation above loyalty to the South and southern institutions. Unionist refugees from Knoxville were among the first to convey this message. Some eighteen months after Lincoln's election, Parson Brownlow identified himself at a northern patriotic rally as "an unconditional, straight-out Union man" and pledged his willingness even to sacrifice slavery in order to subdue the rebellion. German immigrant Hermann Bokum, who fled Knox County during the period of Confederate occupation, reiterated this view. "The Union is with the Union men of East Tennessee the paramount question," the refugee declared in a book published in Philadelphia in 1864. "Every other is secondary."[33] In like manner, after the Union army occupied much of East Tennessee in the fall of 1863, local Unionists were quick to emphasize the population's undying commitment to the Constitution and the Union. In a petition requesting economic assistance for the region, six prominent Knoxville Unionists instructed the U.S. Congress on the depths of East Tennessee's patriotism. When the sectional crisis erupted, they explained, "her people did not stop to consider their local or pecuniary interests. Their innate love of country rose above the narrow and selfish considerations that controlled the people and dictated the policy of other states." Long after the war, amateur historians labored to reinforce this portrayal. In 1888, for example, Knoxville minister Thomas Humes wrote a "four-hundred-page rhapsody" to East Tennessee Unionism in which he attributed the loyalties of his mountain neighbors to their "deep and strong love for their *whole country*."[34]

Such statements need to be examined both contextually and philosophically. The post-1861 claims of southern Unionists came regularly with ulterior motives, whether it was to stimulate patriotism, elicit sympathy, or inspire admiration. They were also part of a broader self-conscious and self-interested struggle between Confederates and Unionists to explain East Tennessee's stubborn dissent. The predominant Confederate interpretation—a bit short on nuance—emphasized the stupidity and ignorance of "Lincolnite" mountaineers. In an article titled "Disloyalty of East Tennessee—How Will It Be Accounted For," the pro-secession *Knoxville Register* pointed to the inability of "Tories" to recognize their own interests or perceive slights to their honor. "How inconceivably great the ignorance of such a people!" railed the editor. "How persistent in adhesion to error!"[35]

Similar views prevailed elsewhere in the South. The *Nashville Banner* lamented the region's shortsightedness. "If East Tennessee could cast her eye ten years beyond the present, there would not be a Unionist in any of her mountain heights," the *Banner* declared. Given the area's fast-moving streams and natural treasures of coal and lumber, her villages would rapidly become "the Lowells and Walthams" of an independent southern confederacy. Less charitable, an Alabama newspaper ridiculed East Tennesseans as "a poor, miserable, ignorant, woebegone set of creatures." Richmond newspaper editor Edward A. Pollard concurred; in explaining the area's sizable Unionist element, it was enough to observe that "this section was inhabited by an ignorant and uncouth population."[36] In short, the Confederate "explanation" was no explanation at all, but rather a demeaning caricature of ignorant hillbillies perfectly consonant with late-nineteenth-century stereotypes of Appalachian isolation and backwardness. But it is only fair to note that the Unionist response was simply to fashion a different kind of crude stereotype, that of the sturdy mountaineer who loved freedom more than life itself and cherished the Union with a blindly patriotic, almost mystical devotion. Neither interpretation is very helpful.

It is also important to think about Unionist claims more philosophically. Whereas Confederates more often than not condemned Unionists for being unable to perceive their true interests, Unionists argued that East Tennessee loyalists consciously denied all other interests in deference to their one supreme loyalty. Implicitly at least, they described unionism as akin to religious faith, an exclusive type of commitment that, if genuine, necessarily supersedes all other forms of attachment. For Americans in 1861, however, commitment to the Union—whether strong or weak—coexisted alongside numerous other forms of group loyalty, which may have either weakened or complemented and reinforced it. Unionist behavior was undeniably widespread in East Tennessee during both the secession crisis and the four years of war that followed. More than thirty thousand voters in the region cast their ballots against secession. Perhaps forty-two thousand Tennesseans served in the Union army, with the lion's share of these hailing from East Tennessee.[37] Yet at no point during the secession crisis could their ideological commitment to the Union be described as "unconditional," whatever Brownlow might later claim, nor, with all due respect to Reverend Humes, was it grounded simply in a "deep and strong love for their whole country." In making such claims, leading Unionists explained the loyal *behavior* of East Tennesseans with reference to a loyal *mind-set* in which commitment to the Union overwhelmed all other attachments. It is just as likely that opposition to secession was strong in East Tennessee because whites could view loyalty to the Union as incorporating, rather than superseding, other bonds that they held dear.

A close reading of Brownlow's *Whig* during the secession crisis suggests just this conclusion. Although we cannot be certain what the rank and file of East Tennessee Unionists were thinking and feeling as they decided to oppose disunion, much can be inferred from the pages of the *Whig*, whose circulation escalated dramatically during the secession crisis. With as many as fourteen thousand readers by the spring of 1861, Brownlow was actually reaching a larger audience than any other southern Unionist, and not even the Parson's most hostile critics could deny the newspaper's influence.[38] "The rabble have it as their guide and textbook," one bitterly remarked. "It enter[s] and pollute[s] every home," another local secessionist complained, "deluding and poisoning the public mind." Incensed by the paper's "treasonous" rhetoric, southern communities from North Carolina to Texas banned the *Whig* as an "incendiary sheet" or burned its editor in effigy.[39]

Whatever Brownlow may have said later, during the secession crisis he recognized the need to fashion an argument against separation that resonated with as many of his readers' attachments as possible. Patriotic rhetoric was far from nonexistent in the *Whig*, but the editor of the most widely read Unionist sheet in the future Confederacy used it sparingly, rarely emphasizing national loyalty per se.[40] Instead, he countered secessionist tactics by arguing that a combination of other allegiances—to slavery, to the white race, to the Whig Party, to East Tennessee, and to the working class—dictated that his readers stand against disunion.

Brownlow's first task was to refute the secessionist argument that opposition to disunion was tantamount to endorsement of the "Black Republican agenda." Countering assertions that southern Unionists were "submissionists" and Knoxville was "a damned abolition hole," Brownlow proclaimed that southerners only "differed as to the *time* and *mode* of resistance." Unlike secessionists, Unionists still believed it possible to defend slavery within the Union, under the Constitution. Yet as the nation teetered on the brink of war, the Parson declared that no white southerner was prepared to submit to the antislavery platform on which Lincoln had been elected. "If we were once convinced in the border Slave States that the Administration at Washington . . . contemplated the *subjugation* of the South or the *abolishing* of slavery, there would not be a Union man among us in twenty-four hours."[41]

At the same time, Brownlow argued anew that slavery was not currently in danger nor were Southern rights in jeopardy. The new Republican president would still be bound by the protections of the Constitution, and the Supreme Court would still remain under conservative control. If the northern states would repeal their "personal liberty" laws (state laws interfering with the return of fugitive slaves) and codify the Supreme Court's ruling on the inviolability of slavery in the states (the decision in *Dred Scott v. Sanford*), slavery would be as secure as southern whites could ever hope for. In early 1861 the prospects for both seemed promising. To underscore this point, Brownlow published a lengthy letter and two speeches from the pen of Horace Maynard, Knoxville's Constitutional Union congressman who was then serving on a special committee in the House of Representatives charged with crafting a legislative compromise to end the sectional crisis.

In a missive dated 14 January, the congressman reported his confidence that Congress would eventually pass the so-called Crittenden compromise, a package of constitutional amendments that would, among other things, explicitly forbid the federal government from interfering with slavery in the states and resurrect the Missouri Compromise line to govern the future expansion of slavery into the territories. In a speech from 30 January to a delegation of "workingmen from Philadelphia," Maynard similarly contended that fully four-fifths of the people of the North favored the repeal of personal liberty laws if doing so would forestall disunion. By reprinting a speech Maynard delivered on the floor of the House on 6 February, Brownlow also reminded readers that southern Unionists were defenders of southern rights as well as advocates of sectional compromise. In his remarks Maynard castigated the Republican Party for being "wholly unable to apprehend the upheaval of a discontented, aggrieved people." True, the driving force behind secession was a small group of clever men who were "disunionists for the sake of disunion," but their arguments for southern independence had been given power by the growth in the "popular delusion" of abolitionism and the "anti-southern crusade" that had culminated in the election of Abraham Lincoln."[42]

Should Congress fail to devise a satisfactory compromise, there was also the possibility that the peace conference scheduled to meet in Washington, D.C., in February 1861 might bear fruit. Responding to a call issued by the Virginia state legislature, fourteen free states and seven slave states had agreed to send delegates to the nation's capital to discuss a range of compromise proposals. Among Tennessee's representatives at the meeting would be Knoxville's own Robert J. McKinney. Born in Londonderry County, Ireland, McKinney had immigrated to East Tennessee in 1809 at the age of six. He began practicing law in 1824 at the ripe age of twenty-one and rose quickly in his profession, ultimately being named to the state supreme court in 1847. McKinney opposed any "further dismemberment" of the Union—which meant that he opposed secession but also objected to any effort on the part of the federal government to "coerce" the lower South into submission. He went to Washington "ready to concur in any plan that will secure us protection in the undisturbed enjoyment of our just and equal rights, in the future; and to leave open the door to the return of those States that have rashly forced themselves out of the Union." After weeks of deliberation, the assembled delegates agreed on a single constitutional amendment that incorporated, in modified form, the signal features of the Crittenden Compromise. McKinney returned to Knoxville in early March, read the text of the proposed amendment to a crowd gathered outside the county courthouse, and declared it more than satisfactory to the South.[43]

The upshot of all this, Brownlow contended, was that, for the moment, slavery was safer within the Union than outside of it, and the true friend of the "peculiar institution" was the conservative who stood firm against the foolhardy, self-destructive agenda of the Fire-Eaters. Echoing an argument common among upper South Unionists, the Parson declared time and again that secession would not remedy any ill facing the South. On the contrary, the disunionist scheme was "a more consummate Abolition contrivance than ever was devised at the North, by the most ultra anti-slavery men." By precipitating civil war and an inevitable invasion of the slave states, it would "bring about the overthrow of Slavery, one hundred years sooner than the Republican Party could have done it."[44] Brownlow also devised his own kind of racist argument, twisting support for secession into an obsession with blacks akin to that supposedly monopolized by abolitionists. Both, the Parson concluded, had a bad case of "nigger on the brain." Indeed, since secessionists and Unionists were both opposed to abolition, it was this fixation on the Negro that primarily distinguished those clamoring for disunion. The confederacy they sought to create would rest on a new reading of the Ten Commandments that stressed that "the chief end of man is nigger."[45]

Given that secession could not possibly benefit slavery—according to the proslavery Parson—the question naturally arose as to why so many southern whites seemed bent on destroying the Union. Brownlow's answer mirrored the Confederate explanation for southern Unionism. The masses who supported secession were sincere but stupid, he averred bluntly, duped by leaders who were insincere and cunning. In fact, the whole movement to break up the Union was "the work of corrupt, designing, and unprincipled demagogues, who seek their own and not their country's good." It was also no coincidence, he noticed, that the individuals who owed the most money to northern merchants and bankers were the most outspoken supporters of disunion, finding in secession the attractive prospect of canceling valid debts.[46]

Brownlow knew beyond question that secessionist leaders were "corrupt and designing" because of what else he knew about them: they were Democrats, and that pretty much settled the matter. It is difficult to exaggerate the importance of partisan themes in the Parson's assault on secession. Granted, in Tennessee as in other upper South states, there was a serious effort in early 1861 to establish a "Union Party" that would encompass loyalists of all political backgrounds. Even after the effort failed in the wake of the attack on Fort Sumter, East Tennessee Unionists often told northern audiences that loyalists in the South had abandoned all of their old party allegiances to unite in the common defense of the Union. For example, a representative of the newly formed East Tennessee Relief Association informed a Boston audience in 1864 that the old parties had all been dissolved by "the great questions that have divided us for the last four years." There were now only two parties, he claimed, "the one known as the Union party, and the other as the Secession or Rebel party."[47] There was a grain of truth in what he said. Neither antebellum party was completely unified during the sectional crisis, which meant that one could find both Whig and Democratic Unionists and both Democratic and Whig secessionists. Sometimes the examples of political reconciliation that resulted were spectacular. The most striking case in point was the tenuous rapprochement between William Brownlow and Andrew Johnson, who suddenly found themselves on the same side after two decades as bitter political rivals. The Parson had once denounced Johnson as a "huge mass of corruption" and a "beast in human form." His opinion was unchanged as late as the 1860 presidential campaign, during which Johnson faithfully supported the Democratic nominee, John Breckinridge. But in mid-December the Greeneville Democrat had delivered a harsh condemnation of secession on the floor of the U.S. Senate, and by the end of the month his longtime enemy was telling Knoxville Democrats that "Johnson is right . . . and I will defend him to the last." When a pro-secession newspaper from upper East Tennessee ridiculed the new alliance, Brownlow admitted in the *Whig* that he had opposed Johnson for twenty years and even now he did not admire him. They were now allies nonetheless, he explained, because they stood together on the same ground. Both were determined to defend the Constitution and the Union in their hour of peril.[48]

The "Constitution and the Union," however, had long been the mantra of the border-state Whigs, who had actually built the Constitutional Union platform in 1860 around an elaboration of the phrase. (Their entire platform consisted of the slogan "The Constitution of the Country, the Union of the States, and the enforcement of the laws.")[49] References to a "Union Party" notwithstanding, Constitutional Unionists in East Tennessee did not view cooperation with Unionist Democrats as the forerunner of a new party, but rather as the enlargement and resurgence of the old Whig Party. Quite accurately, they looked around them and saw that almost every prominent Democrat in the eastern part of the state was going over to secession (with Andrew Johnson the most glaring exception). A local Democrat ruefully admitted as much when he sent word to Johnson that the senator should endorse the appointment of a Whig as the next postmaster of Knoxville. Joseph McDannel, a small businessman and brother of one of Johnson's oldest advisers, indicated that "all the leading democrats about Knoxville, who are qualified, are disunionists."[50] Conversely, although in East Tennessee not all prominent former Whigs were Unionists, almost every prominent Unionist was a former Whig. If some rank-and-file Democrats now chose to follow them, it was misleading to say that they were forging a new party. They were *converting*.[51]

In a word, old partisan divisions may have blurred somewhat, but traditional party allegiances still mattered. Not long after Brownlow vowed to support Andrew Johnson "to the last," Knoxville's Constitutional Unionists became highly agitated by a rumor that Johnson intended to recommend a Democrat as the next local postmaster. A clerk in a dry-goods store wrote to Johnson to complain that the supposed appointee was not a better Union man than several "Whig" aspirants, giving rise to the conclusion that "the only apparent grounds for your favoring his appointment is that he was of the same political faith as you before *the recent overthrow of all parties*." Constitutional Unionists outnumbered Unionist Democrats more than three to one in Knox County, the clerk maintained, and the appointment of a Democrat would "not be very satisfactory to them." (Johnson's young correspondent was oblivious to the obvious contradiction: all the old parties had been "overthrown," but men who had "formerly" been Constitutional Unionists still objected to a postmaster who had "formerly" been a Democrat.) By early April, Parson Brownlow had become convinced that the new Republican president planned to take his cues on patronage appointments in East Tennessee from the Democrat Johnson, and there was probably no other time during the entire secession crisis that his commitment to the Unionist cause was more sorely tested. "Whilst I am a Union man, in every sense of the word," Brownlow editorialized, "I am not to be used in the name of UNION to help re-construct the Democratic party, whose corruptions, insincerity, demagoguism, and general policy, have brought the country to the verge of ruin." If the "Union Party" was to be a vehicle for promoting Democratic ambitions, then Brownlow wanted no part of it, and the sooner it disintegrated the better.[52]

Even after the "overthrow" of the old parties, then, one of the most effective ways for Brownlow to malign the motives of prominent secessionists was merely to observe that they were Democrats. As the Parson employed it, the very term itself became an epithet. While fire-eating secessionists were emphasizing the corruption of the old political parties and calling for "a revolution against politics," the *Whig* editor was attributing the momentum for secession to the demagoguery of political opportunists. Secession would not even be an issue, Brownlow claimed, had not Democratic office seekers irresponsibly agitated abstract sectional issues for partisan advantage. As early as March 1860, he had blamed southern Democrats for the rise of the Republican Party. "If the Union is dissolved," Brownlow had thundered, "and the institutions of the country are overthrown, this vile, designing, corrupt and abominable Democracy are [*sic*] responsible for it."[53]

Brownlow muted his partisan rhetoric as the February referendum approached, but never completely. Even as Brownlow defended Johnson in print, he took the opportunity to contrast the senator with the "hypocritical, insincere, and unprincipled Democrats" with whom he had been allied until just weeks before. He also spoke frequently in code words laden with partisan meaning. After the Unionist victory of 9 February, for example, he exhorted loyalists in an editorial entitled "Put None on Guard but Union Men." Readers immediately recognized this as a variation on the slogan emblazoned across the masthead of the *Whig*. A holdover from the days when the *Whig* had been affiliated with the now-defunct Know-Nothing Party, the masthead read "Put None on Guard but Americans." The replacement of a single word, evidently, would facilitate the latest reincarnation of East Tennessee's Whigs, who in the past five years had also campaigned under the banner of the American (or Know-Nothing) Party, the "Opposition," and most recently the Constitutional Union Party. In calling for his readers to keep Union men "on guard" (on the alert against secessionist intrigue), Brownlow added that no one should be allowed to pass "who cannot give the 'counter sign': the Union, the Constitution, and the enforcement of the laws." How convenient that the "counter sign" of East Tennessee Unionists should be the official motto of the Constitutional Union Party! By March, Brownlow had dropped such "subtlety" and was again openly blasting the Breckinridge Democrats. It was the loss of political spoils, not concern about the security of slavery, that stimulated their demands for secession, he maintained. Indeed, the creation of the Confederacy in February 1861 represented nothing more than "a revival of corrupt Southern Democracy." Support for the Confederacy, by extension, was tantamount to conversion to the Democratic Party, a course that Brownlow politely promised to follow as soon as hell froze over.[54]

If old Whig allegiances helped to blunt secessionist appeals, so too did East Tennesseans' long-standing sense of their region's geographic uniqueness and economic inferiority. The pages of the *Whig* seethed with accusations against the cotton states for their alleged determination to dominate the upper South. While secessionists sought to convince white Southerners that the greatest danger to their liberties lay in an external threat—the abolitionist agenda of the Black Republican Party—Brownlow countered by stressing an internal threat, warning his upper South readers that the chief menace to their liberties would come from within the new Confederacy. Noting that the three-fifths clause gave white voters in the Black Belt an artificial political advantage over their upper South counterparts, Brownlow insinuated that secessionists fomented fear about equality among the races merely to perpetuate inequality among whites. The border states could never live in peace with such men, he concluded. Although he continued to espouse the preservation of the Union as his personal preference, during the first half of 1861 the Parson suggested a variety of alternatives to alliance with the Deep South should a permanent rupture be unavoidable. To begin with, the border states could move to establish a "Middle Confederacy," a proposal also briefly espoused by Unionists in Virginia and North Carolina. If the rest of the upper South refused to cooperate, Tennessee could declare itself an independent republic. Should Middle and West Tennessee oppose such a course, East Tennessee itself could secede and form its own "independent Mountain State."[55]

It is doubtful that Brownlow viewed any of these recommendations as even remotely feasible, but as rhetorical devices they reveal much about his "Unionist" strategy during the secession crisis. The preservation of the Union was greatly to be desired, his readers learned, but Black Belt domination was to be prevented at all costs. As Brownlow put it, "We can never live in a Southern Confederacy, and be made hewers of wood and drawers of water for a set of aristocrats"—an appropriate role for slaves but not for free men. East Tennesseans, at least, stood to gain nothing in exchange for such degradation, for as "a grain-growing and stock-raising people," they shared no common interests with the lower South. Yet, in the war that would inevitably ensue after secession, the "honest yeomanry" of the border states would be "forced to leave their wives and children" and "fight for the purse-proud aristocrats of the Cotton States, whose pecuniary abilities [would] enable them to hire substitutes!"[56]

As these comments make apparent, such charges were designed to stimulate class resentment as well as regional rivalry. Secessionists like William Sneed argued that working-class whites would suffer disproportionately from the Black Republican agenda; Brownlow responded that secession would prove devastating to the common folk. Black Belt leaders intended to roll back the democratic advances of the past two generations, he informed readers of the *Whig*. They wanted "a King, or a limited Monarchy," and they would restrict the franchise to the owners of land and slaves, effectively excluding the majority of East Tennesseans, while reserving to slaveholders all "offices of honor and profit." The result would be a "SLAVERY ARISTOCRACY" that would "overshadow and dishonor poor white men."[57] Slaveless whites in such a confederacy would be socially degraded as well as politically disfranchised. "We never thought it a *disgrace* to labor," he sermonized, "or to eat bread and meat 'by the sweat of our brow.' It may suit the hateful aristocrats, and purseproud nabobs of Cottonocracy, to frown down on laboring men and mechanics," the former carpenter declared, "but we Union men, in the Old Confederacy, learned a different lesson from the signers of the Declaration of Independence, many of whom were mechanics and day-laborers."[58]

These arguments worked in Knoxville during the winter of 1860–61. Secessionists like William Sneed had made the case for disunion by appealing to the townspeople's loyalty to the lower South, to slavery and to white supremacy, and to the welfare of the working class. Unionist leaders persuasively countered with a strategy that emphasized time-tested themes of partisan and regional attachment—to the old Whig Party and to East Tennessee—and insisted that the true friends of slavery and the white worker were those who resisted the self-interested agenda of the Fire-Eaters. Nearly nine-tenths of Knoxville's voters found such contentions persuasive—until 15 April. On the previous day, Major Robert Anderson, commander of the Federal garrison at Fort Sumter, had surrendered his small command after a thirty-three-hour bombardment from Confederate forces occupying Charleston, South Carolina. Twenty-four hours later the new Republican president issued a presidential proclamation calling on the loyal states to provide seventy-five thousand militiamen for ninety days' service, during which time they would put down an insurrection "too powerful to be suppressed by the ordinary course of judicial proceedings." Tennessee's quota of volunteers was to be fifteen hundred. From the pulpit the following Sunday the Reverend Thomas Humes led his congregation in the prescribed first reading in the Episcopalian liturgy for the third Sunday after Easter, from the book of Joel, chapter 3: "Proclaim ye this among the Gentiles; prepare war, wake up the mighty men, let all the men of war draw near; let them come up; beat your plough-shares into swords, and your pruning-hooks into spears."[59]

THE EFFECT OF THESE events in Tennessee—as across the upper South— was immediate and electrifying. Lincoln's militia requisition prompted an uproar in both Middle and West Tennessee and immediately created large secessionist majorities in both regions. Governor Harris's official response encapsulated the popular mood there. Harris informed the president that Tennessee "will not furnish a single man" in support of the federal government, "but fifty thousand for the defense of our rights and those of our Southern brothers." On 18 April the governor called for the legislature to convene in special session a week later, and after some debate the Tennessee General Assembly determined to act unilaterally rather than to call for a special secession convention. On 6 May the legislature approved a "declaration of independence" from the United States, "waiving any expression of opinion as to the abstract doctrine of secession, but asserting the right, as a free and independent people, to alter, reform, or abolish our form of government in such manner as we think proper." The declaration was to be submitted to the people for their approval in a statewide referendum to be held on Saturday, 8 June. Ratification seemed certain.[60]

By early May the question for East Tennesseans, as Oliver Temple recalled, was no longer whether the *state* should secede. It would. Rather, each person now had to ask, "What shall I, as an individual, do? Shall I go with my state into secession, or shall I remain true to the old government?" A related question was even more controversial. Lincoln's apparent determination to use force against the seceded states seemed to vindicate William Sneed's prophecy of "fratricidal war" should the border states not join forces with the Deep South. A policy of "coercion" would lead to the "shedding of southern blood, on southern soil, by southern hands," as a local Whig put it. If secession was an evil, was this not an even greater tragedy?[61] Both questions were viscerally divisive; both dramatically altered the local debate. As late as the first week of April, Knoxville was still a relatively unified community. Sympathy for disunion remained limited to a secessionist clique that commanded the support of scarcely 10 percent of the population. After 15 April the town was split almost evenly down the middle, and a violent civil war seemed not only likely but imminent.

"Original secessionists" (those who had favored secession since Lincoln's election) often took action at once. Within twenty-four hours of Lincoln's proclamation, J. G. M. Ramsey's son Robert was packing his bags for Georgia, where he could enlist immediately in the Confederate service. His father wrote numerous letters of introduction on his behalf, lobbying for his son to be commissioned as an officer and proudly describing him as "the first one of our citizens who expatriates himself for the purpose of defending the Southern cause." Robert Ramsey and perhaps fifteen to twenty other young "resistance men" were on the train to Atlanta two days later.[62] Those unwilling to "expatriate" themselves joined unofficial militia companies or "Home Guards" in anticipation of violent conflict. Unionists did the same. Only four days after the surrender of Fort Sumter, secessionist William McAdoo wrote to John Bell (who was in the process of switching to the secessionist camp) and entreated him to make his views known among East Tennessee's former Whigs. "Here factions rage to an intense degree," McAdoo lamented. Words like "traitor" and "tory" were being applied freely by both sides, and some Unionists had even gone so far as to express the prediction—or wish—"that certain secession speakers here should have their throats cut by their negroes." A mass Union meeting was slated to be held in town shortly, McAdoo related, and he would be "gratified indeed" if the event passed without bloodshed. "We are but a step removed from civil war among ourselves in East Tennessee."[63]

McAdoo did not exaggerate. Bloodshed was only narrowly averted nine days later—27 April—when Unionists and Confederates held simultaneous rallies on opposite ends of Gay Street. Unionists had turned out to hear two out-of-town speakers, Democratic senator Andrew Johnson and Whig congressman Thomas A. R. Nelson, a prominent Unionist representing Tennessee's easternmost district. Johnson was met at the depot (Nelson arrived during the rally) and escorted first to the Franklin House Hotel, and then on a short distance to a speaker's stand that had been erected in front of Unionist Sam Morrow's bank. Johnson (whom Knoxville secessionists had recently burned in effigy) offered a bold antisecession speech, according to Parson Brownlow's account in the *Whig*. About halfway through his two-hour speech, a Confederate band approached from a nearby hotel and struck up a tune with the object of drowning out the speaker. Then from down the street came two companies of Confederate soldiers from

72   LINCOLNITES AND REBELS

nearby Monroe County. The "Monroe Volunteers" had just heard a few rousing speeches themselves and now deemed it a fine time for a parade. A bloody collision seemed imminent until a number of leading townsmen, most notably Unionists Abner Jackson and John Williams and secessionist Joseph Mabry—all three wealthy merchants—stepped in to plead for a peaceful resolution.[64]

THE NUMBER OF LOCAL secessionists grew dramatically during the first few weeks after the attack on Fort Sumter. Four days after the fort's surrender, Oliver Temple reported to Thomas Nelson that the "panic in our ranks" caused by the proclamation was fading. "We have lost a few weak kneed gentleman, who have not been with us in heart for months, and who only acted with us from fear or selfishness. . . . The country people especially are still firm and determined." Temple's assessment was close to the mark concerning the surrounding countryside. The defection from the Unionist ranks among the townspeople was not nearly as slight as he implied, however, nor was it limited to men who were already borderline Unionists, as his description of the apostates was designed to

Simultaneous Union and Confederate rallies on Gay Street two weeks after the surrender of Fort Sumter. Young Knoxville Confederate Samuel Bell Palmer sketched this scene from memory while a prisoner of war at Camp Douglas.

From the collection of Richard P. W. Williams.

suggest. The last time that Knoxville Unionists had met en masse before the attack on Fort Sumter had been on 1 April, when they had gathered to nominate delegates to represent Knox County at a statewide Union convention in Nashville scheduled for early May. That meeting had named twenty-six townsmen among the forty-nine individuals chosen to represent the county at the state capital. Presumably the nominating committee sought to exclude, as much as possible, those "not with them in heart." Of the twenty-six, thirteen ultimately supported the Confederacy, and most of these switched sides shortly after 15 April.[65]

Many of those who defected from the Unionist ranks did so with hesitation and unease. Like William Brownlow, quite often they held both North and South responsible for the current political crisis. Faced with an agonizing decision, they had put off taking sides as long as possible. Physician William J. Baker, for example, believed that both sections of the country had forgotten God and had desecrated the Sabbath by condoning the carrying of the mail on Sunday. "God has a controversy with us," he wrote to Congressman Thomas Nelson, "not on account of slavery, but on account of our ingratitude. . . . We justly deserve his displeasure." David Deaderick, clerk of the Knox County Chancery Court, blamed the country's emergency on a deterioration of political values. Both North and South had abandoned long ago the framework of the Founding Fathers, who had originally erected a "National Representative Republic." Demagogues had converted it into a democracy, however, and now the people had lost all reverence for law and order. Deaderick finally chose to side with the South, perhaps in part at the urging of his sons, the two oldest of whom entered the Confederate army shortly after the state seceded. Even so, he was still second-guessing his decision as late as 1862. Granted, the North had "for years intermeddled with the subject of slavery, which very remotely concerned *them*." But on the other hand, Deaderick could not help noting, Abraham Lincoln had been constitutionally elected, and the South, rather than submitting for four years, had "precipitated war upon us by the first hostile attack." Similarly, prominent Knoxville businessman Hugh Lawson McClung struggled mightily before converting to support of the Confederacy. "I hesitated, long hesitated," he explained to a former political ally, citing "a belief that our difficulties might have been averted" and the suspicion that "they were brought upon us by . . . a party who preferred a disruption of the Union to a loss of office. . . . But, when convinced that it was narrowed down to a sectional strife, that I had to take sides either with the South or the North, I could no longer hesitate." Rather than condone the coercion of their homeland, such reluctant Confederates grimly cast their lot with the Confederacy in what they perceived as an avoidable war that the South had helped to start.[66]

For others the conversion was easier. Martha Hall, whose husband had previously opposed secession, derided those who still supported the Union after the events of April and May. "How any Tennessean can be for the Lincoln government, under all the circumstances, is to me a mystery of mysteries," she confided in a letter to her sister. "They call themselves Unionists but it is a perversion of the term. *There can be no such thing now.*"[67] Attorney John J. Reese had been one of the few prominent Democrats in the Unionist camp during the early stages of the secession crisis. He had chaired a Union meeting in January, made public speeches against disunion prior to the referendum in February, and been named a delegate to the impending state Union convention in April. By late May, however, he was lieutenant colonel of the Third Tennessee Infantry (C.S.A.), and by the time Tennessee formally seceded in June, he was serving with Colonel A. P. Hill's brigade in the vicinity of Winchester, Virginia.[68] William M. Cocke described himself as "an active, ardent, and devoted friend of the Constitution and the Union of the States" until Lincoln's call for seventy-five thousand volunteers. But "being a native of the South," he cast his lot with the Confederacy once he learned of Lincoln's proclamation "calling into active service so large a military force with hostile purposes" toward his native land.[69] Similarly, Reuben Clark, a twenty-seven-year-old clerk in the employ of Cowan and Dickinson, Knoxville's largest mercantile establishment, was a staunch Unionist as late as the Fort Sumter crisis. A self-described member of the "old line Whig party," Clark deplored the secession of South Carolina when he first heard of it while on a temporary assignment in New York City. His first impulse was to wish that the commander at Fort Sumter "would blow Charleston off the ground." Once the die was cast, however, Clark realized that "there was no alternative but to take sides in this bloody conflict." Realizing that "I could not desert my own people," Clark returned to Knoxville in early summer and joined John Reese in the Third Tennessee Infantry. His first night spent in camp was on the field of Manassas.[70]

What unified these personal decisions was an aversion to take sides against Tennessee and the rest of the South once civil war had become a reality and neutrality was no longer an option. In the early weeks after 15 April, Parson Brownlow scrambled to build an effective Unionist argument that would halt the mass exodus from the Unionist ranks. Above all, he sought to counter the secessionists' charge that further opposition to secession was equivalent to support for federal "coercion" of the Confederate states. As early as 18 April, William McAdoo related a rumor that Brownlow and some other "envenomed party leaders" intended to sustain Lincoln's "war policy." In the first issue of the *Whig* after the proclamation, the editor tackled the question head-on, and, at first glance, he appeared to do precisely that. "We have looked the matter full in the face," he declared, "and we are still on the side of the Government. . . . We don't intend to be misunderstood by any one. We shall rejoice in the success of the American arms over these Seceding Rebels, as sincerely as we did in their triumph over the Spanish Rebels on the bloody plains of Mexico." This was pretty tough talk, even for the Fighting Parson. And yet from the moment Brownlow enunciated this defiant position he began to qualify it so completely that it lost much of its defiance—and a great deal of its coherence to boot.[71]

In the very same issue the editor began to develop the practical application of his policy in an editorial entitled "What Shall Tennessee Do?" Brownlow began with the now demonstrably false claim that the majority of the people of Tennessee were still for the Union. Even so, he cautioned, "they will not turn out to fight in this unholy crusade." Tennesseans venerated the Union, *and* they loved the South. As a consequence, they would never join the southern Confederacy and thus fight the battles of a set of ambitious traitors, but neither would they "unite with Northern Republicans in a bloody war upon the soil where repose the bones of Washington, Madison, [and] Clay." Although Brownlow might "rejoice in the success" of Federal forces, he urged that Tennesseans do nothing to help them. Instead, they should "stay aloof" from the struggle and follow a course of "armed neutrality."[72]

Brownlow elaborated his position extensively, if erratically, over the next several weeks, and several key themes emerged. The most predictable was his persistent hostility to secession. He underscored his resolve most memorably in a public letter to Middle Tennessee planter and politician Gideon Pillow. Within days of the battle at Fort Sumter, the soon-to-be brigadier general had begun raising a brigade for the Confederate army. Having heard a false rumor that the Parson had converted to the Rebel cause, Pillow had invited Brownlow to serve as brigade chaplain. The editor published his reply in the *Whig* of 27 April: "In the spirit of kindness in which this request is made, but in all candor, I return for an answer, that when I shall have made up my mind to go to Hell, I will cut my throat and go direct, and not travel by way of the Southern Confederacy."[73]

When not insulting Confederate generals, Brownlow was hard at work attacking the new Republican president. Local secessionists had taken to branding all southern Unionists as "Lincolnites," and the editor was determined to set the record straight. He went to great lengths to distinguish between the federal government, which belonged to "the people," and President Lincoln, "the creature of a sectional party, doomed to overthrow." He blasted Lincoln for appointing men to his cabinet who had devoted their careers to the abuse of the South. "If the Devil himself had been consulted and commissioned to select a cabinet best adapted to the ruin of the country," Brownlow lamented, "he could not have found a body of men, the same in number, better qualified for the work."[74]

Simultaneously, though, Brownlow asserted that the cotton state Rebels—not Lincoln—were the aggressors in the sectional conflict. It was they who had caused this "cruel and unnatural war," and the new president had both the right and the obligation to assert the power of the government and thus "show to the world that it is capable of protecting itself." Lincoln's response to the attack on Fort Sumter in no way portended a war of aggression or subjugation, Brownlow insisted, but rather "a war of protection, to establish the supremacy of the laws."

The president had called for seventy-five thousand troops to defend the capital only. "We have no idea that the Northern army intend to invade Virginia, or any other Southern State," he assured his readers on 11 May. "We have never believed so, or else our course would have been different." It was one thing to deny common cause with your southern brothers, quite another to shoulder a gun and assist in their "subjugation."[75]

LINCOLN'S CALL FOR VOLUNTEERS put southern Unionists immediately on the defensive, and for the next three weeks the most widely read Unionist newspaper in the South equivocated, denouncing Lincoln but endorsing the federal government, condemning secession while opposing the invasion of any seceded state, and calling on Tennesseans to remain neutral while the country was splitting in two. It was the actions of the state legislature in early May, more than any other development, that allowed East Tennessee Unionists to resume the offensive. As early as 30 April, the General Assembly had received a commissioner from the Confederate States of America, who addressed a joint session on the subject of an alliance between the two governments. On 1 May the legislature authorized the governor to appoint a three-man delegation to negotiate an agreement with the Confederacy. Five days later the legislators finally got around to passing their "declaration of independence." Because ratification was a foregone conclusion, they immediately completed the process of allying the state with the southern Confederacy and preparing for war. That very afternoon the Assembly passed an act that would raise and equip a provisional army of fifty-five thousand men and cover the resulting expenses through a variety of tax increases. On 7 May the legislature formally approved a "military league" with the Confederacy, effectively placing all state troops under the direction of Confederate president Jefferson Davis. On the same day they also invited the Confederacy to consider Nashville for its permanent capital. Tennessee's membership in the Confederacy was effectively accomplished—a full month before the 8 June ratification referendum.[76]

Secessionists considered the legislature's course a justifiable response to a state of emergency. Unionists viewed it as a "vile act of usurpation," the "wildest of revolutions," and a "bold attempt . . . to override the free will and real mind of the people."[77] From early May right on through the June referendum, Brownlow hammered away at the high-handed, undemocratic actions of the General Assembly and their likely effects in East Tennessee. The General Assembly had neither a legitimate reason nor the constitutional authority to act as it had done. "No war will be made by the Government on slavery," Brownlow asserted. "No right of the people of the South will be invaded. No peaceful citizen will be molested." Legislators had been driven by political ambitions, and the people would suffer as a result under a "military despotism" that would increase taxes and diminish civil liberties. On 25 May the editor calculated that taxes must necessarily increase at least forty-fold, and in the same issue he related a secret communication from a "reliable source" in Alabama that leading East Tennessee Unionists—including Knoxville residents Maynard, Trigg, Temple, and himself—were to be arrested immediately following the impending election. Should this happen, he thundered, Unionists must seek immediate retribution. "Let the Railroad on which Union citizens of East Tennessee are conveyed to Montgomery in irons, be eternally and hopelessly destroyed! Let the property of the men concerned be consumed, and let their lives pay the forfeit, and the names will be given!" These words would come back to haunt him.[78]

Unionists were especially offended by the pervasive presence of Confederate troops, which they perceived as nothing more than a heavy-handed effort at intimidation. After the June referendum—in which 70 percent of the voters statewide endorsed separation—they sometimes made the preposterous claim that the majority of Tennesseans, including those in Middle and West Tennessee, actually opposed secession but had been "over-awed" by the ubiquitous show of Confederate military force leading up to the election.[79] Nothing could have been further from the truth. The secessionist majorities in Middle and West Tennessee were genuine. And yet Confederate activities in East Tennessee could not have been better calculated to reinforce the perceptions of local Unionists that a tyrannical minority was engaged in a "diabolical conspiracy" to suppress their liberties and thwart the democratic process.[80]

Pro-Confederate militia companies from all across East Tennessee began to concentrate in Knoxville even before the end of April, as the confrontation during Andrew Johnson's speech on the twenty-seventh attests. This trend was amplified after the passage of the 6 May military act. Under authority granted him by the act, Governor Harris named Knox County's William R. Caswell as one of five brigadier generals for the Provisional Army of Tennessee. The Mexican War veteran immediately announced that he was establishing a camp of instruction near Knoxville for the organization and training of volunteers from across East Tennessee. He eventually chose to situate the camp on the fairgrounds east of Knoxville, and for the next twenty-seven months a substantial Confederate military force was always within one mile of town.[81] Within nine days of the act's passage, Knoxville banker William M. Churchwell wrote the Confederate secretary of war, Leroy P. Walker, to tender to the Confederate government six companies of infantry and four companies of cavalry, or nearly a thousand men all told. At the time of the Fort Sumter crisis, the bankrupt financier had been living and working in New York City, perhaps to escape the glare of publicity after the collapse of his bank and the initiation of a lawsuit against him. He returned to Knoxville immediately thereafter, however, and by late May had been elected colonel of the Fourth Infantry Regiment, Provisional Army of Tennessee.[82] Most of Churchwell's force consisted of volunteers from other counties, but local boys were also enlisting in considerable numbers. By the time that the state had officially seceded, two companies with substantial contingents of Knoxville recruits had been mustered into Confederate service.[83]

In the midst of such martial activity, Dr. Ramsey described the environment in Knoxville to his son Robert: "We are all excitement here now—troops passing here constantly by the trains & companies coming into camp every day." On 11 May, Brownlow reported that on the average one thousand Confederate troops were passing through daily en route to northern Virginia. The figure was probably a bit high, but given Knoxville's position astride the major railroad route between Virginia and the western Confederacy, his estimate was probably not far off. The Parson probably felt as if he had encountered each one individually. Given that the rails of the East Tennessee and Virginia and the East Tennessee and Georgia did not actually connect, many of these troops had an extended layover of several hours (or even days) in Knoxville, and one of their favorite pastimes (perhaps with the encouragement of local secessionists) was to parade before the homes of well-known Unionists and serenade them with catcalls and obscenities. Conflict between Rebel troops and local civilians turned bloody in late May, when Confederate officers brawled with a contentious Unionist named Charles Douglas, a thirty-eight-year-old baker known for his "violent disposition" and fondness for alcohol. At least one of the officers took a shot at Douglas, missing his target but accidentally killing a civilian named Ball as he was entering a store on Gay Street. The following day, under circumstances ever after in dispute, Douglas was killed by a musket ball while sitting in his second-story window.[84]

Behind the scenes, local secessionists were lobbying for an even greater concentration of Confederate forces in the area. From their perspective, this was a prudent response made necessary by Unionists' treasonous resistance to the will of the majority. On 25 May, William Churchwell again wrote to the Confederate secretary of war from Knoxville, this time to stress the "importance of a speedy rendezvous here of at least five thousand men." The newly minted Confederate colonel explained that Unionist leaders still had the audacity to speak in public against secession, and in several counties across the region Unionist "Home Guard" companies were continuing to drill in preparation for a possible uprising. Given "the peculiar condition of things here," he concluded, "we must be prepared to crush effectively treason in our own heart." Around the same time, William McAdoo wrote not once but twice to Governor Harris in Nashville to urge that he send more troops to the area. Had J. G. M. Ramsey had his way, there never would have been a referendum to begin with. Convinced that a majority of East Tennesseans would vote against separation, Ramsey wrote to Governor Harris to urge him simply to "declare by proclamation Tennessee absolved from all allegiance" to the U.S. government. No wonder East Tennessee Unionists were sometimes suspicious.[85]

Secessionists were also tampering with the mails. In William Churchwell's second letter to Leroy Walker, he had informed the Confederate cabinet member that "we are now watching the P.O. [post office] closely." Churchwell went on to explain that his brother-in-law was the Knoxville postmaster, and that only yesterday he had intercepted a letter to Andrew Johnson from Boston, Massachusetts, with a check for $1,000 enclosed. What Churchwell did not reveal to Walker was that his brother-in-law, secessionist C. W. Charlton, was actually engaged in an elaborate ploy to bilk a northern industrialist out of a small fortune. Sometime before 15 May the postmaster had intercepted a letter to Johnson from Amos Lawrence, a New England businessman and philanthropist. The letter, now lost, evidently expressed support for Johnson's courageous stand on behalf of the Union and offered "material aid" to support the resistance to treason in East Tennessee. "Guided by a profound conviction of duty," Charlton later recalled, the erstwhile Methodist minister—most probably in consultation with Churchwell and other local secessionist leaders—decided to reply on Johnson's behalf. Over the senator's forged signature, he asked Lawrence for further "assurances" of the material aid alluded to. Lawrence responded immediately with a check for $1,000, made out to "Andrew Johnson," and guaranteed his correspondent that he could raise ten times that amount from other New England patriots in three days' time. Postmaster Charlton intercepted this missive as well and saw to it that "Johnson" replied promptly. In a letter dated 23 May, he thanked Lawrence for the check but noted, presumably with a grin on his face as he penned the words, that "it would not do to attempt to have it cashed, as I would be *suspected*." Charlton (aka Johnson) cagily concluded by encouraging his benefactor to send the promised $10,000 in currency—rather than personal check—and advised him that, to attract as little attention as possible, he should send it via the regular mail, "*not* by express." The postmaster kept Governor Harris apprised of his scheme to provide the state with $10,000 of Lawrence's money, but word of the plan leaked from the governor's office, and it ultimately came to naught, although the *Richmond Enquirer* did later publish the letters from "Johnson" in an effort to impugn the senator's integrity. Although Knoxville Unionists were ignorant of Charlton's shenanigans until after the referendum of 8 June, the revelation of the scheme contributed to their view of the secessionist clique as willing to stop at nothing to plunge the Unionist majority—against their will—into an unwarranted and immoral revolution.[86]

ALTHOUGH NO ONE REALLY doubted the outcome, both secessionists and Unionists campaigned furiously until the final ballots were cast. Secessionists continued to harp on the themes that had been central to their argument all along. The *Knoxville Register* recapitulated them nicely three days before the election. The Union was already effectively dissolved, the editor averred, and the Constitution bequeathed by the revolutionary forefathers had ceased to exist as well, having been trampled underfoot by the "tyrannical despot" now enthroned in Washington. A featured editorial reminded readers that Lincoln had replaced the Constitution "with the inglorious platform of the black republican party, that places the African negro on an equality with you and every white man." Who would suffer most from such a course? the commentator asked. "The answer is, undoubtedly, '*the poor man.*' The poor class would be placed on an equality with the negro in labor, association, and in every other possible way."[87]

Unionists brought in the big guns for the closing days of the campaign. Andrew Johnson and Horace Maynard—who had both been in Washington prior to the February referendum—stumped all over East Tennessee, joined by first district congressman Thomas Nelson. In addition, Knoxville's John Baxter, Oliver Temple, Connally Trigg, and John Fleming all campaigned tirelessly in rural Knox County and in adjacent counties as well. Unionist efforts culminated in a mass meeting held in Knoxville at the end of May, in response to a public call from a dozen or so Knoxville loyalists. The two-day East Tennessee Union Convention attracted 469 delegates from twenty-six counties. No building in town could accommodate them, and so for two days they gathered in a grove outside of Temperance Hall in East Knoxville and listened to a succession of speeches. On the second day they endorsed a series of resolutions that succinctly summarized the Unionist position: secession was a "ruinous and heretical doctrine"; those "in authority" in the state government had labored pertinaciously "to override the judgment of the people," who had overwhelmingly repudiated secession the previous February; the acts of the state legislature earlier in the month had been "hasty, inconsiderate, and unconstitutional"; and, most ominously, "the doctrine of non-resistance against arbitrary power and oppression is absurd, slavish, and destructive of the good and happiness of mankind." Before adjourning, the assembly agreed to reconvene after the referendum of 8 June, with an eye to "the promotion of the peace and harmony of the people of East Tennessee."[88]

The referendum came off pretty much as expected, and Tennessee became the eleventh and final state officially to secede from the Union. During the preceding weeks, East Tennessee loyalists had stubbornly insisted that nothing had happened since the last statewide referendum on secession "which should change that deliberate judgment of the people."[89] Nearly eighty thousand voters across the state—more than half the electorate—heartily disagreed. Only a quarter of Tennessee voters had supported secessionist convention delegates in the referendum of 9 February. Four months later, seven-tenths endorsed the legislature's declaration of independence, which was ratified by a margin of 108,418 to 46,996. Beneath the statewide totals lay a pronounced regional disparity, of course. Roughly 86 percent of voters in Middle and West Tennessee voted to sever their bonds with the Union, whereas 69 percent of East Tennessee voters opposed that fateful step. "A despotism has now been established over the people of East

Tennessee by those of the *West*," Parson Brownlow concluded. In Knoxville "the election passed off very quietly," as Martha Hall observed. It probably did not hurt that the board of aldermen decided at the last minute to prohibit the sale on election day of all "spirituous and vinous liquors."[90] The official returns showed that the town's voters now *favored* secession by the surprising margin of 777 to 377, as the pro-secession *Knoxville Register* proudly announced. It failed to point out, however, that the tally included the votes of 436 Confederate soldiers from other counties currently encamped at the fairgrounds. In reality, Knoxville voters narrowly opposed secession by a vote of 377 to 341. Given that perhaps as many as twenty of the town's young men were already in the Confederate service out of state, the true margin was probably even narrower. Knoxville was a town literally split down the middle.[91]

What this would mean in the near future was anybody's guess. The *Register* celebrated the 8 June election as a free and fair referendum in which the voice of the people had spoken. Erstwhile Unionists, new editor J. A. Sperry maintained, would now yield to the majority, and all Tennesseans would "unite heart and mind in sustaining the government we have asserted our right to choose." In private, secessionists had no such confidence. Nineteen-year-old Eleanor White was glad when she heard of the referendum's outcome but noted in her diary, "I am afraid we will have fighting right amongst us all." Newly-wed Martha Hall lamented "the prospect of civil war right here in our own beloved East Tennessee." William McAdoo was similarly conscious of "the great danger of civil war among ourselves" and shared with his mother an exaggerated rumor of fifteen thousand Unionists supposedly "armed and instructed to resist the laws of Tennessee."[92]

Some Unionists gladly would have vindicated McAdoo's fears, but the large majority probably dreaded the prospect of "civil war among ourselves" as much as he did. A week after the referendum, Knox County Unionist Beriah Frazier informed Thomas Nelson that few men in his district would favor defiance, even though they had voted down secession 166 to 9. A handful would do anything rather than submit, he conceded, "but the majority here are peaceful citizens who could not be induced to adopt any measures calculated to bring on a collision of arms in their midst."[93] The key to his assessment lay in the last three words. All throughout the secession crisis, Knoxville Unionists had argued that secession would likely lead to war with the North. The true advocate of peace, they had claimed, opposed the dissolution of the Union. But Tennessee's formal secession had turned that argument on its head. Whatever should happen on the national stage, peace at home was possible only if Unionists acquiesced to Confederate rule. Overt resistance guaranteed violence and bloodshed in their own community.

In the end, the majority placed their immediate hopes on a secession movement of their own. As soon as the result of the referendum was evident,

Congressman Nelson, who had been elected president of the East Tennessee Union Convention at Knoxville, issued a call for the convention to reassemble on 17 June at Greeneville, a town about sixty miles to the northeast. The Greeneville Convention, as it was usually designated, attracted 285 delegates from across the region. From the first gavel, Nelson sought to lead the convention toward a showdown with Confederate authority. On the first evening he introduced a declaration of grievances, which defined the current emergency, and a series of six resolutions, which charted a course of action. The declaration condemned the recent referendum as fraught with corruption and intimidation in all parts of the state save East Tennessee. Even there, "no effort ha[d] been spared" to "prostrate the freedom of speech and of the press." To avoid "intolerable and relentless oppression" under the despised Confederacy, the Unionist majority must act immediately and forcefully. In the proposed resolutions that followed, Nelson urged the assembled delegates to declare themselves the legal government of the state. They should then immediately organize to resist by force any effort to station rebel troops in their midst and, provided that the Confederacy left them alone, "maintain a position of neutrality between them and the federal government in the existing war."[94]

Nelson's resolutions prompted a heated debate and ultimately proved too extreme for the majority of the delegates. The opposition was led by three Knoxville delegates, John Baxter, Horace Maynard, and Oliver Temple, who maintained that "blood would flow like water" if they were implemented. Given that their hometown had been occupied by Confederate troops for weeks, perhaps they realized better than their colleagues from the more remote counties where Nelson's proposals would lead. The presence of half a regiment of Confederate soldiers in Greeneville during part of the convention likely had an effect as well. In the end their plea for caution carried the day, and the convention voted to retain Nelson's fire-breathing declaration of grievances while rejecting his course of action. Instead they appointed a three-man commission to deliver a memorial to the state legislature requesting permission for East Tennessee to "form and erect a separate State." For the third time in two decades, East Tennesseans looked to independent statehood as a solution to their political weakness. "It is now for the Secessionists in the Legislature to say whether we shall separate in peace," Parson Brownlow concluded, "or have a disastrous Civil War."[95]

"The Secessionists in the Legislature" considered the petition on 29 June. They rejected it. Their report noted that the members of the Greeneville Convention had been elected before the referendum of 8 June. It was unlikely, therefore, the report concluded, that the delegates represented the true sentiments of the masses of East Tennessee, who were bound to the rest of the state "by the closest ties of kindred and interest." They were wrong.[96]

CHAPTER FOUR

The "Reign of Terror" Unfolds

For a considerable time, including that in which these trials, imprisonments and executions occurred, there was a reign of terror over Union people.
—Unionist Thomas W. Humes[1]

The assertion that Union men have been persecuted in East Tennessee is as false as hell; and the Lincolnite who asserts it is a black-hearted, white-livered scoundrel and liar. —Confederate Jacob Sperry[2]

BECAUSE OF THEIR disparate war aims, time seemed to be on the side of the Confederacy rather than of the Union during the latter half of 1861. To suppress the southern rebellion, the North desperately needed battlefield victories. Initially, many northerners had naively assumed that the Rebels would wilt at the first sign of northern resolve, prompting grandiose predictions that the South would be licked and Jeff Davis hanged before the leaves began to fall. The debacle at Bull Run in July had put an end to such nonsense, however, and northerners had finally begun to realize the sheer magnitude of the task before them—that of subduing a well-armed population dispersed across an area twice the size of the original thirteen colonies. In contrast, the South did not need to defeat the North militarily; southerners could secure their independence simply by holding out until the northern will to continue the war withered. Writing in early summer, Knoxville's Margaret Ramsey captured the heart of the difference in a letter to her son Robert, who had rushed to join the army of "our beloved Confederacy" immediately after the fall of Fort Sumter. "Our brave and true hearted soldiers . . . are fighting for liberty, for their homes, their mothers, sisters, etc." she reminded her son. "It is different with the North. We do not invade their territory; we want nothing they have." Jefferson Davis had made precisely the same point in a message to the Confederate Congress at the end of April. "We seek no conquest, no aggrandizement, no concession of any kind from the States with which we were late confederated," Davis had explained to the world. "All we ask is to be let alone."[3]

Although they might not have appreciated the comparison, Knoxville Unionists sounded a lot like the Confederate president during the early summer of 1861. With a large Rebel force already stationed at Knoxville and little realistic hope of military assistance from the North, most concluded that overt resistance was foolhardy. Given the circumstances, they considered a position of neutrality to be honorable as well as prudent, and they hoped that they would be left alone to pursue such a course. Confederate military authorities, for their part, principally desired the pacification of the region and the reliable control of its railroads and foodstuffs. At least in the short run, they were willing to tolerate a measure of disaffection as long as it was not manifested in rebellious *acts*. A rapprochement appeared possible, in other words, that might spare those opposed to the Confederacy from even more agonizing decisions between competing loyalties. The events of war brought their own dynamic, however, and developments between the summer of 1861 and the end of the year—most notably the growth of civilian arrests and a spectacular uprising—steadily undermined the possibility of a meaningful neutrality.

ALTHOUGH BITTERLY DIVIDED over the question of separation, Knoxville did not immediately erupt into civil war once the state was voted out, above all because neither local Unionists nor Confederate authorities outside of Knoxville desired that kind of confrontation. Admittedly, a tiny fraction of male Unionists did make the dangerous trek through Cumberland Gap into Kentucky in order to volunteer for the Union army. The first was likely young Fred Heiskell, who packed his things immediately after the fall of Fort Sumter, was in Louisville by 18 April, and was a member of the First Kentucky Infantry by the twenty-first. The most prominent of the early volunteers was probably Edward Maynard, the oldest son of Knoxville's Unionist congressman. Maynard made his way to Camp Dick Robinson in southeastern Kentucky, where he was appointed adjutant of the First East Tennessee Volunteers, eventually rising to the rank of lieutenant colonel with another Tennessee unit.[4] Comparatively few Knoxvillians followed the lead of Heiskell and Maynard, however—no more than a handful at most. This was consistent with the pattern across the region. In East Tennessee as a whole, perhaps fifteen hundred men had joined the Union service by the beginning of September. It was not a trivial number by any means—especially given the risks involved in the undertaking—but this represented probably no more than 5 percent of the number of East Tennesseans who would eventually enter the Federal ranks. For the present, at least, most who considered themselves loyal to the Union were simply staying put.[5]

Not that they were wholly quiet. Throughout the region, Unionists were forming paramilitary "Home Guard" units and meeting regularly for drill. The men who joined such outfits mightily resented the presence of Confederate troops in their midst, and the potential for an explosion of violence was constant. And yet, when all was said and done, precious few shots were fired in anger during the summer and early fall of 1861.[6] Notwithstanding the small minority who were willing to risk everything and do anything to throw off Confederate rule, the majority of East Tennessee loyalists wanted no part of a bloody uprising. Unlike the Unionists of western Virginia (who had declared their independence from the Old Dominion in mid-June), opponents of secession in East Tennessee were situated in the heart of the Confederacy, and the prospect of Federal military assistance appeared remote.[7] It was easy to conclude that overt resistance was futile, perhaps even insane. If this view made some sense in the more remote counties of upper East Tennessee, where Rebel troops rarely penetrated, it seemed doubly true in Knoxville, where Confederate military mobilization in the region was centered.

For weeks after the referendum of 8 June, armed companies of Confederate volunteers arrived in Knoxville almost daily. Some were merely passing through en route to Virginia, but numerous others took up residence at the camp of instruction at the fairgrounds east of town. The number of troops in and around Knoxville fluctuated greatly. When Confederate generals used the town as a staging ground for an assault on Kentucky—as was true in the fall of 1861 and summer of 1862—the number of Confederate soldiers on site was double or even triple the town's population. Although typically the total was much smaller, equivalent to a regiment or even less, not a day would pass for the next two years when less than a few hundred troops were camped within a mile of town.[8] Even with most troops posted beyond the town limits, the Confederate military presence was ubiquitous. The general commanding the District of East Tennessee—seven officers held this assignment in a little more than two years—typically had his headquarters adjacent to the Bell House Hotel. The commandant of the post (the officer specifically in charge of the Knoxville garrison) and the Confederate recruiting and conscription officer—not the most popular man in town—both worked out of meeting halls nearby. By 1862 the courthouse, the Deaf and Dumb Asylum, and the university buildings on College Hill all housed military hospitals. The Ordnance Bureau was ensconced in buildings near the railroad depot, and the merchants on Gay Street shared office space with the Confederate provost marshal as well as with agents of the quartermaster, commissary, and niter bureaus. It was an exaggeration, but only a slight one, when a visitor to Gay Street observed that if he were forced to salute every officer he met, his arm would soon fall off like an old pump handle. For Unionists, there were reminders everywhere that they lived in an occupied town.[9]

It comes as no surprise, then, that most of them chose to define loyalty to the United States as the absence of active support for the Confederacy. Parson Brownlow continued to breathe fire, admittedly, but his threats concentrated on how Unionists would retaliate against possible Confederate repression, not on a patriotic revolt against Confederate rule per se. Although he urged Unionist "Home Guards" in the region to continue to drill, the editor repeatedly stressed that Unionists would attack no one without provocation. Civil war, he maintained, could only break out as a result of Confederate aggression. The Unionists of East Tennessee "only ask to be let alone," the Parson explained. "They claim the right of free speech and free thought, and if left alone in the enjoyment of these constitutional rights, they will go quietly along, and disturb no man."[10]

But what Brownlow defined as "constitutional rights" looked a lot like treason to local Confederates. In truth, the town's Confederate leaders had little patience with the Unionist brand of free speech and free thought, and if they had had their way they would have cracked down immediately on those they denounced as "Lincolnites." William McAdoo, for instance, wrote to Governor Harris before the second secession referendum and urged him to arrest all prominent Unionists in East Tennessee the moment that the outcome was official. In so doing, he foreshadowed a trend that held throughout the period of Confederate ascendancy in Knoxville: it was local residents, not outsiders from Nashville or Richmond, who consistently led the way in calling for a severe policy toward Unionists. J. G. M. Ramsey, John Crozier, William Swan, William Churchwell, and *Knoxville Register* editor J. A. Sperry, in addition to McAdoo, all sought at various times to convince Confederate military and civil authorities to take off the kid gloves and deal more harshly with area Unionists.[11]

They did so, at least in large part, because they were scared, especially as the troops that had been training at the fairgrounds began to ship out for points farther north. Although not outnumbered in the town itself, Knoxville's Confederates knew full well that they were surrounded by a large, hostile, and potentially dangerous population of "Tories." They also recognized East Tennessee's strategic significance to the Confederacy. Whoever controlled the East Tennessee Valley would control the major railroad line between Virginia and the Deep South and one of the Confederacy's leading food-producing regions to boot. In the minds of local Confederates, the region's military importance, combined with the presence of a potential "fifth column" of "Lincolnite" traitors, made East Tennessee an irresistible target for a Federal invasion.[12]

Many northerners arrived at the same conclusion. As soon as Tennessee joined the Confederacy, northern newspapers identified East Tennessee as both vitally important and potentially vulnerable. The *Washington National Republican* pointed to the critical value of the great rail line running through its midst and called for the summer's campaign to focus on East Tennessee, the population of which was "not only loyal, but belligerently loyal." (Old Dr. Ramsey clipped the article and mailed it to the Confederate secretary of war, in case it had escaped his attention.) The *New York Times* offered a similar opinion. Only two weeks after the state seceded, the *Times* spoke at length concerning "the great importance of organizing and supporting the Union Party of East Tennessee." The proposition was beyond debate, the paper declared, for even a brief glance at a map of southern railroads would confirm it. The writer then became more specific. A Union army stationed at Knoxville could cut off reinforcements to the Confederate army in Virginia and leave Jeff Davis at the mercy of the Union forces. "It would appear," the paper concluded, "that Knoxville, Tenn. . . . is the key to the whole situation, and when once in the grasp of the Government the utter ruin of the rebels is only a matter of a few months' time."[13] Abraham Lincoln generally sympathized with this view. After the Federal defeat at Bull Run, he composed a memorandum in which a Federal thrust toward Knoxville figured prominently in his vision for future Union strategy.[14]

In sum, local Confederates had good reason to be apprehensive, and their urgent pleas to Richmond for a show of force in the region were undoubtedly sincere.[15] Yet there were other factors at work as well, as even some Confederates were quick to admit. Partisan rivalry, which had played such a huge role during the secession crisis, did not disappear after the outbreak of war. Neither did the personal animosity that was so often inseparable from the region's intense partisanship. W. Y. C. Humes, a former Knoxville attorney who eventually rose to the rank of brigadier general in the Confederate service, linked the two factors when he blamed wartime conflict in East Tennessee on "old party and private animosities."[16] With rare exceptions, Knoxville's most rabid Confederates were Democrats, and several of these "original secessionists" now held positions of power in a town that had traditionally been predominantly Whig. John Crozier Ramsey, oldest son of the doctor and historian, was Confederate district attorney for East Tennessee. His father would soon be an agent of the Confederate Treasury Department and, briefly, Confederate tax collector for the entire state. C. W. Charlton was the Confederate postmaster. William Churchwell would eventually serve as the Confederate provost marshal for East Tennessee. William Swan, whom Oliver Temple remembered as "exceedingly ultra" and intense in his "condemnation of the Union people," now had the ear of the government in Richmond and would soon gain a seat in the Confederate Congress.[17]

The correlation between party affiliation and Unionism had never been perfect, and as more old-line Whigs resigned themselves to the demise of the Union after 8 June, it became even less so. With that said, men like Churchwell, Swan, and others could still take it for granted that most local "Lincolnites" had long opposed them politically. Not only that; each had been the unfortunate beneficiary of Parson Brownlow's special treatment, that is, the editor had abused them publicly in his own inimitable way. Swan, for instance, had been at odds with Brownlow ever since the latter moved to Knoxville and challenged the supremacy of the *Knoxville Register*, at that time a Whig sheet that Swan partially owned. When Swan converted to the Democrats in the mid-1850s, Brownlow publicly denounced him as an unprincipled politician who bolted the party when Whig voters denied him office. Two years later the Parson filed a suit in chancery court that implicated both Churchwell and J. G. M. Ramsey for their involvement in the bankruptcy of the Bank of East Tennessee. On behalf of some six hundred depositors, the editor sued the bank's trustees, including the elder Ramsey, charging them with systematically directing the failed institution's remaining assets toward a handful of influential creditors, hanging the remainder (including Brownlow) out to dry. In the course of the prolonged proceedings, the Parson also eventually claimed that Churchwell, the bank's president, had pocketed $102,000 rightfully belonging to depositors before absconding to New York City.[18] The Parson had also attacked postmaster Charlton, most recently for his likely perpetration of mail theft and forgery in the "hell-born and hell-bound expedition against the reputation and life of Andrew Johnson."[19] Nor did he leave out Crozier Ramsey. Indeed, in many respects Brownlow seemed to take particular relish in abusing the man whom he later described as "but a few degrees removed from an idiot." In the spring of 1860 the *Whig* devoted three full columns to allegations of pension fraud that another local Democrat had lodged against him. The following March the editor chided Ramsey—who was finishing up a term as U.S. district attorney—for not immediately resigning after Lincoln's inauguration. When Jefferson Davis later appointed him to the same post under the Confederacy, the *Whig* mocked Ramsey's appointment as "Confederate Southern Rights Southern Independence District Attorney for the Kingdom of East Tennessee."[20]

Such men did not call for a heavy-handed policy in East Tennessee solely because they had "private griefs and malice to gratify," as one moderate Confederate put it.[21] At the same time, they would have been less than human had the memory of such public attacks played no role in their thinking, and less than savvy not to recognize that the official policy toward dissenters could have a lasting impact on the political balance of power long after the shooting stopped. In retrospect it is impossible to disentangle all the factors that led local Confederates to call for a crackdown on "Lincolnites." Legitimate security concerns were surely at work, as was the desire for partisan advantage. The key point is that, from the perspective of Knoxville's original secessionists, the two were complementary and reinforcing.

In the early summer of 1861, however, authorities from outside Knoxville tended to favor a conciliatory rather than a repressive policy. Both civil officials and military commanders regularly rejected demands for a show of force in favor of a strategy aimed at winning over the Unionist element. Thus, when William

McAdoo wrote to the governor in June to urge that he arrest Unionist leaders, Isham Harris replied that he had actually been encouraged by the size of the pro-secession vote in East Tennessee and would prefer not to order troops into the section until absolutely forced to do so. "I wish to give them every opportunity and inducement to come in and submit gracefully to the will of the majority," he wrote in reply, "and to make no show of force until it is necessary to use it." In keeping with this approach, Harris encouraged the Confederate War Depart-ment in mid-July to employ troops from other parts of Tennessee to defend East Tennessee's crucial railroads from attack. As he explained somewhat naively, "It will exasperate East Tennesseans more to have troops from other states quartered among them than from other portions of their own state."[22] For similar reasons, Harris recommended to Richmond the appointment of Brigadier General Felix Zollicoffer as commander of the newly created District of East Tennessee. The former U.S. congressman was a Tennessean, a lifelong Whig, a supporter of John Bell in 1860, and an opponent of secession until after the fall of Fort Sumter. Before entering politics he had been a newspaperman and had even served as a journeyman printer at the *Knoxville Register* back in the 1830s. If any commander could pacify East Tennessee's disaffected majority, Zollicoffer seemed the most likely candidate. His instructions from the War Department stressed that he was to protect the railroads, keep the peace, and, as much as possible, reconcile Unionists to Confederate rule.[23]

ZOLLICOFFER TOOK COMMAND of the district on 1 August and was im-mediately made aware of the depth of the region's persistent Unionism. On the very day that he assumed command, East Tennesseans went to the polls to exercise their constitutional rights "of free speech and free thought" with regard to three questions: they were to cast their ballots either for or against the new Confederate constitution, they were to elect a governor, and they were to choose among candidates for the provisional Confederate Congress, which would sit until the following February. Noting that the Tennessee General Assembly had at least expressed a willingness to consider separate state-hood for the region if its members were convinced that the majority desired it, Parson Brownlow billed the election as an opportunity for East Tennesseans to register their opposition to Confederate rule. Register it they did. On 1 August, 68 percent of East Tennessee voters rejected the Confederate constitution—almost the same proportion as had repudiated secession two months earlier. By a similar ratio they opposed the reelection of Isham Harris to another term as governor, preferring a moderate Confederate, Middle Ten-nessean William H. Polk, to the fire-eating incumbent. Finally, they under-scored their intransigence by electing openly Unionist congressional candidates in each of the state's three easternmost congressional districts. To put an ex-clamation point on this message of defiance, all three attempted to escape from the Confederacy in order to represent their constituents in Washington, rather than in Richmond.[24]

The vote in Knoxville and in Knox County closely resembled that of the preceding June. In the county as a whole, 78 percent of voters hewed the Unionist line. The townspeople, in contrast, were again almost evenly split. In the congressional race, for example, Horace Maynard defeated local secessionist J. H. Shields by a vote of 371 to 345 (51.8 percent to 48.2 percent), a tally remarkably similar to the 377 to 341 margin against secession in early June. The mere fact of Tennessee's secession had produced few Confederate converts, despite the *Register*'s optimistic prediction that erstwhile Unionists would bow to the will of the majority and "unite heart and mind" in support of the new government. While Brownlow was crowing about Unionists' steely resolve, Horace Maynard slipped through the mountains into Kentucky and made his way to Washington, where northern congressmen accepted his qualifications for a seat in the House, even though he technically represented a state now a part of the Confederacy.[25]

The Confederate response to this manner of defiance was inconsistent. Rebel patrols immediately sought to intercept the three Unionist congressional candidates and ultimately succeeded in capturing both Thomas A. R. Nelson, who had won handily in Tennessee's First District, and George Bridges, who had claimed a narrow victory in the Third. Embarrassed and angered by the election, Isham Harris, who was reelected governor despite the overwhelming opposition of East Tennessee, reversed his course and reported to Richmond on 3 August, "I fear we will have to adopt a decided and energetic policy with the people of that section." Shortly afterward he appealed to Leroy Walker, Confederate secretary of war, to send more troops to the East Tennessee Valley. Harris contended that the minimal force currently in the area—no more than a few thousand men—was enough to irritate the Unionist population but too small to produce genuine submission. "Twelve or fourteen thousand men in East Tennessee would crush out rebellion there without firing a gun," he told Walker, "while a smaller force may involve us in scenes of blood that will take long years to heal." The requisite show of force, Harris concluded, combined with the arrest of the Unionist ringleaders, "will give perfect peace and quiet to that division of our State in the course of two months." Walker immediately ordered three more regiments into the area—two from Mississippi and one from Alabama—and assured the governor that the government in Richmond endorsed his determination to pursue a "decided policy to insure the public safety."[26]

The man charged with implementing this policy was still committed to conciliation, however. Felix Zollicoffer was not naive. From the beginning he understood that the Confederate commander in East Tennessee faced a peculiar challenge. He must guard against not one but two dangers—subversion from within as well as invasion from without. Within five days of assuming command he forwarded reports to Richmond that Union forces were massing in southeastern Kentucky—little more than sixty miles from Knoxville—and likely receiving arms and ammunition from the federal government. Their goal, he had no doubt, was "to force a passage into East Tennessee." To compound the danger, there were "Federalist" civilians who would surely aid them as soon as they penetrated the region. "My impression is that a large number of Union men are opposed to it," he informed Confederate adjutant general Samuel Cooper, but many others would be "restrained from cooperating only by considerations of policy or apprehensions of the consequences."[27]

Zollicoffer's strategy for dealing with these twin perils was straightforward. He was determined to act aggressively to prevent an invasion from Kentucky, all the while pursuing a conciliatory policy behind the front lines with the goal of pacifying Unionist civilians. As soon as logistical difficulties allowed, he began positioning his troops along the Kentucky border. On 9 September he crossed into Kentucky in force and moved to seize control of Cumberland Gap, the most likely avenue of a Federal invasion into East Tennessee. By the twenty-fourth of the month he had concentrated some forty-six hundred soldiers near Cumberland Ford, Kentucky, fifteen miles north of the Gap. By contrast, on that date there were no more than seven hundred armed Confederates in Knoxville, and probably no more than fifteen hundred soldiers (many of them unarmed) throughout all the rest of East Tennessee.[28]

Zollicoffer hoped that no more would be needed. Within a week of assuming command of the district, the general issued a proclamation, "To the People of East Tennessee," in which he set forth his policy toward civilians. Treason would not be tolerated—he could not allow noncombatants to give material aid and comfort to the enemy. On the other hand, he assured them that Confederate troops had been sent to East Tennessee to defend the region from invasion, not to oppress the civilian population. Consequently, no one who submitted to Confederate authority need fear that their rights or property would be disturbed. "All who desire peace can have peace, by quietly and harmlessly pursuing their lawful avocation." Zollicoffer followed his proclamation with a general order to all military personnel calling for a "scrupulous regard" for the property of civilians and stressing that "the Confederate Government seeks not to enter into questions of difference of political opinions heretofore existing." In effect, he was offering Unionists the option of neutrality that so many desired; they must submit to Confederate authority, but otherwise they would not be required to endorse or support the Confederacy in any way.[29]

It was a common saying among Civil War soldiers that there is nothing so close to God on earth as a general on the battlefield, but Knoxville was not a battlefield—not yet anyway—and Zollicoffer's instructions were not universally obeyed. Depredations against property holders were pretty limited in the summer and fall, but "difference[s] of political opinions heretofore existing" loomed larger than the general had proclaimed that they should. This was predictable. Many of the enlisted men under Zollicoffer's command were openly contemptuous of area Unionists. One wrote to the folks back home that the "traitors" in East Tennessee deserved "to be loathed of earth, scorned by heaven and kissed by the serpents of hell." As the summer progressed, the troops stationed in Knoxville came increasingly from outside of the area, and these soldiers typically brought with them a view of the region as synonymous with disloyalty. As a Confederate officer from a nearby county recalled, "To hail from East Tennessee was a reproach in the South."[30]

The presence of a large body of soldiers with time on their hands and disdain for the surrounding population made conflict with Unionist civilians almost inevitable. Unionists frequently complained after the war that instances of harassment and intimidation had been widespread under Confederate occupation. They most commonly made these charges as part of formal applications for reimbursement for damages, so their accusations must be taken with a grain of salt, but the theme is too prevalent to be dismissed. A Knoxville carpenter named Simeon Dawson, for example, remembered being abused regularly by Rebel soldiers for being a "damn Lincolnite." Unionist John Griffin claimed to have been "molested" on the street by Confederate soldiers who only relented when a schoolmate of his in the Rebel army intervened to protect him. A farmer living just south of town recalled being accosted in Knoxville by Confederate soldiers who "drew their knives on me and threatened to kill me" until he admitted that he "was not a Union man."[31]

Add alcohol to the mix, and the potential for conflict multiplied exponentially. From the beginning, military authorities found it all but impossible to restrain soldiers from drinking to excess, in no small part because it was so difficult to discourage tavern keepers from serving thirsty men in uniform with money in their pockets. In an editorial lamenting "Whiskey Drinking in Knoxville," the *Whig* complained that there were far too many soldiers drinking in town. It was when they were drunk, the paper observed, that soldiers were the most likely to abuse the law-abiding citizenry. "The best thing the Military authorities could do for this town," the editorial concluded, would be to close up "the numerous *breathing holes of hell*, called *doggeries*." Although not in the habit of taking suggestions from Parson Brownlow, the army in fact did try—repeatedly— to shut down the sale of alcohol to soldiers. At various times during the twenty-seven months of Confederate occupation, post commanders issued general orders threatening to close down offending businesses and arrest the merchants involved. Even Jefferson Davis eventually got in the act. As part of a proclamation in the spring of 1862 in which he declared martial law in the Department of East Tennessee, Davis also completely prohibited both the distillation and the sale "of spirituous liquors of any kind."[32]

Although it is not certain, intemperance may have played a role in a major brawl between soldiers and civilians in late October 1861. The colonel in charge of the Knoxville garrison, W. B. Wood of the Sixteenth Alabama Infantry, reported to General Zollicoffer (then in southeastern Kentucky) that "eight or ten of the bullies and leaders" among the Union men "made an attack" on some of his soldiers near the Lamar House Hotel. These "bullies" included several of the town's policemen, however, suggesting the possibility that the Confederates who were accosted were not as innocent as Wood intimated. Wood reported that "gentlemen who witnessed the whole affair" insisted that his troops were "not at all to blame," but at least one other bystander maintained that the soldiers "were creating a disturbance" and that the police were attempting to take them to jail. Whatever the actual situation (and it is impossible to tell), when Wood learned that civilian police were attempting to arrest members of his command, he immediately called in the cavalry—literally—although the "assailants" successfully made their escape. The aroused soldiers did not give up easily, however. A week later the records of the town council indicate that some of the town's policemen were in "military custody," and a blacksmith who had been called to assist in the arrest of the Rebel soldiers reported that they had since threatened to kill him.[33]

WHILE DRUNKEN SOLDIERS were occasionally undermining Zollicoffer's conciliatory policy, sober civil servants in Richmond and Knoxville were positively eviscerating it. The very day after the general issued his conciliatory proclamation, the Confederate Congress passed the Alien Enemies Act, which had ominous implications for East Tennessee loyalists. According to the measure, all "natives, citizens, denizens, or subjects" of any nation hostile to the Confederacy were ordered to remove themselves within forty days, after which time they were "liable to be apprehended, restrained or secured and removed as alien enemies." The act was ambiguously worded, and it was never entirely clear just who qualified as an "alien enemy." If interpreted broadly, it could be understood to declare every southern Unionist as potentially subject to imprisonment or deportation.[34] To raise the stakes even higher, at the end of August the Confederate Congress passed a sequestration act that authorized the confiscation of all real and personal property owned by "alien enemies," whoever they might be. (To oversee such confiscation in East Tennessee, the government appointed Landon Carter Haynes of Washington County, a Democratic journalist and politician who had shot Parson Brownlow in a street brawl in the 1840s.)[35] Local civil authorities were also doing their part to increase the pressure on persistent Unionists. On 6 September the Confederate District Court for East Tennessee opened its first session since Tennessee's separation, and for the next three weeks Judge West H. Humphreys listened as District Attorney Crozier Ramsey brought charges against 109 civilians for alleged acts of disloyalty.

These legal efforts to crack down on disloyalty affected Knoxville's Unionists more indirectly than directly. Only two of the town's citizens were actually charged during the September session of the court. The court minutes are so terse that in many instances it is difficult to discern the nature of the defendants' alleged treason, but it appears that it usually entailed some kind of overt resistance, such as continuing to drill in Unionist "Home Guard" units, attempting to reach the Union lines to enlist in the Federal army, or giving "aid and comfort" to those involved in such activities. In sum, they involved the kind of out-and-out defiance of Confederate authority that was far less risky in the more remote recesses of East Tennessee than it was within a stone's throw of the Confederate headquarters for the region. Much to Ramsey's chagrin, Judge Humphreys consistently refused to find such activities treasonous, regularly ordering the release of the defendants upon taking an oath of loyalty and, in the majority of cases, posting a bond for good behavior. Although the hapless DA failed to secure even a single conviction during the September term, his efforts were not entirely for naught; in three weeks the court took in more than $46,000 in bonds for good behavior.[36]

The first Knoxvillian to be charged was John Bell Brownlow, the Parson's son. His alleged crime was circulating a copy of Hinton Rowan Helper's book *The Impending Crisis of the South*. The author of this inflammatory work, a native North Carolinian, had had the gall to claim that slavery was a drag on the southern economy and an obstacle to the economic advancement of nonslaveholding southern whites. Republicans had applauded Helper's conclusions—they published a condensed version of the book as a campaign tract in 1860—while white Southerners had condemned him for writing a polemic "calculated to excite discontent and insurrection," to quote Crozier Ramsey. After spending several days and nights in custody, the younger Brownlow finally appeared before Judge Humphreys, who concluded that he had committed no offense against the Confederacy. Young Brownlow had indeed perused a copy of the forbidden book, but he had borrowed it from none other than William McAdoo, whom Humphreys would soon appoint as clerk of the Confederate Court. Beyond that, no one for a moment seriously believed that the Parson's son espoused Helper's views. His father was in the habit of referring to the author as the "Hell-deserving Helper," and the *Whig*'s assertion that both father and son found the book "infamous" was entirely convincing.[37]

Equally groundless were the charges against Perez Dickinson, the second town resident hauled into court and the only individual tried specifically in response to the Alien Enemies Act, which was rarely applied in the Confederate District Court prior to 1862. Citing the law, in mid-September District Attorney Ramsey issued a warrant for the arrest of the forty-eight-year-old Dickinson, a Massachusetts-born merchant who had resided in Knoxville since 1829 and gradually built up the largest mercantile house in East Tennessee. The dry-goods salesman was a "dangerous man," Ramsey told the grand jury. The evidence of his guilt was twofold. First, Dickinson had recently taken a business trip to the North where he had had "intercourse among northern people." (Ramsey neglected to mention that the merchant had secured written permission from Governor Harris prior to leaving.) Second, and just as damning, Dickinson had been heard to declare before his departure that he would rejoice to see a northern army in East Tennessee when he returned. Judge Humphreys, a Middle Tennessee Democrat who had sat on the Federal bench in Knoxville prior to secession, did not find Ramsey's case persuasive. When Dickinson appeared before him, the judge acknowledged that the businessman was an upstanding citizen and offered to drop all charges and release him without bond if he would simply swear an oath of loyalty to the Confederacy. Dickinson was opposed to the Confederacy and made no effort to deny it, yet he avowed that he had done nothing illegal and "declined" to take the oath. He informed the judge that his mother, sisters, and brother were all buried in Knoxville; that he had been a law-abiding citizen there for more than three decades; and that he should not have to take an oath to re-main peacefully in his home. Humphreys initially ordered Dickinson's removal from the Confederacy but soon thought better of it and allowed the merchant to remain after posting a $10,000 bond for good behavior.[38]

The official Confederate policies in August and September pleased almost no one in Knoxville. Confederates frequently criticized Zollicoffer's leniency, whereas Unionists—and even some moderate Confederates—roundly condemned Ramsey's aggressiveness. William McAdoo could not contain his contempt for the Con-federate brigadier. He quickly became convinced that the former Whig congress-man was determined to stay on good terms with the local Whig leadership, so that they could deliver him votes when he ran for office after the war. "General Zollicoffer is proving himself totally unfit for the duty of quelling this Lincolnism in East Tennessee," McAdoo wrote in mid-August. He was patrolling the Ken-tucky border to prevent "Tories" from joining the Federal Army, but was doing nothing to quiet the Unionist leaders who were encouraging them to do so. The former were merely the "sincere dupes" of "deluding villains" such as Maynard, Brownlow, Baxter, Trigg, and Temple. Worst of all, McAdoo la-mented, "Brownlow's newspaper is to be tolerated, nay encouraged." If the popularity-hunting politician was sincere about subduing the Lincolnites, he "would promptly put down that paper. Brownlow governs by fear," the attorney maintained, "and the moment he goes down, thousands who now act with him will feel *relieved*, and *rejoice*." Dr. Ramsey harbored a similar suspicion of the Whig general. "We need here commanders and officers who have no sympathies with their Union and disloyal acquaintances and relatives and associates," Ramsey ex-plained to the Confederate secretary of war, Judah P. Benjamin. The ideal com-mander in East Tennessee would be "a stern man from one of the cotton States, who has no knowledge of our people and their past political affinities."[39]

Unionists, for their part, deeply resented the mass arrests as bald-faced efforts to persecute law-abiding citizens. The *Whig* denounced the "indiscriminate arrests" as stemming from old grudges rather than serious crimes. Robertson Topp, a prominent Memphis secessionist who had traveled through East Tennessee at the behest of Governor Harris, reported in October that nothing had thwarted the efforts to pacify the Tory element more than the arrests of civilians during the preceding month. They "have gone far to poison the minds of the people against the Government," he concluded, "and if tolerated and persisted in the people of that end of the State at a critical moment will rise up enemies instead of friends." Topp called for Ramsey's immediate removal and blamed "a few malicious, troublesome men in and around Knoxville" for egging him on, naming in particular William Swan, William Churchwell, John Crozier, and C. W. Charlton. Although no one in Knoxville went to prison as a result of their efforts, the widespread arrests created a chilling climate that both angered and intimidated local Unionists. As a Knoxville Confederate observed, "Almost every hour of the day presented the spectacle of small bodies of armed men in the streets, in soldiers uniform, with fixed bayonets, marching . . . people in citizens clothes to or from the Court House." And as Unionist Reverend Thomas Humes now sadly realized, "Even the citizens of better social position" would not be immune.[40]

Prominent Unionists did their best to convince the Confederate authorities that such a heavy-handed policy was unnecessary. In an editorial in mid-August, Parson Brownlow again defined "the Position of East Tennessee Unionists." The editor ridiculed rumors that large numbers of Union men were heading almost nightly into Kentucky to join the Union army, and he claimed that Unionist leaders were trying to discourage such resistance, "exerting all the influence they have, to quiet the common masses." Brownlow even asserted that Unionist leaders had contemplated going to Washington to seek assurances from the Lincoln administration that it would not attempt to send a Federal army into the region. Even though critics were accusing them of going over to secession, they were telling the rank and file "that it is madness to rebel, and the worst of folly to contribute to the getting up of a Civil War in East Tennessee." A few weeks later, seventeen leading Unionists from across East Tennessee, seven of them from Knoxville, published a public letter to Felix Zollicoffer in which they assured him that he need not fear an uprising. The signatories—who included Brownlow, Frederick S. Heiskell, John Baxter, Oliver Temple, Connally Trigg, and John Fleming—informed the general, "We should deplore civil war in our midst and we believe that we but reflect the feeling of the Union people in East Tennessee in avowing that sentiment." By this point Brownlow had adopted an even milder tone in the pages of the *Whig*. Indicating that he had no desire for martyrdom, the editor explained that he would now "surrender to a necessity they have forced upon us" and retire "to a position of neutrality." The Fighting Parson would fight no longer, or so he claimed.[41]

IT IS TEMPTING to speculate on the causes of the combative editor's sudden moderation. The least probable explanation is the one circulated later by his enemies, namely, that Brownlow had concluded that Confederate independence was all but certain and was in the process of shifting his allegiance. In May 1862, by which time the Parson was touring the North and colorfully denouncing the "imps of hell" who had fomented the southern rebellion, the *Knoxville Register* ridiculed Brownlow's pretended constancy to the Union. The *Register* claimed that he had been poised to convert to the southern cause the preceding fall, and would have done so if the newspaper had not predicted his conversion and ridiculed him for it. Only his pride, the paper alleged, combined with his deep-seated animosity toward his political enemies, had prevented the Parson from becoming a Rebel. Perhaps. The charge was raised more than once, and it is impossible to rule out. The explanation seems so obviously politically motivated, however, that it fails to convince. Indeed, as late as the end of August 1861, the *Register* was denouncing Brownlow's pledge to adopt merely a neutral stance. "The fact is patent to every observer," the editor fumed, "that while he means to keep his promise . . . to keep under his Lincolnism, it is ever in his heart, as it ever has been."[42]

There are at least three possible explanations other than the one proffered by the *Register*, and a combination of the three likely offers the best interpretation of Brownlow's behavior at the end of the summer. First, it is entirely conceivable that Brownlow meant just what he said. Tired of the battle, holding out less and less hope of victory, he may have viewed neutrality as his best remaining option. Certainly he had every reason to be discouraged by this point. Ever since the state's secession he had been financially hard-pressed, as his advertising revenue dwindled and it became increasingly difficult to circulate his paper. Then there had been the surprising news from Bull Run. The Parson had originally damned the *Register* for printing a dispatch claiming that the Confederates under General Beauregard had won a huge victory at Manassas Junction. "We have no other expectation but that the Confederate forces will fall back from there upon Richmond, and there make their last and desperate stand," he proclaimed. By early August his hopes for the Confederacy's quick demise were fading. "When will the war end?" he asked his readers. His own prediction was gloomy: "Our candid opinion is that the war will not terminate under three or five years, and then only, when the money and men are consumed on both sides." Casualties, he observed, would be in the "hundreds of thousands." It is also likely that Brownlow felt keenly the fate of his good friend Thomas Nelson, who had been arrested while en route to Washington after his victory in the congressional race in Tennessee's First District. General Zollicoffer had sent Nelson to Richmond, where after a few days' confinement he negotiated his release with Jefferson Davis by pledging to submit to the Confederate government and to refrain from using his influence in any way to encourage resistance among his constituents.

Indeed, the Parson must have felt increasingly isolated in his crusade against the Confederacy. The *Whig* had long since become the only Union sheet still in publication within the seceded states. Locally, his allies seemed to be falling away. Nelson had acceded to an enforced silence. Horace Maynard was in Washington. John Baxter had resigned himself to southern independence and was campaigning for a seat in the Confederate Congress. Oliver Temple had fled north shortly after the election of 1 August (although only temporarily, as it turned out), and Connally Trigg would eventually follow suit.[43]

On the other hand, the cagey editor may have been trying to drive a wedge between the Whig Zollicoffer and the local Democratic leadership. Repeatedly in August and September he praised the Confederate general for his judicious policy and maintained that his fair-minded approach would be rewarded. In mid-August the Parson described Zollicoffer as a "man of fine sense, of great firmness of character and of true courage." The townspeople would "find him generous and reasonable," the editor assured his readers, "not disposed to oppress anyone because he may have the power to do so." In mid-September, when the general ordered a detail of soldiers to protect Brownlow's house and office from vandalism, the Parson lauded him for his "dignity, promptness, and impartiality." For his part, Zollicoffer expressed himself "gratified at the preservation of the peace and the rapidly increasing evidences of confidence and good-will among the people of East Tennessee." While not dismissing the reality of Unionist opposition, he increasingly sensed that local civil authorities were exaggerating the seriousness of the threat to Confederate rule. At the end of October he instructed the post commander W. B. Wood to "restrain our ultra friends from acts of indiscretion." Although Wood must be prepared to suppress any overt resistance, he must not be overly alarmed. "I have observed heretofore that a few of our friends about Knoxville are unnecessarily nervous," the brigadier cautioned. "Give their expressions of apprehension only their due weight."[44]

Finally, there is a good chance that Parson Brownlow was genuinely fearful of being arrested. Although he relished the role of martyr after it was thrust upon him, he did not invite it, as he himself was quick to admit at the time. Acknowledging that some of his friends expected him to attack the Confederacy in every issue, he was adamant that the military authorities were not "fool enough" to tolerate such a course. "Not being impressed with any such sense of duty," he informed his readers, "I most respectfully decline the honors and hazards of so brave and independent a course." It is certainly no accident that the moderation in his tone, which began in mid-August, followed closely on the heels of Nelson's capture and roughly coincided with the decision by the secretary of war to transfer three more Confederate regiments to East Tennessee. Nor is it surprising that it continued throughout September, as the Confederate District Court considered charges against more than one hundred civilians in the courthouse only two blocks from the Parson's office. Finally, it is telling that, when Brownlow at last resumed his caustic criticism of the Confederacy, he did so at the end of September, by which point the quarterly session of the Confederate Court had ended and the lion's share of Zollicoffer's command was encamped in southern Kentucky rather than on the outskirts of town.[45]

His strategy this time around was different. Rather than attack the Confederacy directly, the Parson filled the columns of the *Whig* with criticism of the Confederate government taken from other southern newspapers. After quoting a letter critical of Jefferson Davis in a Richmond paper, he informed his readers that he could not agree with it for fear of being arrested. He assured them, however, that he had had an opinion on the matter "*before* this reign of terror set in" and that his opinion remained unchanged. While holding back (somewhat) from attacking the government in Richmond, he still felt no compunction about lambasting the character of local Confederates. In October his favorite target was Jacob Sperry, the fire-eating editor of the *Daily Register*. Sperry was a "low-down, ill-bred, lying, debauched, drunken scoundrel," the editor railed, "alone worthy of the company of the VILLAINS and COWARDS who write the dirty, slanderous editorials for his paper." (The latter was intended as a shot against William Swan and John Crozier.) Warming to his subject, Brownlow revealed that Sperry had been beaten up in a "doggery," thrashed in a "Ten-Pin Alley," picked up from the sidewalk dead drunk, and recently driven "out of a neighboring lot, from the embraces of a filthy negro wench!"[46] In what was ultimately the most explosive element of his new strategy, the Parson also penned two sarcastic editorials chiding local Confederate leaders for not volunteering for military service. Under the heading "To Arms! To Arms! Ye Braves!" he urged the champions of southern rights to "come to your country's rescue." Many of those who had "made big speeches in favor of the war" had been willing to sell supplies to the government or to stoop to fill well-paying civil offices far removed from harm's way. But "there is more honor in serving as a private," Brownlow taunted them.

> Come, gentlemen, *do* come, we insist, and enter the army as volunteers. You will feel badly when *drafted*, and pointed out as one who had to be *driven* into the service of your country! Let these Union traitors submit to the draft, but let us who are true Southern men *volunteer*. Any of us are willing to be Judges, Attornies [*sic*], Clerks, Senators, Congressmen, and camp followers for *pay* when out of danger, but who of us are willing to shoulder our knapsacks and muskets, and meet the Hessians? Come, gentlemen, the eyes of the people are upon you, and they want to see if you will pitch in.[47]

This was the unkindest cut of all, in large part because it carried a certain ring of truth. Volunteering was slow among all ranks of society after the initial passions engendered by Fort Sumter began to cool. J. G. M. Ramsey admitted as much in a letter to Jefferson Davis in the middle of the autumn. "The spirit of volunteering . . . I am humiliated to say is very low," he confessed to the Confederate president. A Chattanooga newspaper soon made the same discovery, chiding the secessionists of Knox County for profiting from the war without sacrificing for the cause.[48] No one knows precisely how many men and boys from Knoxville went into the Rebel armies in the summer and fall of 1861. Because no rosters of local recruits have survived, the most systematic source of information is an alphabetical listing of nearly 187,000 individuals who served in Confederate units from across the state. Even though other sources help to pinpoint the specific units raised in or near Knoxville, almost all companies in East Tennessee included men from multiple communities, and verifying the identity of soldiers with common surnames such as Smith or Jones is nearly impossible. It is, however, unlikely that as many as 100 of the town's 950 white men of military age had volunteered by the end of the year. Probably half of the town's military-age men had opposed secession, of course, but it is still doubtful that more than one-fifth of those supporting separation in June had entered the army by December.[49]

The underrepresentation of the town's most outspoken secessionists was particularly glaring, and Brownlow's taunts must have struck a nerve. John Crozier, William Sneed, and J. G. M. Ramsey were all too old to enter the ranks, but most did not have that excuse. Whatever their reasons, however pure their motives, most of Knoxville's leading secessionists of military age still slept in their own beds at night. C. W. Charlton was serving his new country in the post office rather than on the battlefield. Crozier Ramsey was battling Lincolnites from the district attorney's office. J. A. Sperry was fighting the good fight from his editor's desk. Campbell Wallace, whom Brownlow described jeeringly as "one of the great lights of Secession," was serving as president of the East Tennessee and Georgia Railroad. The Reverend Joseph Martin decided to minister to his flock at home rather than to the soldiers at the front. William McAdoo accepted a position as clerk of the Confederate Court. William Swan briefly volunteered and then resigned to run for the Confederate Congress. Joseph Mabry, whom the *Daily Register* called "one of the earliest and staunchest advocates of the Southern cause in this city," offered to provide free uniforms for two companies of volunteers, but by staying out of the army found time to do perhaps a million dollars' worth of business with Confederate purchasing agents. The list of stay-at-home patriots was long.[50]

Oliver Temple later maintained that the editor's attacks on those reluctant to volunteer were the last straw for the heretofore patient Confederate authorities. "There were so many prominent men in Knoxville . . . to whom these taunting, bitter reproaches manifestly applied," he recalled, "that a cry of rage was at once raised against Brownlow." Within a week the editor received word from allies in Nashville that he would soon be charged with treason by the grand jury impaneled there. Unknown to him, Crozier Ramsey was also preparing to indict him in the Confederate District Court when it was scheduled to reconvene in Knoxville in November. The Fighting Parson did not go quietly into the night, however. The editorials in question had appeared in print on 12 and 19 October. In one last act of defiance, Brownlow reprinted the offending essays in the issue of 26 October and then announced to his readers that he was closing down the *Whig* in anticipation of his imminent arrest. He was not guilty of any offense against the Confederacy, he maintained; he was being persecuted simply because the Confederate government was intent on shutting down the last Union newspaper in the South. He was certain that he would be allowed his freedom if he would only swear his loyalty to the Confederacy, but he was determined to do nothing to assist in the destruction of the best government on earth and would languish in jail instead. "I am encouraged to firmness," the Parson concluded, with a biblical allusion calculated to enrage his political enemies, "when I look back to the fate of Him 'whose power was righteousness,' while the infuriated mob cried out, 'crucify Him, crucify Him!'" The "infuriated mob" would have to find Brownlow before they could crucify him, however. Convinced that his life was in danger, he left Knoxville. He first attempted to make his way north into Kentucky; when he became convinced that the mountain passes were guarded too closely to allow that, he changed his course and headed east into the Smoky Mountains along the Tennessee–North Carolina border.[51]

Only three days after the Parson slipped out of town, events transpired that permanently altered the already tenuous position of local Unionists. On the night of 8 November, small bands of Unionists, anticipating a Federal invasion from Kentucky, attempted simultaneously to burn nine strategic railroad bridges along the main trunk line between Bristol, in extreme northeastern Tennessee, and Bridgeport, Alabama, some 270 miles to the southwest. They were successful in five of nine instances. The anticipated arrival of a Union army did not materialize, however. On the verge of a nervous breakdown, the Union commander in Kentucky, William Tecumseh Sherman, had called off the invasion at the eleventh hour and left the bridge burners to go it alone.[52]

IN THE AFTERMATH of the uprising, Confederate authorities almost universally concluded that Zollicoffer's conciliatory policy had been a failure. Governor Harris fumed that the "rebellion must be crushed out instantly" and promised to send ten thousand troops to the region to ensure that the ringleaders were arrested and "summarily punished." From Richmond, Secretary of War Judah Benjamin vowed to "crush the traitors" and instructed the post commandant at Knoxville that all individuals suspected of bridge burning were "to be tried summarily by drum-head court-martial" and executed on the spot if found guilty. "It would be well," he added, "to leave their bodies hanging in the vicinity of the burned bridges." Zollicoffer himself agreed that a draconian response was now imperative. "The leniency shown them has been unavailing," he concluded bitterly. "They have acted with base duplicity, and should no longer be trusted." He called immediately for the arrest of resistance leaders and ordered his subordinates to begin disarming the Unionist population generally. In sum, those still antagonistic to the Confederacy must be made to feel "that their hostile attitude promises to them nothing but destruction."[53]

Such determination notwithstanding, Zollicoffer was still careful not to exaggerate the extent of the uprising. He took pains to distinguish between those who had taken up arms against the Confederacy and the rank and file of the Unionist population. Almost alone among Confederate officials, he argued that one of the salient features of the bridge burnings had been that "comparatively a small proportion" of the population had actually supported them. Weeks after the attacks, a lower-ranking officer stationed at Knoxville reached the same conclusion. An assistant to the post commandant blamed the bridge burnings on a "few leading miscreants and a handful of ignorant and deluded followers." The overwhelming majority was not only "entirely ignorant of their designs," he contended, but also "utterly opposed to any such wickedness and folly."[54] Such dispassionate assessments were rare. As a Knoxville grocer recalled, the bridge burnings "startled the whole Southern Confederacy" and evoked a reaction within Tennessee akin to panic. Isham Harris concluded that "a deep-seated spirit of rebellion" permeated East Tennessee. Colonel W. B. Wood, the post commander at Knoxville, informed Richmond that "the whole country is now in a state of rebellion" and warned of a "general uprising in all the counties." Brigadier General William H. Carroll, who would soon succeed Wood in command at Knoxville, told Judah Benjamin that the region was plagued by a "traitorous conspiracy . . . extensive and formidable."[55]

Harris, Wood, and Carroll were certainly correct in asserting that sympathy for the Union was still widespread across East Tennessee. Since taking command of the district, Zollicoffer had undoubtedly exaggerated the degree to which he was actually winning the loyalty of erstwhile Unionists through his conciliatory approach. It did not take the bridge burnings to establish this, however. Only days before the uprising, area Unionists had almost unanimously boycotted the elections for the first full session of the Confederate Congress (which would succeed the short-lived provisional Congress elected in August), unwilling to cast their ballots for representatives who acknowledged the legitimacy of Confederate rule. On the other hand, taken literally, the wave of dire pronouncements about rampant "rebellion" were gross exaggerations. The total number of saboteurs involved in the attacks was well under one hundred, and they hailed almost entirely from three or four of the most remote and isolated counties of East Tennessee, areas in which the Confederate military presence had been minimal or nonexistent. As word of the attacks spread, between one and two thousand others mobilized in scattered locations up and down the East Tennessee Valley, including a large group of men from Sevier County who briefly threatened the bridge over the Holston River at Strawberry Plains, only fifteen miles east of Knoxville. When all was said and done, however, the number of civilians who had actively supported the uprising represented no more than 2 to 3 percent of the region's military-age white males.[56]

Reminded daily of the potential power of the Confederate army, Knoxville Unionists had been consistently counseling against an armed revolt since the time of the Greeneville Convention. Resistance not only would fail, they argued, but would actually harm loyalists by inviting a crackdown on civil liberties. Their predictions were dead on target. It appears that not a single person in Knoxville was implicated in the assault on the bridges, and yet the environment in the town was immeasurably altered as a result of the uprising.[57] Knoxville again became a heavily occupied town. General Zollicoffer dispatched a regiment to Knoxville at once, and over the next few days reinforcements poured in from West Tennessee, Middle Tennessee, and Georgia. By early December, troop strength in Knoxville had quadrupled to more than four thousand, or roughly one soldier for every man, woman, and child in the town.[58] Upon hearing of the uprising, the post commander, Colonel Wood, immediately placed the town under martial law (albeit temporarily) and announced that no one would be allowed to enter or leave the town without a pass. To procure such a pass, citizens would have to be willing to swear an oath of loyalty to the Confederacy. (When old Frederick Heiskell refused to swear such an oath, the seventy-four-year-old Unionist was arrested and charged with "inciting rebellion" and held in jail for ten days until Zollicoffer ordered his release.) Within twenty-four hours Wood had also sent squads of men door to door to confiscate firearms from not just Unionists but the entire population. Convinced that "the whole country is now in a state of rebellion," Wood was leaving nothing to chance.[59]

For the second time that fall, local Unionists watched as the town filled with political prisoners. In the weeks after the 8 November uprising, as many as one thousand prominent and not-so-prominent East Tennesseans were arrested, and the great majority of these were taken to Knoxville. There they awaited trial before a military court established for the purpose, although many never received an official hearing. The volume of those arrested was so great that the county jail rapidly filled up and a temporary prison was established in a house on the corner of Main and Prince streets to accommodate the overflow; even then, it was necessary to board some at the Bell House Hotel while they awaited trial. The Confederate District Court reconvened in late November. When Judge Humphreys began to issue writs of habeas corpus ordering the release of certain prisoners, Wood's successor as post commandant, General Carroll, again declared martial law and refused to turn over to the civil authorities any of those suspected of disloyalty.[60]

The charges against those in custody varied widely. A handful were alleged actually to have participated in the attacks, a larger number to have had prior knowledge of the plot, a yet larger group to have taken arms in support of the uprising after the bridges had been burned. Others still, there can be no doubt, were arrested simply because of their known Unionist sympathies. A Confederate officer at Knoxville suspected that "old political animosities and private grudges" precipitated many of the arrests and concluded that "bad men among our friends" were taking the opportunity to hunt down "all those against whom they entertain any feeling of dislike." Months later, the War Department acknowledged that "it is not only possible but probable that in the confusion and disorder of the times some innocent men have been confounded with the guilty."[61] As in September, many of those arrested were allowed to go free upon taking the oath of loyalty, but others were pressured to volunteer in the Confederate army. Those considered more serious offenders, somewhere between two and four hundred, were shipped off to the Confederate prison in Tuscaloosa, Alabama. Those found guilty as bridge burners—seven in all—were sentenced to death. Two were ultimately spared, but the other five were hanged, two near the railroad bridge in Greene County that they were alleged to have destroyed, the others in Knoxville on a gallows erected for that purpose. The first, a Greene County Unionist named A. C. Haun, was executed on the outskirts of town on 11 December. Six days later, Greene Countians Jacob Harmon and his son were hanged on the same spot, with the father forced to watch the execution of his son because the scaffold could accommodate but one noose at a time. The gal-

"Removing Prisoners from Knoxville Jail," from Parson Brownlow's Book.

Photograph courtesy of Special Collections, University of Tennessee Libraries.

lows were used rarely thereafter, but they stood as a constant and silent reminder of the penalty for treason against the southern Confederacy.[62]

DURING THIS TIME the best-known prisoner in Knoxville was none other than William Brownlow. To local Confederates, the Parson's departure from town just before the burning of the bridges looked awfully suspicious, and the rumor emerged almost immediately that the editor was somehow involved in the plot or, at the very least, knew about it ahead of time. Whether he had advance knowledge of the scheme is impossible to verify, but if he did, then he almost certainly tried to discourage it. He had opposed an uprising consistently for several months, denounced it immediately after the fact, and never once thereafter even hinted that he had been involved, even long afterward when it might have enhanced his reputation to take partial credit. The most likely explanation for his absence was the one he himself offered: his fear of arrest for his long-standing opposition to the Confederacy. After the events of 8 November, however, his situation became desperate. He was convinced that he could not make it to Kentucky, and should he be caught in the effort, his flight would almost certainly be used as circumstantial evidence against him. But his efforts to hide out in the Smokies might also be construed as an admission of guilt. Confederate troops

"Execution of Jacob Harmon and his son Henry," from Parson Brownlow's Book. *The sketch incorrectly shows the two alleged bridge burners being hanged simultaneously. In fact, the scaffold had but one noose, and Jacob Harmon was forced to watch his son be executed before him.*
Photograph courtesy of Special Collections, University of Tennessee Libraries.

were combing the coves and hollows in search of him, and he was concerned that
if they succeeded, they might not be overly preoccupied with the finer points of
the law, for instance, the maxim that the accused is innocent until proven guilty.[63]

Searching for a way out of his predicament, on 22 November Brownlow sent
a letter to the post commandant, General Carroll, by way of Knoxville Unionist
John Williams, son of a former U.S. senator and member of one of the oldest
families in town. He had no advance knowledge of the plan to burn the bridges,
the Parson assured Carroll, and he condemned the act "most unqualifiedly."
Getting to the heart of the matter, he let it be known that he was willing to stand
trial before a court of law but wished to avoid being "turned over to an infuriated mob of armed men filled with prejudices by my bitterest enemies." Six days
later Carroll sent word back to Brownlow. If the Parson's statements were true,
he could return to his home without fear of personal violence. "I desire that every
loyal citizen regardless of former political opinions shall be fully protected in all
his rights and privileges," he assured his correspondent. (The general's magnanimity was not quite so unbounded, for only two days earlier he had confiscated
the building and machinery of the *Knoxville Whig*, which would henceforth be
used to turn smoothbore muskets into rifles for the Confederate army.)[64]

Roughly at the time of this exchange, Knoxville attorney John Baxter traveled to Richmond to speak to the Confederate authorities on Brownlow's behalf.
Since the Rebel victory at Bull Run, Baxter had made peace with the idea of
Confederate independence, and he used the opportunity to urge a lenient policy
in East Tennessee as the best way to win the loyalty of the region's Unionist
majority. Regarding Brownlow specifically, he suggested that the fugitive editor
would be happy to leave the South, and if the government would provide a passport for his removal, he would cease to be both a constant irritant and a potential martyr for the Unionist cause. Secretary of War Judah Benjamin saw the
wisdom in Baxter's recommendation, agreeing that he would rather have
Brownlow "as an open enemy on the other side of the line than a secret enemy
within the lines." Benjamin then wrote to Major General George B. Crittenden,
who had just arrived in Knoxville and would soon supersede General Zollicoffer
in command of the Confederate forces near Cumberland Gap. Although he
stopped short of ordering Crittenden to grant Brownlow safe conduct to the
North, Benjamin intimated that he "would be glad to learn that he has left Tennessee." Crittenden had no problem reading between the lines. He promptly sent
word to the Parson through John Bell Brownlow, offering him a passport to
Kentucky—and a military escort to ensure his safety—if he would turn himself
in within twenty-four hours.[65]

Brownlow assented immediately and reported to Crittenden's headquarters
in Knoxville on 5 December. He and the commander agreed that he would de-
part for Kentucky on the seventh, giving him twenty-four hours to pack his bags
and bid farewell to his family. On the sixth, however, District Attorney Ramsey

swore out a warrant for Brownlow's arrest for treason against the Confederacy, and the Parson was hauled off to jail, where he joined more than a hundred other political prisoners awaiting trial. Ironically, on the very same day the *New York Times* reported as true an egregiously false rumor that "Federal forces under Parson Brownlow" had just attacked and stampeded a Rebel force northeast of Knoxville. Citing a dispatch from the *Memphis Avalanche*, the newspaper related that "the gallant Parson" had led some three thousand Unionists into battle and won the "most important victory the Union has yet gained." The *Times*'s account even got the attention of President Lincoln, who promptly ordered General George McClellan to investigate the report about Brownlow's exploits and, "if it prove true . . . push a column to join him."[66]

It did not "prove true," of course. Rather than wielding the sword, the imprisoned editor was busy wielding his pen, firing off a letter to Judah Benjamin, inquiring of the secretary of war whether a "dirty little drunken attorney" really had the authority to override his wishes. In the meantime, local Confederates launched a campaign of their own to make sure that the Parson stayed in jail. For public consumption, the *Knoxville Register* announced the patent falsehood that area *Unionists* were particularly incensed by the rumor that the War Department favored Brownlow's release. This was true, the editor explained, because so many of them had "friends and relatives now languishing in prison on account of his teachings." Although the *Register* did not really wish to see Brownlow "pull Tennessee hemp," it did recommend his incarceration in Tuscaloosa for the duration of the war. Once Confederate independence was secure, "the enviable gentleman can go over by himself and see Abe Lincoln and abide with him forever."[67]

Privately, leading Confederates were also writing to Richmond with a similar recommendation. Campbell Wallace, president of the East Tennessee and Georgia Railroad, wrote to Secretary Benjamin to say that he had been making a superhuman effort to keep the trains running for the Confederate army. He was now tempted to resign, however, since hearing that Benjamin was contemplating the release of the "prince of bridge-burning Lincolnites." On the day after the Parson's arrest, three other Knoxville Confederates wrote to Jefferson Davis, each stressing the popular furor that would erupt if Brownlow was allowed to go free. William Swan related to Davis his "utter surprise" that Judah Benjamin had even considered allowing the Parson to leave East Tennessee. The "citizens and soldiers" of Knoxville, he reported, were "almost unanimously indignant" at the prospect. J. G. M. Ramsey similarly informed the president of the widespread "feeling of indignation" sparked by rumors of clemency for the outspoken Lincolnite. Brownlow "was the prime mover and instigator of all this rebellion against the South," he explained to Davis. The wise course would be to "let the civil or military law take its course against the criminal leader in this atrocious rebellion as it has already done to his deluded and ignorant followers." The

doctor's son Crozier also wrote to Davis, assuring him that the Parson had knowledge of the bridge burnings and calling attention to the numerous editorials he
had published against the Confederacy since Tennessee's secession. "His newspaper has been the great cause of rebellion in this section," the district attorney
maintained, "and most of those who have been arrested have been deluded by
his gross distortion of facts and incited to take arms by inflammatory appeals to
their passions." The younger Ramsey went so far as to argue that many Confederate soldiers from East Tennessee had become greatly discouraged by the
thought of Brownlow's release; indeed, he told the president, they would likely
lay down their arms if the government they were defending should allow such a
villain to go free.[68]

Brownlow was not without his advocate. John Baxter continued to work
behind the scenes on Brownlow's behalf, assuring officials in Richmond that only
those who thirsted for the Parson's blood would be disappointed by his release,
whereas "the more enlightened, liberal and brave Southern men among us take
a different view." John Craig, the cashier of a Knoxville bank and a Unionist who
generally kept a low profile, wrote to Judah Benjamin to pose a question that the
secretary must have found unsettling. Craig observed that, in making his case
for Brownlow's guilt, the Confederate district attorney had conspicuously cited
an editorial Brownlow had published *before* Tennessee's secession. "Is it the purpose of the Government," he asked Benjamin, "to arrest and try for treason
gentlemen who may have expressed hostility to the Southern cause before the
State was formally voted out?" Craig assured him that "the reports of great excitement about the Brownlow affair are greatly exaggerated." As a matter of fact,
the banker maintained, "all disinterested parties" regarded the peculiar circumstances of his arrest as shameful and injurious "to the fair name of the Confederacy." Brownlow himself chose to appeal to Jefferson Davis. Admitting that he
had "resisted with his whole strength the revolution which your excellency is now
conducting," the Parson asserted nonetheless that he was not guilty of treason
against the Confederacy. He reminded Davis that the warrant issued against him
concentrated on his activities as an editor, and however objectionable its content,
"the publication of a newspaper . . . cannot amount to treason."[69]

In the end these arguments won out. Strictly speaking, neither Carroll nor
Crittenden had promised Brownlow that he would be immune from civil prosecution if he returned to Knoxville. For his part, Brownlow conveniently forgot
that he had promised Carroll that he was willing to defend himself in the courts
if the general would protect him from a mob. Even so, Judah Benjamin recognized that it would appear to all the world that the Confederate authorities had
entrapped Brownlow, luring him with promises of safe passage to the North in
order to facilitate his capture. Shortly before Christmas the secretary concluded
that Brownlow would have to be released. Although he lacked the authority to
order the district attorney to withdraw the charges, he informed Crozier Ramsey

that if he persisted in prosecuting Brownlow, he would feel obliged to recommend that the president pardon him for any crime of which he should be found guilty. Two days after the holiday Ramsey capitulated and informed Judge Humphreys that the government would not pursue its case against the editor. Technically, Brownlow was a free man, although he was immediately placed in military custody by the commandant of the post, both to protect him from attack and to preserve the peace until he could be sent beyond the Confederate lines. In part due to his own serious illness, in part because of the glacial pace of the Confederate authorities, the Parson remained under house arrest for more than two additional months. Finally, at the beginning of March, he was escorted to a point "within the Hessian lines" near Nashville, where he was reunited with neighbors Horace Maynard and Connally Trigg, as well as with his old nemesis Andrew Johnson, now military governor of the Union-occupied portions of the state. Although the *Knoxville Register* condemned the decision to release Brownlow, it did note one silver lining: "We presume we shall in future hear less of him in East Tennessee."[70]

NOT LONG AFTER BROWNLOW's release, the *Register* reviewed the treatment of local Unionists and repudiated the assertion that they had been persecuted. Exhibit A for the defense was the patience and restraint exhibited toward Brownlow himself. Confederate authorities had allowed him to continue to publish his paper long after Tennessee had formally separated from the Union. Indeed, this "most noxious and pestiferous sheet" had actually been borne by the *Confederate* mail service throughout the region. This despite the fact that it was "filled with information for the public enemies—teeming with falsehood for the people—inviting invasion—teaching rebellion—urging resistance to the late action of the people of the State." Badly outnumbered, the true southern men had gradually awakened to the danger posed by reckless men seeking to foment civil war within their midst. Even then, the *Register* observed, Confederates had not clamored for their exile or the confiscation of their property but had only called on them to submit to the will of the majority. They had stubbornly refused to do so, however, "and the consequence was their arrest and coercion into good behavior." Even this had not transpired until the Tories had engaged in a violent uprising. No republic could pretend to sovereignty while tolerating such open rebellion among its populace. In sum, local Confederates were to be applauded for their liberal policy, and the Unionists themselves were alone responsible for any hardship they ultimately experienced.[71]

Needless to say, Unionists understood the situation differently. Where Confederates saw toleration and restraint, Unionists discerned a "reign of terror" aimed at depriving them of their most basic rights of free expression. Most Unionists had consciously pursued what they considered to be an honorable neutrality, a path in which they would neither support the Confederacy directly nor bear arms against it. Felix Zollicoffer had seemingly offered them just such an option, and they had upheld their part of the bargain, going about their vocations peacefully and doing nothing tangibly to give aid or comfort to the enemies of the Confederacy. Almost from the beginning, however, Confederate civil authorities had embarked on a policy that threatened the systematic repression of those who merely sympathized with the Union. Then, when a tiny fraction of foolish men had risen in rebellion, the Confederates had used the uprising as an excuse to eliminate all dissent. The *Knoxville Register* might congratulate the Rebels for their long-suffering toleration of Parson Brownlow, but the Parson was gone, and the machinery that had printed the last Unionist newspaper in the Confederacy was now being used to manufacture rifles for southern soldiers. Confederate rule had led to a "time of darkness and oppression," as one Knoxville Unionist described it. Although not technically illegal, public expressions of support for the Union had entirely vanished; since every Unionist was now a suspected saboteur, such open avowals were simply too dangerous.[72]

Not everything about their situation was grim, thankfully. In mid-January the Confederate forces under Crittenden and Zollicoffer had been defeated in southern Kentucky at the Battle of Mill Springs, and less than a month later the fall of Forts Henry and Donelson had rendered much of West and Middle Tennessee vulnerable to Union invasion. Only a week afterward, Nashville had been evacuated by the Confederates, becoming the first Confederate state capital to fall to Union forces.[73] Yet there was no sign of a Union offensive into East Tennessee. The disloyal sections of the state were now being occupied by Federal troops, but the Unionist regions were apparently being ignored. They would not be ignored much longer. Parson Brownlow was introducing the entire North to the plight of East Tennessee's Unionists, in the process making Knoxville one of the best-known southern towns in all the Union.

CHAPTER FIVE

"Prudent Silence" and "Strict Neutrality"

I have only done my duty; and the man who is not prepared to submit to insult, the confiscation of his property, the incarceration of his person, or even to death itself, in defense of this glorious Union, is not worthy of the name of an American citizen.   —William G. Brownlow[1]

ITHIN A MONTH of his banishment, William Brownlow had become a celebrity of the first rank throughout the loyal states. As the editor of the last Unionist newspaper in the Confederacy, he had already been well known in the North by the fall of 1861, but his subsequent arrest and imprisonment transformed him into a martyr as well as a patriot, and northerners immediately clamored to see and hear the "celebrated exile."[2] Invitations poured in from groups as diverse as the Albany Independent Lecture Committee, the Brooklyn Athaneum, the students of Yale College, and the Smithsonian Institution, and Brownlow responded with a triumphal speaking tour during the spring and summer of 1862. It is impossible to retrace his steps completely, but his itinerary included speeches in Cincinnati, Columbus, Dayton, Chicago, Detroit, Indianapolis, Bloomington, Pittsburgh, Philadelphia, Washington, Buffalo, New York, Boston, Hartford, and Portland. Beyond these major stops were countless appearances at smaller venues, including five county fairs in Michigan and lectures to seventeen communities in Iowa and Illinois in the span of fifteen days.[3]

Everywhere crowds received him enthusiastically. In Cincinnati an audience estimated at five thousand filled the opera house to overflowing and listened as a choir of schoolchildren paid tribute to Brownlow in song: "All hail! All hail the hero unflinching! / The pure patriot we sing, unwavering and bold."[4] In Chicago's Metropolitan Hall a cheering throng praised his "independent, manly, and patriotic course" and lauded him as one who had "stood firm and unmoved" when all about him were deserting the flag of their fathers. His admirers packed New York City's Academy of Music to honor "the sturdy and much-suffering lover of the Union." There was not an empty seat in the house, and the audience's unabashed adulation prompted a *Times* reporter to conclude that "seldom has more triumphant welcome been vouchsafed to warrior or statesman." Another reporter characterized the scene when Brownlow was led upon the stage: "The whole assembly sprang simultaneously to their feet; the clapping of hands seemed almost to shake the very walls; gentlemen waved their hats and ladies their handkerchiefs; and all this was followed by cheer upon cheer."[5]

Northerners who did not hear Brownlow in person learned about the "martyr missionary" in countless other ways. Responding to an invitation from Philadelphia publisher George Childs, Brownlow hastily assembled a narrative of his "personal adventures among the Rebels" by combining a couple of hundred pages of material previously published in the *Whig* with the text of a diary that he had kept during his incarceration. Known popularly as *Parson Brownlow's Book*, the volume had sold one hundred thousand copies by the end of summer, prompting the *Saturday Evening Post* to predict that the "book will take rank among the great literary successes of modern times."[6] Brownlow's speeches were also widely reprinted in pamphlet form. An author with a good imagination wrote a mostly fanciful drama about the Parson's daughter, based loosely on her reported efforts to discourage Confederate soldiers from hauling down a Union flag flying in front of the Brownlow home in Knoxville. *Vanity Fair* put a cartoon of "Our Fight-

The "Fighting Parson" graced the cover of Vanity Fair in May 1862, not long after his banishment from the Confederacy.
Photograph courtesy of University of Washington Libraries, Special Collections, uw25982.

ing Minister from Tennessee" on the cover of its 31 May issue, and the publisher of Beadle's Dime Novels came out with a short biography of the hero. For those who wished to own a picture of the southern patriot, photographers in New York and Philadelphia were selling "carte de visite" portraits of the Parson, and a Cincinnati company sold stationery bearing Brownlow's likeness. Finally, a Pennsylvania firm even came out with a new musical ditty entitled "The Parson Brownlow Quick Step." If they were hearing less of him in East Tennessee, in the North Brownlow had become "an historic character," as the *Post* put it, his name so nearly a household word that at least one newspaper had to caution its readers against "idol worship."[7]

What triggered such phenomenal popularity is open to conjecture. Democratic societies engaged in war need to believe in the moral superiority of their cause, and certainly Brownlow was adept in presenting the current conflict in terms of moral absolutes. The preservation of the Union was "the cause of God and humanity," he declared, while those who would rend it asunder were "for the cause of the devil and his imps." It was that simple. The Parson was also definitely "a good hater," as the *New York Times* observed after he spoke in that city—his speeches were replete with tales of Rebel "atrocities" against loyalists and scathing condemnations of the "rebel usurpers."[8] Yet northern civilians did not need a southern minister to teach them how to despise the instigators of the

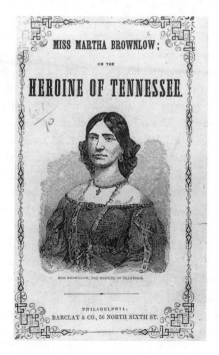

Parson Brownlow's daughter traveled throughout the North with her father and soon became famous as well.

Photograph courtesy of Special Collections, University of Tennessee Libraries.

rebellion. Nor did they need a polemical speaker to stimulate volunteering or promote greater sacrifice among a war-weary populace. In the spring of 1862 Union armies were riding a wave of battlefield successes. Forts Henry and Donelson had fallen. Nashville and New Orleans had been captured. Grant's victory at Shiloh had secured western Tennessee and much of northern Mississippi, and in Virginia McClellan's enormous Army of the Potomac was approaching the outskirts of Richmond. To many who heard Brownlow lecture or who purchased his book, the end of the war seemed imminent. Brownlow agreed. "The game of the rebellion [is] pretty near played out," he assured them. A little more grapeshot and the war would be over.[9]

For all his condemnation of secession and of the Confederacy, Brownlow's popularity may have stemmed more from the hope for national restoration that he symbolically represented. Certainly Confederate "atrocities" loomed large in his narrative, but they could be portrayed as evil only because they were inflicted on a loyal and innocent people. In his special message to Congress during the first summer of the war, Abraham Lincoln had questioned whether there existed "a majority of the legally-qualified voters of any State, except perhaps South Carolina, in favor of disunion."[10] Many conservative and moderate northerners shared his skepticism. Born of wishful thinking, their hope in a loyal but silent southern majority bore little semblance to reality across most of the Confederate states. East Tennessee was a conspicuous exception. Therein, perhaps, lay the greatest source of the Parson's appeal. As he reminded northern audiences repeatedly, Brownlow hailed from a land of widespread, fervent, "unconditional" Unionism.

In order not to complicate the point, Brownlow consistently passed over the extensive divisions within his own hometown and instead lumped bitterly divided Knoxville with the rest of predominantly Unionist East Tennessee; indeed, he often spoke of the town as a proxy for the region. Thus, whenever he referred to Confederate strength in Knoxville, he typically alluded only to the small "clique" of Crozier Ramsey, John Crozier, William Swan, William Sneed, and C. W. Charlton that had constituted the core of the town's "original secessionists." Occasionally he added potshots against other prominent Confederates, for example, "that prince of hypocrites" Campbell Wallace, the president of the East Tennessee and Georgia Railroad, or the town's two pro-secession Presbyterian ministers, Joseph Martin and William Harrison. This emphasis on a few prominent leaders perfectly complemented President Lincoln's portrayal of secession as an undemocratic movement actively fomented by a tiny elite. As Brownlow described it to northern audiences, the Confederate cause in Knoxville appeared to rest on the shoulders of a mere handful of malevolent instigators, supported by a small number of nameless followers.[11]

The remainder of the townspeople—the vast majority, the Parson implied—were courageously, defiantly loyal. When northern audiences praised him for his

unparalleled heroism (after he had eliminated from his frequent autobiographi-
cal sketches every element of personal hesitation or equivocation), Brownlow was
wont to deflect their applause by modestly denying that he deserved any credit
for the battle he had waged on behalf of the Union. "I have done nothing more
than my duty," he regularly asserted, "and the man who is not prepared to submit to insult, the confiscation of his property, the incarceration of his person, or
even to death itself, in defense of this glorious Union, is not worthy of the name
of an American citizen."[12] If this was heroism, Brownlow averred, then East
Tennessee was filled with heroes. The Parson made clear that he had left behind a legion of "ever-true and now suffering patriots"—men and women distinguished by an "uncompromising devotion" to the Union, "unmitigated
hostility" to those who would destroy it, and a willingness to risk life and property "in defense of the glorious stars and stripes." It was an inspiring message,
and northern civilians far removed from the theater of war cheered the messenger. How many of Brownlow's former neighbors would have recognized themselves in his descriptions is less certain.[13]

HOWEVER IT WAS DESCRIBED at patriotic rallies, the true breadth and
depth of Unionism in Knoxville evolved under the watchful eye of Confederate
soldiers. Brownlow's optimism notwithstanding, the rebellion was far from
"played out," and another year and a half would pass before Knoxville's "liberation" from Confederate rule. If anything, the circumstances of the town's Unionists worsened during the eighteen months after the Parson's banishment to the
North. "Hard as was the lot of the refugees," one Unionist who stayed in Knoxville would recall, "the condition of those who remained at home, in mental
anxiety and fear, was even harder."[14]

To begin with, those who stayed put still shared their town with Rebel troops.
The size of the occupying force continued to fluctuate greatly. At the end of
spring 1862 there were only four companies assigned to the Knoxville post—
probably no more than three hundred men. "We see a few soldiers about the
streets now," Confederate sympathizer Martha Hall informed her sister in early
May, "but we scarcely ever hear a gun fired or the sound of a drum." The number of troops continued to dwindle in early summer, as General Kirby Smith concentrated the forces under his command north of Knoxville, in preparation for
an invasion of Kentucky in coordination with General Braxton Bragg. Sick and
wounded soldiers filled the university buildings, and there were several convalescent camps situated around the outskirts of town, but otherwise the military
presence was minimal. "Our town is more empty than it has been for some 8 or 9
months," attorney Henry Elliott reported in early July to his friend William
McAdoo, who had relocated to Marietta, Georgia. In mid-August Smith led his
army of twenty-one thousand into Kentucky; for most of the next two months his
command operated 150 miles or more away from Knoxville, and East Tennessee

was as devoid of Confederate soldiers as it had been since the war began. The invasion of Kentucky was brought to a halt at the Battle of Perryville in early October, however, and soon Smith's divisions were streaming back toward town. By the beginning of November, Knoxville was once again literally overrun with troops. A local attorney described the situation in a letter to a close friend: "All the public & most of the private buildings have been appropriated by the military, and the disorder and confusion exceeds any thing you can imagine—no place to sleep & nothing to eat; still they come."[15]

Even when their numbers were small, the constant presence of soldiers severely taxed the town's resources and exacerbated shortages of basic commodities. Sugar was becoming scarce as early as the fall of 1861, and salt was soon in short supply as well. By spring of the following year, leather was extremely hard to come by, paper was almost impossible to purchase, and manufactured fabrics had nearly disappeared from the store shelves. In May 1862, a Knoxville housewife complained to a relative that "there are no new goods in town, many of the stores are shut, and the others might almost as well be for all they have in them." Indeed, she remarked, "I have heard that there is not a yard of calico in town, & there is nothing at all that will do to make a frock or apron." According to another account, the price of boots in Knoxville had tripled since the war began, and there was not a fine-tooth comb to be had in the entire town. More alarming, food of any kind was now selling at a premium—when it could be purchased at all. In late April a Knoxville resident observed to a Georgia correspondent that "there cant hardly be anything got to eat" in town. That autumn an employee of the *Register* sounded the same alarm, informing William McAdoo that "it is almost impossible to get food at *any* price." The latter blamed the predicament on the prevalence of Unionists. Knoxville labored under two great disadvantages, he noted in his diary near the end of 1862. The town is "too disagreeable from toryism, & from our troops eating up everything, such large numbers being required in E. T. by the tory abolitionist which still threatens mischief."[16]

In addition to food shortages, which affected Confederates and Unionists alike, three crucial developments in 1862 significantly exacerbated the hardships of Knoxville's loyalists. The first, ironically, resulted from the major Union military victories during the first half of the year. Although its larger strategic significance was negligible, the lopsided Federal victory at the Battle of Mill Springs in mid-January produced a new sense of vulnerability that permanently changed the war from the perspective of Knoxville Confederates. Subconsciously, at least, the bridge burnings had convinced them that the greatest threat to their security was internal. By comparison, the danger of invasion from outside of the region seemed remote, inasmuch as East Tennessee was protected by mountain ranges, natural "ramparts reared by the great Engineer of the universe" for defense "against the mighty hosts of the North." Only days before news of the conflict in southern Kentucky arrived, the *Register* had been promoting Knoxville as an ideal site for the permanent capital of the Confederacy, in part because the region was inaccessible to invading armies. Then retreating Rebel soldiers began to pour into Knoxville, and the paper's headlines trumpeted the shocking news: "CRITTENDEN'S COMMAND ROUTED! Gen. ZOLLICOFFER KILLED! Federalists advancing into East Tennessee!"[17]

Close on the heels of this reverse came word of the fall of Forts Henry and Donelson in mid-February. On 19 February the *Register* reported that the enemy had unexpectedly obtained a foothold in Middle Tennessee, and this "same exultant and powerful foe" now threatened the homes and firesides of East Tennesseans. Prominent secessionists such as John Crozier, William Sneed, and William McAdoo quickly moved to relocate their wives and children farther south, prompting the *Register* to complain that a wave of terror was sweeping Knoxville. Enhancing the psychological impact of the defeat was the news that twenty-two-year-old Captain Hugh L. McClung Jr., scion of one of the town's oldest and most prominent families, had perished in the fighting at Fort Donelson. "Another bright offering on the sacred altar of the South," McClung was the first town resident to fall in battle. Although the Union high command eventually opted to concentrate on Middle Tennessee, Federal troops retained control of Cumberland Gap until late that summer, and the possibility of an unchecked Federal strike toward Knoxville remained constant.[18]

In this environment, the pressure on Unionist sympathizers to convert to the southern cause entered an entirely new phase. It was one thing for local loyalists to endorse the "coercion" of the Confederate states when it involved the clash of arms in northern Virginia, quite another for them to acquiesce in the invasion of East Tennessee itself by Federal forces. Confederate leaders hoped that the specter of Lincoln's "Hessian" hordes descending on Knoxville would finally unify the town. During the first summer of the war, the *Register* had predicted that two-thirds of those who had voted against secession would volunteer in the Confederate forces should "Lincoln's thievish and mercenary forces . . . attempt to pollute the soil of East Tennessee with their unholy feet." What had then seemed remote now appeared imminent, and the *Register* hammered away at the point without ceasing. Everywhere Federal forces have penetrated, an article insisted shortly after the fall of Fort Donelson, "a dark and sombre desolation has followed." In a letter "To the Present Union Men of East Tennessee," a correspondent maintained that all who continued to oppose the Confederacy necessarily desired the countless deaths of neighbors and friends. An editorial the following week asked local Unionists, "Are you willing to subject the innocent wives, mothers and daughters of your secession neighbors to be turned over to the tender mercies of a brutal, mercenary foreign soldiery?" A number of new units were being organized in town—attorney W. C. Kain was raising a company of artillery, for example, and A. A. Blair, a minister and professor at East

Tennessee College, was forming an infantry company. It was time for Knoxville's Unionists to abandon their futile opposition to the Confederacy and join forces with their neighbors in driving out "the foul invader."[19]

The increasing stress on local Unionists also resulted from the policies of Confederate civil and military authorities. The most important initiative came from the Confederate Congress. On 16 April, legislators in Richmond passed the first of three conscription acts. The initial measure made every white male between the ages of eighteen and thirty-five subject to military service, although draftees were accorded the privilege of hiring a substitute from the pool of "persons not liable for duty." Only five days later the Congress modified the law by automatically exempting members of a number of skilled and professional occupations. Five months afterward it altered the act yet again, raising the upper limit of those eligible for the draft to forty-five but also adding an exemption of one white male on every plantation with twenty slaves or more. Many East Tennesseans now began to suspect that the government in Richmond intended to force poor Appalachian whites to finish a war that Black Belt slaveholders had begun. Anticipating the furor that the new policy would evoke, on 8 April Jefferson Davis had effectively declared East Tennessee an enemy territory, suspending the writ of habeas corpus and imposing martial law throughout the area. Martial law notwithstanding, East Tennesseans resisted the draft so vehemently that the Confederate military commander on the scene convinced Davis to suspend enforcement of the act temporarily throughout the region. As a result, the draft was not permanently applied to the area until October 1862, some six months after it was implemented elsewhere in the Confederacy.[20]

In Knoxville, the effect of the conscription policy was uneven. Although not a single individual escaped military service due to the so-called Twenty Negro Law, there were still numerous opportunities to avoid the draft, especially for Confederate sympathizers. Although they lacked twenty slaves, many of Knoxville's commercial elite—James D. Cowan and Charles McClung, for example—possessed the financial means to hire a substitute and apparently did so. Several of the town's merchants also used their bookkeeping talents to procure draft-exempt jobs in the Confederate Ordinance Department. Frank and Pleasant McClung both worked with the Ordinance Department locally, while Sam B. Boyd labored in a similar capacity in Bristol, Virginia, just across the state border. All five of these men were well connected and wealthy, hailing from families with nearly $60,000 worth of property on average. For such men, staying out of the army was no difficult task.[21]

Blue-collar workers were also able to stay out of the army in large numbers. Those with skills considered vital to the war effort frequently procured exemptions. Alfred Buffat, a naturalized immigrant from Switzerland, was exempted due to his "being a miller skilled in his profession and actually engaged in working for the publick." Emmanuel Bolli stayed at home by working in a government machine shop, whereas Nicholas Lewis avoided service by laboring as a carpenter for the East Tennessee and Virginia Railroad. Even wood choppers for the ET&V were excused from the draft, at least once president John R. Branner convinced the War Department that they were essential to the smooth operation of the line. A significant number of these may have been Unionist in sympathy, for Branner was accused by a correspondent of the *Register* of hiring numerous Tories as railroad hands. A different correspondent raised the same charge concerning the East Tennessee and Georgia.[22]

Even though manual laborers could and did frequently avoid the draft, conscription still affected the poor disproportionately. Conscription records do not survive for East Tennessee, but the fact is still obvious from a comparison of men who entered the army before and after the passage of the first Conscription Act.[23] Men who volunteered before the end of March 1862 were predominantly young, single males, and more than half hailed from white-collar households, making their living as clerks, merchants, and attorneys (see Appendix, Table 1). In contrast, Knoxville males who entered the service under the threat of the draft (whether as conscripts or as volunteers) were slightly older, considerably more likely to be married, and far more likely to work with their hands. Above all, they were almost universally poor. The median household wealth of men who joined the army before the end of March 1862 was nearly $1,200; for those who became soldiers after the implementation of conscription, the figure declined to a mere $75. Of the former group, 20 percent came from slaveholding households; of the latter, only 3 percent did so. Parson Brownlow had long ago predicted that if the state seceded, the "honest yeomanry" would ultimately be "forced to leave their wives and children" and "fight for the purse-proud aristocrats of the Cotton States, whose pecuniary abilities [would] enable them to hire substitutes!" The prediction now appeared prophetic.[24]

Potentially the greatest strain on Unionists' loyalties stemmed from the changing policies of the federal government with regard to southern slaves. Since President Lincoln's first call for volunteers, Confederates had been declaring that the "Black Republicans" in Washington would use the pretense of a war to preserve the Union in order to wage a war against slavery. In the summer of 1861 congressional Republicans explicitly repudiated such a charge, supporting overwhelmingly a resolution sponsored by John J. Crittenden and Andrew Johnson (both border-state Unionists) which declared that the sole object of the war was to preserve the Union, and not to interfere with "the rights or established institutions" of the seceded states. Had the war ended with a northern victory in 1861, they very well may have honored that pledge. But as the war waxed long, and as its cost in blood and treasure mounted to unimagined heights, Republican legislators increasingly supported aggressive measures against the South's "peculiar institution." Within weeks of the Crittenden-Johnson resolution, the Republican majority passed the First Confiscation Act, which authorized the seizure of all property—including slaves—used in direct military aid of the rebellion. In March of the following year they passed a new article of war forbidding Union military commanders from returning fugitive slaves to their masters. The following month they abolished slavery in the District of Columbia, in June they prohibited slavery in all federal territories, and in July they passed the Second Confiscation Act authorizing the seizure of all property, however employed, owned by persons actively in rebellion against the United States. Shortly thereafter, an anonymous correspondent to the *Register* implored East Tennesseans to "open your eyes to the true object and purpose of this war. It is not for the restoration of the Union. It is for the consummation of the hellish purposes of abolitionism."[25]

When Abraham Lincoln issued the Emancipation Proclamation in late September 1862, Knoxville's Confederates rejoiced that the Black Republicans had at last honestly avowed their insidious agenda. This "damnable exhibition of barbarity," they were certain, would backfire against the man they ridiculed as "Uncle Ape." Thanks to this "culminating act of unparalleled lawlessness," Republican tyranny now stood unmasked "in its most hideous form." "Is there a Tennessean who will not now take up arms against the North?" asked J. A. Sperry of the *Register* incredulously. "Shall we not stand up as one man, and bid defiance to the plundering horde of abolition fiends who would not only deprive us of our rights as freemen, but make us the slaves of slaves?" Given Lincoln's proclamation, which would "convert a Paradise into a very Hell," the editor wondered aloud who could possibly still attempt to remain neutral in the life-or-death struggle before them. Such a one was "either a miserable, skulking coward, or a traitor to his country and his God." His epitaph should read "Here lies the body of a cowardly wretch, who trembled and obeyed a tyrant."[26]

Sperry received unexpected help in his campaign against East Tennessee's persistent Unionists. On 5 October, the *Register* prominently published an address from Thomas A. R. Nelson, Parson Brownlow's longtime ally and the most outspoken advocate of defiance at the Greeneville Convention in June 1861. "Of all the acts of despotism of which the civil war in which we are now engaged has been the prolific source," Nelson wrote, not one "equals the atrocity and barbarism of Mr. Lincoln's proclamation." The once-zealous loyalist observed that Lincoln had violated the platform on which he had campaigned and had broken the personal promise not to interfere with slavery which he had solemnly offered in his inaugural address. Even worse, he made no distinction whatever between the property of the loyal and the disloyal within the Confederate states. If the North was really willing to sustain him in this foolhardy policy, "then we have no Union to hope for, no Constitution to struggle for . . . no peace to expect, save such, as with the blessing of Providence, we may conquer." Nelson conceded that the Confederacy was also guilty of its share of wanton crimes against the persons and property of those heretofore loyal to the Union, but none of that mattered in the aftermath of the president's proclamation. "The Union men of East Tennessee," Nelson proclaimed, "are not now and never were Abolitionists."[27]

Consequently, at the same time that Parson Brownlow was boasting to northern audiences about East Tennessee's overwhelming and unwavering Unionism, J. A. Sperry was exulting that a "revolution" of conviction was under way throughout the section and declaring that the combined effects of invasion, conscription, and emancipation would constitute "the death blow of Toryism in this unhappy division of the State."[28] Neither characterization held true in Knoxville. Something approaching a "revolution" in sentiment had occurred there, all right, but it had taken place more than a year earlier, in the immediate aftermath of the attack on Fort Sumter. As late as February 1861 no more than one-eighth of the town's voting population had advocated disunion, but four months later almost one-half had endorsed the state legislature's "declaration of independence." Unionism did continue to erode gradually thereafter, but "Toryism" far from disappeared. We know this thanks to the survival of a variety of civil and military records that shed light on local patterns of loyalty and divulge, in particular, who leading Unionists at the time considered to be loyal among their neighbors.[29] These sources—which offer insight into the sympathies of more than half of the town's households—suggest that the proportion that Unionists represented of the town's white population fell from just more than one-half in the middle of 1861 to just more than one-third two years later. This was a significant decline, but hardly the precipitous collapse that the *Register* had predicted.

This was true, at least in part, because conscription failed to produce the effect that the *Register* had expected. Once it was implemented, editor J. A. Sperry had anticipated that the draft law would force many fainthearted Rebels into open support for the Confederacy. It may have done so, but it also pushed many of those with Unionist leanings into a position of overt resistance. Even after the mass arrests in the summer and fall of 1861, Oliver Temple believed, most local Unionists still were willing "to remain quietly at home until the national government should be able to come to their relief and restore its authority." This was not simply an expression of indifference on their part, much less cowardice. Union men who tried to join the Federal forces in Kentucky not only risked arrest and imprisonment but also jeopardized the loved ones they left behind. Unlike loyalists in the more remote reaches of upper East Tennessee, they would be leaving their families not among overwhelmingly Unionist neighbors but in a bitterly divided community under the constant surveillance of Rebel soldiers. All things considered, it is small wonder that the vast majority of Unionists had opted to stay put and pray that the region would soon be liberated.[30]

After the implementation of conscription, however, remaining "quietly at home" was no longer a possibility, at least for men not old enough, rich enough, skilled enough, or clever enough to avoid the draft. No more than a handful of

Knoxville men had enlisted in the Federal forces during the first year of the war, but probably at least sixty made their way to Union camps in Kentucky during the spring and summer of 1862. Many others likely wished to go but were deterred by Confederate patrols on the lookout for "stampeders." Knoxville druggist Edward Sanford would later recall that a group of Knoxville Unionists had joined an informal "company" with the intention of escaping together to the Federal lines on the night of 18 April. Confederate authorities evidently got wind of the plan, however, and the post commander placed a heavy guard around the town that successfully deterred some seventy-five of the town's men from leaving. Most areas in East Tennessee were not so closely watched, of course, and General Kirby Smith, who replaced the ill-fated Felix Zollicoffer as commander of the Department of East Tennessee, estimated toward the end of April that perhaps as many as seven thousand East Tennesseans had fled the region to avoid the draft. Most of these made their way to Kentucky, where they eventually enlisted in Federal units. With regard to East Tennessee, at least, the primary beneficiary of the Confederate conscription policy was the U.S. Army.[31]

Nor did emancipation generate the popular backlash that Confederates had hoped for. Indeed, Thomas Nelson's high-profile conversion was the exception that proved the rule during the winter of 1862–63. Shortly after the congressman's address, the *Register* declared that "thinking, intelligent" members of the former Union party were "rapidly declaring their adhesion to the cause of the South." This was so much wishful thinking. William McAdoo's assessment was far less sanguine—and much more accurate. "The *masses* of the Unionists are not in the least moved from their devotion," he noted in his diary before the year was out. "Nelson's letter produced no effect." In February 1863 the *Register* finally acknowledged as much, observing incredulously that the followers of Johnson and Brownlow intended to "persevere in their course to the bitter end." An anonymous correspondent reached the same conclusion not long thereafter, complaining that East Tennesseans had become "radically, thoroughly abolitionized."[32]

This was surely an exaggeration, but it captured an important truth: the Emancipation Proclamation per se appears to have pushed few loyalists into the Confederate camp. For one thing, those most susceptible to appeals to southern white solidarity in defense of the peculiar institution had probably long since cast their lot with the Confederacy; the idea that the fate of slavery hung in the balance was hardly new, after all. Beyond this, those still hoping to preserve both the Union *and* slavery could take solace in the fact that Lincoln's decree did not even apply to Tennessee, which was excluded on the grounds that two-thirds of the state was already occupied by Federal forces and theoretically no longer in a state of rebellion. Parson Brownlow wrote to President Lincoln on Christmas Day of 1862 to affirm the decision to exclude Tennessee from the final proclamation, an act that would "secure her co-operation in the work of restoring the Union, and add strength to your administration." Slavery was still alive and well in East Tennessee, and although a day of decision would eventually come for the most staunchly proslavery Unionists, in early 1863 it was still possible to think of the president's decree as a weapon wielded solely against traitors.[33]

This was precisely how Parson Brownlow viewed it. Four days after Nelson announced in Knoxville that he was reversing his course to stand with the Confederacy, Brownlow declared to an audience in Grand Rapids, Michigan, that he was willing to endorse the president's proclamation as a military measure, although "in no other sense." Although he doubted that the decree would have any practical effect (it was too much like "the Pope's bull against the comet"), he nevertheless endorsed its sentiment. "I say confiscate the land, the money, the negroes of all rebels in rebellion against this Government," the proslavery Parson proclaimed, "and then turn round and confiscate the necks of the infernal leaders." Another Knoxville exile, Horace Maynard, took a similar tack in a speech in Nashville, where he was serving as the attorney general for Union-occupied Tennessee under military governor Andrew Johnson. Emancipation was an act "purely of military expediency," Maynard averred, and President Lincoln had "the same rightful power to deprive the rebels of their slaves that he would have to stampede their horses." There is evidence that a growing proportion of East Tennessee Unionists not only tolerated but actually advocated emancipation on precisely such grounds. Extensive hardship under Confederate rule had apparently transformed thousands into "practical abolitionists" willing to strike at slavery in order to cripple the rebellion. Some ten thousand East Tennesseans in the Army of the Cumberland met in March 1863 to voice their hearty approval of the Emancipation Proclamation. In a series of formal resolutions they announced that they were "for a vigorous prosecution of the war, until the rebels throw down their arms without condition." More specifically, they favored "depriving the rebel master of his slaves and every other species of property, so far as may be necessary to effect such object." The momentum of events unleashed by the war had carried Unionists to a position unimaginable only three years earlier.[34]

AND YET FOR ALL of Parson Brownlow's boasting to northern audiences, in his own hometown the ranks of the faithful had fallen off sharply after Fort Sumter and continued to dwindle gradually thereafter, so that by the summer of 1863 probably no more than one-third of the white population stood firm. What compelled this minority to follow a path at odds with their neighbors? Answers are elusive, even for the leaders; for the rank and file they are particularly so. Yet if the surviving records do not afford conclusive insight regarding individual motives, they do allow the construction of a suggestive *collective* profile of "Lincolnites" and "Rebels."

When scholars have tried to pinpoint the foundations of East Tennessee's divided loyalties, they have most commonly seized upon an urban-rural distinction, noting, as contemporaries were fully aware, that pro-Confederate support was always most pronounced in the region's towns, especially those along the major railroad lines, whereas the countryside tended to be staunchly pro-Union.[35] The generalization is beyond dispute, but it offers little help concerning the divisions within Knoxville itself. When contemporaries sought to explain the region's wartime divisions, they pointed just as frequently to the persistent strength of long-standing party ties. Although they disagreed over what to make of the fact, both Rebels and loyalists agreed that East Tennessee Unionism was grounded solidly in the prewar Whig Party. Confederates condemned the connection. As an anonymous correspondent charged in the *Register*, "With shame it must be confessed [that] Unionism in East Tennessee [is] the expiring struggle of the Whig politicians." Conversely, Unionists accused secessionist leaders of political opportunism and proudly boasted that the antecedents of the Union party were "for the most part the old Whig party of 1835–6—the party that sprang up in opposition to General Jackson." Oliver Temple estimated that 80 percent of East Tennessee Whigs had voted against secession in June 1861, while John Bell Brownlow boasted that some seven-tenths of Union soldiers from Tennessee had roots in the party.[36]

No voting records survive that would allow a systematic assessment of the correlation between Whiggery and Unionism in Knoxville, but the connection was undoubtedly strong. Given the almost total dearth of acknowledged Democrats who remained true to the Union, a reasonable conjecture would be that local Democrats eventually sided with the Confederacy almost universally, while little more than half of local Whigs did so. And yet an explanation based solely on partisan ties is still insufficient. It is obviously incomplete, given the likelihood that a majority of Knoxville's Whigs ultimately joined with the town's Democrats in support of the Confederacy. Party loyalties mattered, but there were still a lot of former Whigs wearing gray uniforms. To some degree the appeal to party ties also begs the question, ignoring as it does the manifold factors that undergirded partisan attachment. Although in the absence of individual voting records it is impossible to determine the socioeconomic differences between Democrats and Whigs, there is sufficient evidence to speak broadly about differences between Confederates and Unionists.

Some of the distinctions are predictable.[37] The number of individuals involved was small, but Unionists apparently were more likely to have been born in the North; 12 percent of identified Unionists hailed from one of the free states, as compared with only 4 percent of Confederates (see Appendix, Table 2). Even so, the correlation was not as pronounced as might have been expected. Among the northern-born whose loyalties could be ascertained, nearly one-half (44 percent) ultimately sided with the Confederacy. Both Thomas Humes and Oliver Temple maintained that Knoxville was home to a large number of "Northern men with Southern principles," and the evidence seems to bear this out.[38] Foreign nativity, on the other hand, appears not to have been a factor, at least among those whose loyalties could be determined. On the contrary, the foreign-born seem to have divided in roughly the same proportions as the community as a whole.

It also makes sense that the ownership of slaves would predispose masters to support the Confederacy. Certainly slaveholders were told repeatedly that a Union victory would lead to the abolition of their peculiar species of property. Whether they wholly bought into this view is uncertain, but the correlation between slave ownership and Confederate sympathy indicates that local slaveholders and their dependents sided disproportionately with the Confederacy. Members of slave-owning households are the most overrepresented group among those whose loyalties can be identified; evidence exists to determine the sympathies of ninety-five such individuals, and fully four-fifths of these can be classified as Confederates. And yet a significant proportion of Unionists (17 percent) still hailed from slaveholding families, a fraction not dramatically different from the proportion of Confederates (25 percent) who did so.

Figures on wealth and occupational status are also revealing. Reflecting on patterns of wartime loyalty, Thomas Humes later remembered that "as a general rule, secessionists . . . were more numerous in East Tennessee among the rich and persons of best social position, and were greatly outnumbered among the middle and poorer classes."[39] However accurate the reverend's observations may have been for the overall region, the reality in Knoxville was more complicated. Strictly speaking, Knoxville Confederates were not outnumbered in any major wealth or occupational category. Even so, there was a *relative* correlation between socioeconomic status and support for the Confederacy. An analysis of the wealthiest 10 percent of Knoxville households in 1860 shows that Unionists were a small minority among the town's leading citizens. Of the fifty-nine who can be classified (out of a total of sixty-nine), only fifteen can be labeled as Unionist, suggesting that roughly three-quarters of the economic elite sided with the Confederacy. It must be remembered, however, that probably two-thirds of the community as a whole eventually took this position, hence the very wealthy were only slightly overrepresented in the Rebel ranks. Among all the townspeople who can be classified, however, the median household wealth of Confederates ($3,250) did exceed that of Unionists ($2,200) by nearly 50 percent. On the whole, Rebels had greater means than their Lincolnite neighbors.

A similar kind of correlation emerges when occupational patterns are considered. Both Confederate and Unionist leaders had gone out of their way to attract the support of Knoxville's working classes, who after all did constitute nearly three-quarters of the town's adult white males. The *Register* had insisted that "the poor man" would suffer most from the North's abolitionist agenda, while Parson Brownlow—the self-appointed champion of the "Mechanics, Farmers, and laboring classes"—had countered by emphasizing that secession would serve the cause of the "purse-proud aristocrats" of the Black Belt at the expense of the hardy laborers of East Tennessee.[40] In the end, the Unionist message seems to have resonated strongly among Knoxville's blue-collar laborers, for men who worked with their hands accounted for more than three-fifths of the town's known Unionists, but only one-third of identified Confederates. This *relative* correlation aside, it appears likely that Confederates predominated numerically even among blue-collar laborers, for nearly three-fifths of those whose loyalties have been identified can be classified as pro-Confederate. Among white-collar workers the proportion rises to fully four-fifths. Without a doubt, Knoxville's merchants, clerks, bankers, and attorneys overwhelmingly cast their lot with the Confederacy. More directly involved in commercial or professional relationships with southerners from outside the immediate vicinity, they may have felt less threatened by the specter of Cotton Belt aggression and more optimistic about the prospect of prosperity as a peripheral region within a slave-state confederacy.[41]

In sum, the evidence points consistently to a socioeconomic difference in the bases of Confederate and Unionist support. Compared with their Confederate neighbors, Unionists possessed less wealth (including slaves) and were more likely to hold blue-collar jobs; Confederates were somewhat wealthier and considerably more likely to work in white-collar professions. Yet it is possible to exaggerate these relative distinctions. The *typical* Confederate, like the *typical* Unionist, was a southern-born, nonslaveholding male of modest means. The *typical* blue-collar laborer, like the *typical* professional, ultimately sided with the Confederacy, not the Union. Differences of wealth and occupational status are clearly correlated with identifiable patterns of loyalty, but in no way do they explain them fully. In the final analysis, the overall similarities in wealth and occupation between Confederates and Unionists are as striking as the relative differences.[42]

For all the populist rhetoric on both sides, it appears that Knoxville's civil war was not solely, or even primarily, a class conflict. Like partisan affiliation, perceptions of class interest also surely influenced patterns of wartime allegiance, but they were not determinative. Still other factors must have been at work. Specifically, the townspeople were also members of other smaller, overlapping subcommunities that may have helped to shape their response to the national crisis. Always more than just the sum of their possessions and political ties, the people of Knoxville experienced the events between 1861 and 1865 as members of families, churches, and neighborhoods, not to mention a host of other communities or reference groups that are beyond our power to reconstruct.

Kinship was undoubtedly a potent influence. Although it is impossible to gauge the power of extended family ties with any exactness, it seems clear that *nuclear* families were rarely divided in sympathy. The tragic frequency with which "brother fought against brother" during the Civil War has always captivated the popular imagination, but instances of such divided households were probably never as numerous as legend insists.[43] As badly split as Knoxville was, most individual households appear to have remained unified during the conflict. Of the 323 households for which information survives, only 14 were definitely divided, and only 7 of these (scarcely 2 percent of the total) contained *family members* living under one roof and yet taking opposite sides in the struggle. (In the other 7, an unrelated household member, probably a boarder, held sympathies at odds with those of the nuclear family.)

To the degree that the war split Knoxville families asunder, it was much more likely to pit father against son than brother against brother. Of the divided nuclear families that have been discovered, only one actually fits the classic stereotype of the "brother's war." In the remaining six instances, the primary line of conflict was intergenerational, that is, between fathers and sons. The lone exception was the family of Knoxville's mayor, moderate Unionist James C. Luttrell, who had sons in each army. When war broke out, John Luttrell left his studies at the University of North Carolina to enlist in the Confederate army and ultimately died in the service. His younger brother, James Jr., likewise sided with the Confederacy. Enrolling in an artillery company in Knoxville in the summer of 1861, he rose to the rank of lieutenant and survived to surrender with Joseph Johnston in North Carolina in the spring of 1865. The youngest Luttrell brother, on the other hand, seventeen-year-old Samuel, initially stayed at home but later joined the Twelfth Tennessee Cavalry (U.S.A.). Both surviving sons—Confederate Jim and Unionist Sam—eventually followed in their father's footsteps to serve as mayor of Knoxville.[44]

Church affiliation also must have played a role in shaping sympathies. Knoxville had seven congregations when the war broke out—two Presbyterian, one each of Methodists, Baptists, Episcopalians, and Catholics, and another, possibly nondenominational but more likely Methodist—that met in Temperance Hall in East Knoxville. Probably a minority of the free population attended church regularly, but it was a sizable minority, and disproportionately influential. Long after the war, Thomas Humes maintained that "friends of secession" had been "largely in the majority among church-goers." Extant membership rolls for three of the seven congregations indicate that the Unionist clergyman was almost certainly correct. Humes's own congregation, for example—St. John's Episcopal Church—was dominated by supporters of the Confederacy, many of whom boycotted the rector's sermons when he persisted in praying for Lincoln after the fall of Fort Sumter.[45]

The First Presbyterian Church was similarly a secessionist bastion. Its pastor, William Harrison, reportedly proclaimed from the pulpit that "Jesus Christ was a Southerner, born upon Southern soil; and so were his disciples and apostles—all, except Judas, and he was a Northern man." Probably most of his audience enjoyed the joke, for Confederates in the congregation outnumbered Unionists more than five to one (among those whose loyalties can be identified), and all seven members of the board of elders had favored separation in the June 1861 referendum. The Second Presbyterian Church was probably more divided, though also tilting toward the Confederacy. Its pastor, Joseph Martin, was also an outspoken champion of the southern cause, and Confederate sympathizers appear to have predominated among his flock. The elders and deacons, however, were split almost evenly between Confederates and Unionists; when Pastor Martin prayed that Horace Maynard's "bones shall bleach upon the Cumberland Mountains," enough members were offended by this attack on one of their ruling elders that attendance thereafter was noticeably diminished. Almost nothing is known about the Baptist and Catholic congregations, but the pastor of the Methodist Church on Church Street later recalled that his flock was "in full sympathy with the Confederacy." Anecdotal evidence also suggests, to no great surprise, that the group meeting in Temperance Hall—whose most prominent member had been Parson Brownlow—was largely Unionist. In sum, although every congregation surely contained both Unionist and Confederate members, there is some indication that most, if not all, of these religious bodies identified disproportionately with one or the other side.[46]

When all is said and done, a conclusive explanation of Knoxville's conflicting loyalties remains elusive. Partisan ties, perceptions of class or individual economic interest, family bonds, and church affiliation all undoubtedly played a role in shaping the innumerable decisions that resulted, cumulatively, in the division of this southern town. And yet, because these decisions were ultimately individual and personal, they were subject to the infinite vagaries of human nature and circumstance. No simple generalizations will suffice, and the possibility remains that, despite the relative distinctions between them, "loyalists differed *with* the rebels much more than they differed *from* them."[47] This nagging impression is strengthened by examining the spatial distribution of definite Confederates and Unionists. Drawing on information from an 1859 city directory, the map on the following page shows the approximate location of the residences of all townspeople whose loyalties can be identified. With the exception of northwestern Knoxville—a less densely inhabited area dominated by the railroad depot and the Deaf and Dumb Asylum—it is hard to argue that there are clearly discernible Confederate and Unionist neighborhoods. Rebels and loyalists lived and worked in close proximity. The Civil War in Knoxville may not have been a "brothers' war," but it was definitely a war among neighbors.

BUT HOW DID LINCOLNITE and Rebel neighbors differ in *behavior* and *experience*, if at all? According to the exiled William Brownlow, any "Unionist" worthy of the name gladly risked life and property rather than abandon the cause. It necessarily followed that "true" Unionists suffered under Confederate rule, whereas the fidelity of those not "hurt with loyalty" was suspect.[48] The Parson's rhetoric played well in front of northern audiences who had little experience of

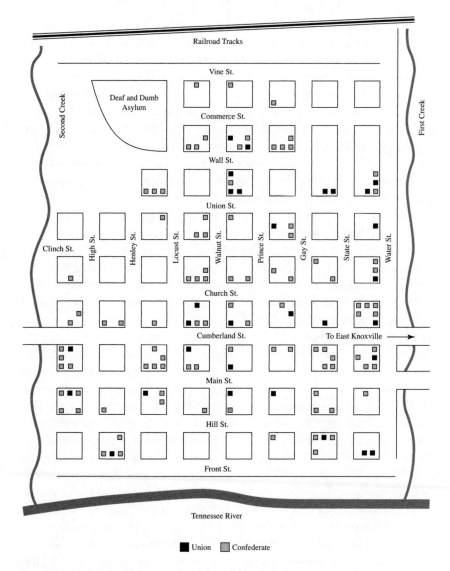

Knoxville's Identifiable Union and Confederate Households.

The location of households is derived from *Williams' Knoxville Directory, City Guide, and Business Mirror* (Knoxville: C. S. Williams, 1859). For sources employed in determining individual loyalties, see Appendix.

civil war within the Civil War. Crowds cheered his strict standards, and during Reconstruction the federal government largely adopted them to determine the wartime sympathies of southern civilians.[49] But how well did they apply to his own hometown? What did it mean to be a Unionist in a Confederate-occupied town?

By the time that his northern lecture tour was well under way, those who most closely conformed to Brownlow's severe definition of loyalty were no longer even in Knoxville. Gone were the sixty or so men and boys who had shown their "uncompromising devotion" to the Union by fleeing their homes to enlist in the Federal forces in Kentucky. Also absent were outspoken Unionist leaders such as Horace Maynard and Connally Trigg. These men braved considerable dangers and experienced great hardships, but they at least escaped the morally troubling questions haunting those who remained behind: Did duty truly require resistance to Confederate rule, or was some measure of submission consistent with the dictates of conscience? When did submission shade into tacit cooperation? What *were* the acceptable boundaries of loyalty?

Significantly, neither Oliver Temple nor Thomas Humes had much to say about how Union sympathizers addressed these thorny issues. Both remained in town for most of the period of Confederate occupation, and both later wrote lengthy histories of the war, yet each was strangely reticent regarding the period between Brownlow's arrest in late 1861 and the "liberation" of Knoxville by Federal troops more than twenty months later. What little they offered was frustratingly vague. Temple characterized the period as "gloomy beyond description." There was danger at every hand. "It was no longer safe to speak except in a whisper," and despair, "darker than midnight," threatened to overwhelm even the most resilient. The anxiety was almost unbearable, especially for men of prominence, and most formerly outspoken Unionists adopted a path of "prudent silence." Humes observed that a patriotic spirit remained strong "among the country people," and although he did not emphasize them, he alluded to incidents of guerrilla warfare and partisan violence in the more remote recesses of East Tennessee. Closer to home, however, he was chiefly struck by the "comparative quiescence" that characterized the routine of most Union men. Admittedly, soldiers were constantly on the streets, and "friendly social intercourse" had largely ceased between Confederates and Unionists, but otherwise "the current of life in the community, with its mingled civil and military elements, flowed on in wonted channels."[50] Other witnesses offered corroborating testimony. A Knoxville Confederate suggested that most leading Unionists were characterized by "strict neutrality" in public, while an area Unionist later remembered that his loyal neighbors had followed a simple survival strategy: "We stayed at home and kept our mouths shut." A Union officer stationed in Knoxville after the fall of 1863 concurred, explaining that "there were a great many persons in East Tennessee whose sentiments were well known, but who had to modify their public expressions as a too open and too continued expression would imperil their lives."[51]

"Prudent silence." "Comparative quiescence." "Strict neutrality." These phrases more aptly embodied the day-to-day routine of suffering Knoxville Unionists than the bluster and brag with which Parson Brownlow regaled northern audiences. In actuality, instances of resistance or open defiance in Knoxville were rare. Oliver

Temple could later recall only two individuals who publicly acknowledged their affinity for the Union after the fall of 1861. The first was Mrs. George Mabry, a headstrong Scot who threatened to return to her homeland should the rebellion succeed and informed her husband that she would not live in the southern Confederacy even if "Washington and Jefferson were both raised from the dead." Although "widely and . . . favorably known" as "unflinchingly true to the Union," Jeannette Mabry was shielded from persecution in part by her sex, in part by her wealth, and in part by her political connections. (She was the sister-in-law of Joseph Mabry, a leading "original secessionist.") The second outspoken Unionist, according to Temple, was "Colonel" John Williams, son of a former U.S. senator and related by blood or marriage to most of the town's leading families. Not gifted as a public speaker or writer, Williams had limited influence after Tennessee's separation; his family connections, combined with the very audacity of his outspoken loyalty, likely protected him from harassment as well. Apart from Williams, no other leading Unionist dared to avow his sympathies openly. In public, at least, most instead effected a posture of strict impartiality. The *Knoxville Register* noted as much, observing in early 1863 that Unionism had just about vanished, only to be succeeded by "its bastard and most malignant offspring NEUTRALITY."[52]

For all the Parson's rhetoric about "uncompromising devotion" and "unmitigated hostility," the boundaries of Unionism among the civilians who remained at home were always blurred. The extremes of loyalty were easy to categorize. At one end of the continuum was the handful of open Unionists like Jeannette Mabry and John Williams who were universally recognized as loyal. At the other end was a larger group of outspoken "original" secessionists—the Ramseys, Croziers, Swans, and others who had been zealous advocates of disunion from the moment of Abraham Lincoln's election. After Fort Sumter, the latter had been joined by nearly half the townspeople, and the actual secession of the state and the reality of Confederate power had prompted yet more conversions, until two-thirds or more of the town's whites had cast their lot with the Confederacy. And yet many of the last group had done so with considerable misgivings. Unionists who testified before a Federal claims commission in Knoxville in 1864 regularly distinguished between civilians who had been "thoroughly disloyal"—that is, who had actively promoted the Confederate cause—and those who had been disloyal but "quiet," or "peaceable," or "undemonstrative." Although the latter thought of themselves as loyal Confederates (and were perceived as such by their Unionist neighbors), they rarely saw the South as blameless in the sectional dispute, they often sought to avoid military service, and they typically left Unionists in their neighborhood alone, perhaps even treating them with a modicum of respect. A more bitter Rebel condemned these moderates "as striving hard to keep in with their Union friends, so that if Old Abe should pay us a visit, they can say, 'we have not been Southern to hurt!'"[53]

The "quiet and peaceable" Rebel was but a step removed from the position of neutrality so heartily damned by the *Register*. There was more than one kind of neutrality, however, for as contemporaries well understood, public impartiality could conceal a whole range of private motives and sympathies. Loyalists who remained in Knoxville insisted that a rigorous determination not to support the Confederacy in any positive way represented an honorable form of Unionism, in fact, the only honorable form realistically open to them. At the same time, they realized that ostensibly neutral behavior need not stem from Unionist sympathies at all but could reflect instead a lack of commitment to either side. The problem for both contemporaries and historians, of course, is that on the surface both kinds of neutrality could look pretty much alike. When all was said and done, the line between loyalty and disloyalty in Confederate-occupied Knoxville was defined less by overt acts than by private commitments, and these were (and are) difficult to pinpoint.

Although rare in Knoxville, neutrality could be based on ideological conviction, a conscientious refusal to support either side. This, at least, was the position that Robert J. McKinney claimed to hold. As part of his application for a presidential pardon in the fall of 1864 (in response to Lincoln's Amnesty Proclamation of the previous December), the state supreme court justice stressed that principled convictions prevented his identifying wholly with either the Union or the Confederacy. He did not believe that secession was constitutional, but neither did he have the slightest sympathy with the "doctrine of 'abolition' and other views subversive of the Constitution which have characterized the course of the Republican Party." A delegate to the Washington Peace Conference in February 1861, he had done all that he could to forestall disunion, and he could truthfully say that he sympathized with both North and South "in the common calamity which Divine Providence, in his inscrutable wisdom, has been pleased to visit upon our devoted Country." When all efforts to avoid war had failed, McKinney informed President Lincoln, he had "resolved to stand aloof from, as far as possible, and to have neither part nor lot in this unnatural strife." As proof of his "attempted course of neutrality," he noted that he had never taken an active public role in supporting the Confederacy. What is more, he had adamantly objected when General Kirby Smith had "imperatively demanded" that he swear an oath to uphold the Confederate constitution, and although he had finally yielded, he had done so "under solemn protest."[54]

Given the circumstances—McKinney was applying for a pardon, after all—it is prudent to take the judge's declaration with more than a grain or two of salt. He may have been more sympathetic with the Confederacy than he was willing to admit. Not only had his eighteen-year-old son joined the Confederate army in 1863, but McKinney had also brought suit against Horace Maynard as an "absconding debtor" less than three weeks after the Unionist congressman escaped through the mountains to take up his seat in the U.S. House of Representatives.

Yet there is one compelling reason to believe that he was telling the truth: ardent secessionists and Unionists both denounced him. In his deposition to the federal government, McKinney ruefully admitted that his "aloof" stance had "unfortunately drawn down upon him the displeasure of some extreme men of both parties." The evidence corroborates his account. Confederates routinely saw him as duplicitous. The *Knoxville Register* opposed his reelection to the state bench, and editor Jacob Sperry suspected that the judge's "neutrality" masked a "secret preference for the Federal cause." Attorney Henry Elliott agreed, and William McAdoo bitterly denounced McKinney as "the high tory judge . . . of the Supreme Court of Tennessee." As McAdoo viewed the situation in late 1862, McKinney was leading the Confederate commander "by the nose," making him "a mere tool of the Union or Tory faction." In contrast, Unionists regularly classified McKinney as disloyal. John Bell Brownlow remembered him as a Rebel, and both Laura Maynard and her son Edward grouped him among the town's Confederate elite. Oliver Temple recalled him as having "cast his lot with the secessionists," while Andrew Johnson actively opposed McKinney's application for pardon, informing the attorney general that the judge's influence "until now has been decidedly hostile to the Government." Neither side had much respect for McKinney's brand of impartiality.[55]

This kind of neutrality grounded in conviction—if such it truly was—shaded gradually into something more opportunistic. Seemingly neutral public behavior might reflect a genuine ambivalence, even an indifference to the outcome of the national struggle. Although he finally acquiesced in Confederate rule, George Mabry later recalled that he did his best to stay at home and out of the way of Confederate authorities. He never spoke out in support of the Confederacy and expressly refused to swear an oath of loyalty to the Confederate government. He hired a substitute rather than serve in the Confederate army, and he tried as much as possible to avoid selling foodstuffs to Confederate purchasing agents. (Although he spent much of his time in town, he also owned a large and productive farm west of Knoxville.) Yet the reasons for this neutral behavior were more pragmatic than principled. Even as he was trying to establish his Unionist credentials before the U.S. Court of Claims after the war, Mabry could come up with no better explanation for his course than his belief that secession would ultimately fail. "I just didn't have any hope of success," he explained with a candor unlikely to elicit admiration from Federal attorneys. He had disliked selling his crops and livestock to the Confederate government, he admitted furthermore, "because their money wasn't worth much at the time." He was averse to joining the army because he was not cut out for it, having "never carried a pistol in my life nor a knife of any kind." Finally, he had refused to swear an oath of loyalty to the Confederacy at least in part because of the circumstances in which he was asked to do so. Because Mabry traveled frequently between Knoxville and his farm, William Sneed had demanded that he take the oath to make sure that he

was not communicating with the enemy. Sneed was a heavy drinker, Mabry remembered, and "I told him that no man who would boo-hoo around at the hour
of mid night . . . could make me swear allegiance to the Southern Confederacy."
The cantankerous Mabry was allowed to leave town without taking the oath, but
his defiance apparently had less to do with devotion to the Union than an un-
willingness to be pushed around by a man given to late-night binges.[56]

Public neutrality could also mask a very conscious determination to keep a
foot in both camps until the outcome of the war was more certain. Although it
is difficult to know for sure, this may explain the behavior of East Tennessee and
Virginia president John R. Branner. Certainly Branner had much tangible at
stake. He had worked hard to build up the ET&V into a viable concern, and
the war threatened to undo all that he had labored to accomplish. If he tried to
prevent the Confederate military from using the railroad, there was a good chance
that the authorities might take possession of the line, but if he was perceived as
too enthusiastic in support of the Confederacy, he ran the risk of losing the road
should Union forces gain control of East Tennessee. There is some evidence that
Branner hired large numbers of Unionist employees and lobbied to shield them
from the draft, but at the same time he had a son who enlisted early in the Confederate army, he identified himself as a "Southern man" and a "good and true
citizen of the Confederacy," and when the Confederate military tried to interfere with his operations, he protested to Secretary of War Judah Benjamin that
he was already doing "all any man can to promote the interests of the Government." Once Knoxville was evacuated, however, he immediately began to offer
the same kind of cooperation to the Federal military, successfully convincing
several Knoxville loyalists (unaware of his correspondence with Secretary Benjamin) of the sincerity of his Unionist sympathies. His heirs could not convince
the U.S. Court of Claims of this, however. "If John Branner was loyal," an official
of the court concluded, "so was President Jeff Davis and Gen. Lee, and Stonewall Jackson and all the balance of the Confederates."[57]

McKinney, Mabry, and Branner were all ultimately considered disloyal by
Federal officials, but their *behavior* did not differ drastically from that of most
of those deemed to have been authentically Unionist. A commitment to "strict
neutrality" offered loyalists a fair degree of latitude. It was not inconsistent with
swearing loyalty to the Confederacy, for example, and numerous Unionists did
so. Some agreed to take the oath in order to retain positions of influence from
which they might protect other Unionists from official repression. A Knox
County loyalist who accepted a position as postmaster in 1862, even though it
required his taking the oath, recalled that Union friends and neighbors had encouraged him to do so. In agreeing to take the job, he had done "only what was
common in this section of the State with Union men. They accepted offices, and
were encouraged to do so by their Union friends, because those offices protected
them from military duty, and often from arrest and imprisonment, and because

in the discharge of the duties of those offices, they were often able to favor Union men." Beyond this, as he explained, "the refusal to any office was clear evidence of Union sentiments, and subjected the person so refusing to Rebel persecutions." This may well explain the behavior of the Knox County Court after the state voted out. All thirty-three justices of the peace who constituted the court swore loyalty to the Confederacy when required to do so in early 1862. Twenty-one of the thirty-three appear in the records of the various Federal claims commissions established during and after the war, and of the twenty-one, seventeen were determined to have been always loyal to the United States. The same held true for approximately one-third of the members of Knoxville's board of aldermen, including the Unionist mayor, James Luttrell, who held the town's top post throughout the entire war.[58]

It was also considered acceptable to make public declarations of loyalty to the Confederacy, or at least of acquiescence to Confederate rule, in cases in which prison seemed the likely alternative. When wealthy merchant and slave owner Abner Jackson was arrested and charged with disloyalty, for example, he refused to swear an oath of loyalty under compulsion, but wrote local authorities from jail to say that since Tennessee's secession he had been a "loyal citizen of the Confederate States, and would allow his arm to be severed before he would raise it against this government." Similarly, when suspicions were aroused regarding Oliver Temple's loyalty, he asked the editor of the *Knoxville Daily Register* to inform the public that he had "already taken the oath to support the Confederate States, and intends to demean himself as a loyal citizen thereof. He wishes quietly to pursue the practice of his profession, without being drawn into the arena of public discussion."[59] Both declarations were made under duress, of course, and may have been examples of what could be called "survival lying"; a Knox County man later testified before a Federal military commission that "the great law of self-preservation" forced even the most loyal "to practice dissimilation."[60] One thing is clear, however: in Knoxville such pronouncements did not necessarily violate community standards for Unionism, for neither Jackson nor Temple was discredited as a Unionist leader after the town was "liberated" by Federal troops. It is worth noting, as well, that neither Jackson nor Temple actually pledged to support the Confederacy through positive actions. Both professed to be "loyal citizens," but their concrete pledges amounted to little more than a promise to go about their business as usual. A correspondent to the *Register* observed as much after Temple's declaration, acknowledging what everyone knew—the loyalty oath alone meant little. "If Mr. Temple is *for* the South now let us know it," the correspondent demanded. Temple did not respond.[61]

No individual case better illustrates the complexity of "Unionism" under Confederate occupation than that of John Baxter. A prominent Knoxville attorney, banker, and old-line Whig politician, Baxter was one of the town's most forceful opponents of secession until Tennessee's formal separation in June 1861.

Oliver Temple doubted whether "any man in the state . . . was so bitter in denunciation of secession and its leaders." His contempt for the Confederacy continued into July, when, according to the *Register*, Baxter boasted that "in a few weeks we will have the rebels like partridges in a trap, and I expect to be obliged to go to Richmond to use my influence with Mr. Lincoln to prevent my secession relatives in Virginia from being hanged."[62] The Confederate victory in late July at Bull Run evidently changed his perspective dramatically, however, for at that point Baxter appears to have adopted the position that Confederate independence was inevitable. John Bell Brownlow later claimed that Baxter "turned Rebel" immediately after the battle, telling him "that the cowardice of the Yankees on that occasion proved that they would not fight & that the South could easily gain its independence." The most sensible course for sincere Unionists, Baxter began to maintain, was to resign themselves to Confederate rule and work within the system to minimize the power and abuses of "original secessionists" in the new government. Baxter voluntarily took an oath of loyalty to the Confederacy in mid-September, nearly three months before the bridge burnings, at least in part to be able to defend Unionists in the local Confederate court. That same month he ran unsuccessfully for a permanent seat in the Confederate Congress against original secessionist William G. Swan. Early the next year he briefly published a newspaper in Knoxville, the *East Tennessean*, through which he attempted to "harmonize the discordant elements among us, and reconcile the disaffected to the Government of the Confederate States."[63]

The range of responses to Baxter's strategy is instructive. Temple counseled against it and considered Baxter to have converted to secessionism. Although a year later Brownlow would describe Baxter as a "moderate secessionist," in the fall of 1861 he publicly endorsed Baxter's candidacy for the Confederate Congress, exclaiming that "a more honorable, high-minded and patriotic gentleman than he, never presented himself as a candidate to the people of Tennessee." When Baxter took the oath in order to practice in the Confederate court, Brownlow declared it "most fortunate for the Union prisoners that he [has] done so." In private, the editor maintained that Baxter was "making a good impression" in the campaign and lauded his brave defiance of Confederate soldiers who tried to break up his speeches.[64] Baxter's law partner, Confederate senator Landon Carter Haynes, on the other hand, praised the lawyer's courageous, if tardy, stand with the South, while another Confederate lawyer in town blasted him as "the worst of all the traitors and tories." For its part, the *Register* was suspicious if not outright dismissive of Baxter's purported submission to the Confederacy. "How many believe in the sincerity of his new faith and would trust him in the new position to which he now aspires?" the *Register* asked contemptuously.[65] Confederate general Edmund Kirby Smith, who was still receiving "repeated accusations" against Baxter some six months after he took the loyalty oath, was similarly skeptical. Fearing that Baxter might be attempting to communicate with Unionists in West Tennessee, and incensed by a recent "disloyal if not treasonous" speech in which Baxter held out "not one hope for the future success of the Southern cause," Smith wrote to General Albert Sydney Johnston in late March 1862 to suggest that Baxter be arrested and searched while en route to Memphis on business. Angered by such insulting treatment (and possibly impressed as well by Union military victories during the first half of 1862), by June 1862 Baxter had switched course again. Temple described his new path as a reversion to "stalwart Unionism." Jacob Sperry, editor of the *Register*, characterized Baxter's behavior as "that of strict neutrality of conduct, though of secret preferences for the Federal cause." In the context of Confederate-occupied Knoxville, "stalwart Unionism" and "strict neutrality" were largely synonymous.[66]

Again, it is significant that such dramatic political shifts during the period of Confederate occupation did not disqualify Baxter from a position of influence as a leading "Unionist" when the Union army later gained control of the town. After Knoxville's occupation by Federal forces in September 1863, the Union provost marshal's office readily accepted him as loyal, and less than six months later he became a charter member of the East Tennessee Relief Association, a charitable organization created to publicize the sufferings of Unionists in the region. Although Parson Brownlow broke bitterly with Baxter after the war and took to ridiculing the latter's "treason" during the twenty-seven months of Confederate rule, the rift between them stemmed mainly from partisan rivalry. Baxter's real crime, in Brownlow's eyes, was his shift to the Democratic Party. Both Oliver Temple and Thomas Humes—less politically radical and personally vindictive than the Parson—persisted in classifying Baxter as a sincere Unionist, albeit, as Temple put it wryly, with "a mental agility that is somewhat remarkable."[67]

Given the range of political behavior reconcilable with "Unionism," it is not surprising that Unionists among the Knoxville elite pursued a variety of economic strategies as well. Within weeks of Tennessee's separation from the Union, Parson Brownlow had declared that secession "has been the ruin" of Knoxville. "It has destroyed business of every kind," he proclaimed, "reduced the price of real estate, fully one half, and thrown almost every laboring man out of employ." Whether *secession* had had such an impact is hard to say, but the war that followed it definitely stimulated business in countless ways. It had disrupted the local economy, to be sure, but it had also created numerous new opportunities for both workers and entrepreneurs. The convalescent camp offered to buy all the vegetables that local farmers could spare. The town's hotels and restaurants were overwhelmed, and a number of "eating saloons" sprang up overnight to meet the demand of hungry soldiers. Hardware stores did a booming business selling to purchasing agents of the Confederate Ordnance Bureau and Quartermaster Corps. The meatpacking business grew rapidly as the Confederate government purchased thousands of hogs slaughtered and packed at Knoxville. A government shoe shop regularly employed forty to fifty hands and contemplated doubling its workforce. A makeshift Confederate armory hired thirty or more females to make cartridges and percussion caps for rifles, while dozens of poor women and girls found work sewing uniforms for the Confederate army. The pages of the *Knoxville Register* were regularly filled with advertisements from employers in search of additional kinds of laborers: wood choppers, railroad hands, blacksmiths, machinists, gunsmiths, carpenters.[68]

In this booming economic environment a number of Knoxville's leading Unionists traded openly—and apparently willingly—with the Confederate government. John S. VanGilder, a New Jersey–born boot and shoe and hat maker, started the Knoxville Leather Company during the war—in partnership with one of the town's Confederate elite, Frank Scott—and manufactured infantry brogans and cavalry boots for the Confederate military. By December 1862, the future Knoxville mayor was selling between two thousand and twenty-five hundred pairs of boots and shoes monthly to the local Confederate quartermaster. Yet after the Federal occupation of the town, VanGilder was immediately accepted as a "respectable Union man," according to the records of the Union provost marshal general. Furthermore, it is clear that his business continued to prosper. By 1869, VanGilder was not only president of the Knoxville Leather Company but also principal owner of the Bank of Knoxville, and his net worth had increased from $15,000 at the beginning of the war to approximately $100,000.[69] Although the historical record does not afford a detailed account of VanGilder's business dealings during the period of Confederate rule, the following poem, sent after the arrival of Union troops by an ardently pro-Confederate female to his son and future business partner, Thomas VanGilder, is suggestive:

> Oh! Tommy dear, you used to talk
> Ere Blue Coats came this way
> As if you were the best of Rebs
> Why are you Yank today?
>
> . . . .
>
> And you were always wont to say
> You loved the Rebels dearly.
> So a man may change his politics
> As he does his dress coat—yearly.
> I think that all you want just now
> Is to make plenty money.
> Whichever army should be here
> You'd call them dearest honey.[70]

Although few were as open in their business dealings as the VanGilders, it appears that most Unionist merchants continued to do business with Confederate clients. Retail merchant Jefferson Powell did more than $40,000 worth of business with Confederate purchasing agents prior to the arrival of Union forces. Similarly, Perez Dickinson and James Cowan, partners in the largest wholesale firm in town, continued to trade extensively with pro-Confederate retailers, even though, as a business associate later testified, there was probably not "a man in the community but what knew the fact that they were Union men." The loyalty of the Massachusetts-born Dickinson was especially unimpeachable; former associates remembered him as "an unconditional Union man" and "intensely loyal." Yet he was also a "prudent, careful kind of man." "As loyal as General Grant," he nevertheless "did not talk much when it was not safe to do so." Dickinson had a great number of friends and business associates who were Confederates, and it appears that these relationships mostly survived intact. The superintendent of the East Tennessee and Virginia later testified that the merchant conducted his business affairs "without reference to politics." Unconditional Unionism notwithstanding, Dickinson "dealt with his customers, a portion of whom were Union men and a portion of whom were Southern men, just as he did for years."[71]

Cowan and Dickinson also found time to speculate heavily, if discreetly, in cotton. Cotton exports had been prohibited since early in the war, and the price of the white fiber in northern markets had soared as a result. As early as the spring of 1862, the *Knoxville Register* printed a letter charging "East Tennessee Lincolnite Cotton Speculators" with buying cotton in Georgia and South Carolina and shipping it to East Tennessee, where they intended to store it until the region was overrun by the Union army. The letter claimed that such men were making as much money out of the Confederacy as they could while all the time professing privately to Union sympathies. Although the newspaper never named names while it was operating in Knoxville, after it relocated to Atlanta in the fall of 1863 the *Register* identified Cowan and Dickinson as among the chief offenders. Writing only a month after the evacuation of Knoxville by Confederate forces, editor J. A. Sperry alleged that the wholesale merchants, along with "other noted Unionists," had already shipped several hundred bales of cotton to the North. The editor explained that Cowan and Dickinson, as well as other prominent "Tories," had initially refused to accept Confederate currency in their business dealings. They then began to accept it and, as a hedge against depreciation, used it to buy cotton, which they stored in Knoxville in anticipation of its eventual liberation.[72]

Sperry claimed to have seen cotton piled conspicuously near the railroad depot when he took one of the last trains out of town before the arrival of Federal troops. Apparently, the hastily evacuating Confederate soldiers made no effort to destroy it, prompting Sperry to complain that "the traitors of East Tennessee have thus profited by the mistaken leniency of our military authorities." Such profits could be considerable. It is unknown just how much cotton Cowan and Dickinson had under their control at the time of the Confederate evacuation, but

Union military records show that in October 1863 the firm forwarded at least 111 bales of cotton to Cincinnati and New York, and by early November it had another 256 bales ready for shipment northward. A conservative estimate is that these 367 bales could have sold in New York for between $140,000 and $150,000 in gold, promising a fair rate of return for goods that were, in all likelihood, purchased with now worthless Confederate paper.[73]

Thanks to wartime shortages, salt was almost as valuable as cotton, and there is evidence to suggest that Oliver Temple was able to profit from its scarcity. Temple's brother, Major S. Temple, had a contract worth $150,000 annually to manufacture salt at Saltville, Virginia, for the Confederate state government of Georgia. Major Temple wrote to his brother in September 1862 to describe the arrangement and to invite him to "unite your destinies with me at this place." The attorney's response to this invitation has not survived, but William McAdoo, who had relocated to Georgia in early 1862, insisted in his diary in December of that year that both Temples were extensively involved and asserted that Oliver Temple was spending most of his time at Saltville. The contract was "immensely profitable," according to McAdoo, and would "make millionaires of these Temples of Mammon." McAdoo was undoubtedly predisposed to think the worst of the Temples, and there is no definite proof that Oliver Temple was ever formally involved with the Saltville project.[74] On the other hand, there is no question that in 1864—after Knoxville had been occupied but much of East Tennessee was still under Confederate control—Temple bankrolled the efforts of his brother to buy both cotton and tobacco behind Confederate lines in upper East Tennessee, with an eye to eventually selling those precious goods in the North.[75]

The point of these examples of economic opportunism is not to question the loyalty of purported Unionists such as VanGilder, Cowan, Dickinson, or Temple, but rather to show clearly the range of economic behavior consistent with local perceptions of "Unionism." Northern audiences cheered when William Brownlow told them that "a man who would not sacrifice his property" in defense of the Stars and Stripes "deserves not the protection of that flag."[76] The Parson's allies who remained in Knoxville, however, rejected his definition of "ever-true" Unionism as ill-suited to the complexities of life in a bitterly divided community under constant Confederate surveillance. Instead, they largely acquiesced to Confederate rule and exhibited a "Unionism" characterized primarily by "prudent silence," "strict neutrality," and a willingness to make money while awaiting Federal deliverance.

CHAPTER SIX

Liberation, Occupation, and Twenty Minutes of Carnage

On reaching Knoxville . . . the northern soldiers were both surprised and carried away by the grateful enthusiasm of the people. . . . Their deliverers shared their joy & felt more than ordinary pride in being permitted to free such a people from the harsh rule under which they had been forced to live.
—Union brigadier general S. P. Carter[1]

I think it is outrageous. The Yankees are here. Just think, here—here in Knoxville. Walked in without the least resistance on our part. . . . How I hate them.
—Knoxville civilian Ellen House[2]

ACCORDING TO THE 1662 Anglican Book of Common Prayer, the prescribed first reading for the morning liturgy on 6 September 1863 began with Psalm 30, verse 1. As he announced the text to the congregation of Knoxville's St. John's Episcopal Church, the Reverend Thomas Humes surely felt a deep sense of thanksgiving as well as a measure of personal vindication. Humes had served the church as rector from 1846 to 1861, an extended tenure that had ended abruptly a few months after the fall of Fort Sumter. From the moment the first shots were fired, the middle-aged minister had felt pressure to support the movement for southern independence. Certainly family ties pulled in that direction. A half brother soon served as the medical director for the Confederate army in East Tennessee, a nephew would rise to the rank of brigadier general in the Confederate service, and another would enlist in the Rebel ranks in Mississippi. Compounding the bonds of kinship was the fact that, as a Knoxville housewife observed, Humes's congregation was "mostly Southern in sentiment." A glance at the list of communicants verifies that Humes led a congregation top-heavy with ardent secessionists.[3]

Unionist minister Thomas W. Humes,
from a postwar portrait.
Photograph courtesy of Special Collections,
University of Tennessee Libraries.

And yet the soft-spoken reverend had firmly resisted the growing momentum for separation. As long as Tennessee remained in the Union, he angered
many in his flock by continuing to pray for President Lincoln. When Jefferson
Davis called for a national day of prayer and fasting on the Thursday after Tennessee seceded, Humes refused to observe the day, and from that point on he
took to praying for "those in authority" rather than refer to the Confederate president by name. When the patience of his presiding bishop finally ran out later in
the summer of 1861, Humes submitted his resignation and retired into private
life. Only a severely broken leg thwarted his plan to leave the place of his birth
in search of a more congenial home beyond the borders of the Confederacy.[4]

Now, after two long years of "silent submission," the fortunes of war had
turned. In late August 1863 the Confederate high command had decided to abandon Knoxville, and by 1 September Federal cavalry under Colonel John Foster
had begun pouring into town, followed within forty-eight hours by the veteran
infantrymen of Ambrose Burnside's Army of the Ohio. After twenty-seven
months of Confederate occupation, the Union army now controlled the "metropolis of East Tennessee." The "reign of terror" was over. Enjoying his role as
liberator, General Burnside moved quickly to reward the town's loyalists, and one
of his very first acts had been to invite Thomas Humes to return to the pulpit
from which he had been banished two years earlier. And so it was that Humes
now stood before his former congregation and led them in a responsive reading
prescribed for this day by the Church of England some two centuries before: "I
will magnify Thee, O Lord," Humes read from the thirtieth Psalm, "for Thou
hast set me up, and not made my foes to triumph over me."[5]

Not everyone in Humes's congregation was present to hear this psalm of praise. Earlier that morning, twenty-year-old Ellen House had heard rumors concerning the reverend's return and had boycotted the service in disgust. "I am not going to hear him," she vowed to her diary. "That much is certain." House knew Humes well. To begin with, he had been her minister for more than a year and a half, from March 1860 when she and her mother and sister had joined St. John's, until his resignation in August of the following year. Apparently, he was also her neighbor; evidence suggests that they lived just a few houses apart near the corner of Cumberland and Locust streets.[6] Finally, Humes was her landlord. It must have galled her that her father, once a prosperous small slaveholder but now a bookkeeper in straitened circumstances, had to rent their home from a man whom she described as "the grandest old rascal that ever was."[7]

But more than class resentment fueled her contempt. Ellen House detested Yankees with every fiber of her being, and she scorned the local traitors who welcomed them even more. Union military authorities quickly categorized her as a "very violent rebel," a label that Ellen proudly accepted. She began a daily record of events upon the arrival of Burnside's army, and although she later claimed to have done so for the sake of her brother, who was away in the Confederate army, it is apparent that the journal served a kind of therapeutic purpose as well. In its pages she regularly vented her deep-seated animosity toward the Yankee invaders. She wrote that the Union soldiers she encountered were "wicked" and "vile." They were "animals" and "devils." The sight of their "abominable" flags "completely nauseate[d]" her, whereas the sight of wounded Yankees gladdened her heart. "They have my best wishes to die," she confided to her diary.[8]

Reverend Humes's tenant and parishioner, the "very violent Rebel" Ellen House.

Photograph courtesy of Ellen Allran and Victoria Guthrie.

There was more to this Rebel spitfire than anger and defiance, however. Ellen House's world was being turned upside down, and the pages of her journal exude fear as much as hatred. Terrifying rumors had begun to swirl among the town's Confederates as soon as the first blue-coated cavalrymen had ridden into Knoxville. All Rebel civilians were to be banished, it was whispered; all Rebel property was to be confiscated. J. G. M. Ramsey's house had been torched to the ground, and reports of additional burning and looting outside of town seemed to lend credence to these grim predictions. Only time could tell whether such prophecies would prove true, but in the meantime there was more than enough cause for worry. Yankee soldiers were everywhere: they had taken over the hotels, the boardinghouses, the university, and the hospitals. They were attending the churches in large numbers (although Ellen was sure it would do them little good). Some were even camped in a vacant lot right across the street from Ellen's home. "We are completely surrounded by them," she lamented. "How I hate them."[9]

Two interwoven lives, two dramatically different responses to the same event. Thomas Humes celebrated the arrival of Union troops and praised the Lord for His mercy and goodness. Ellen House—Humes's parishioner, neighbor, and tenant—mourned when the Yankees marched into town, and she sank temporarily into a depression. Each understood what Burnside's soldiers sometimes failed to realize: they were coming to Knoxville as *both* deliverers *and* conquerors, as an army of occupation as well as of liberation. In the long run, their arrival would present the townspeople with a different set of challenges than any the war had yet produced. In the short run, they would have to battle to keep the town. At the end of August, a garrison of scarcely a thousand Confederates had abandoned Knoxville without a fight. Within a few weeks, an army of nearly twenty thousand Rebels would seek to reclaim it.

ONE OF THE IRONIES of the Civil War in Tennessee was that Union armies quickly occupied much of Middle and West Tennessee—where support for secession had been overwhelming after Fort Sumter—whereas the liberation of staunchly Unionist East Tennessee was of relatively low priority during the first two years of the war. If armchair tacticians writing for northern newspapers viewed the region as vitally important, military officers were struck by the logistical obstacles to a successful invasion of the Valley of East Tennessee. Formidable mountain barriers loomed to the east and west; states solidly in Confederate control lay to the north and south. "East Tennessee is my horror," William Tecumseh Sherman would later confess to Ulysses Grant. "That any military man should send a force into East Tennessee puzzles me." Major General Don Carlos Buell, the Federal commander in Middle Tennessee until after the Battle of Perryville, was so slow to strike eastward that Republicans in Washington began to question the depth of his commitment to Union victory. His successor, Major General William S. Rosecrans, proved almost as lethargic, even after Secretary of the Treasury Salmon Chase wrote to encourage him to drive vigorously toward the eastern section of the state, "the proud central fortress—the keys of the whole position of the rebellion." While Rosecrans prepared leisurely and methodically for such a campaign, East Tennessee loyalists despaired of his ever moving decisively and questioned the sincerity of Lincoln's pledge to act on their behalf. Frustrated to the breaking point, in the fall of 1862 Horace Maynard wrote directly to Abraham Lincoln to express his deep disappointment in the government's apparent indifference. "Having provided for the freedom of the slaves," Maynard wrote, "can you not, I beg you, in God's name, do something for the freedom of the white people of East Tennessee? Their tears & blood will be a blot on your administration that time can never efface, & no proclamation can cover up." The following August, Knoxvillians John Fleming and Robert Morrow carried a petition to the president calling on the government finally to act to liberate those who had "so long waited in vain" for deliverance. Hoping to present the petition in person, they waited five days for an audience with Lincoln before finally giving up.[10]

What loyalists longed for, Rebels feared. If Unionists felt abandoned and forgotten by the government in Washington, Knoxville Confederates were frequently convinced that an invasion was imminent. For months after the Federal victory at Mill Springs in early 1862, the *Knoxville Register* regularly alerted readers to the possibility of an attack. The Union army was making "great preparations" to push into the region, the paper warned. Soon the time would arrive when "we must make a stand here." An editorial suggested that local mechanics set about making pikes, "the most potent of all weapons in a charge on infantry," and it called on the townspeople to "raise a regiment of pikemen at once." In March the newspaper reported that "Hessians" were massing along the Kentucky border west of Cumberland Gap, and in June it published a (false) rumor that some eight thousand Union soldiers were marching on the town. The following month it called attention to the presence of four to five regiments of Union soldiers from East Tennessee among the Federal forces in southern Kentucky, "their minds and hearts demonized with the glow of intense hatred."[11] The success of Braxton Bragg and Kirby Smith in drawing the Union Army of the Cumberland back into Kentucky in late summer seems to have quieted local anxieties during the fall of 1862, but in the spring of 1863 old fears resurfaced. In April a Richmond correspondent announced that Union general Ambrose Burnside had been given thirty thousand men and ordered to gain control of East Tennessee. (His force was little more than half that large.) The *Register* acknowledged the report and noted that, as a result, the Tories were more "bold and defiant" than usual. The following month the paper conceded the likelihood that Burnside would soon strike toward Knoxville with his army of "Northern barbarians and renegade [i.e., Unionist] East Tennesseans."[12]

Throughout these tense months the *Register* alternated between dispiriting suggestions that the Confederate military might decide to abandon East Tennessee entirely and optimistic assertions that they would defend the region vigorously. As early as the summer of 1862, an editorial had posed the question "Are We to Be Defended?" The column had hinted darkly at the possibility that the region's faithful Confederate minority might be abandoned to the mercies of the Lincolnite invaders. In May 1863 the paper returned to this unthinkable prospect, expressing the hope that, should East Tennessee fall, it would not fall due to mere "listlessness," as had been the case allegedly with Nashville and New Orleans. Conversely, the paper continually opined that East Tennessee was impregnable if energetically defended. Should Burnside dare desecrate the valley, "every tree should protect a patriot who would send a bullet to the heart of some one of our infamous invaders." Against such "energy, enterprise and courage," the Hessians could never prevail. As a correspondent to the *Register* declared in the issue of 18 June 1863, "Eastern Tennessee is the last, greatest and surest stronghold of the South."[13]

The following evening some fifteen hundred Federal cavalrymen camped on the outskirts of Knoxville. The Union troopers, under the command of Colonel William P. Sanders, had been ordered into the valley by Ambrose Burnside with instructions to tear up the railroad both above and below the town. They approached Knoxville from the southwest, having spent most of the day of the nineteenth cutting telegraph lines and ripping up rails every mile or so between Knoxville and Lenoir's Station, a stop on the East Tennessee and Georgia some twenty-four miles away. At daylight on 20 June they briefly threatened the Knoxville depot, engaging in an hour-long artillery exchange with Confederate batteries posted on a series of low hills in north and east Knoxville, before turning northeast along the East Tennessee and Virginia to torch the crucial railroad bridge at Strawberry Plains, nearly twenty miles up the line toward Bristol. The raiders then escaped back through the mountains into Kentucky, having captured ten pieces of artillery and approximately three hundred prisoners during their ten-day jaunt. So much for the South's "greatest stronghold."[14]

For Knoxville's anxious Confederates, there was good news and bad news in the military response to Sanders's raid. On the positive side, the Confederate forces in Knoxville had quickly orchestrated a vigorous defense of the town, driving the Federal cavalry away with the loss of only two dead and two wounded. With scarcely one thousand soldiers at his disposal, the post commandant, Colonel R. C. Trigg, had moved with alacrity to prepare for the invaders. He ordered that the streets be barricaded with cotton bales and positioned artillery on hills behind the Deaf and Dumb Asylum on the north side of town and near Temperance Hall in East Knoxville. To augment his force, he mobilized as many convalescent soldiers from the town's hospitals as could rise from their beds and commanded the local recruiting and conscript officer to muster in every available civilian. A sizable number answered the call. A local Methodist weekly later listed sixty-one civilians who mounted the barricades—a hodgepodge of government shoemakers, ordnance workers, carpenters, butchers, merchants, clerks, druggists, doctors, and ministers. If "a great many Secessionists contented themselves with guarding their cellars," as a Confederate physician wryly observed, the official Confederate report on the skirmish lauded those who presented themselves for duty, mentioning by name original secessionists John Crozier and William Sneed. Given that the clash was mostly an artillery duel, the town's civilian defenders never "had the opportunity to discharge [their] muskets on the Abolitionists," as one participant complained, but this did not mean they escaped unscathed. One of the last volleys from the Federal guns claimed the life of ordnance supervisor Pleasant McClung, who along with other government employees had been stationed near one of the Confederate batteries. McClung fell when an artillery shell severed both legs below the knees. He survived but two hours, maintaining consciousness long enough to pray with his wife and children—and with Unionist minister Thomas Humes.[15]

Such bravery notwithstanding, the Confederate military had also shown a distressing readiness to abandon the town, if necessary. When word of the Yankees' approach arrived on the morning of 19 June, soldiers and government employees had worked frantically to load up military supplies—throwing goods down stairs and out windows in their haste—ultimately filling eight trains and a handful of steamboats, which they immediately sent upriver. The banks sent off their specie and paper money as well, old Dr. Ramsey leading the way with the assets of the Knoxville branch of the Bank of Tennessee. The *Knoxville Register* renewed its campaign to rally popular resolve, warning the townspeople that the "large army of wanton enemies" just across the mountains would "ravage, devastate, and ruin your country." They would inflict "cruelties, atrocities and barbarities" just as they had in the other regions they now occupied. If the people meekly submitted to this fate they would prove themselves once and for all unworthy of freedom, but rather "fit only to be the slaves of the Yankees." It was not the townspeople, however, but the Confederate government that ultimately determined the fate of the region. As the Union Army of the Cumberland under William Rosecrans finally drove toward Chattanooga in late August, the Confederate commander in East Tennessee, Major General Simon B. Buckner, was ordered to join Confederate general Braxton Bragg in defending that city. By the final week of August, the last Rebel soldiers marched out of Knoxville, accompanied by many of the town's leading Confederate sympathizers. The road was now clear for Ambrose Burnside's Army of the Ohio, twelve thousand Union soldiers marching rapidly from Cumberland Gap to "liberate" the region.[16]

NORTHERNERS AWAITED THE OUTCOME of the campaign for East Tennessee with keen interest, thanks in no small part to the region's most famous refugee. Since his exile eighteen months earlier, William Brownlow had come to personify southern Unionism in the minds of many northerners. In the process, he had helped to popularize one of the earliest—and most enduring—Appalachian stereotypes. As the Parson portrayed him, the typical southern "mountaineer" lacked the refined sensibilities of the plantation aristocrat, but underneath his crude exterior was a fiercely independent lover of freedom who clung staunchly to the Union.[17] Now, as the war's third summer was drawing to a close, the North would finally have the opportunity to test that stereotype. "East Tennessee is practically relieved of rebel domination," the *Chicago Tribune* observed, "and we shall see how far the boasts of Brownlow . . . will be made good."[18]

The Army of the Ohio was positioned to provide an answer for the *Tribune*'s readers. Its march into East Tennessee was a homecoming for a small portion of Burnside's command, which included the First East Tennessee Mounted Infantry, as well as a smattering of other units mustered in the area. The vast majority, however—men hailing from Massachusetts to Michigan—were beholding a land and a people entirely foreign to them.[19] If those who recorded their thoughts were representative, then the Yankee "liberators" were simultaneously inspired, disappointed, and repulsed by what they saw. On the one hand, the natural beauty of the landscape was undeniable. Although they would later remember the trek across the mountains as one of the most arduous of the war, they recalled the splendor of their surroundings just as vividly. A New York private "could not help admiring the wild and picturesque scenery through which we passed," while the adjutant of his regiment spoke of the "grandeur" of the panorama unfolding before them. The view from Cumberland Gap "must be seen to be realized or imagined," a Michigan soldier gushed to his parents. "All I can say is it was more sublime, grand & beautiful than anything I ever saw painted or pictured." Such impressions persisted as rugged mountains gave way to alternating ridges and valleys as the army approached Knoxville. All praised the town's setting, which the soldiers variously described as "lovely," "charming," and "magnificent."[20]

The town itself, on the other hand, was another story, an eyesore in the midst of nature's splendors. Encamped nearby, Massachusetts surgeon Robert Jameson explored "the famous town of Knoxville" and decided afterward that one visit was enough. There were a few "fine looking dwelling houses," Jameson observed in a letter to his mother, "but the most of them present a dilapidated tumble-down appearance." Another Massachusetts officer gave the town a second chance. On his first visit, William Draper noted "many fine residences in the suburbs" and concluded that Knoxville must have been "a very pretty place before the war." The town's principal streets were "rather deserted," however, and few stores were doing business. Returning the next day, he "was not any more favorably impressed." As Draper explained to his (hopefully trusting) wife, "The only institutions that seem to prosper are houses of ill fame and there are 39 of those doing a large business." Rhode Island officer Daniel Larned found "nothing inviting or cheering" in the town's appearance: "the streets are rough, the side walks broken, & everything looks forsaken and neglected." Ohio captain Orlando Poe was even more dismissive. "We have always heard of this place," he observed to his wife, "and from the stir it made in the world, one was led to believe that it was a great place." In fact, precisely the opposite was true, he explained. "It is a small, insignificant, worthless town." Darker still in his assessment, another Yankee visitor pronounced Knoxville to be "wretched, unhealthy, unhandsome, [and] uninteresting."[21]

Although Jameson and Draper were willing to attribute Knoxville's decay to the war itself, Larned and Poe discerned a deeper, cultural cause. Larned pointed to "the same evidence of shiftlessness and poverty" that characterized all the other southern places he had visited. Poe agreed with the diagnosis but coined a new word to describe it. "You can scarcely imagine such utter stand-still-a-tive-ness," he declared to his wife. "A strong infusion of Yankee blood is needed to give things some life here." A northern civilian reached a similar conclusion while visiting Massachusetts regiments camped northeast of Knoxville. The entire region had great potential, he determined, but "another race than its present occupants, or a new inspiration animating them, will be needful to its full development."[22]

Interaction with the "natives" further convinced Yankee outsiders of the region's backwardness. From the moment they began their descent into the East Tennessee Valley, Burnside's men had been struck by the peculiarities of the civilians they encountered. They could understand (and even admire) their ubiquitous fondness for "apple-jack" (homemade apple brandy), but they shuddered in disgust at the sight of women chewing tobacco.[23] Half a day's march south of Cumberland Gap, the men of the Seventeenth Michigan came upon a delegation from "up in the mountains" who had come to see real live Yankees, and the encounter left the soldiers dumbfounded. A private in the regiment later recounted the scene: the women and children were riding on the backs of cows, accompanied by "men in ancient raiment, unshaved and unwashed. . . . One look at such a grotesque group," he concluded, "was enough to make one doubt his mother country." These were mountain folk, of course, and the typical inhabitants of cosmopolitan Knoxville were surely less rough around the edges. Even the townspeople, however, were occasionally the objects of derision, especially among the Union officers. Daniel Larned sniffed that "the costume of the women is ludicrous in many cases," whereas Orlando Poe concluded uncharitably that "there is not a handsome woman in Knoxville." The former was further repulsed when he attended services of the Second Presbyterian Church. The minister "jerked & twitched till I thought he would fly in pieces," Larned exclaimed to his sister. The congregation was no better. They "made me think of a factory village meeting, only I never saw such odd wearing jeans as they had on—nor such ill-behaved people."[24]

When all was said and done, however, the local population did exhibit one redeeming quality in the eyes of their liberators: the vast majority were passionately, courageously devoted to the Union. Of this the Yankees had no doubt. When the conversation shifted from the region's poverty to its patriotism, the tone of the soldiers' remarks shifted from condescension to awe. Literally thousands of civilians turned out to welcome the Army of the Ohio, one soldier reported, transforming the entire march from Kentucky into a continuous celebration, "a perfect ovation." Whole families lined the route, a New York cavalryman explained, bringing fresh water and fruit to the weary soldiers, waving U.S. flags that they had long kept hidden, and conveying stories of suffering under Confederate rule. Time and again the Union soldiers were humbled by what they saw and heard. "I wish you could see the delight of the people—such loyalty to the Union I have never seen in my life before," Orlando Poe related to his wife. "We don't know at the North what loyalty means." Unlike most northerners, a Massachusetts officer marveled, "these people know what war is in its worst shape," and yet "they are true to the old flag." After watching old men step forward to shake General Burnside's hand, another soldier concluded, "I never knew what the *Love of Liberty* was before."[25]

Although local loyalists had long agreed that Unionism in East Tennessee was stronger in the countryside than in the towns, Burnside's soldiers discerned no slackening of enthusiasm as they approached Knoxville. If anything, they claimed to observe the contrary. As they approached the town, their reception "was past all description." The people seemed "frantic with joy" and "wild with delight." "I thought I had seen loyalty in the mountains," Poe wrote to his wife from Knoxville, "but it is not so intense as that we find here." Almost a half century later, Ohioan Joseph Wilshire still vividly remembered riding down Gay Street as Ambrose Burnside first entered the town. "The thronging multitude" shouted and wept and hailed their deliverers, he recalled, while "every window in the houses on either side were filled with faces on most of which beamed happy smiles and expressions of cordial welcome." Summing up, Robert Jameson voiced the near-universal conclusion. "Knoxville," he declared flatly, "is a Union town."[26]

A *Union* town? In February 1861 the label may have fit, but it had ceased to apply when the first shot had been fired at Fort Sumter. This was, after all, the same community in which one-half of voters had cast ballots for secession the following June. Since that time, moreover, perhaps two-thirds had supported the Confederacy, while scarcely a handful had actively opposed it. How could these Yankee "liberators" have reached such a conclusion? No one factor but rather the combination of many offers the most likely explanation.

To begin with, many of Knoxville's Confederates were no longer around. More than one hundred were serving in the Rebel army, and these were scattered from Chickamauga to northern Virginia when the Army of the Ohio invaded their home. Numerous Rebel civilians had also fled in anticipation of the Confederate evacuation. As the Federal column approached from the northwest, most followed the railroad toward either the northeast or the southwest. A train full of refugees, including William Sneed and John Crozier, set out for Bristol, Tennessee, a staunchly pro-Confederate community on the Virginia border. By all accounts an even larger contingent headed in the opposite direction. Editor J. A. Sperry took one of the last southbound trains out of town, and in a little more than two weeks he was publishing the *Knoxville Daily Register* from Atlanta, Georgia. Sperry's office became a common gathering place for East Tennessee refugees, with the *Register* regularly listing the names of the most recent arrivals from Knoxville. These included many of the town's most ardent original secessionists. William G. Swan, Campbell Wallace, J. G. M. and Crozier Ramsey, and Bill Williams, among others, were now refugees, although the sixty-six-year-old Dr. Ramsey, who had left his wife and teenage daughter behind, vowed that he would "yet return with the army and try to recapture Knoxville."[27]

It is also true that many of the Unionists in town were not locals. News of the arrival of Federal troops spread rapidly, and from all across East Tennessee loyalists flocked to Knoxville to get a glimpse of their deliverers. Probably typical was James McMillan, a Unionist from north Knox County who had not set foot in Knoxville for more than a year and a half when Burnside's troops marched into town. Interrupting a string of terse entries in his journal pertaining to crops and the weather, the laconic farmer briefly noted the arrival of the Union army on 1 September, then recorded on 10 September: "I went to Knoxville to see Yankeys." According to Oliver Temple, the impulse to do so drew countless other Unionists out of the hills and hollows and into town. The people began "pouring in" on the day Foster's cavalry arrived, Temple later recalled. "On the next day, the crowd had swollen to thousands," and by the third day "the streets were literally packed with human beings." By 4 September, when General Burnside delivered an "awkward, stammering" public speech from the balcony of the Mansion House Hotel, local Knoxvillians were a distinct minority among his enraptured audience. Federal soldiers like Robert Jameson had no way of knowing this, of course, and it is small wonder that they commonly walked away marveling at the intensity of Knoxville's loyalty.[28]

Finally, it is also possible that Burnside's men simply "saw" what they had been taught to expect. For more than two years they had been hearing of Knoxville as a Unionist stronghold within the Confederacy. No one had been more instrumental in propagating this image than Knoxville's most celebrated exile. William Brownlow had regularly damned the Democratic demagogues who had engineered Tennessee's separation and then initiated a "reign of terror" over the masses of loyalists. Apart from frequent references to a tiny clique of original secessionists, however, the Parson had promoted an illusion of overwhelming loyalty in his hometown, the community that he in turn employed as a proxy for East Tennessee as a whole. If undiluted loyalty existed anywhere in the South, the soldiers of the Army of the Ohio expected to find it in the town they had come to liberate.

As soon as possible, Parson Brownlow would do all within his power to set them straight. As he lectured across the North, Brownlow had occasionally fantasized about accompanying the Union army when it liberated his home. He would don a military uniform and ride "a big war-horse" into Knoxville, he told cheering audiences, "and I do believe the scoundrels had rather see the Devil coming after them!" His actual arrival was a bit less dramatic. When Burnside first arrived in Knoxville, it was not at all certain that he would stay. General William Rosecrans's Army of the Cumberland entered Chattanooga on 9 September, and the War Department repeatedly instructed Burnside to drive southward and assist him in striking at the Confederate Army of Tennessee near Rome, Georgia, roughly 170 miles away. The possibility that Knoxville might soon be evacuated—perhaps to be reoccupied by Confederate troops currently in southwestern Virginia—was too real to ignore.[29]

When it finally was apparent that the Army of the Ohio would remain in upper East Tennessee, at least for the foreseeable future, Brownlow moved with alacrity to return to Knoxville. He and Maynard brought their families from Cincinnati by means of Federal ambulances (courtesy of Secretary of War Edwin Stanton) and arrived in Knoxville on 17 October.[30] Both men hit the ground running. They delivered passionate speeches to the crowds that serenaded them by torchlight on their first evening in town, and they agreed to serve as the principal speakers at a Unionist rally the next Saturday. ("I've no doubt but they will get somewhat excited," Orlando Poe predicted to his wife.)[31] Brownlow also immediately acted to make good on his promise to northern audiences to resurrect his newspaper at the earliest opportunity. With the *Whig* again "in full blast," he had explained, he could resume his crusade against the fiends who had fomented this unholy war, and if he could not actually place the rope around their "infernal necks," he would at least "'spress my opinion of some of them."[32] That he would. The first issue of the paper came out scarcely three weeks after his arrival. That the editor could proceed so quickly was due, at least in part, to the assistance of the federal government. Perhaps responding to a petition from several Tennessee Union regiments calling for the resumption of the Parson's newspaper, the government provided Brownlow with $1,500 in start-up capital, five wagons with which to haul newsprint and ink from Cincinnati, and quite possibly a printing press as well. The newspaper bore a new title, calculated to reflect its editorial strategy and to capitalize on the editor's name recognition among northern readers. On 11 November the first issue of *Brownlow's Knoxville Whig and Rebel Ventilator* hit the streets.[33]

In the first weekly issue the editor concentrated on condemning secession and defending the policies of the Lincoln administration, but by the second issue Brownlow began broadening his emphasis to remind readers how many local townspeople had actively supported—and continued to support—the "wicked and uncalled for rebellion." In the 18 November issue the editor blasted by name the "scoundrels" and "beasts" who had favored the arrest of leading Unionists. He announced that Knoxville was "full of spies," both male and female, and he called for their immediate arrest. To highlight the extent of this fifth column, he re-published the list of civilians who had assisted in the defense of Knoxville against Sanders's cavalry raid the previous June. As a final case in point, the Parson re-ported that Rebel sympathizers were regularly meeting in private homes and ex-ulting over the prospect of regaining control of the town.[34]

Taken literally, Brownlow's claim that Knoxville was swarming with spies was far-fetched, but his observation that the town was still replete with Confederate sympathizers was on the mark. Whether they met clandestinely to dream of their deliverance from Yankee occupation is unknown, but surely they looked south-ward and hoped. Even as Brownlow was composing the 18 November issue, an army under the command of Confederate general James Longstreet was prepar-ing to cross the Holston River near Loudon, roughly thirty miles to the south, with the intent of striking immediately toward Knoxville. By the fourteenth, Ellen House (who "hate[d] the Yankees more every day") recorded hearing the sound of Confederate cannon and noted swelling rumors that the Rebel army was ap-proaching the city. On the following day, General Burnside—at that moment near Lenoir's Station just north of Loudon—sent word to his chief of staff in Knoxville to inform "Dr. Brownlow" and other prominent Unionists that the Federal army might soon be "compelled to leave the city." By the time the 18 November issue rolled off the press, the *Rebel Ventilator*'s editor was on his way back to Ohio, exiled a second time from the metropolis of East Tennessee.[35]

JAMES LONGSTREET APPROACHED KNOXVILLE a frustrated and disgruntled commander. For months, Robert E. Lee's most trusted subordinate in the Army of Northern Virginia had been lobbying the Confederate War Department for reassignment to the western theater. Principled conviction and personal ambi-tion both pointed him westward. On the one hand, the forty-two-year-old lieu-tenant general genuinely believed that the Confederacy needed to shift its focus from the battlefields of Virginia. Long an advocate of a western strategy, he was convinced that George Meade and the Army of the Potomac presented no im-minent threat to the Confederate capital. "The enemy intends to confine his great operations to the west," he had maintained to Lee in early September, and "it is time that we were shaping our movements to meet him." Toward that end,

Longstreet had recommended that Lee take up a strong defensive position north of Richmond and send a large portion of his army—Longstreet suggested his own First Corps—to help destroy Rosecrans's Army of the Cumberland near Chattanooga. "Our best opportunity for great results is in Tennessee," he had assured Lee.[36]

On the other hand, as the highest-ranking officer in the Confederate army without an independent command, Longstreet surely recognized in his proposal an opportunity for self-advancement. The Confederate general currently contending with Rosecrans was Braxton Bragg, a commander whose ineptitude and unpopularity rendered him ripe for removal. Thus, the possibility that he might be called on to replace Bragg surely crossed Longstreet's mind. Indeed, on 5 September he had written to Lee and magnanimously offered to exchange places with Bragg (assuming command of the Army of Tennessee while Bragg would serve Lee as a corps commander). Assuring Lee that he was "influenced by no personal motive" in making this suggestion, Longstreet shared his opinion that Bragg lacked confidence both in himself and in his army. "He is not likely to do a great deal for us," the disinterested patriot concluded.[37]

In the end, Longstreet had received his reassignment to the western theater—but as a corps commander under Bragg, not as the new chief of the Army of Tennessee. After a lengthy council of war with Robert E. Lee in Richmond, Confederate president Jefferson Davis, with Lee's apparent acquiescence, had decided to adopt Longstreet's western strategy for the time being. Davis had balked, however, at handing command of Bragg's army over to Longstreet and instead ordered that Longstreet and two divisions of the Army of Northern Virginia be assigned temporarily for service with the Army of Tennessee. Because Union control of upper East Tennessee had severed the main railroad connection between Virginia and Georgia, Longstreet's troops had been routed through the Carolinas; after a circuitous journey of roughly nine hundred miles over multiple rail lines, they had arrived just in time to make a decisive contribution to the Confederate victory at the Battle of Chickamauga, a day's march below Chattanooga, on 20 September.[38]

In the aftermath of the battle, however, the indecisive Bragg had done nothing to follow up the victory, apparently content to allow Rosecrans to retreat unhindered back to Chattanooga. In the opinion of several of his subordinates, Longstreet conspicuously among them, the befuddled Bragg had squandered an unprecedented opportunity to turn the tide of the war in the West. Longstreet wasted no time expressing his disdain. On 26 September he had written to Confederate secretary of war James A. Seddon: "Our chief has done but one thing that he ought to have done since I joined his army. That was to order the attack upon the 20th. All other things that he has done he ought not to have done. I am convinced that nothing but the hand of God can save us or help us as long as we have our present commander." Rancor among Bragg's generals soon approached open mutiny, with a dozen signing a petition to Jefferson Davis in early October calling for Bragg's removal. In a display of colossally poor judgment, the Confederate president had traveled to northern Georgia personally on 9 October, listened as Bragg's generals unanimously expressed their lack of confidence in him (with Bragg seated before them), and then returned to Richmond, leaving Bragg in command with a blank check to replace his critics. Longstreet had survived the subsequent "purge," however, in part because of his popularity with his troops, but even more so because he was technically "on loan" from Lee. Among Bragg's most outspoken critics, he would remain under the command of a man who now disliked him intensely.[39]

It was the decision to strike against Burnside that ultimately rescued him from this fate. Jefferson Davis had written to Bragg at the end of October, suggesting offhandedly "that you might advantageously assign General Longstreet . . . to the task of expelling Burnside" from East Tennessee. The president had not ordered Bragg to do so, but the latter clearly liked the idea and had informed Longstreet in person of his new assignment by 3 November. Bragg's plan called for Longstreet to move speedily northward along the East Tennessee and Georgia Railroad, strike Burnside immediately and decisively—either driving his army from East Tennessee or destroying it—then return southward before the Federal forces at Chattanooga could be reinforced sufficiently to break the Confederates' hold on the city. The success of the plan, Bragg emphasized in a written communication that followed, depended on "rapid movements and sudden blows," but he trusted that Longstreet would meet with "the same success which has ever marked your brilliant career."[40]

The sincerity of the compliment seems doubtful. It is only a slight exaggeration to say that the primary justification for the entire Knoxville campaign was the opportunity it afforded both Bragg and Longstreet to be shed of each other. Militarily, the undertaking made little if any sense. Longstreet's chief of artillery kindly labeled the plan "as remarkable a piece of strategy as the war produced." To begin with, the position of the Union Army of the Cumberland was growing steadily stronger. In early October, Joseph Hooker had reported to Chattanooga with twenty thousand veterans from the Army of the Potomac. Later that month Ulysses Grant, now commander of all Federal armies between the Appalachians and the Mississippi River, had arrived to assume direction of Union efforts to break the siege, and within a week he had opened up a new supply line for the hungry Yankees. At Grant's direction, William Sherman and an additional seventeen thousand troops were also on their way from Memphis and might arrive at any moment. Given that Bragg would soon be greatly outnumbered, sending Longstreet with a sizable force into upper East Tennessee was a gamble indeed. What is more, even if the scheme should succeed, it was difficult to make a case that the benefits would justify the risk. Should Burnside be driven from upper East Tennessee, the Union position at Chattanooga would not be seriously weakened. On the other hand, if Bragg should be routed at Chattanooga, Confederate control of upper East Tennessee would be all but impossible, no matter what Longstreet might temporarily accomplish there.[41]

To minimize the risk in the undertaking, Longstreet had immediately sought to modify Bragg's proposal. In the council of war on 3 November, he had recommended that Bragg move southward to a strong defensive position behind Chickamauga Creek, a shift that would free him to detach at least twenty thousand troops for the strike against Burnside. To Longstreet's chagrin, Bragg had adamantly objected. The Army of Tennessee would not withdraw in the face of the enemy, the general had insisted. It would remain in close proximity to Chattanooga, and Longstreet, of necessity, would press northward with a comparatively smaller force: two divisions of infantry (under Generals Lafayette McLaws and Micah Jenkins), two battalions of artillery with approximately thirty-five guns, and four cavalry brigades led by "Fighting Joe" Wheeler. In all, the expedition would total around fifteen thousand men, exclusive of camp guards and foraging parties. Bragg had spoken vaguely of the possibility of reinforcements at a later date, should circumstances permit.[42]

Longstreet had left the meeting on the third deeply pessimistic about the prospects of the undertaking, convinced that Bragg had denied him the manpower and matériel essential for victory, and perhaps suspecting that his antagonist was setting him up for failure. The general's intelligence indicated that Burnside could muster more than twenty thousand troops against him. This meant that his own force was simply too small to succeed. Thus twice before leaving Chattanooga he had protested to Bragg that he required more men. On the second occasion, he had noted that "if I am feeble my movements must be slow and cautious," an ominous assertion—almost a threat, even—given that the success of the mission depended so utterly on speed. Perhaps seeking a sufficient paper trail to exonerate himself, one of his last acts before breaking camp—while sitting on an empty flour barrel in a light drizzle, he later recalled—was to dash off a note to his friend General Simon Buckner. Bragg was being willfully obtuse, Longstreet implied, and due to his stubborn refusal to support the expedition properly, no great results could be expected. Not one to give up easily, however, six days later Longstreet had again written to Bragg and officially requested another division of infantry and additional artillery. "There are many reasons for anticipating great results from the expedition against General Burnside's army with a proper force," he lectured Bragg, "but with the force that I now have I think it would be unreasonable to expect much. In fact," Longstreet concluded in a tone calculated to infuriate his nemesis, "it will, in all probability, be another fine opportunity lost."[43]

If there was a silver lining in the path ahead—not that Longstreet was inclined to search for one—it was in the low quality of Union leadership the Confederates would soon confront. The brigadiers in the Army of the Ohio were comparatively inexperienced, while its commanding officer, though personally brave, could be spectacularly incompetent. Ambrose Burnside had demonstrated as much the preceding winter, shortly after Abraham Lincoln had chosen him to replace George McClellan as commander of the main Union army in Virginia. It was Burnside who had led the Army of the Potomac to the lopsided and dispiriting defeat at Fredericksburg the previous December, ordering innumerable frontal assaults against one of the strongest defensive positions of the war. Time after time, he had sent courageous Federal troops across open ground against dug-in Confederates on Marye's Heights west of the town, and time after time, ranks of North Carolina and Virginia marksmen concealed behind a stone wall had cut down their assailants until the Union dead covered the field like windrows of hay. The Confederate position was so strong, and the futility of the Federal assault so apparent, that the Rebel commander behind the stone wall had assured Robert E. Lee that from it he could kill every man in the Union army. That commander was James Longstreet; for the remainder of the war the bloodbath at Fredericksburg would epitomize to him the superiority of defensive tactics. Now, nearly a year later, the proposed thrust toward Knoxville offered him another shot at Burnside, but this time their roles would be almost completely reversed. For the campaign to succeed, the defensive-minded Longstreet would have to attack Burnside, and he would have to do so quickly.[44]

THE BLITZKRIEG BRAGG ENVISIONED never materialized. Longstreet delivered neither "rapid movements" nor "sudden blows," and from the Confederate perspective the entire Knoxville campaign can only be adjudged an abysmal failure. Things went badly from the beginning. Burnside had more than twenty-two thousand troops under his command in upper East Tennessee, but they were scattered across 80 miles between Cumberland Gap on the Kentucky border and Lenoir's Station, 25 miles south of Knoxville. According to the original plan, Longstreet's infantry and artillery would move swiftly by railroad to Sweetwater, the northernmost station safely under Confederate control. Having covered two-thirds of the 120 miles to Knoxville in two to three days, they would then strike across country toward Knoxville, threatening the town and ideally destroying Burnside's force piecemeal before he was able to concentrate effectively. What should have been the shortest part of the journey turned out to take the longest, however. The East Tennessee and Georgia Railroad was already overtaxed, the necessary cars were slow to arrive, and when they did materialize, they ferried the Rebel troops at a speed scarcely averaging five miles per hour. (The trains had to stop regularly while soldiers chopped fence rails to fuel the engines, and even a gentle incline often forced all aboard to get out and walk.) As a result, the last of Longstreet's infantry and artillery did not reach Sweetwater until 12 November, and what ought to have taken two or three days at most instead took eight. Longstreet and Bragg blamed one another, but whoever was at fault,

Longstreet was surely correct when he grumbled that "my troops could have marched up in half the time that has been consumed in transporting them by rail." Longstreet's state of mind hardly improved when he found no rations awaiting him at Sweetwater, thus requiring that he lose at least another precious day while foraging parties canvassed the countryside so that his soldiers would not starve.[45]

For all the delay, Longstreet still came very near catching Burnside off guard. Late on 13 November, Confederate engineers began laying a pontoon bridge across the rain-swollen Holston River west of Loudon, and by early the next morning the first Confederate soldiers were beginning to file across it. Whereas most of the Federal Twenty-third Corps was in camp near Knoxville or at points farther north, Burnside's depleted Ninth Corps—forty-five hundred men or so—had gone into winter quarters near Lenoir's Station, not a day's march from where Longstreet's engineers were now busily at work. Anticipating that there would be no more campaigning until spring, Union soldiers in the Ninth had for some time been building snug little huts, each complete with fireplace, table, and bunk, and in some instances even a wooden floor. This was not quite all the comforts of home, but about as good as it got for an enlisted man in the Civil War. "We thought ourselves the happiest of soldiers," recollected a member of the Thirty-sixth Massachusetts. Then at 4:00 A.M. on the fourteenth came the order to break camp and be ready to march at daybreak. "A thunderbolt from a clear sky would not have astonished us half so much as did the order to move," a soldier in the Seventy-ninth New York recalled. "We were disgusted. Why couldn't the 'rebs' behave themselves and let us enjoy our snug quarters for a while?" In the mad scramble to evacuate, the astonished and disgusted Yankees were forced to leave behind much of their baggage and equipment. The Federal artillery was badly short of horses (some of the heavier cannon required as many as sixteen horses to pull them over the muddy roads), and it soon became necessary to shift teams from the baggage wagons to the caissons and field pieces. The Union soldiers destroyed as much as they could, but when Confederate troops entered Lenoir's the following day, they found some eighty to a hundred wagons of abandoned food, ammunition, and personal effects.[46]

Burnside considered a variety of responses during the night of 13 November, having learned of the Rebel movement from Federal pickets posted on the northern bank of the Holston. His initial intelligence placed the strength of Longstreet's force at anywhere from twenty to forty thousand, and in the face of such superior strength his first impulse was evidently to retreat northward toward Cumberland Gap.[47] Writing home the same day, an officer on Burnside's staff informed his sister that his next letter would likely come either from Kentucky or from a Confederate prison. Although his boss clearly had contemplated a withdrawal toward the gap, it seems certain that Burnside always hoped not to evacuate East Tennessee entirely. Indeed, a representative of the War Department then in Knoxville "found him possessed by the idea that he must expose his whole force to capture rather than withdraw from the country." Perhaps with that in mind, Burnside also considered a rapid movement to the southeast, throwing his entire command across the Holston River into Blount County, a more isolated area between Knoxville and the Smoky Mountains where he hoped his army could subsist until Grant could come to his rescue. His communications would have been severed at once under this dubious stratagem, however, and an officer just arrived from Chattanooga convinced him "that Grant did not wish him to include the capture of his entire army among the elements of his plan of operations."[48]

Finally, Burnside concluded that he could best serve Grant by withdrawing slowly toward Knoxville and holding out there for as long as possible. Compared with other points along the route to Kentucky, he could concentrate his forces more rapidly in Knoxville and supply them more effectively, thanks to the easy access to river and rail transportation. The town was also potentially, if not immediately, strongly defensible. In the best-case scenario, by making a stand at Knoxville he could also draw Longstreet another thirty miles away from Bragg and weaken the Army of Tennessee sufficiently to allow Grant to break the siege at Chattanooga. Burnside telegraphed Grant the proposal sometime during the night, and the commander in chief wired back his approval the next day. Anticipating the arrival of Sherman's corps at any time, Grant confidently expected to drive Bragg from Chattanooga within a week, after which he promised to come swiftly to Burnside's aid. In the meantime, Burnside should "harass and embarrass" Longstreet's progress "in every way possible," rendering his invaluable corps useless to Braxton Bragg.[49]

It was Longstreet's job to prevent this, of course. Orders to "harass and embarrass" the enemy notwithstanding, Burnside opted not to seriously contest the Confederate crossing near Loudon. A division of the Ninth Corps turned toward the river and skirmished briefly with the Rebels on the afternoon of 14 November, but by dawn the next day the Union troops were retreating in earnest, following the path of the East Tennessee and Georgia Railroad through Lenoir's Station and then veering toward the north to strike the road from Kingston into Knoxville. Longstreet sent Jenkins's division in pursuit along the same path and ordered the division under McLaws to drive toward Campbell's Station, a crossroads sixteen miles southwest of Knoxville at which the Federal column would intersect the Kingston road. Had McLaws moved more promptly, the Rebels might have blocked Burnside's retreat and smashed the Union troops from both front and rear. As it turned out, Burnside won the race to Campbell's Station—barely—his advance units arriving there late in the morning on the sixteenth, scarcely half an hour ahead of McLaws. At that point a portion of the Ninth Corps, no more than thirty-five hundred soldiers, was able to hold back the converging Confederate divisions from noon until dusk, by which time the remainder of the Union force was well down the Kingston road toward Knoxville.[50]

All through the night, exhausted Union soldiers (many of whom had been on the alert since dawn on the fourteenth) slogged through ankle-deep mud to distance themselves from their Rebel pursuers. Autumn is often a dry season in East Tennessee, but in 1863 the winter rains had begun in mid-October, and the retreating column soon churned the already soft road into a "bottomless" quagmire. A New York soldier recalled the march as "damp and disagreeable"; a member of the Seventeenth Michigan remembered the "long, muddy miles" as among the "longest, weariest miles that it has ever been my misfortune to travel." Most of the Union column reached Knoxville between 2:00 and 5:00 A.M. on the seventeenth. Ellen House was awakened around 2:30 by the sound of wagons lumbering down Cumberland Street and watched as they filled, first, a vacant lot next door, then the family garden, then finally her own front yard. Throughout the day "the excitement and commotion beat any thing" Ellen had ever seen. "Cavalry and footmen [were] racing backwards and forwards. . . . None seem to know what they are after, or where they are going." Most were surely headed to work on the town's fortifications. As an officer in a Massachusetts regiment observed, "Knoxville at this time was by no means in a defensible condition." The range of hills that framed the town offered a variety of potentially strong positions, but apart from two incomplete earthen forts begun by the Confederates (one west of Second Creek and the other in East Knoxville), the town lacked any formal defenses. And now "Longstreet was coming sure with the flower of Bragg's army," as a private in the Nineteenth Ohio Artillery realized that morning. The Army of the Ohio was woefully unprepared.[51]

Orlando Poe worked feverishly to change this. Fighting Longstreet "with brain and spade," as he put it, Burnside's chief engineer set to work. Poe met each Federal unit as it arrived, directed the troops into a predetermined position, and told them to dig with all their might. As Poe supervised the hasty entrenchment, his West Point classmate, cavalry commander William Sanders (who had led a raid of the town in June), bought him more time by fighting a stubborn delaying action against Longstreet on a hill just north of the Kingston road, a mile or so west of town. With scarcely seven hundred troopers, some armed with repeating rifles, the Kentuckian won an invaluable thirty-six hours for the Union defenders before being mortally wounded around 4:00 P.M. on the eighteenth. Almost simultaneously, his dismounted cavalry broke against the Rebel onslaught, and the main body of Longstreet's army swept toward the outskirts of town just before sunset.[52]

At this point Longstreet did a curious thing. Rather than press his advantage, he entrenched. The Confederate commander later claimed that he was searching for a favorable point of attack while awaiting promised reinforcements. In effect, he was undertaking a partial siege or, in military parlance, an "envelopment." Longstreet ordered his infantry and artillery to dig in to the west and north of town, sent Wheeler's cavalry to patrol the northeast, and gradually began to push his picket lines forward. In fairness, one can understand why he hesitated to call for an immediate assault—Burnside's force inside Knoxville was nearly as large as Longstreet's and occupied most of the high ground—but that or a prompt withdrawal were the only two options consistent with Bragg's orders. And an immediate attack just might have worked. At this point the Yankees had done little more than dig shallow rifle pits. "We expected at every moment to be obliged to throw down our tools and take up our rifles," an infantryman recalled, hence "our first desire was only to effect a temporary protection, and the trenches were of the most simple character." Even Captain Poe conceded that the Federal soldiers were only "tolerably well under cover."[53] Another Federal officer at the time gave the Confederates a "good chance" at succeeding, whereas a staff officer in Union general S. P. Carter's brigade later offered that Longstreet "ought to have taken Knoxville, and it was generally thought by us that he would." Confederates both inside and outside of Knoxville agreed. On 16 November rumors began to swirl that the Rebels had "whipped" the Yankees "terribly down at Campbell's station," and when the Union sutlers began to sell out and flee northward, Ellen House and "all the rebel Ladies" turned out to pick up some bargains, each "looking as smiling as possible." Traveling with Longstreet's army, old Dr. Ramsey was confident that a vigorous attack on the seventeenth or eighteenth would carry the town. When Longstreet hesitated, Ramsey bitterly blamed the Confederate commander for his tardiness, although in fairness to the general the physician noted that such was "the fault of fat men generally." Although they did not blame his obesity, several of Longstreet's lieutenants similarly concluded that their commander had lost a great opportunity by not striking at once.[54]

Hindsight is twenty-twenty, of course, but this much is clear: while Longstreet waited, the Federal defenses grew steadily stronger. On 19 November Poe began putting the townspeople to work on the fortifications, pressing into service not only "citizens of the town" but also nearly two hundred local slaves, or "contrabands," as they were labeled in the official reports. Poe particularly praised the latter; during the first week of the siege they willingly put in eighteen-hour days "without murmur." With the former he was less pleased— many of the drafted civilians were Rebels who "worked with a very poor grace which blistered hands did not improve." In tandem with the Federal soldiers, these black and white laborers transformed the ring of crude rifle pits into a formidable defensive line. Over the course of the siege, they completed two nearly continuous lines of trenches, strengthened the existing earthwork forts and erected new ones, constructed in front of the entrenchments "chevaux-de-frise" (sharpened stakes placed in the ground at a forty-five-degree angle), and dammed First and Second creeks on the north side of town in order to flood that avenue of approach. "The earth-works on each side seemed to grow like magic," Orlando Poe remembered, "but we were apparently doing more digging than they."[55]

After halfheartedly probing the Union defenses, on the twentieth Longstreet cabled Bragg that a frontal assault would be futile. Without reinforcements, his best course was to *starve* Burnside out. How long that might take Longstreet did not venture to guess, but any thought of striking quickly to help Bragg at Chattanooga had obviously vanished from his brain. What is more, he made clear that even a siege would require additional troops to succeed. Although he had shut down the major roads into town, he did not control the south side of the Holston (Knoxville's southern boundary), nor had he made any effort to destroy the Federal pontoon bridge recently laid at the foot of Gay Street, which afforded the Yankees easy access to food and forage southeast of town. More troops, in sum, were needed "to help . . . shut up the place." Longstreet reiterated the point in a telegram the following day: another division, he informed Bragg, would "shorten the work here very much." Bragg had heard all this before.[56]

In actuality, the Confederate blockade was even more porous than Longstreet realized. Because Wheeler's cavalry was patrolling the northern bank of the Holston well east of Knoxville, Longstreet assumed that he had effectively cut off the flow of supplies from upriver. He was convinced of this thanks to a faulty map that incorrectly showed the French Broad River intersecting the Holston west of Knoxville, whereas the two rivers actually joined several miles east of town. (Dr. Ramsey and other local Confederates called attention to the error, but Longstreet ignored their warnings.) As a result, throughout the siege Unionists from nearby Jefferson and Sevier counties sent goods by raft down the French Broad and then on into Knoxville under cover of darkness. This "cracker train" brought cattle, hogs, and thousands of bushels of corn and wheat within the Federal lines, and may well have proved the difference between survival and starvation for Burnside's command. As it was, the men of the Army of the Ohio still spent the siege on one-half to one-quarter rations, and the bulk of the army's mules and horses had to be destroyed for lack of forage. On Thanksgiving Day (the ninth day of the siege), a Union major celebrated the holiday with a piece of bread the size of his fist. Shortly thereafter an enlisted man in a Michigan unit recorded his daily ration as twelve ounces of pork and one-eighth of a loaf of bread. The latter, he told his parents, was made from a mixture of graham flour, corn and cob meal, and molasses. The result was "black and solid." Having left Kentucky in August, many of the Yankee soldiers were also without overcoats or satisfactory shoes, prompting the commander of a Massachusetts regiment to describe his men as "half fed, half clothed, and half frozen."[57]

Many of Knoxville's civilians were little better off. With a lengthy supply line over almost impassable roads, the Army of the Ohio had primarily subsisted off of the countryside since it had first entered the region nearly three months earlier. It had descended on Knoxville like a plague of grasshoppers and promised to eat the townspeople out of house and home and burn every fence rail for fuel in the process. Within hours of their arrival, Union soldiers were knocking on Ellen House's door to ask for food, a ritual that immediately became a daily occurrence. Federal troops had dispersed across upper East Tennessee shortly thereafter, bringing some relief, but Longstreet's thrust toward Knoxville had brought them streaming back, effectively quadrupling the town's population in forty-eight hours. Elizabeth Crozier, whose husband and son were with Longstreet's army barely a mile away, left her home temporarily on the seventeenth and returned the day following to behold a scene she could scarcely have imagined: "Every lock in the house was broken open, the contents of every wardrobe, bureau, closet and side board, the front of which had been broken out, were scattered over every room. I was overwhelmed with amazement not knowing what to do. My wine all drunk, my hams, bacon, butter and sugar all gone." Years later, the daughter of pro-Confederate Swiss immigrants living just beyond the Union lines remembered how Union foraging parties had come frequently during the siege to take whatever they could find. They acted "just as if they had bought it," Margaret Klein recalled bitterly, "and the tears would run down my mother's face."[58]

Union soldiers did not prey solely on Confederate sympathizers. Federal foraging parties around Knoxville had a standing order to "collect from every possible quarter every pound of subsistence you can," which meant that Unionists also shouldered the burden of feeding their deliverers. Thomas Edington, a Knox Countian in the Federal army, reflected shortly after the siege that the region's Unionist faithful had "looked forward to the coming of the Union army as a time when they and their property would be protected," but instead "they have lost all their property and subsistence and have got naught in return but a very fair promise of starvation." When in January he finally managed to visit his parents, after an absence of twenty-three months, he returned to find that "the roguish yankees ha[d] robbed them of nearly all subsistence." Writing long after the war, Thomas Humes acknowledged that the town's loyalists suffered greatly during the struggle for Knoxville, but he insisted that they "were contented over their losses, knowing the army's need." This sounded noble, and it certainly fit nicely into the author's tribute to East Tennessee's "loyal mountaineers," but the good reverend's memory was a bit selective. Within days of Knoxville's "liberation," Union brigadier general S. P. Carter—newly appointed provost marshal general for East Tennessee—was fielding complaints by local Unionists concerning the army's "depredations." The town's loyalists had gladly shared of their surplus when their liberators first marched into town. As days turned into weeks, though, and the burden of Union occupation worsened, their enthusiasm waned, and many grew resentful. By mid-September General Burnside had established a commission to review claims for damages filed by area Unionists, and the commander who succeeded him shortly after the siege reported that more than

$200,000 in claims had already been filed. Several of these claims were filed by local slaves or free blacks, who also were not immune from the demands of cold and hungry Union soldiers. Slave Isaac Gammon and his freeborn wife, Nancy, lost twenty-two hogs to soldiers of the Twenty-third Corps. Free black Anthony Humes watched as members of the Ninth Tennessee Cavalry (U.S.A.) tore down his stable for firewood. Wiley Mabry, who had bought his freedom from J. A. Mabry, stood by helplessly as an officer from the hospital at the Deaf and Dumb Asylum confiscated nearly one hundred bushels of apples.[59]

Even so, Confederates surely suffered disproportionately. If Federal foraging parties often visited Confederate and Unionist households indiscriminately, they at least held out to the latter the possibility of repayment at some vague future date. Undoubtedly, they were also more zealous in impressing the goods of known Rebels. Not long before the siege began, Knox Countian Michael Rule—now Private Michael Rule, U.S. Army—explained to his parents that "the Rebels don't fare very well where we stay." After relating secondhand accounts of the Confederates' "savage barbarity" toward Unionists, Daniel Larned similarly assured a relative back home in Rhode Island that "one feels but little hesitation in appropriating the property of rebels in this vicinity." Northern soldiers who wished to single out Confederate sympathizers when foraging could turn for assistance to local Unionists, who were often happy to oblige. When Federal commissary agents knocked on the door of Unionist Sam Morrow in search of sugar, Morrow directed them down the street to the home of a Confederate neighbor, whom he knew to possess a barrelful. As the Yankee lieutenant knocked on the door pointed out to him and demanded the sugar, the entire Morrow household turned out into the street to enjoy the scene. Knoxville's slaves and free blacks were apparently also willing to help in this way. A slave named Titus, for instance, claimed that he "often informed Union officers as to who were Rebels, and where their property was." Union captain H. H. Thomas was amused when the efforts of a wealthy widow to conceal extra bedding were thwarted by a knowing wink and nod from her household slave.[60]

Upheaval and suffering increased for both sides as Longstreet's army crept forward. Known Confederate sympathizers were ordered to stay off the streets or face arrest. The First and Second Presbyterian, Methodist, and Baptist churches were all being used as hospitals, as well as the courthouse, the college, the Female Academy, the Lamar House and Mansion House hotels, and the Deaf and Dumb Asylum. Union soldiers were camped everywhere, occupying gardens, front porches, and woodsheds when they could not manage more comfortable quarters. And countless families were now homeless. Bookseller J. A. Rayal sought refuge with friends when Yankee cannon were planted in his yard. Merchant Jefferson Powell likewise left his newly built brick residence—a mansion by Knoxville standards, complete with marble fireplaces and a spiral staircase— when two companies of the Thirty-sixth Massachusetts moved in and began knocking loopholes into its outer walls. When Burnside's troops had withdrawn within their hurried fortifications on the seventeenth, they had created a kind of "no-man's-land" on the town's northern and western outskirts. The numerous houses dotting this neutral ground fared especially poorly. Union pickets often sought shelter in them first, drawing fire from the enemy in the process. They then burned them when forced to fall back so as to deny shelter to Confederate pickets. By the eighteenth, Rebel skirmishers had advanced to within sixty yards of David Deaderick's house, for example, and by the following morning bullets were beginning to strike about it occasionally. Union pickets returned fire from behind Deaderick's smokehouse, and four or five acted as sharpshooters from his attic, finally prompting the owner to flee to his son-in-law's home. Within twenty-four hours Union troops were ordered to burn his house and outbuildings.[61]

Among others, the residences of banker John L. Moses, physician Carrick Crozier, tailor Peter Staub, businessman William Branner, attorney W. B. Reese Jr., and widow Eliza Coffin eventually suffered similar fates. On the evening of the twentieth Ellen House recorded that the whole country north of the railroad was evidently aflame, and about that time (coincidentally?) the two Union bands in town struck up a merry tune. "It made me perfectly furious," she fumed to her diary. "I could have seen every Yankee here murdered and not shuddered." When Rebels made a dash toward the railroad depot three days later, the Union defenders again burned everything of value before falling back, setting fire to fifteen to twenty houses, the Humphreys Hotel, the roundhouse and machine shops of the East Tennessee and Georgia, and the nearby arsenal. The sight was "magnificently beautiful," a private in the Seventeenth Michigan observed. Less appreciative of the aesthetics, Ellen House was again "boiling over" at the destruction of southern property and consoled herself with the rumor that the Yankees had buried sixty-one of their number the day before.[62]

WHEN HE FIRST HEARD word that he might be sent into East Tennessee, James Longstreet had derided Braxton Bragg for not acting more decisively. "I came to the conclusion, as soon as the report reached me," he wrote to a friend and fellow Bragg-hater, "that it was to be the fate of our army to wait until all good opportunities had passed, and then, in desperation, seize upon the least favorable movement." A psychiatrist might label this a case of "projection": while Longstreet had Bragg's indecisiveness in mind, the prediction aptly described his own leadership around Knoxville. Precious days were passing. After learning of Longstreet's decision to institute a siege, Bragg wired him on 22 November, informing him that reinforcements were on the way from both Georgia and Virginia and urging him "if practicable to end your work with Burnside promptly and effectively. . . . I fear," he surmised correctly, that "he has already grown much stronger than when you drove him to cover." To prod his subordinate into action, on the same day Bragg also dispatched to Knoxville his chief engineer, General Danville Leadbetter, whose job it was to persuade Longstreet in person of the imperative need to strike quickly.[63]

It took three days for Leadbetter to reach Knoxville. As soon as he showed up with renewed pleas for an attack, Longstreet invited him to "make the reconnoissance [sic] and designate the assailable points." Leadbetter had been stationed for a time in Knoxville, and perhaps Longstreet genuinely desired his advice, but that seems a bit of a stretch. Porter Alexander, his trusted chief of artillery, insisted that Leadbetter had absolutely "no appreciation of ground," and it is unlikely that his boss viewed the interloper any differently. At their first conference, Longstreet questioned the wisdom of an assault given that Burnside would be starved out within two weeks. When Leadbetter pressed for an attack (in keeping with his orders), Longstreet appears to have thrown up his hands and said, in effect, "Fine. Tell me where to attack so that you (or Bragg) can bear the blame later on." After a bit of waffling, Leadbetter determined that the Yankees would be most susceptible to a thrust from the north aimed at Mabry's Hill, in East Knoxville. Alexander was incredulous, noting that a column charging from this direction would have to cover more than a mile of open ground without cover of any kind, cross a creek and several man-made ponds along the way, and then dash uphill against a heavily fortified position—all the time under enemy fire. A second examination of the ground finally convinced all involved in the decision that an attack along this line would be a nightmare. After wasting two full days, Longstreet and Leadbetter agreed that the assault should instead come from the west of town and focus on the earthwork fort positioned at the northwest corner of the Federal line, a bastion known as Fort Loudon when begun by the Confederates but now rechristened Fort Sanders.[64]

Porter Alexander had long since pinpointed Fort Sanders as the weakest point in the Federal line. There were compelling reasons to attack there. To begin with, not far in front of it the ground began to fall off in a concave arc toward Third Creek, and the valley was deep enough that an attacking column could actually form under complete cover within 150 yards of the fort. The Yankees had posted skirmishers in rifle pits along the edge of this "dead space," but they could be easily brushed aside at the moment of the attack. Second, the configuration of the fort, a slightly irregular quadrilateral roughly 95 yards by 125 yards, rendered its northwest salient particularly exposed. Due to the thickness of the parapet, the defenders inside of the fort would find it very difficult to fire at an angle. They could cover the ground directly in front of them well enough, but a column striking directly at the juncture of the northern and western walls would lie outside of their field of effective fire. Fortuitously, the shortest path of approach from the declivity to the fort would take the Confederates directly toward this vulnerable salient. Finally, because the fort was defended by no more than a few hundred men within its two acres, it might be possible for the Confederates to bring a crushing superiority of numbers to bear almost before the Yankees knew what was coming, and if the fort was overrun, the entire Federal line would likely crumble as well.[65]

Alexander was not the only man on the field who recognized this. His colleague from the peacetime army, Orlando Poe, was equally aware of the potential Achilles' heel and did his best to remedy its defects. He made certain that the ground in front of the fort was strewn with obstacles to slow down an attacking force. First came an abatis, felled trees placed lengthwise one over the other with their branches facing the enemy. Next came a network of nearly invisible wire. The trees covering the slope in front of the fort had been leveled by the Confederates when they had initially begun work on the fort, and now Poe ordered that telegraph wire be strung from stump to stump in front of the salient. Next, immediately in front of the fort was a ditch twelve feet wide and six to eight feet deep. (Longstreet and Alexander were both aware of the ditch but mistakenly believed it to be much shallower, possibly no more than three feet deep.) The earthen walls rising over the ditch were also twelve feet high on average and very nearly vertical, and on top of these the Yankees had piled five-hundred-pound cotton bales for additional cover. Any attackers who made it as far as the ditch would have to find some way to scale what amounted to a twenty-foot wall, made slick by frequent rains and frigid temperatures. Twelve cannon and more than four hundred soldiers would be posted inside to ensure that they did not succeed.[66]

On 27 November—the tenth day of the siege—Longstreet finally made up his mind. The attack would come the next morning. After Alexander's artillery had softened the Union defenses, the three brigades of McLaws's division would drive back the Yankee picket line and then charge in two columns, converging on the salient from the northwest and southwest. If all went as planned, they would overwhelm the fort's defenders, and brigades held in reserve would rush forward to exploit the breakthrough and roll up the Federal line. Cold rain and heavy fog that obscured the fort on the twenty-eighth led to yet another postponement, however, and the assault was rescheduled for the twenty-ninth. In the meantime, Longstreet altered the plan to try to increase the element of surprise. Now the skirmishers were to be driven back before midnight, the attacking columns were to form under the cover of darkness, and the assault was to step off before sunrise.

Having received his orders, General McLaws expressed reservations to Longstreet in writing. Rumors had reached the Confederate camp of a major battle between Bragg and Grant at Chattanooga, and McLaws now wondered whether it was wise to launch a major offensive until the outcome of the battle was known. If Bragg had suffered a serious defeat, then their position in upper East Tennessee was no longer tenable and it made no sense to risk casualties when they would not be able to remain on the field, even if victorious. Having finally resolved to act, however, Longstreet was in no mood to reconsider. The attack must be prosecuted "with a determination that will insure success," he replied to McLaws. "There is neither safety nor honor in any other course than the one I have chosen and ordered." That evening around 11:00 P.M. the Confederates pushed back the Union pickets and occupied their rifle pits between 80 and 120 yards in front of Fort Sanders, effectively broadcasting to the enemy that an attack was imminent. The long drumroll sounded within the fort accompanied by cries of "Fall in, boys! They're coming!" as the Union defenders raced to their posts. In the darkness before them, more than four thousand Rebel soldiers had formed ranks and now shivered and waited for the sign to attack. With the first gray of dawn the awaited signal finally came: around 6:00 A.M. a lone Confederate cannon near the home of Robert Armstrong on Kingston Pike sent a shell screaming over the fort.[67]

The twenty-ninth was a Sunday, and on this Sabbath morning "the services opened at daylight," as a Michigan captain inside Fort Sanders wryly put it. After the first cannon shots erupted from Armstrong's Hill, the remainder of the Confederate artillery opened fire, joining in a brief and largely ineffectual bombardment of the fort. "We could hear [the shells] coming before they got anywhere near us," an artillery private related to his parents, "and what a noise they make." McLaws's division then burst forward in the gloom, racing forward in two columns, bayonets fixed. They withheld their fire as they advanced, while sharpshooters in the newly captured rifle pits kept up a murderous fire concentrated on the parapet and the embrasures for the cannon. Their volleys were so effective that the fort's complement of twenty-pound Parrott guns and twelve-pound Napoleons were practically silenced, and the muskets very nearly so, prompting Porter Alexander to surmise from his remote vantage point that the fort was actually surrendering. The attackers slowed briefly as they struggled through the abatis and the wire entanglements, but in two or three minutes they had reached the ditch in front of the northwest corner with minimal losses, and a number had even planted battle flags on the outer wall of the fort.[68]

What followed was courageous but pathetic. The Rebel infantrymen had brought no scaling ladders, no cutting tools, and no plan whatsoever for surmounting what amounted to a two-story-high barrier. When they arrived at the ditch they simply piled into it, and then the ditch became a grave. A few weeks later an artist for *Harper's Weekly* gave northern readers a highly dramatized view of the "Battle at Fort Saunders." In a full two-page spread, the artist's sketch showed the Federal defenders all standing with their upper bodies exposed above the parapet as they aimed their muskets at the oncoming gray line. The Confederates were leaping across a shallow ditch and scrambling up a wall little taller than their heads. At the center of the drawing, the artist positioned three defenders actually standing *on top* of the parapet to repulse the bayonet-wielding Rebels—one brandishing an ax, another swinging his rifle like a club, the third preparing to heave an artillery shell into the mass of humanity below. Before the war's end, a popular print of the battle scene would actually place the *majority* of the Union defenders on top of the wall. It was an inspiring image.[69]

It was not, however, remotely accurate. A handful of brave Confederates did make it to the top of the earthen wall, and an equally small number of Union soldiers actually sprang atop the parapet. Few in either group survived as long as it takes to read this sentence. To climb on top of the wall was "certain death" for the attacking Confederates, a Georgia sharpshooter explained. The Yankee veterans inside the fort also understood that to expose themselves above the cotton bales for more than an instant was suicidal. Even in the days leading up to the attack, Rebel pickets had convinced them that to take a peep above the parapet in daylight was to risk getting their heads blown off. Once the assault was under way the danger only increased. Some of the attacking Confederates took cover behind stumps only a few yards in front of the fort, and along with the sharpshooters to their rear, they sent a dozen bullets toward every head that peered above the wall. Seeing two of his company shot down while trying to fire over the cotton bales, a sergeant in the Seventy-ninth New York ordered his men not to expose themselves so recklessly. One foolishly sprang upon the parapet nonetheless but fell back the moment his head appeared above the wall, having taken a bullet through his brain.[70]

From then on the company returned fire by passing loaded muskets to the sergeant, who posted himself next to an embrasure cut in the wall for one of the cannon. The sergeant, without exposing more than his right arm and shoulder, could then fire into the ditch; even without taking careful aim, almost every bullet he fired "found a death mark." In similar fashion, men in other units held their guns over their heads and discharged them over the wall without actually ever seeing the enemy. Most of the hand-to-hand fighting that occurred during the battle took place not on top of the wall but around the artillery embrasures, where the attackers stood a fighting chance of survival. Even that was deadly danger-ous. Rebels who tried to slip through one of the openings were met by waiting Union marksmen or, worse yet, ran head-on into the yawning mouth of a loaded cannon. Lieutenant Samuel Benjamin, commander of a battery of Parrott guns within the fort, reported later that "I put my pistol within 6 inches of a rebel's face and pulled trigger three times." When a half dozen Confederates made it to the porthole in front of a twelve-pound howitzer and demanded that the "damned Yankees" surrender, the gunner replied, "Yes! we'll surrender *this* to you" and pulled the lanyard.[71]

Actually, the most devastating fire came from Federal positions on either side of the fort. Union infantrymen to the east of the bastion poured volley after volley into the left flank of the Confederate column approaching the salient from the northwest, while Federal batteries posted to the south were able to rake the southwestern approach with double and triple loads of canister. Meanwhile, the

"Attack on Knoxville," print taken from an original sketch by Thomas Nast and published by Johnson, Fry & Co., New York, 1865.
Photograph courtesy of Special Collections, University of Tennessee Libraries.

defenders within Fort Sanders added their own "artillery barrage" without revealing themselves to the enemy—and largely without firing their cannon. Anticipating that he might need them, Lieutenant Benjamin had stockpiled twenty-pound artillery shells equipped with unusually short fuses. When the withering Rebel fire on the embrasures made it too dangerous to man his Parrott guns, the resourceful artilleryman took up a position against an interior wall and began to shotput these makeshift bombs over the top of the parapet, after which they would roll to the bottom of the ditch and wreak unspeakable havoc. "Yells, shrieks and groans attested to the bloody work," a New York infantryman remembered. Soon, those in the ditch who were still alive began to call for quarter. Those who could, retreated; those who could not, surrendered. It was not yet 7:00 A.M. A half hour later a telegram arrived to inform General Longstreet that Bragg "had retired before superior numbers," a polite way to characterize his humiliating defeat at Chattanooga four days earlier. Bragg's Army of Tennessee was now in headlong retreat toward Atlanta.[72]

Longstreet and Burnside agreed to a flag of truce, and for the remainder of the day the armies buried the dead and tended to the wounded. Soldiers on both sides gravitated toward the no-man's-land between the lines, talking and swapping stories with men they had tried to kill that morning. Members of the Twenty-first Massachusetts and the Palmetto (South Carolina) Sharp-shooters caught a pig and divided it for dinner. Orlando Poe chatted with Porter Alexander, whom he had known at West Point before the war, and the latter produced a "convenient flask" from his overcoat for their mutual enjoyment. Many of Fort Sanders's defenders were also drawn irresistibly toward the bloody ditch they had so recently defended. There for the first time they actually viewed the carnage they had helped to create. "Such another sight I never wish to see," a Union captain confessed to his diary. It was "like living murder sculptured by Perfection's Artist," a Michigan sergeant wrote to his brother. It was a "sad scene of slaughter," a soldier in the Fifty-first New York recalled. "At every footstep we trod in pools of blood." Ohio artilleryman John Watkins described the sight in numbing detail to a friend back home. "As soon as the firing was stopped I went up and got onto the parapet to look at them," he explained, "and such a sight I never saw before. . . . The ditch in places was almost full of them[,] piled one on top of the other, and such groaning I never heard. The dead were lying in all imaginable shapes[,] the wounded on top of them and dead on top of them again, and the ground was strewn with them all along their route up to the fort." In his subsequent report on the battle, General Longstreet would reduce this vision of horror to a bloodless enumeration: Confederate losses, he informed Richmond, were 129 killed, 458 wounded, and 226 missing—813 total casualties in roughly twenty minutes of fighting, or one casualty every second and a half. In contrast, Union losses inside of Fort Sanders totaled five dead and eight wounded. The fort's defenders had escaped relatively unscathed, not because of their valor on top of the parapet but because of their skill in staying behind it.[73]

Only with hindsight did it become clear that the twenty minutes of carnage on 29 November marked the defining moment of the Knoxville campaign. Unable (or unwilling) to go to Bragg's aid, General Longstreet did not immediately break off the siege. The Yankee soldiers in and around Fort Sanders fully expected the Confederates to renew the attack. The day after the battle Orlando Poe wrote home that the siege was "not by any means terminated." On the next day he wrote again, observing that "everything is now very quiet, but that quiet is ominous. Forty-eight hours more must tell the tale of the siege of Knoxville." Poe called it about right. On the evening of 2 December word arrived at Burnside's headquarters that General Sherman was approaching Maryville with twenty-five thousand troops. Longstreet was already apprised of the same information, and on the third his supply trains began to move as unobtrusively as possible toward the northeast, followed after dark on the fourth by the main body of the Confederate corps. The siege of Knoxville was over. Longstreet's men would go into winter quarters not far north of town, and their commander would devote his energies during the winter lull to finding a scapegoat for the Rebel defeat. On 17 December he ordered Lafayette McLaws relieved from further duty on the grounds that he had "exhibited a want of confidence in the efforts and plans which the commanding general has thought proper to adopt." Precisely the same could have been said concerning Longstreet's own lack of confidence in Braxton Bragg.[74]

On 5 December the guns around Knoxville were silent, and the townspeople left their cellars and gathered on street corners and front porches to discuss the rumor that the Confederates were actually in retreat. The same report had circulated daily for the last week, but on this morning there was no firing in the distance to prove otherwise, and by afternoon the rumor had been confirmed. Within thirty-six hours the news had reached Washington; Ulysses Grant cabled the War Department late on 6 December to report that Longstreet was in full-fledged retreat toward Virginia. When Grant had recently informed the president of his victory at Chattanooga, President Lincoln had responded tersely, commending Grant for a job well done but concluding with instructions to "remember Burnside." Now, finally, Lincoln could relax. Grant's telegram arrived in Washington around 2:00 A.M. on the seventh, and on the same day the president issued a rare proclamation calling for a national day of thanksgiving. Deeply committed to the region's liberation—"the project nearest and dearest" to his heart, according to his private secretaries—Lincoln proclaimed the outcome of the fighting in East Tennessee a "great advancement of the national cause" and urged all loyal citizens to "assemble at their places of worship and tender special homage and gratitude to Almighty God."[75]

Knoxville's Unionists needed no encouragement. The sixth was a Sunday, and most of the town's loyalists had attended church with grateful hearts and then made a holy pilgrimage of sorts, strolling out the Kingston road to view the site of the battle on the previous Sabbath. Few Confederates cared to make the excursion. For three weeks they had held their breath, looking to Longstreet's seasoned veterans to "remove the iron heel of despotism from the necks of an innocent people," as Elizabeth Crozier put it. Those hopes were now frustrated, and the future appeared bleaker than ever. "A leaden cloud hangs over our spirits," Ellen House acknowledged as the year drew to a close. "God grant the next year may end more pleasantly, more hopefully to us."[76]

CHAPTER SEVEN

A New Set of Strains

Alas, has it come to this? The troops are leaving and we are left in the hands of the tyrants! . . . What a triumph for our enemies.
—Confederate sympathizer Elisa Bolli[1]

I am as firm in my principles as ever, but never will I sanction the abolition policy of Abraham Lincoln. We will be obliged to submit because we cannot help ourselves. —Union sympathizer Rhoda Williams[2]

WHEN AMBROSE BURNSIDE first rode into Knoxville at the head of the Army of the Ohio, an artist for *Harper's Weekly* sought to capture the scene for northern readers. His sketch soon appeared on the cover of that popular magazine and in short order became one of the best-known visual images of southern Unionism in the wartime North. Entitled "Reception of General Burnside by the Unionists of Knoxville," the drawing featured the "deliverer of East Tennessee" surrounded by a mass of adoring admirers who were waving handkerchiefs and hats and babies while the general gazed stoically toward the horizon.[3] In hindsight, the significance of the cover lies as much in what it omits as in what it includes. There are no Confederates in the picture, for one thing. Neither Ellen House nor any of her compatriots can be seen scowling from the shadows, muttering their undying hatred for "vile" Yankees. Nor are there any disgruntled Unionists in the sketch, even though a significant minority of the loyalists in the crowd were surely troubled by the possible implications of their "liberation." Finally, there is not a single slave in the drawing, even on the periphery of the celebration. This is more than a bit curious, since there is no doubt that slaves were in fact present. When the Forty-fifth Ohio Infantry crossed Second Creek into Knoxville, one of their officers recalled that they were met at the bridge by a large number of blacks shouting and singing. Hours later, when an enthusiastic throng of whites and blacks had gathered to hear a speech from General Burnside, what impressed this observer most was the haunting strains of an

"Reception of General Burnside by the Unionists of Knoxville," Harper's Weekly,
October 24, 1864.

Photograph courtesy of Special Collections, University of Tennessee Libraries.

African American spiritual. "What do you do when the Redeemer comes here
on earth?" a young black woman sang from the roof of a nearby building. From
the street below a "swelling chorus" of kindred spirits responded in a hymn of
praise.[4]

Astutely selective, the *Harper's Weekly* artist portrayed the occupation of
Knoxville in a manner calculated to appeal to his northern audience. For nearly

two years, northern "Copperheads" (antiwar Democrats) had been ridiculing the idea of forcing unwilling southerners to rejoin a fraternal Union at the point of a bayonet. For the previous twelve months, the entire Democratic Party in the North had been condemning emancipation as monstrous. But what northerner could not be heartened by the liberation of Knoxville? The Army of the Ohio had freed a "renowned Union stronghold" inhabited by an all-white citizenry unburdened by slavery and untainted by treason.[5] Stripped of complexity in this way, Knoxville could serve as a proxy for East Tennessee as Abraham Lincoln and other northern Republicans wished to perceive it—and as Knoxville Unionists actively labored to depict it.

In reality, however, the arrival of Burnside's army aggravated tensions within an already divided community. Federal occupation presented Knoxville Confederates with the same basic moral dilemma that had confronted local Unionists for the previous twenty-seven months: what would it mean to remain faithful to their convictions in a town now controlled by the enemy? But Federal military success also presented Unionists with a quandary of their own. Knoxville's loyalists had opposed secession while upholding slavery, and those who had remained at home during the Confederate occupation had clung tenaciously to that increasingly untenable position. Even though Tennessee had been exempted from the Emancipation Proclamation, the inundation of Yankee soldiers immediately threatened the preservation of slavery locally, and Knoxville's proslavery Unionists would find their political commitments challenged as never before.

No MATTER HOW MUCH they flocked to the site of the recent battle, the townspeople of Knoxville could never fully comprehend what had occurred in the bloody ditch before Fort Sanders. In that sense there had been not one but two campaigns around Knoxville—the one that the soldiers had fought and the one that the civilians had witnessed. And yet it would be wrong to characterize the townsfolk as mere observers of the conflict. Granted, they had suffered minimal loss of life. Miraculously, there had been but a single civilian casualty during the seventeen-day siege, a little girl struck down in her garden by a stray bullet. Even so, they *had* felt the heavy hand of war, of that they were sure.[6]

The very landscape testified to this. "I hardly knew our poor Knoxville," French-born teenager Elisa Bolli observed when she and her sisters hitched a ride into town after the siege. All the timber on the surrounding hills had been cut down, and numerous forts and innumerable trenches now encircled the community. When David Deaderick returned to his home on the outskirts of town, he counted forty-four rifle pits in his yard and thirty-eight bullet marks on the west side of the house alone. All across town the costs of the campaign were evident, and few households if any had escaped entirely. The heart of the town was now

"completely ruined," according to Ellen House. Scarcely a fence remained standing, the sidewalks resembled "a stable yard," and the nauseating odor from the
churches and schools now serving as hospitals would have been unbearable, had
it not been overwhelmed by the stench from the hundreds of dead horses and
mules now littering the streets. Filth had become the town's defining charac-
teristic, and it surprised no one that smallpox was beginning to spread.[7]

Homelessness compounded the effects of disease. "A great many houses"
had been burned to the ground, Bolli sadly observed. William Brownlow later
claimed that one-third of the town had been destroyed, perhaps an overstate-
ment, but not greatly so. At the close of the war, a *New York Times* reporter
found "burnt houses and solitary chimneys over one whole quarter of the city."
A northern correspondent with the Army of the Ohio during the siege condemned the "wanton" and "useless" destruction of property that had produced
so many "houseless wretches." Those dwellings still standing were far from
unscathed. Horace Maynard's son Edward (now an officer in the Union army)
returned to find his father's home "much abased"—the fences were destroyed,
the yard ruined, and "things wrecked generally." The roof of John Knox's modest house had been torched during the siege, and after Longstreet's evacuation
he watched as the Federal hospital corps dismantled the surviving walls brick
by brick. Confederate sympathizer Isabella Boyd looked on helplessly as hospital orderlies in search of firewood gradually tore down her corncrib, cowshed,
smokehouse, carriage house, and stable. A swarm of locusts could not have been
more thorough.[8]

The war's most pressing reminder, though, was hunger. Food prices soared
to three times prewar levels, and a Unionist housewife complained (with a bit
of exaggeration) that it cost ten times more to live than it had only three years
earlier. In truth, food was scarce at any price. "The principal thing with all," Laura
Maynard observed in January 1864, "is *something to eat.*" Just because the siege
was broken did not mean that food suddenly became plentiful; if anything, food
shortages worsened for a time. It was still next to impossible to haul supplies in
large quantities across the mountains from Kentucky, so the Army of the Ohio
continued to live off the countryside. Union soldiers stationed in Knoxville received no more than half rations throughout the winter, and much of what they
consumed came from local civilians. Confederate sympathizers tried to hide their
stores (usually unsuccessfully): the Buffats built a false wall in their attic for a
cache of provisions, for example, while the Chavannes family hid corn in the
woodpile and bacon under the lining of the roof. Unionists were generally more
forthcoming, although increasingly embittered by the Yankee soldiers' apparently
insatiable demands. Seventy-seven-year-old Frederick Heiskell lodged several
angry protests with Federal authorities. He claimed that for months his family
rarely sat down to dinner without the table being crowded with "needy warriors"
to whom he could not, realistically, refuse access to his "humble supply." Ex-

congressman Thomas Nelson, who relocated to Knoxville during the war, filed a formal complaint with the Union provost marshal general, Brigadier General S. P. Carter. "The Union Army is more destructive to Union men than the rebel army ever was," he contended. "Our people are stripped in many instances of the last vestige of subsistence, our means to make a crop next year are being rapidly destroyed, and when the best Union men in the country make appeals to the soldiers they are heartlessly cursed as rebels." Before resigning his command in mid-December, Ambrose Burnside established a commission to review the claims of area Unionists for uncompensated contributions to his army, but the claims approved by the "Burnside Commission" were never honored, and East Tennessee Unionists pressed their demands for reimbursement literally for decades after the war.[9]

The Confederate army also depleted the area's store of foodstuffs. After breaking off the siege, James Longstreet retreated only a couple of days' march toward Virginia. When neither Burnside nor his successor, newly promoted General John W. Foster, acted aggressively to expel him, the Confederate commander decided to spend the winter in the region, with the result that Confederate foraging parties regularly ranged within a few miles of Knoxville. The area to the north and east of Knox County had been relatively untouched by foragers, but the Rebel troops so systematically stripped the fields over the next three months that Longstreet reported to General Lee in late February that there was literally nothing to feed man or horse between Knoxville and Greeneville, a distance of seventy miles.[10] To aggravate the situation, once it became clear that Longstreet's Confederates would be occupying the region indefinitely, hundreds and then thousands of Unionists poured into Knoxville. Most of the refugees eventually resumed their journey, taking a roundabout path by rail to Louisville or Cincinnati via Chattanooga and Nashville, but many remained for an extended period. A local Unionist estimated that on any given day there were several hundred transients adding to the town's already hungry population. Some slept on the ground around the railroad depot, and as late as May at least 150 destitute refugees were crammed into the Summit House Hotel.[11]

In short, the area around Knoxville was forced to feed not one but two armies during the winter of 1863–64, and the result was predictably devastating. Many of the townspeople were "now wanting the actual necessaries of life," Orlando Poe explained to his wife. "This destitution is going to lead to all sorts of crimes," he predicted, "for people *will* live." Thomas Nelson agreed, writing to Federal military authorities, "If nothing is done & promptly done, starvation and ruin are before us." As a stopgap measure, the Army of the Ohio stepped into the breach and shared some of its own scarce supplies, distributing rations to destitute civilians on nearly three thousand occasions between November 1863 and the end of 1864. As a rule, these meager handouts were restricted to Unionists and reserved for the hungriest of the hungry. On a typical day the army shared its bread with only five to ten families, a mere fraction of those in genuine need.[12]

In search of a more satisfactory solution, in February 1864 a group of prominent Unionists—two-thirds of them from Knoxville—gathered at the local Methodist church to form the East Tennessee Relief Association (ETRA). The goal of the organization was to coordinate and promote charitable assistance from outside the region. In large part the association built on the efforts of Nathaniel Taylor, a Unionist minister and politician from nearby Carter County who had already begun soliciting donations across the Northeast. Within the next twelve months, the ETRA would serve as the conduit for nearly $170,000 in donations, mostly from Massachusetts, Pennsylvania, and New York. Agents for the association used the funds to purchase basic commodities and oversaw their distribution, in theory at least, across all of upper East Tennessee. Much of the region was either still occupied by James Longstreet or inaccessible by railroad, however, so during the first half of 1864 a disproportionate share of the ETRA's supplies remained in and around Knoxville. This welcome relief did not eliminate suffering entirely, but it did allow the townspeople to turn their attention to less tangible matters.[13]

YANKEE OCCUPATION ELICITED a broad range of responses from Confederate civilians. For a sizable minority, the advent of Federal troops triggered an immediate conversion. Recent refugees from Knoxville informed William McAdoo that "many Southern men remain there, and seem quite prepared to be on amiable terms with the Yankees." If Ellen House can be trusted, merchant Thomas Van Gilder was a "little Turncoat" who embraced the Union as soon as it no longer paid to be a Confederate, which was roughly the moment that the last Rebel troops evacuated the town. In like manner, after waffling repeatedly during the first two years of the war, John Baxter worked his way into the good graces of Federal officers within days of their arrival. The prize for most brazen opportunism went to Joseph Mabry, however. In 1861 Mabry had offered to help equip Confederate volunteers, and numerous local Rebels had marched off to war as members of the "Mabry Greys." The day after the Army of the Ohio entered Knoxville, Mabry introduced himself to Burnside's quartermaster, Captain H. S. Chamberlain, who still vividly remembered the encounter decades later. "I am a notorious rebel," Mabry confessed, explaining that he had done hundreds of thousands of dollars of business with the Confederate government. Even so, he averred, "I am here to tell you that whatever I have that will be of use to your army you can have." The cagey merchant understood that the Yankees would take his property if they needed it—with or without his encouragement. Only by establishing his newfound "loyalty" would he have any chance of eventual compensation. Mabry took the oath of allegiance to the United States as soon as

possible and then began applying to Federal military authorities for reimbursement for provisions taken since Burnside's arrival. Incredulous, the assistant provost marshal for the Army of the Ohio rejected his claims, reminding the
erstwhile secessionist of what he had already admitted, namely, "You have given
all the moral and material aid to the rebellion that your high social position and
great wealth would enable you to give."[14]

At the other extreme, the most ardent Confederates had typically fled before
the arrival of Burnside's troops. Gone were almost all of the community's clique
of "original secessionist" leaders: J. G. M. and Crozier Ramsey, William Swan,
John Crozier, Bill Sneed, Campbell Wallace, and Jacob Sperry, among others.
They likely feared personal violence or official punishment if they remained, but
each was also determined to continue the struggle for Confederate independence
within the Rebel lines. Swan continued to represent East Tennessee in the Confederate Congress at Richmond, for example, whereas Sneed was serving in
Bristol as a commissioner helping to enforce the Confederate Impressment Act.
The elder Ramsey was in Atlanta working for the Confederate Treasury Department, while Sperry was editing the fire-eating *Knoxville Register* in the same city.
Other lesser-known Confederate sympathizers also became refugees, preferring
to abandon their homes rather than submit to Federal authority as long as there
was any alternative. Still others, less prominent and therefore less fearful of retribution, lingered until certain that Union control was permanent, leaving only
after Longstreet had definitely abandoned his efforts to reclaim the town. Elizabeth Crozier headed toward Middle Tennessee and the charity of friends,
Jefferson Powell packed up for Cincinnati, merchant Sam Hamilton hastened to
Washington, D.C. (notoriously southern in sentiment), physician R. O. Currey
relocated to North Carolina, and a number of the McClungs settled temporarily
in New York, comfortably mingling with that city's large Copperhead element.[15]

The majority remained behind, however, unwilling to leave and loath to cast
off their convictions. Relatively few men were publicly defiant. Since arriving on
the scene, Federal officers had shown no hesitation in arresting male civilians who
were too outspoken in their sympathies. By Christmas they had jailed at least
two dozen "active" or "violent" Rebels. Occasionally the specific charges included
overt acts, such as trying to smuggle mail through the lines, assaulting Union
citizens, or harboring Confederate soldiers. The majority, though, were apparently arrested for words rather than deeds, accused of "disloyal talk," "expressing
treasonable sentiments," or "preaching secession." Most eventually gained their
release after taking the oath and posting a sizable bond, usually $1,000 to $2,000,
but the message was clear. Men who were too open about their Confederate convictions could wind up behind bars. Relatively few were inclined to seek such
martyrdom. On the contrary, if pressured to do so they would pledge their fidelity
to a government they had come to despise. When the Union provost marshal

called on the townspeople to take advantage of President Lincoln's recent offer
of amnesty to southern Rebels, more than one hundred men voluntarily swore
oaths of loyalty to the United States by the end of January.[16]

Fully four-fifths were insincere, according to Parson Brownlow, who had
returned from his second exile from Knoxville by the end of December and within
a week was back at the task of "ventilating rebels." As Confederate civilians came
forward to take the oath, the editor listed their names for all the world to see
and encouraged loyalists to scrutinize their behavior closely. Some of the "peni-
tent" intended to use the oath as a cover for continued disloyalty, he declared.
Others were primarily hoping to avoid prosecution and protect their pocketbooks.
He was probably right. Since the passage of the Second Confiscation Act in July
1862, the real and personal estate of Confederate sympathizers had been legally
subject to seizure, but by taking the president's amnesty oath they could secure
a pardon and preserve their property (excepting slaves). Not that this was a pain-
less solution. Although he finally swallowed his pride and took the amnesty oath,
David Deaderick seethed at the contention that Rebel civilians had forfeited legal
claim to their property due to disloyalty. The doctrine was simply a specious
justification for robbery, he fumed, a shocking abuse of a constitutional right he
had done nothing to forfeit. To his mind, at least, the fact that he had supported
secession after Fort Sumter, or that he had given material aid to four sons now
serving in the Confederate army, had no bearing on the federal government's
obligation to respect his possessions. For men such as Deaderick, taking the oath
represented a pragmatic necessity, not an admission of guilt, much less repen-
tance. In the view of pro-Confederate civilian Nathan Gammon (who himself
had three sons in Confederate uniform), his only crime lay in "exercising his high
constitutional privilege [of] thinking for himself." Such men took the oath "from
the teeth out," hoping to nurture their loyalties and nurse their grievances in
private.[17]

In theory, the army reserved the right to expel any Confederate sympathizer
who refused to take the oath. When they ultimately acted on that prerogative,
Confederate critics claimed that "every family of Southern proclivities" had been
ordered to leave. With "utter disregard . . . to all the decencies of civilized life,"
the *Bristol Gazette* announced in horror, the Yankees had inaugurated in Knoxville "a system of cruelty . . . unprecedented in the annals of modern warfare."
In reality, Provost Marshal General Carter, the officer responsible for policing
local civilians, acted only against individuals he deemed especially egregious in
their persistent support for the rebellion. Quiet Rebels were to be left alone, with
banishment reserved for persons who, in the words of a military directive, "aver
their sympathy for the rebellion or its supporters openly . . . or who use language
or act in such manner as to show contempt for the U.S. Government."[18]

Parson Brownlow used the pages of the *Whig* to make sure that no offenders escaped the general's attention. Carter had numerous East Tennessee rela-

tives in the Confederate service, and one of Brownlow's goals was to make sure that the general's policies were not influenced by a "too gentle regard for his rebel Kin." In the first issue after the Parson's return, he listed by name those most deserving of expulsion, starting with three ministers of the gospel: the "impudent" scoundrel Joseph Martin, the "hell-deserving secessionist" William Henderson, and the "vile old traitor" Isaac Lewis. In a departure from custom, the editor also focused considerably on *female* wrongdoers. A minority of Rebel women were quiet and ladylike, he admitted, but the majority were "as brazen as the devil, full of impudence, with but little sense, and less prudence." He was particularly incensed by the spectacle in mid-January of a porch-full of Rebel females cheering Confederate prisoners of war as they marched through town on their way to the train station. It was a "bold, impudent, and *flirting* demonstration," and Brownlow demanded that the "*she* rebels" involved be expelled immediately, without respect to rank or association.[19]

The Parson soon had his way. Within a month General Carter had ordered at least twenty offenders (of both sexes) banished beyond the lines. Eventually, the total grew to more than fifty. Typically, individuals "sent South" had only two to three days' advance warning and were forbidden to take more than a few personal items with them. At the encouragement of Thomas Humes, they were allowed to sell their personal property before leaving, although it is doubtful that such hasty transactions generated fair sums. The motive for deportation seems to have been primarily punitive, as few of those banished could have seriously been deemed a threat to the security of the community. The list of early deportees included two preachers, a doctor, a druggist, and a merchant, and all of the men involved were middle-aged or older. The Union army was punishing them for their sentiments, not their actions.[20]

The majority of those sent south were women, most of whom had husbands, sons, or brothers in the Rebel army and would neither take the oath nor hide their Confederate sympathies. Their deportation represented a major alteration in the nature of Knoxville's war. Reflecting long-standing cultural attitudes concerning the acceptable treatment of "ladies," Federal military authorities had initially tolerated acts of petty defiance from females, many of which would have landed their menfolk in jail. Confederate women sometimes made a show of walking in muddy streets rather than using sidewalks festooned with Union flags. They regularly collected food and clothing for Confederate prisoners of war and religiously visited the Confederate wounded in the town's numerous makeshift hospitals. They took pride in showing disdain for local boys in blue, and they repeatedly insulted Yankee officers with unblushing candor. When a Union officer called on Mattie Luttrell, the teenage daughter of Knoxville's mayor, she refused to come downstairs but instead called out loudly to her slave Betty: "You are his equal in this house—go & entertain him. But be sure to see that he doesn't steal anything." In like manner, when a Yankee lieutenant spent the evening in Ellen

House's parlor, she "peppered him well," lecturing him on the absurdity of trying to restore the Union by force and explaining to him that "Southern children
hated the Yankee nation from the time they were born, and the hatred grew with
their growth and strengthened with their strength."[21]

In the months following the siege such overt demonstrations became unac-
ceptable, and the cultural conventions that had traditionally protected female
noncombatants gradually eroded. General Carter did not immediately heed
Brownlow's call to strike at the "she rebels." An East Tennessean himself and
viewed by local Confederates as a "gentleman," he was initially hesitant to take
action. Upon receiving a complaint, Carter's standard response was to warn the
offending party first. When directly challenged, however, he would stand his
ground, as Ellen House found out when she called his bluff. Carter twice warned
House about her outspoken behavior, once through her father and a second time
through Charles McAlister, a Union officer who (much to Ellen's chagrin) was
boarding with the House family. Through the latter she sent word back to Carter
that "I certainly would lay down my life willingly did I know by so doing I would
do the Confederates the least good." To her diary she defiantly declared, "I am
not afraid of him or any other Yankee living or dead." She meant it, too, but a
month later she was on a train bound for Abingdon, Virginia, ordered beyond
the Federal lines by the Union provost marshal. There were numerous charges
against her, but the final straw had been reports that she had insulted Captain
McAlister's wife. Exiled at the same time was J. G. M. Ramsey's youngest daughter, Susan, who defied the assistant provost marshal in asserting her "right" to
visit her sister at Lenoir's Junction without a pass. When told that she would
have to sign a loyalty oath if she wished to travel freely in and out of town, the
sixteen-year-old secessionist protested. "I owe allegiance only to Tennessee and
the Southern Confederacy," she informed the Yankee major—and then left town
without his permission. Immediately arrested and ordered out, she soon joined
the household of her uncle and fellow refugee, John H. Crozier, then living in
southwestern Virginia.[22]

Years later, old Dr. Ramsey still bitterly resented the treatment of his daughter. At the time of her exile, he himself was a refugee in Atlanta and only learned
of her banishment after the fact, via telegram. While proudly acknowledging that
Susan was "enthusiastic for the Southern cause," Ramsey lampooned the Yankee paranoia that had transformed his "little Rebel" into a Joan of Arc ready to
lead an uprising against Federal authority. The "genteel and refined" members
of Knoxville society rightly saw such charges as "puerile and ridiculous." The real
cause of the Yankees' "war against women," the doctor contended, was that the
town's Confederate belles spurned the attentions of Union officers. How could
they have done otherwise? "Southern ladies" were "aristocratic" in the fullest sense
of the word, Ramsey noted. They cherished integrity, high-souled honor, and a
cultivated intellect. The Yankee officers, in stark contrast, were "low and vulgar,"

knowing nothing of the "manly virtues" that distinguished the chivalrous southerner. Not only were they "enemies of enlightened liberty" and "the tools of tyrants"—worse yet, they were ill-mannered. In her father's opinion, Susan Ramsey's only real "crime" was that she preferred to associate with "gentlemen."[23]

Parson Brownlow never had the opportunity to read Ramsey's memoirs, but he would not have been surprised by the doctor's defense of his daughter. In the first issue of the *Whig* after his return from exile, Brownlow observed that a certain class of women insisted on maintaining that, whatever the loyalties of the masses, "all the *respectable* ladies are Secessionists, and do not sympathize with the low-flung Unionists." For Brownlow—who proudly identified with the "low-flung Unionists"—one of the glorious consequences of Union victory would be the humiliation of such arrogant traitors. "Thanks to God," he gloated in a tribute to "Our Poor Women," when the war is over "the scornful, proud and bitter rebel woman will find herself upon a level with the poor Union woman, without a gang of negroes at her command." Although the condescending "*Slaveocracy*" had long "pointed the finger of scorn against the virtuous laboring woman," the day was not far distant when "it will not be a disgrace to labor" and "the rich and poor, the loyal and disloyal" will compete on terms of equality.[24]

As THESE PASSAGES SUGGEST, even though President Lincoln had excluded the state from his Emancipation Proclamation, by the end of 1863 Parson Brownlow could take for granted that slavery in East Tennessee was doomed to be a casualty of the war. For Brownlow, the irony of it all was delicious. Slavery had been absolutely secure under the Constitution, but secessionist leaders had consciously fomented fears concerning its security in order to undermine democracy and further magnify the power of plantation-owning nabobs. For years they had claimed that the election of a Republican president would be the death of slavery, and in a sense they had been correct. "Wherever the Federal Army goes," he observed without a hint of regret, "the negroes walk off from their owners and claim to be free."[25]

In truth, the Army of the Ohio had liberated not only white Unionists when it marched into Knoxville. Just as surely it had also emancipated Knoxville's slaves, regardless of what Lincoln might proclaim from his desk in Washington. The end came gradually, but the beginning of the end came immediately. The first sign was a change in attitude among those held in bondage. Local slave owners noticed it right away. Many of their "servants" were discarding traditional masks of deference, becoming bolder, more assertive, sometimes more menacing. Within three days of Burnside's arrival, Mrs. Sophronia Strong "was worried almost to death" by the behavior of her slaves. Six days later one of her male slaves threatened to shoot her. Initially, Ellen House praised the behavior of the two slaves now in her household—"if left to themselves"—but acknowledged that they might be "enticed off." Only ten days into the Federal occupation, however, she ruefully conceded "that the negroes are getting pretty high." About this time, Mary McPherson's cook became "so impudent" that she had to send her away. J. G. M. Ramsey's coachman continued to serve the doctor's wife and daughter dutifully, but even this "faithful" slave now openly sympathized with the Union.[26]

Such ingratitude must have come as a rude shock to local whites who had viewed the slaves among them as "happy and contented." During the period of Confederate occupation, local slaves had not dared to show open support for the Union. Long afterward Anthony Humes, former slave of the Reverend Thomas Humes and a preacher himself, recalled how the slaves "used to have secret meetings and pray for the Union army and Lincoln." When he expressed as much in a public sermon, however, the Confederate authorities quickly put an end to his preaching. Similarly, Isaac Gammon's master whipped him when he overheard him discussing the whereabouts of the Union army. Gammon claimed that his owner punctuated the punishment with another threat, namely, "if he thought I was Union he would take me to the wood pile & chop my head off." The advent of Federal troops eliminated this environment of fear, and those who had for so long concealed their true sympathies could now begin to act on them. In so doing, they revealed the truth of former slave Chesley Jarnigan's recollection that "there were mighty few colored men" who were not longing for the arrival of the Yankees. This was so, former slave Titus Robinson explained matter-of-factly, because they were "in favor . . . of being free."[27]

But did the Army of the Ohio favor the same thing? The majority of Union soldiers in the American Civil War did not champion emancipation on moral grounds. Even so, a small fraction did enlist in the service as principled opponents of slavery, and a far larger proportion gradually became "practical abolitionists" who favored the liberation of slaves as a tangible means of weakening and punishing the Confederacy.[28] Overall, the soldiers who marched into Knoxville with Ambrose Burnside probably mirrored this larger pattern, although we cannot know for sure. Some held truly "radical" views, at least in the opinion of the local whites whom they offended. Young Mattie Luttrell was repulsed by one of the officers on General Carter's staff, who "made himself very obnoxious in talking of 'Negro Social Equality.'" In like manner, Ellen House came to loathe General James Shackleford, a brigade commander in the Ninth Corps. "It is perfectly disgusting to see a man touch his hat to every negro he meets as he does," she fumed. In contrast, some Yankees were repulsed by the slaves whom they encountered. Staff officer Daniel Larned, for instance, wrote his sister that he was appalled by "such niggers as we see here" and described them as "stupid & lazy." A few Union officers even held slaves themselves, for example, Horace Maynard's son Edward, now a lieutenant colonel in the Sixth Tennessee Infantry (U.S.A.). The younger Maynard kept two slaves with him while in the service. Jerry and Ben were both faithful "boys," he explained in a letter to his brother at the U.S. Naval Academy, and he did not know how he could get along without them.[29]

Whatever their views on slavery in the abstract, the Federals in Knoxville enjoyed the sport of antagonizing local Rebels through their treatment of blacks. Union soldiers told "Old Buck," the slave of Mrs. W. C. Kain, "that they would not be satisfied till they had him waiting on them," rather than his Rebel mistress. She no longer owned anything, they maintained, and must in future do her own work. An aide to General Burnside knocked on the door of Margaret Ramsey and ordered a favored slave to leave her owner and cook for the general. When the slave declined, the officer rebuked her in front of her mistress "for preferring to live as the slave of rebels when she was really free." When Thomas Humes refused to renew their lease and the House family was forced to look for other lodgings, Federal officers agreed to allow them to occupy a vacant house, but only if they were willing to share it with "several negro women & children" already squatting there. They were "good girls," a Yankee captain explained, and he would not turn them out to accommodate a family of secessionists. Similarly, when Confederate Nathan Gammon took steps to evict a black woman from one of his properties, he was told by a Union soldier that she was "under the protection of military authorities." Finally, in a move calculated to humiliate recipients, Federal officers sometimes assigned "insolent negroes" the task of doling out rations to indigent whites. To local Confederates, it appeared that the Union army was determined to shift the bottom rail to the top.[30]

Officially, at least, this was never the case; the army's overall policy toward local slaves was chiefly self-interested and pragmatic. Union officers sought to maximize the contribution of "contrabands" to the war effort and minimize their burden on the army's resources. Even so, the army unavoidably undermined slavery by its very presence. All across the Confederacy, the arrival of Union troops in a given neighborhood regularly triggered a wave of runaways toward the Federal lines, each fugitive convinced that freedom and security awaited him there. The same scenario unfolded in and around Knoxville, even though the legal context was technically different due to Tennessee's exclusion from the Emancipation Proclamation. In practice, the distinction proved to be meaningless because Federal officers were still bound by a new article in the U.S. military code of conduct (amended by Congress in March 1862) that forbade them from returning fugitive slaves to their masters.[31]

Slaves began running away almost as soon as the Army of the Ohio marched into Knoxville. Those already living in town often left their masters to unite with loved ones. Mrs. Frank Ramsey's house slave abandoned her mistress to marry a local free black man. Slave William Bradley walked away from his owner and went to live with his free black wife on a farm outside of town. More commonly, slaves living in the surrounding countryside flocked into town. Hungry and homeless, they sought food, jobs, and protection from their owners. In the early days of the occupation, Federal authorities considered their presence a nuisance, but as it became clear that Burnside would not soon be heading toward Chattanooga to reinforce Rosecrans, their value to the Union army grew significantly.[32] Military authorities increasingly impressed local slaves as laborers, prompting others to offer their service voluntarily when it became evident that they would not be turned away. They worked in a variety of capacities: Anderson Moffitt left his master's farm a mile west of Fort Sanders to "wait on" Union officers in Knoxville. Isaac Gammon ignored his master's threats and got a Union friend to tell the Yankee soldiers that he wanted to work for them; in short order a Union detail came to his house and "impressed" him into the service of the Commissary Department. Titus Robinson left his owner, Unionist John Williams, and went to work building breastworks for the defense of the town. According to the estimate of General Burnside's chief engineer, he was one of at least two hundred "contrabands" who did so. Finally, many local slaves ran away to enlist in the Federal army. Jake Luttrell, for example, had the pleasure of marching past his owner's house as part of a column of black soldiers, stopping to greet his master's three-year-old daughter when she recognized the family's "dining-room boy." Times were changing.[33]

How many Knoxville slaves and free blacks ultimately entered the Federal service is unknown. Through the end of 1863 the demand for black laborers was so great that Federal officers in Knoxville recommended against establishing a recruiting office for black soldiers there. Burnside's successor, General Foster, justified this position by noting in mid-December that already there were "not enough negroes in Knoxville to drive the teams and do the work about the city which is assigned to them." The army's official policy changed within a month, however. The near completion of the town's defenses significantly reduced the demand for slave laborers, and by early January the *Whig* was complaining of "the idle and pilfering gangs of rebel slaves loafing about town." Evidence that James Longstreet intended to leave Knoxville alone also meant that much of the town's Federal garrison would be freed up to join the spring offensive under General William Sherman in Georgia, further reducing the need for black workers. By mid-January the army had officially reversed its position on black recruitment. In his "General Order no. 6," General Foster announced that all "able-bodied colored men" between eighteen and forty-five were to report to headquarters to be enrolled in a regiment of heavy artillery soon to be formed as part of the U.S. Colored Troops. The only exceptions to this compulsory draft were black men already employed in civilian capacities by the army and the slaves of Unionists who "preferred" to stay with their masters.[34]

The Union army's new policy was wholly pragmatic, applying only to those slaves considered of value to the military. Less than a week later, for instance, Federal authorities gave the notorious Confederate Joseph Mabry written authorization to reclaim any of his "female slaves, or children *under fifteen* years of age wherever they may be found." In its effect on local secessionists, Foster's order could be defended as justified by the Second Confiscation Act passed by Congress in the summer of 1862, which authorized the confiscation of all slaves owned by masters who supported the rebellion. In its effect on Unionist masters, on the other hand, the edict was probably of dubious legality. The *Whig* endorsed it nonetheless, along with "the employment of every agency this side of hell" that promised to contribute to Union victory.[35]

Whatever their numbers, nothing more vividly testified to the death of slavery than the sight of former slaves in blue uniforms. Parson Brownlow hammered home the fact at an outdoor rally later in the spring. As Oliver Temple was addressing the crowd on the subject of emancipation, the Parson spied a squad of the First U.S. Colored Artillery passing along the outskirts of the gathering and shouted out, "There is the local institution now!" The audience turned to behold a traveling exhibit of the consequences of Union victory—consequences that went well beyond the collapse of slavery and pointed, potentially at least, toward a radically new relationship between the races. As the famous black abolitionist Frederick Douglass put it, "Once let the black man get upon his person the brass letters, U.S.; let him get an eagle on his button, and a musket on his shoulder and bullets in his pocket, and there is no power on earth which can deny that he has earned the right to citizenship." Citizenship might have to wait, but in the short term black soldiers often asserted themselves in ways that deeply offended white sensibilities, starting with their demand for an equal place on the sidewalk. Parson Brownlow complained of "ill-bred soldiers and insolent negroes" elbowing civilians into the streets and viewed that as part of a larger failure of the Federal authorities to make both "white folks and negroes . . . know their places."[36]

The editor's dissatisfaction with the military authorities reached a head in the spring of 1864, when the U.S. Treasury Department—which Brownlow now served as "assistant special agent"—ordered him to investigate charges that had been lodged against a local employee, William Heiskell, for "inhumane treatment of a boy claimed as his slave." Approximately seventy years of age, William Heiskell was the younger brother of prominent Unionist Frederick Heiskell. He had moved to Knoxville from a nearby county during the war, and Brownlow had appointed him as his assistant shortly after he returned to town. Toward the end of March, one of Heiskell's slaves, thirteen-year-old Jim, filed a complaint before the army post commander in which he claimed that his owner had kidnapped and beaten him. According to his statement, after Burnside's arrival Jim had run away from Heiskell and hired out as a waiter for the officers' mess in the Union quartermaster's office. Heiskell's overseer had caught him, unfortunately, and had taken him to his master's home on Cumberland Street. There, according to Jim, William Heiskell and the overseer had clamped irons on his legs, thrown him down, and whipped him for what seemed like half an hour. That night Jim's older brother, Bob—who had also been working for the army—helped him sneak out of an upstairs window, and after evading a number of shots from the overseer, the older brother carried his manacled and bleeding sibling to safety. Although Jim found a temporary hiding place, his rescuer was soon arrested by Union soldiers and thrown in jail.[37]

Unfortunately for Heiskell (and for the reputation of Knoxville Unionists generally), a special correspondent for the *New York Daily Tribune* caught wind of the story and submitted the details as he understood them to the most widely circulated newspaper in the United States. On 9 April a *Tribune* headline screamed: "Knoxville the Scene of a Disgraceful Slave Hunt—United States Officers Implicated." Readers learned that an employee of the Treasury Department—a prominent Unionist and an associate of the famous Parson Brownlow—had dragged a young slave by the hair of his head, stripped him naked, and then "applied a rawhide to the naked flesh of the prostrate lad." Sympathetic gentlemen who visited Jim after his escape "saw the scarred back, face, and head of the poor little slave, with the partially detached irons still clinging to his ankle— a fitting emblem of the only half-broken chain which . . . still holds the slave in a hateful servitude in Tennessee."[38]

Jim's statement was "a batch of falsehoods from beginning to ending," the Parson declared to his superior in Washington, and wrongly impugned the honor of "as loyal a man as lives in East Tennessee." Far from the monster the *Tribune* described, William Heiskell "was notorious for his kind treatment of his slaves." Jim deserved punishment for his "insolent conduct," and Heiskell had responded with restraint, chastising him "in moderation." If not for Jim's troublemaking brother the matter would have ended right there. Bob, however, had been carrying a revolver about the streets of Knoxville, threatening his master and cursing his mistress as "a damned old freckle-faced bitch." Brownlow included in his report a statement from Provost Marshal General Carter, who explained that he had ordered Bob's arrest after hearing of his threats against William Heiskell, not to punish him for assisting his brother to run away. After confirming Carter's account, Brownlow concluded by blaming "the bad conduct of some of our Federal officers and soldiers" in exacerbating relations between the races. At least two white Union soldiers had married "negro wenches," he pointed out. A black soldier had recently killed a white soldier from a Michigan regiment, "the pistol having been handed to him by a Northern officer to do so!" Finally, black women "of notoriously bad character" were cruising the streets, and the Federal authorities were doing nothing about it; indeed, there was a colored "house of ill fame" operating in the basement of the Baptist church. The situation was rapidly becoming intolerable.[39]

The two accounts of the episode could not have differed more starkly, and without corroborating testimony it is impossible to determine which is more truthful. Even so, two points are obvious: Knoxville's slaves were becoming more and more assertive, whether by slipping away from their owners or by threatening them with bodily harm, and it was the presence of Union troops that was emboldening them to do so. The resolution of Jim's complaint underscored the army's disruptive influence. Four days after Jim's alleged kidnapping, the Army of the Ohio's new commander intervened in the affair. Major General John Schofield ordered the provost marshal general to intercede immediately on behalf of the two slaves, and soon thereafter General Carter dispatched a guard to bring both of Heiskell's slaves to his office. There Jim and Bob each received papers stating that he was "hereby declared free from the control of his late master" and was now "under the protection of the United States Government." The Army of the Ohio was liberating the slaves of loyalists.[40]

Neither Heiskell nor Brownlow could have been pleased with how the incident was resolved. Heiskell professed to be willing "to give up all he had to put down the rebellion" but drew the line at submitting to threats from impudent blacks. Brownlow continued to defend his assistant and to call attention to the obnoxious behavior of supposedly demoralized former slaves. Freed slaves were "lazy and profligate . . . thriftless for the present and recklessly improvident for the future." As a result, the editor predicted, their condition on average "will be worse than it had been during their servitude." And yet "we are for emancipating every negro in the South," the Parson declared defiantly. "A man with one eye, and a sorry one at that, can see that this rebellion is obliged to work out the overthrow of slavery." It was the "nigger question" that had brought on the war, and that question must be resolved forever to bring it to a victorious conclusion. It was unfortunate that loyal slaveholders must suffer along with the guilty, but the war had unleashed forces beyond anyone's control. "The hundreds of thousands who have gone to their graves on account of slavery; the oceans of blood that have been spilt, and the millions of treasure that have been expended to perpetuate slavery, have destroyed the institution, and the man is dull who does not see that it will go by the board in Tennessee as well as in all other states."[41]

A DIVISION HAD BEEN emerging among the ranks of leading Knoxville loyalists ever since Parson Brownlow and Horace Maynard had returned from exile. The schism partly reflected differences in conviction and temperament, but differing experiences over the last two years were surely instrumental as well. Oliver Temple would recall years later that the rift among Unionists pitted those who had stayed at home during the war against "a new set of men who to a large extent belonged to the army, and who had imbibed by suffering and persecution, feelings quite unlike those of the men who had neither suffered nor entered the army." Undoubtedly, military service had converted thousands of East Tennessee Unionists to a pragmatic support for emancipation. In early 1863 some ten thousand East Tennesseans in the Army of the Cumberland had endorsed a resolution supporting the Emancipation Proclamation as a measure calculated to force the Rebels to "throw down their arms without condition." Concerned about opposition to the policy among Unionists on the home front, an officer in the

First Brigade East Tennessee Volunteers (U.S.A.) wrote to the *Whig* a year later to denounce the "dangerous and hateful" doctrine that slavery must be protected or the Union was not worth preserving. In a similar vein, soldiers from the Third and Sixth Tennessee Volunteers (U.S.A.) publicly denounced all who "would rather have the negro without the Union than the Union without the negro."[42]

Neither Brownlow nor Maynard had entered the military, of course, but each had two sons who had enlisted in the Federal service, and both personally identified with the thousands of fellow East Tennesseans who had left home and hearth rather than be drafted into the Rebel army. Banished from their homes, separated from their families, deprived of property, wrenched from their professions—in their mind's eye they had been as sorely injured by Confederate oppression as any of their compatriots in uniform. And like the majority of those in the military, their experience of persecution and hardship had gradually "radicalized" both men. They had left Knoxville as conservative proslavery Unionists, detesting abolitionists and Fire-Eaters with the same heartfelt revulsion. They had returned as radicals, clamoring for revenge against secessionists, advocating emancipation, and defending Abraham Lincoln. The Unionist leaders with whom they were reunited had undergone no such transformation.

A rift began almost immediately, but it was not until the following spring that it became open and irreparable. The break came in April 1864, at a convention of East Tennessee Unionists dominated by stay-at-home conservatives. The previous month the executive committee of the original Knoxville-Greeneville Convention of May–June 1861 had issued a call for that body to reconvene in Knoxville on the third anniversary of the attack on Fort Sumter. The announced purpose of the meeting was to discuss the reorganization of a loyal state government as outlined under President Lincoln's recent "Ten-Percent" proclamation. Issued the previous December, this executive order had authorized federally occupied states within the Confederacy to hold elections for state offices whenever the number of men willing to take the oath of loyalty equaled one-tenth of the prewar voting population. When the meeting convened on 12 April, scarcely one-third of the original delegates were present. Some of the original delegates were now dead, many more were now Confederate sympathizers and not welcome, while many others were Unionists away in the Federal army. In the end some 160 delegates, representing twenty-three counties, gathered in the Knox County Courthouse and deliberated for four days. Their proceedings are mostly shrouded in mystery. Neither Thomas Humes nor Oliver Temple discussed the meeting in histories they wrote after the war, and Brownlow afforded it surprisingly little coverage in the *Whig*, perhaps because it would have weakened the case for Tennessee's rapid readmission to the Union to do so.[43]

The seriousness of the division among the assembly is undeniable, however. Conflict erupted immediately when one of the delegates introduced a motion that only loyal men be allowed to serve in the convention, obviously implying that some of the delegates failed to meet that test. After a protracted debate—in which John Baxter's wartime record was evidently discussed at length—the assembly tabled the proposal by a close vote. The delegates then foundered on the even more intractable question of emancipation. At stake was whether the convention would endorse President Lincoln's Ten-Percent Plan, thus paving the way for the rapid formation of a new loyal state government. The sticking point was that Lincoln's recent proclamation had required Unionists not only to support the U.S. Constitution but also to "abide by and faithfully support all proclamations of the President made during the existing rebellion having reference to slaves." As Lincoln had redefined it, in other words, "loyalty" now included support for emancipation, and proslavery Unionists who objected would be barred from voting in any election for a new state government. The delegates were irreconcilably divided over whether to accept the president's plan, which many understandably found insulting—"you must be a Radical Black Republican, or you are not a Union man," one protested—and after a protracted debate they adjourned without agreeing on a response.[44]

Before doing so, they issued two competing sets of resolutions that foreshadowed a division in the impending presidential campaign. The minority, led by Brownlow, declared their unqualified support for "immediate and unconditional emancipation," "fully endorse[d]" the arming of black soldiers, and called for Lincoln's reelection. The majority—following the lead of Baxter, Thomas Nelson, and Frederick Heiskell, among others—condemned emancipation and effectively repudiated Lincoln's Ten-Percent Plan. They opposed any form of property confiscation as certain to "complicate, increase, and prolong indefinitely the troubles of our unhappy country." Southerners should be required to swear their loyalty to the Constitution and to the Constitution alone. It was the duty of the government to punish treason, they acknowledged, but beyond that it must not go. Finally, in a series of resolutions aimed squarely at the Parson, the majority called for "magnanimity and forbearance" toward Rebels and condemned the use of "derogatory language towards . . . our erring countrymen."[45]

The convention's majority couched their resistance to emancipation largely in pragmatic terms—it was an imprudent policy designed to increase Confederate resolve and thus postpone Union victory—but behind the scenes opponents were often bitterly resentful. Two weeks afterward, Mrs. John Williams, whose conservative Unionist husband was one of the convention's vice presidents, wrote to her son that "a great many of our friends here" had deeply disappointed her. She refused to believe that there was any honorable argument for emancipation. "I don't hesitate in saying that any man born and raised in the South that will embrace abolitionism now at this late day, is not actuated by his honest convictions of right[,] but when you come to sift him you will find that he is after place and power. . . . I do not care a cent about the value of the negroes," she assured her son. "It is the principle I look at and object to." As the months passed her animosity grew. Although as firmly opposed to secession as ever, she confessed to "utterly loathe and abhor this diabolical heresy of abolitionism," and she warned her son not "to engage in any way with this unholy war." Old Frederick Heiskell similarly denounced both emancipation and its primary defender in East Tennessee. Reflecting afterward, he damned Brownlow as a wanton opportunist and viewed him "with contempt and scorn." Penniless when banished to the North, the shameless Parson had "sold his books and his soul (if he had any soul) to the abolitionists . . . and filled his pockets with greenbacks." Upon his return he had garnered support primarily from unscrupulous "cowards" and "lick spittles" willing to do any "dirty work their dirty master commanded them."[46]

For all their passion, the Unionist delegates who rejected President Lincoln's Ten-Percent Plan were stubbornly refusing to acknowledge that three years of bloody civil war had dramatically altered the political, military, and social terrain. Rejecting Brownlow's contention that it was the *secessionists* "who had struck the shackles from your slaves," they blamed emancipation on "Black Republicanism" and insisted that the only honorable position was the proslavery, pro-Union stance that they had staked out in 1861. More bewildering still, they seemed willfully blind to the indisputable fact that slavery was visibly collapsing around them. Perhaps they yet hoped to negotiate some sort of federal compensation for loyal owners, or perhaps, as Rhoda Williams put it, it was simply "the principle" that they looked at and objected to. Whatever the case, their intransigence put them in an awkward place politically. Overwhelmingly Whigs (or Constitutional Unionists) before the war, they had taken a stance on union and slavery identified primarily with northern Democrats. To complicate matters further, at their national convention in Chicago that August, Democratic delegates nominated a "War Democrat" for president—Union general George McClellan—but allowed the "Peace Democrats" (or "Copperheads") to insert an antiwar plank into the party's platform. Condemning the past "four years of failure to restore the Union by the experiment of war," the plank called for an immediate cease-fire followed by negotiations with the Confederate states in an attempt to restore the Union. When McClellan seemed to repudiate the plank, however, Knoxville's anti-emancipation Unionists were ready to embrace him, and most of their leaders—including Baxter, Fred Heiskell, and John Williams—came out openly as McClellan Democrats. Indeed, Williams declared publicly that the Democrats could defeat Lincoln with the devil on the ticket. Equally confident, his wife, Rhoda, had "no doubt" that McClellan would be elected. The result would be a godsend, she explained to her son. "I think our Nations Salvation depends on his election."[47]

Ruefully, Parson Brownlow conceded that such sentiments were now common among Knoxville's Unionist elite. In a letter to Andrew Johnson marked "private," he confided, "The truth is, the Rebels and those in sympathy with them, bear sway here." The good news was that "the *People* are right." Referring to the common folk across East Tennessee, Brownlow was convinced that, when given the opportunity, they would "sustain us at the ballot box, against these copper-head leaders."[48] His task was to make sure that they did so. Having suffered a temporary setback in the Knoxville Convention, Brownlow and the pro-emancipation faction went on the offensive immediately, attacking their Union-ist opponents at a mass meeting on the day after the convention adjourned. Speaking to a large audience from the corner of Gay and Main streets, the Par-son opened the meeting with a "forcible speech" and then introduced a series of resolutions authored (anonymously) by military governor Andrew Johnson. Echo-ing the minority report of the day before, they applauded President Lincoln's war policy and called for a constitutional convention for the purpose of abolishing slavery in Tennessee. The latter institution "was incompatible with the perpetu-ity of free and republican institutions," and "as it has now been strangled in the house of its own friends," no effort need be made to resurrect it. Lest the pre-dominantly white audience be concerned, the resolutions concluded by asserting that both the federal and state governments "*are the Governments of the free white man*, and to be controlled and administered by him." Speaking in support of the resolutions were Oliver Temple, a late convert to emancipation, and Governor Johnson, who had traveled to Knoxville from the state capital in Nashville to attend the convention. "This thing called Slavery is lying dead; we can't hold on to it any longer," Johnson declared. "It only remains for you to legalize freedom." According to a sympathetic correspondent to the *New York Tribune*, when Brownlow put the resolutions to a vote, "there was one long and unanimous 'Yea' from the assembled multitude. . . . It was a triumph for Freedom in Tennessee."[49]

Shortly thereafter, Brownlow and Horace Maynard helped to form a state executive committee for the National Union Party, the label that Republicans had chosen to employ in the upcoming national elections. Both were named delegates to the party's national convention in Baltimore that June, and both proudly en-dorsed the ticket of Abraham Lincoln and native son Andrew Johnson.[50] In the months following, Brownlow mounted a relentless attack in the *Whig* against Knoxville's McClellan Democrats. First, he stressed that the vast majority of loyal East Tennesseans did not share their hypersensitive concern for the fate of slav-ery. Employing an antislavery populism that was becoming second nature, he observed that nine-tenths of local Unionists had never owned slaves in the first place. These "long abused masses" knew full well that they had suffered only "to benefit a few aristocrats in the towns and villages who own slaves." If "the negro is troubling a class of Union men among us much more than the rebellion is," then the "rabble" of East Tennessee would show them how to vote in the im-pending election.[51] Second, the editor repeatedly linked the Unionists who clung to slavery with northern Copperheads, villains who were just as guilty of trea-son as the most rabid secessionist. Not *all* Democrats were traitors, he acknowl-edged, but the Chicago Convention had been dominated by them. Its platform "ignominiously and wickedly betrays to our common enemy the sacred cause for which we have now fought for the last four heroic years," and any man who would support their ticket must secretly prefer Jeff Davis to Abraham Lincoln. In sum, every vote for McClellan was a vote for the rebellion; Lincoln's defeat would mean the establishment of the southern Confederacy. The fate of the country hung in the balance.[52]

These were powerful rhetorical arguments, but the radical faction's most potent weapons were its allies in Nashville and Washington. From Nashville, Governor Johnson issued a proclamation that effectively prohibited McClellan supporters from voting. Responding to a call from a state Union convention held in early September, Johnson specified that all voters in the upcoming election must swear not only that they "ardently desire[d] the suppression of the present rebellion" but that they also "cordially oppose[d] all armistices or negotiations for peace with rebels in arms, until the Constitution of the United States and all laws *and proclamations* made in pursuance thereof, shall be established over all the people of every State." In essence, any loyal white male could vote—once he had pledged to support emancipation and repudiate the platform of the Democratic Party.[53]

Understandably incensed, the state's McClellan Democrats protested to Washington, but they found that Johnson's running mate was decidedly unsympathetic. In a petition to President Lincoln, the state's ten McClellan electors (including John Williams and Thomas Nelson) condemned the prescribed test oath as "irrelevant, unreasonable, and not in any sense a test of loyalty." Passing over the requirement to endorse emancipation, which they also detested, they focused instead on the stipulated opposition to an armistice or negotiations. "As Christians, as patriots, and as civilized men," they were duty bound to support any initiative that might bring the war more rapidly to an "honorable and lawful conclusion." Ignoring the fact that there was no functioning state government, they attacked on principle Johnson's interference "with the freedom of the elective franchise in Tennessee" and demanded that Lincoln revoke the governor's proclamation. For his part, Lincoln conveniently ignored that he had appointed Johnson and maintained that under the Constitution the executive had "no duty in the conduct of a presidential election in any State." In a model of disingenuousness, he reminded his petitioners that no one was actually being forced to subscribe to Johnson's test oath (unless they actually wanted to vote). "Except . . . to give protection against violence," Lincoln concluded, "I decline to interfere in any way." It paid to have friends in high places.[54]

Having appealed in vain to the president, the petitioners announced that they were withdrawing the McClellan electoral ticket across the state, and when election day came, only Abraham Lincoln's name appeared on the ballot in Tennessee. In Knoxville all 943 votes cast went for the candidate whose election the residents of Knoxville had viewed as a calamity only four years earlier. In terms of national import, the significance of Johnson's test oath was nil. Given that

Tennessee lacked a functioning civil government, the chance of the state's electoral vote actually being accepted had always been slim, and in the end Congress refused to do so. It certainly did not affect the outcome. As late as August, Abraham Lincoln had assumed that he would be defeated at the polls, but a string of major Union military victories in late summer and early fall—at Mobile Bay, Atlanta, and in the Shenandoah Valley—had dramatically reversed his political momentum and resulted in a lopsided victory, not just for Lincoln but for Republican candidates generally across the North.[55]

The election had more tangible consequences close to home. First, it intensified the division among Unionists, infuriating McClellan supporters who were convinced—without evidence—that they would have won in a fair fight. Lincoln's purpose was "to crush the South and make us all slaves," Rhoda Williams observed bitterly the week after the election. Because "the southern people will never come to any terms with Lincoln," his reelection had destroyed all "hope of peace for at least four long years."[56] Second, the Republican victory effectively assured the legal demise of slavery in Tennessee as elsewhere across the Confederacy. With Lincoln's urging, the Republican-dominated Congress would immediately reconsider a constitutional amendment to abolish slavery throughout the land. Parson Brownlow welcomed that prospect. "It was the *nigger question* that brought on this infernal war," Brownlow reminded his readers yet again. It was the slave owners who "got up all this row because of their niggers," who drove thousands of Union men away from their homes and filled the jails with political prisoners. "Now let us make them sick of it," the Parson blustered:

> Let them howl when their niggers leave them; and let them cry over a violated Constitution, when their niggers are armed and dressed in the Federal uniform. The people, even in East Tennessee, have said at the ballot box, down with slavery, and down with the rebellion, and let us all work for our meat and bread. And the set of men who suppose that they can excite the people to quarrel and vote to save their niggers, have to learn what public sentiment is, and what the people think.[57]

Before a national amendment could be imposed on the state, however, a convention of Unionists gathered in Nashville and proposed an amendment to Tennessee's constitution that would henceforward prohibit all laws "recognizing the right of property in man." On 22 February 1865, loyalists willing to swear Governor Johnson's test oath went to the polls and ratified the amendment by a vote of 25,293 to 48. "The people" had spoken, endorsing emancipation with a vengeance—or, to be more precise, a vengeful emancipation.[58]

CHAPTER EIGHT

Retribution and Reconciliation

We have had wild times here, with rebels. . . . You know they used to say that the Union men and "Southern" men could not live here together, & the former now take them at their word, & send them away rather hurriedly.
—Laura Maynard, 1865[1]

Often the Union soldier and the Confederate soldier settled side by side. . . . They had been neighbors before the war. Each had chosen his side from honest convictions. When they returned they respected each other, and met as old friends.   —Oliver P. Temple, 1899[2]

A MONTH AFTER ABRAHAM LINCOLN'S reelection, two of Knoxville's best-known Rebel refugees sat in the office of the *Bristol Gazette* and contemplated the prospects of returning home. Editor J. A. Sperry and former district attorney Crozier Ramsey had both taken roundabout paths from Knoxville to this small railroad town, situated some 110 miles to the northeast on the Virginia border. Fifteen months earlier they had fled Knoxville for Atlanta, catching a southbound train shortly before the Army of the Ohio marched into town. Neither was ready to abandon "the Cause." Sperry took his printing press with him and continued publishing the *Knoxville Register* in exile, while Ramsey assisted his father (also a refugee in Atlanta) with his duties for the Confederate Treasury Department. After several months the younger Ramsey relocated to Bristol, where he could be nearer to his mother and sisters; Sperry followed not long afterward, driven from Atlanta by the approaching Federal army under William Sherman.[3]

In the autumn of 1864 the Confederate military still held sway in the uppermost reaches of East Tennessee, and both Sperry and Ramsey must have felt reasonably secure in Bristol. Both longed to return to Knoxville, however, and as winter approached they had reason for optimism. In mid-November, Confederate general John C. Breckinridge had led several thousand Rebels in a bold thrust from southern Virginia into East Tennessee. The only sizable Union force in their path was a brigade of inexperienced Tennesseans under General Alvin C. Gillem, and in short order they had driven that unseasoned unit streaming back toward Knoxville. Breckinridge immediately took control of the railroad from Strawberry Plains to Bristol, effectively reestablishing Confederate ascendancy over all of East Tennessee north and east of Knox County. The former vice president of the United States had initiated such a dramatic shift in momentum that Ramsey closed the conversation with Sperry with a prediction and an invitation: "I believe we shall be in Knoxville on Christmas," he informed the editor, "and I venture to invite you to dine with me on a fat turkey on that day."[4]

Ramsey's prediction was on the mark, although the circumstances were rather different from those he had envisioned. Immediately after Gillem's defeat, Union general George Stoneman, commander of the Department of the Ohio, had traveled to Knoxville to reorganize and refit Gillem's brigade. Then, in tandem with a force in southern Kentucky under Major General Stephen Burbridge, he had directed a coordinated counterattack that drove Breckinridge all the way into North Carolina in less than a week. Unbeknownst to them, on the very day that Sperry and Ramsey were planning their Christmas meal in Knoxville—13 December—Burbridge's cavalry was less than a day's ride from Bristol, and before dawn the following morning they had surprised the small Rebel garrison there, in the process cutting off any chance of escape for the unsuspecting refugees. Within another twenty-four hours Sperry and Ramsey, along with another civilian from Knoxville, Robert Fox, were part of a column of prisoners of the U.S. government tramping through the snow en route to a reunion with their former neighbors.[5]

It was not a joyful homecoming. Arriving in Knoxville on the twenty-first, the unhappy trio spent the first seventy-two hours in the county jail, now being used for the temporary incarceration of Confederate prisoners of war. Fox was particularly familiar with their new surroundings, inasmuch as he had been the jailer in charge of the facility during the period of Confederate occupation. Then on Christmas Eve, when more than 150 captured Confederate soldiers were marched to the train depot for the trip north to a federal prison, the three civilians were instead transferred under guard to the old Temperance Hall, which now served as a jail for political prisoners and Union soldiers charged with petty crimes. On Christmas morning they feasted not on turkey but on an ounce of boiled beef and half a hardtack biscuit. They then concluded their holiday by trying on a new gift from Uncle Sam: a twelve-pound ball and chain to wear while working on the town's fortifications.[6]

Predictably, Confederate officials were incensed. Generals Breckinridge and J. C. Vaughn both lodged formal complaints, with Vaughn assuring the Union provost marshal general that he would "arrest man for man one Union citizen for every Southern man arrested on your side." From Richmond, Knoxville's Confederate congressman William Swan made strenuous efforts to effect their release, his "blood boil[ing]" from reports that the three prisoners were marched with ball and chain "thro the streets of Knoxville to be hooted at." Less predictably, a number of local Unionists shared his consternation. Admittedly, *Brownlow's Knoxville Whig and Rebel Ventilator* applauded the policy, and yet when the three prisoners were at last turned over to the Federal district court, other local Unionists led the way in pleading for their release and posting bond for their good behavior.[7]

In sum, the capture of Sperry, Ramsey, and Fox forced the people of Knoxville to confront the second major question raised by Federal military success in East Tennessee. The first, which concerned the local fate of slavery, had arisen the moment the Army of the Ohio marched into town and began to undermine the institution. The second, which concerned the future of Knoxville's leading Confederates, had also emerged immediately but had remained somewhat hypothetical, in part because the outcome of the war seemed in doubt, but primarily because the town's leading Rebels had largely disappeared. Now this seemed to be changing. Rhetorically, the debate of the matter revolved around irreconcilable abstractions—justice and mercy, retribution and reconciliation—but at bottom the issues were pragmatic and the stakes were high. The treatment of leading secessionists would go a long way toward shaping the political and social consequences of Union victory.

ONLY ONE POLICY was acceptable in Parson Brownlow's opinion—swift and severe retribution. From the moment that he returned from exile, the editor had been calling for the heads of the town's original secessionist clique. Shortly after the siege of Knoxville he enumerated the secessionist ringleaders by name—Sneed, Swan, Crozier, Charlton, Sperry, "and others too tedious to mention"—and proclaimed that they should never again be allowed to return to East Tennessee. "Indeed," the reverend declared, "we regard Union men who have suffered at their hands, and because of their counsels, as justified in shooting them down on sight. . . . Let such imps of Hell die the deaths of traitors," he thundered, "and upon the shortest possible notice." The editor held to this position throughout the remainder of the war. "Shoot them down like dogs," he pithily recommended early in 1865. A few months later he added an eternal dimension to their sentence: "Let them be slain," he thundered, "and after slain, let them be damned." Whether the Parson was truly this bloodthirsty, or whether his bloodcurdling rhetoric was calculated for effect, he was clear about one thing: the secessionist "chivalry" must not be allowed to dominate postwar Knoxville.[8]

Nor should their misguided followers escape the consequences of treason. In his more magnanimous moments, Brownlow differentiated between the aristocrats who had actively fomented secession and the "deluded masses" who had sustained them. Provided that they repented of their sins, the common folk might be treated with charity, whereas "the halter should be summoned to do its appropriate work among the leaders." As early as January 1864, however, he was calling for retribution against everyone who had voted for "separation and representation" back in 1861. "Let them have separation," he thundered, separation from their "lands, houses, rails, timbers, corn, stock, negroes [*sic*], and all! And as to *representation*," the editor went on, warming to his task, "let them be represented in every grave yard South, and every prison North, and finally in *Hell*, where they are bound to have a large representation, and even have it *now*!" If the rank and file were spared the gallows, they should count their blessings and "be content to *breathe* in this country." In sum, support for secession was treason pure and simple, and any traitor who escaped the hangman's noose should count his blessings.[9]

The Parson failed to gun down even a single "imp of Hell," but as a newly appointed "assistant special agent of the Treasury Department," he had both the authority and the inclination to separate traitors from their possessions. Indeed, one of his primary responsibilities, tailor-made for a man bent on punishing rebellion, was to "receive and collect all abandoned or captured property" of disloyal persons throughout East Tennessee. Not one to shirk his duty, Special Agent Brownlow immediately began to initiate confiscation proceedings against prominent Knoxville Confederates who had fled town; by the end of the summer of 1864 he had already confiscated the property of at least forty. Abandoned real estate (residences, stores, workshops, warehouses) he rented out to loyal tenants until it was certain that legal title could be securely conveyed. Movable property (mattresses, bedsteads, bookcases, carpets) he auctioned off immediately to the highest bidder.[10]

Brownlow also used the courts to wage war against local Rebels. Shortly after first returning to Knoxville, he had filed a lawsuit in the local circuit court, seeking damages of $25,000 from the four Knoxville Confederates whom he deemed most responsible for his imprisonment and subsequent banishment: John Crozier, William Sneed, Robert Reynolds, and Crozier Ramsey. The Parson urged other injured Unionists to follow his lead "until we have bankrupted the last thief and assassin in their ranks." One of Brownlow's bitterest critics later claimed that he was motivated only by avarice; having made a fortune in the North, "he was greedy for more [and] thought he could swindle some absent rebels out of their property." It would be naive to discount the lure of riches entirely, but to emphasize it in Brownlow's case is to miss the depth of his hunger for personal revenge and his determination to punish the Democratic scoundrels who had brought so much suffering upon the land. A lawsuit was one way to satisfy both. The strategy seemed to be working when a jury of loyalists found in his favor early in 1865. When the defendants did not promptly pay up—three were not even present at the trial—the court ordered that their property be auctioned to the highest bidder. Brownlow himself won the bidding on the Reynolds farm. The editor exultantly announced the verdict in the *Whig* and promised that this was "only the beginning of the end. Other suits are on the docket, and others are to come," he noted with grim satisfaction. "Let them be made beggars, going from door to door for their bread. . . . They instructed the Southern mind, and fired the Southern heart. Now, let them feel the consequences of their wicked and rebellious conduct."[11]

Knoxville's loyalists generally did not imitate Brownlow in suing for damages, but they did use the courts to strike at Confederates in other ways. The docket of the Knox County Chancery Court quickly began to fill up with lawsuits against "absconding" debtors. Coincidentally, the defendants were almost always Rebels, either men serving in the army or civilians who had left town rather than live under Yankee occupation. Typically, the Unionist clerk of the court announced all pending suits in the local Unionist newspaper and ordered that the defendants appear in court to answer the charges against them. When to no one's surprise they failed to appear, the Unionist judge (appointed by military governor Andrew Johnson) treated their absence as tantamount to a confession. He then ordered the Unionist sheriff (chosen in an election from which Confederates were excluded) to auction off their property in order to cover the unpaid debts. The process was patently unfair and could be devastatingly effective. Dr. J. G. M. Ramsey, for example, lost a three-story house and town lot on Gay Street valued at $8,000 to $10,000 because of an unpaid debt of $300 owed a local Unionist. A refugee in North Carolina at the time of the trial, Ramsey most certainly did not subscribe to the *Whig and Rebel Ventilator* and was unaware of the suit filed against him. Even had he known of it, he would have been arrested on other charges had he tried to appear.[12]

Dr. Ramsey would have faced arrest because the newly appointed U.S. district attorney, James P. Swan, was aggressively charging local Confederates with treason in the Federal Circuit Court for the Eastern District of Tennessee. When the court reconvened in Knoxville in mid-May 1864, after a hiatus of nearly three years, District Attorney Swan set his sights high. He began by pursuing indictments against twenty-two top Confederate civil and military leaders, including President Jefferson Davis and Generals James Longstreet, Kirby Smith, and Nathan Bedford Forrest. He then turned to notorious Confederates from across East Tennessee, presenting 752 indictments to the grand jury during the spring session alone and ultimately some 2,014 by the spring of 1865. Of these, upwards of seventy-five were from Knoxville. The Knox County Circuit Court got in the act as well, its grand jury approving indictments for treason against some fifty local Confederates. It also levied charges against a number of local Rebels for what amounted to war crimes. J. G. M. Ramsey's son Robert was charged with complicity in the alleged murder of a Union civilian early in the war. J. A. Mabry was indicted as an accomplice in the murder of Charles Douglas back in May 1861, and Reuben Clark, formerly a clerk with Cowan and Dickinson, was charged with "bushwhacking" a Federal officer. Prominent Knoxville attorney Claib Kain was similarly charged with multiple offenses for his role on a Confederate military tribunal in 1862.[13]

Although it discouraged many absent Confederates from returning home soon, in the long run this judicial war accomplished little. Postwar juries proved hesitant to send soldiers to the gallows for alleged crimes on the basis of typically thin evidence. The charges against Ramsey were dropped in 1867, without his ever returning to Knoxville. Less fortunate, Clark and Kain both languished in jail for months while awaiting trial, but both ultimately escaped conviction. Juries were more willing to award damages in civil suits, but litigation in the local courts often dragged on for years, and state or federal courts frequently overturned initial decisions on behalf of plaintiffs years later, after wartime tempers had cooled and political circumstances had changed. In 1868 the state supreme court even reversed the Parson's lucrative victory over Reynolds et al. Long after the war, John Bell Brownlow ruefully concluded, with only slight exaggeration, that "loyal men never gained, finally, by these suits."[14]

More discouraging to his father was the abysmal lack of success in the federal court. Parson Brownlow had looked forward to the reopening of the U.S. Circuit Court, and he initially expressed confidence in its newly appointed judge, Knoxville attorney Connally F. Trigg. Originally from Abingdon, Virginia, Trigg had been a relative newcomer to Knoxville before the war, but he had proved himself a stalwart defender of the Union in 1861 before fleeing to the North after the state's separation. He and Brownlow had actually traveled together briefly on the northern lecture circuit in 1862, during which time the Parson had publicly praised him as a man "of great moral and personal courage," and Brownlow later even journeyed to Washington to endorse Trigg's application for a judgeship. When Abraham Lincoln appointed Trigg to the federal district court, Brownlow predicted that East Tennessee Rebels would soon learn "that it is no small matter to engage in an effort to overthrow this government." Trigg disappointed the Parson deeply. Rather than make the traitors howl, in the fall of 1864 the new judge instead began to dismiss treason charges whenever the defendant had taken—or agreed to take—President Lincoln's amnesty oath. In public, Brownlow tried to minimize the effects of such leniency. The traitors really had not gotten off that lightly, he told readers. They had been eaten up by two contending armies and been forced on top of that to pay court costs and lawyers' fees. "In a word, they are pretty well broken up," he observed reassuringly, "and have got their 'southern rights' upon a large and *feeling* scale." In private, Brownlow was far less sanguine. In a letter to Andrew Johnson he informed the governor that "the worst rebels and traitors" were being turned loose. "I think I am not saying any thing more than the loyal people say," he confided, "when I state that it is a *complete farce.*" His contempt only mounted the following spring when Trigg declared unconstitutional a recent act of Congress banning formerly disloyal attorneys from practicing in federal courts.[15]

What disgusted the Parson most was that prominent Unionists seemed to be lining up to help Confederates escape justice. When Union men in the countryside began to seek personal revenge against the Rebels who had persecuted them, many of Knoxville's leading loyalists decried such extralegal violence and blamed the *Whig and Rebel Ventilator* for promoting mob rule with its incendiary rhetoric. When loyal men sought redress through the courts, on the other hand, other so-called Unionists seemingly went out of their way to thwart them. Several Unionist attorneys defended Confederate clients in court, prompting Brownlow to complain to a correspondent about the "set of Union Lawyers" in Knoxville "whose whole business is to make fees, and to make friends by getting every rascal released." Other prominent loyalists posted bond for Confederates under indictment or attested to the recent "loyalty" of Rebels filing claims against the government. Brownlow railed that these *"pretended* Union men" were helping "to save the lives and the property of the worst men in the country." Their only possible motives, Brownlow concluded, were either fear or greed. Either they expected the Confederate army to reclaim control of the region and hoped to protect themselves when the tables were turned, or else they were being paid for their assistance. "When we find men thus engaged," Brownlow editorialized in February 1865, "we do not attribute it to goodness of heart, but to a *love of money!*"[16]

THE PARSON WAS AIMING his darts squarely at the same conservative Unionists who had broken with him over emancipation. As with that issue, the demand for a severe policy against prominent Confederates had driven a wedge between conservative and radical loyalists. The editor was not exaggerating about the frequency with which prominent Unionists stood up for prominent secessionists. Probably the chief "offender" was the Whig-turned-McClellan Democrat John Williams. The prosperous merchant regularly endorsed petitions for the release of Knoxville Confederates from northern prisons. He put up bail for notorious Rebels like Joseph Mabry and Crozier Ramsey. Finally, as one of the three members of the commission established by General Burnside to adjudicate the damage claims of Unionists, Williams appeared to be helping claimants of dubious loyalty procure compensation for losses from the federal government. Brownlow accused the commission of endorsing the claims of numerous petitioners who had "acted with the rebel party" until Burnside's arrival, including Williams's brother-in-law, hardware merchant John L. Moses. Particularly galling, after Williams and paper manufacturer Gideon Hazen attested to his loyalty, the commission approved the claim of railroad executive John R. Branner—the same individual who had identified himself as a "Southern man" and a "good and true citizen of the Confederacy" while the Rebels controlled Knoxville.[17]

Williams and other leading conservatives also frequently came to the aid of those charged with treason in the federal or state courts. They posted bond for the alleged traitors as they awaited trial, and after the war they regularly endorsed their petitions for an executive pardon. Indeed, the names of those assisting local Confederates in this way constitute a veritable who's who of the town's conservative Unionists: Williams, John Baxter, Abner Jackson, John Fleming, Gideon Hazen, Thomas Nelson, and Fred and William Heiskell, among others. After Judge Trigg made clear his intention to dismiss charges against any alleged traitor willing to take the loyalty oath, they publicly praised Trigg for his "wisdom, discretion, and imminent legal ability" and thanked him for protecting the "interests and integrity of the Government." Privately, Frederick Heiskell assured Trigg that "the true friends of the Union" now dismissed Parson Brownlow as "an unmitigated humbug."[18]

It surely galled Brownlow to hear his former allies claim the moral high ground. He scoffed at efforts to portray Trigg as a fair-minded jurist operating above the fray of wartime passions, driving "from the temple of justice the spirit of hate and revenge," as one admirer put it. To the Parson's mind, the judge had become little more than a "sycophant of the slaves of Jeff. Davis," a shameless drunkard who borrowed money from Rebels to pay off his tab at the houses of ill fame that he frequented in broad daylight. Publicly, the Parson proclaimed that none but the "fence-riding, half Union, half rebel" McClellanites could have the audacity (not to mention the hypocrisy) to praise such a perfect specimen of corruption and debauchery. In reality, however, as the editor well knew, the advocates of a liberal policy toward local Confederates were never limited to the McClellan Democrats who had parted ways with Brownlow over abolition. Men like Oliver Temple, Thomas Humes, and Perez Dickinson—each of whom accepted the demise of slavery and might have been styled a "Radical"—nevertheless worked to ameliorate the treatment of Rebels. Indeed, among the ranks of the most prominent loyalists (excluding the rank and file), Brownlow and Horace Maynard were almost alone in calling for a draconian policy.[19]

Reuben Clark, the alleged bushwhacker, explained this by concluding that the leading citizens who deplored the persecution of Confederates "had the manliness to live above prejudice and passion" and the courage to stand up to "the mob." There is surely a grain of truth to this, but there were other, more complicated factors also at work. To begin with, through ties of kinship, friendship, and commerce, Knoxville's leading Unionists had long been intimately connected with leading Confederates, both locally and across Tennessee. John Williams had many powerful Rebel relatives, not only in Knoxville but across the state. The Reverend Thomas Humes was a stalwart Unionist, undoubtedly, but his nephew was a Confederate general. Perez Dickinson was widely recognized as "intensely loyal," but his son-in-law was a Confederate major, one of his chief business partners was prominent Confederate C. J. McClung, and one of his most trusted employees was Reuben Clark. Gideon Hazen's son rode with Confederate general John Hunt Morgan. Frederick Heiskell had a son, stepson, and son-in-law in the Confederate army and another son in the Confederate Congress. Unionist John Fleming had been a law partner of Confederate congressman Landon C. Haynes. Oliver Temple had studied law under Judge Robert McKinney, had subsequently entered into a partnership with William Sneed, and remembered Crozier Ramsey fondly for having been an attendant at his wedding.[20]

Such men could not have received with equanimity Parson Brownlow's demands for the harsh punishment of Confederates. (One can only imagine what Frederick Heiskell thought when Brownlow recommended that his son be hanged!)[21] Nor could they have appreciated Brownlow's arguably self-serving contention that the extent of suffering under Rebel rule was the best evidence of an individual's loyalty. It was not that they were opposed to employing the language of victimhood. Each of these men was a central figure in the establishment of the East Tennessee Relief Association, one of the primary tasks of which was to educate sympathetic northerners concerning the patriotism and poverty of East Tennessee. In its address to President Lincoln of February 1864, the ETRA had reminded the president that East Tennesseans "did not stop to consider their local or pecuniary interests" when the country began to break apart. Rather, "their innate love of country rose above the narrow and selfish considerations that controlled the people and dictated the policy of other states." Moved by their pleas, the *New York Daily Tribune* had asked its readers, "Where is the State which, like East Tennessee, has counted its own interests, its own prosperity—nay, its own existence—as nothing, and has gone forward forgetting all private claims, and given *all* for the Union?"[22]

Such rhetoric was all well and good when directed toward northern philanthropists, but it was another thing entirely when directed too close to home. As a group, the mass of loyal East Tennesseans had undeniably suffered for their convictions, but the majority of Knoxville's Unionist leaders had not been hurt by their loyalty during the period of Confederate occupation. Unlike Brownlow and Maynard, who had been driven into exile, they had remained at home and pursued a course of "strict neutrality." Even as the refugee martyrs were enthralling northern audiences with accounts of East Tennesseans' undying devotion to the Union, those left behind were swearing oaths of allegiance to the Confederacy to avoid persecution. While the Parson was insisting that any Unionist worthy of the name was willing to sacrifice all for the cause, they were conducting business "without reference to politics" and making a decent living in the process. Many could have echoed the assessment of Oliver Temple, who after the war conceded that, notwithstanding the widespread oppression of loyalists in the countryside and the climate of fear that obtained in town, "he never had any cause of complaint against the Confederate authorities. [I] was always treated kindly by them," Temple recalled, "and enjoyed as many privileges as were consistent with a state of civil war." One can only speculate whether such men wrestled with guilt over their wartime compromises. Whatever the case, and to their credit, they were unwilling to condone a policy that treated Rebels more harshly than they themselves had been treated under Rebel rule.[23]

Finally, they could not have been thrilled by the particular brand of populist rhetoric that now infused Parson Brownlow's case for harsh justice. The editor had long employed class-based appeals, of course, but in the current context of punishment and expropriation they conveyed a more alarming message. What had once seemed relatively innocuous—the sort of ritual homage to the common man that was a staple of antebellum politics—now threatened to justify a genuine assault on the sanctity of property. In the spring of 1864, for example, Brownlow called for the punishment of all who had voluntarily supported the Confederate conscription policy. Such villains should be made to atone for their crimes in "purse and property. They have boasted that all the wealth of the South was on their side," the editor observed bitterly. "It is time the wealth was changing hands." Similarly, in the fall of 1864 the *Whig* reported on the whereabouts of several prominent Rebel refugees, including those whom the editor had attempted to bankrupt via lawsuit. Reveling in their destitution, the newspaper exulted in the "falling to the ground of the odds and ends of a hateful aristocracy, that once insulted propriety on the streets." Just before Thanksgiving, Brownlow featured a letter from an anonymous correspondent ridiculing the Copperhead complaint that the war had become a crusade for "negro equality." Nothing could be further from the truth, the correspondent explained. "It is a war to vindicate the rights of the plebeian population, and make the poor the equal of the rich." When Connally Trigg began to dismiss treason charges in federal court, the *Whig* observed that the judge had "never had any sympathy with the laboring, unpretending loyal masses." When local Unionists tried to defend prominent Confederates, the Parson griped that "rebel wealth is too much respected" and denounced the general disposition "to grant peculiar favors and extra privileges to money and property holders." Privately, he informed Governor Johnson that Rebel men and women were "tolerated, even *advocated* by Union men, because they *belong to the first families of the country*."[24]

The problem in all this was that many of Knoxville's leading Unionists also belonged to the "first families of the country," and almost all had benefited personally from the "peculiar favors and extra privileges" that money could command. Prosperous merchants and professionals, they were considerably removed from the "mechanics, farmers, and laboring classes" that Brownlow rhetorically equated with true Unionism. Thomas Humes, James Cowan, and John Williams, for example, were literally descended from the town's "first families." And even though the wealthiest households in Knoxville were disproportionately pro-Confederate, Cowan, John Baxter, and Perez Dickinson each ranked among the top 2 percent of wealth holders, and almost all of the town's leading Unionists ranked within the top tenth.[25] That such men genuinely welcomed the kind of democratic leveling that the Parson was advocating is highly dubious, to say the least, and the obvious enthusiasm for the Parson's populism among the rank and file of Unionists only added to their sense of unease.

For all these reasons, then, the rapid developments of the war's final spring brought both joy and alarm to many of the town's most prominent Unionists. On the battlefield there was great cause for celebration. On 3 April, word reached Knoxville that Robert E. Lee's ragged and half-starved army had abandoned the defenses around Petersburg, Virginia, forcing the immediate evacuation of Richmond, the Confederate capital. "Babylon the Great, the Mighty, has Fallen," John Bell Brownlow exulted in a *Whig* editorial. Unionists celebrated with fireworks and dancing, the post commandant ordered a thirty-six-gun salute from each of the surrounding forts, and the town's black population paraded through the streets behind a brass band and a detachment of the Fortieth U.S. Colored Infantry. Seven days later came the "glorious news" of Lee's surrender to Ulysses Grant at Appomattox, and the townspeople reenacted the jubilant scene of the week before. Scattered Confederate units remained in North Carolina and elsewhere, but all understood that, after four long years, the war was essentially over.[26]

Sandwiched around Lee's surrender, on the other hand, were two events that transformed the political landscape and promised to shape the practical implications of Union victory. On 5 April, only two days after the fall of Richmond, William G. Brownlow was inaugurated governor of Tennessee before a "large and brilliant assemblage" at the state capitol. He had been nominated by the same statewide convention of Unionists that, the previous January, had recommended that Tennessee's constitution be amended to prohibit slavery. As the state's best-known loyalist other than Andrew Johnson, Brownlow had been the only candidate seriously considered, and because Confederates were prohibited from voting in the election of 4 March, his victory had been a foregone conclusion. Scarcely three years after his banishment as a traitor, the "Fighting Parson" had become the most powerful man in the state. Nine days later, an assassin's bullet at Ford's Theater made his predecessor, Andrew Johnson, the most powerful man in the country.[27]

THE EVENTS OF APRIL 1865 ushered in the last phase of Knoxville's civil war. Ironically, the end of the war brought not peace but an escalation of violence. Heretofore, the town had mercifully been spared the brutal and intensely personal episodes of violence that had long plagued the upper reaches of the East Tennessee Valley, where Rebel guerrillas and loyal Home Guards had struggled savagely for supremacy.[28] Now, however, bloody encounters erupted frequently, as the return of large numbers of Confederate and Union veterans combined with the presence of U.S. Colored Troops to create an explosive mixture.

The East Tennessean in the White House had little to do with this growing conflict. Those familiar with his background had had every reason to expect otherwise. In his youth the poorly schooled tailor had sworn that someday he would "show the stuck-up aristocrats who is running the country"; for decades thereafter, Andrew Johnson had perfected a hard-edged populism on the political stump, and he had ascended to the military governorship of Tennessee vowing that "treason must be made odious." Traitors "must be impoverished," he had declared, and "their social power must be destroyed." When news arrived of Lincoln's murder, the *Whig* had warned gloating Rebels that Johnson would not be as merciful as his martyred predecessor, and that they would soon "have occasion to call on the mountains and the rocks to hide them from his wrath." Once elevated to the presidency, however, Johnson fashioned a surprisingly lenient restoration policy, immediately offering a blanket pardon to all but approximately fifteen thousand southerners, nine-tenths of whom he subsequently pardoned individually. With hindsight, Johnson's moderation appears almost predictable, given the myriad of political, economic, and racial convictions that separated him from the Republican majority in Congress. Perhaps Johnson was also swayed by the blandishments of obsequiously repentant southern Democrats who sought his pardon and lauded him as the South's true champion. Knoxville's Nathan Gammon, for example, concluded his application for clemency with a personal note sharing his opinion that, "in the course of events," Johnson "*could* stand foremost in the South on the list of presidential aspirants." Similarly, hardware merchant James C. Moses, in endorsing the pardon application of his son, Frank, informed the new president "that your humane and magnanimous and wise policy . . . is almost unanimously approved here."[29]

This was flattering but untrue. Whatever the East Tennessean in Washington might proclaim, it was the policy of the East Tennessean now in Nashville that set the tone back home. If local Unionists from "the first families of the country" were disproportionately Conservative, the mass of loyalists were now overwhelmingly Radical. Traveling through Knoxville in the fall of 1865, northern reporter Whitelaw Reid found that the townspeople were "inclined to reserve their praises" of President Johnson. Few supported him without reservation, Reid discovered, most believing that "more hangings and fewer pardons would . . . better suit the existing wants of the South." While they still held out hope that Johnson would do right by them, Reid found that the people of Knoxville "had more faith in Parson Brownlow."[30] The latter's views had not changed since taking the oath of governor, although in his official pronouncements he sometimes expressed them with more restraint. In his first message to the new state General Assembly (also installed in April), Brownlow informed the loyal legislators that "secession is an abomination that I cannot too strongly condemn, and one that you cannot legislate against with too much severity." Specifically, the governor called on the legislature "to guard the ballot-box faithfully and effectually against the approach of treason." After some deliberation the assembly responded to Brownlow's satisfaction, passing an act in late May that disenfranchised the most prominent Confederates for fifteen years and the mass of their followers for five.[31]

Although he professed to be pleased with the outcome, mere disfranchisement fell far short of the severe punishment of East Tennessee Rebels that Brownlow had been demanding for years. The Parson continued to monitor the situation in his hometown closely, and both directly and indirectly he continued to lobby, at least unofficially, for a far harsher policy against returning Confederates. The vehicle for his sentiments continued to be the *Whig*, which he now served as a regular "correspondent," but the primary spokesman for his views now became his son, John Bell Brownlow, who took over as editor when his father left for Nashville. The younger Brownlow lacked the father's flair for invective but equaled him in hostility toward Rebels, an antipathy strengthened by more than two years' service as lieutenant colonel of the Ninth Tennessee Cavalry (U.S.A.). As he had explained to a Knoxville Unionist during the war, he had learned that "nothing can be made for our cause by attempting to *conciliate* rebels. The only way to restore *peace* is to kill and subjugate them." His father could not have said it better.[32]

For weeks after the Parson's inauguration, Lieutenant Colonel Brownlow (who somehow retained his officer's commission for several months after assuming his new journalistic post) impressed on his readers that the town's secessionist leaders must not be allowed to return to their homes in peace. After repeating a rumor that John Crozier and William Sneed were hoping to be allowed to take the oath and return to Knoxville, the new editor offered his readers a lesson in arithmetic. Yes, the infamous pair deserved to be tried for treason and hanged, but a long trial could end up costing the taxpayers thousands of dollars. A bullet from a loyal gun, on the other hand, would cost no more than two cents. "Pardon boys and uninformed men who were led into this rebellion," the younger Brownlow concluded, "but kill the leaders." A week later he noted a second time that several prominent Rebels were on the eve of returning to East Tennessee, and again he left nothing to his readers' imagination, inquiring, "Can't some Union soldiers or citizens dispose of them before they get here?"[33]

In the end there were no such summary executions—inexpensive as they might have been—in large part because the town's most outspoken secessionists had the good sense to stay far away from Knoxville for several years after the war's conclusion. In August 1865 a Confederate sympathizer lamented that "no prominent Southern men have returned," and the facts bear out his report. William McAdoo, for example, who had relocated to Marietta, Georgia, in 1862 and then moved farther south to Milledgeville, contemplated returning to East Tennessee to be near his aged mother. After some agonizing he decided against it. It was not that he was bitterly averse to returning. He had sided with the Confederacy out of a "conviction of right," but the "all wise Ruler of the destinies of nations" had decided the conflict, and McAdoo was resolved to reconcile himself and "cheerfully acquiesce."[34]

McAdoo knew that his former neighbors were of a different mind, however. To begin with, he was charged with treason in the federal district court in Knoxville. Beyond that, there was the threat of extralegal violence. "Do not go to E. Ten.," Knoxville colleague J. G. Whitson warned his friend in a letter toward the end of the summer. "Let no one deceive you into the belief that you would be safe in so doing." That autumn he received a less direct, if more ominous, warning. When two Union veterans from his boyhood home came to dine with his mother, she asked him their opinion of what might happen to her son should he return to the region. Their reply was unexpectedly blunt: they would "send [him] to hell where all such people go." McAdoo deplored the unfeeling coldness of such a comment to a defenseless old woman, but he did not dismiss it as false bravado. "I do not know how great would be the risk of my life if I were to go," he wrote to his mother. "I suppose Brownlow's influence would be in favor of assassinating me, and that he has supple tools enough to do it." McAdoo did finally return to Knoxville—twelve years later.[35]

Similarly, Campbell Wallace remained in Athens, Georgia, where he had fled in 1863, "even though he would rather live in East Tennessee than any place in this world." One month after Lee's surrender the former president of the East Tennessee and Georgia Railroad wrote to Governor Brownlow, offering to turn over to the state the property of the company, either at Knoxville or at Social Circle, Georgia, where the remaining locomotives and cars were currently located. The man whom Parson Brownlow had once denounced as "that prince of hypocrites" showed not a hint of remorse in addressing "His Excellency the Governor," but he did take the time to instruct Brownlow in how best to preserve the state's capital investment in the ET&Ga. The Parson was not interested in financial counseling. In a scathing reply (published prominently in the *Whig*), Brownlow reminded Wallace that he had "basely prostituted" the ET&Ga. "to the cause of treason," using the line to transport thousands of Rebel soldiers and thousands of tons of Rebel munitions. The governor warned Wallace not to return to Knoxville, informing him that he was sadly mistaken if he expected to atone for his "high crimes" by merely returning "a few old passenger cars and trucks." Thinking of Wallace's response to the bridge burnings of November 1861, the governor suggested that the individuals who had been imprisoned because of Wallace's directives would be waiting for him, "and they will make your home anything but a 'social circle' for you."[36]

Shortly thereafter Wallace wrote to Andrew Johnson, relating his newfound belief that secession had been "an unmitigated evil" and assuring the president that the charges recently levied against him "in a certain paper in Tennessee are without the shadow of foundation." In particular, Wallace emphasized the "multitude of instances" in which he had "exerted . . . influence for the release of Union men," conveniently forgetting that in 1862 he had threatened to resign from the railroad in protest against the release from jail of one William G. Brownlow. Wallace ultimately received the pardon he was seeking, and he did quite well in his new home. By 1866 he was both superintendent of the Western and Alabama Railroad and president of the Atlanta State National Bank; four years later a federal census marshal estimated his wealth at $61,000, a sum greater than he had ever commanded before the war. He was not welcome in East Tennessee, however, and he did not return there.[37]

J. G. M. Ramsey stayed away as well, albeit for somewhat different reasons. In the fall of 1864 the old doctor had settled his wife and a widowed daughter in the vicinity of Charlotte, North Carolina, and after finishing up his duties with the Bank of Tennessee and the Confederate Treasury Department, he had rejoined them a few weeks after Lee's surrender. Although he was resolved to face the future with "Christian fortitude," it was no easy task to remain "hopeful, trustful & resigned." One of his daughters had succumbed to typhoid not long before the siege of Knoxville; not long afterward, another had died in childbirth. One of his nephews had been killed by a Yankee bullet at Chickamauga, while his youngest son, seventeen-year-old Arthur, had had his leg ripped off by a cannonball at the battle of Piedmont, Virginia, lingering for an agonizing ten days before dying among strangers. Another son was in jail in East Tennessee under charge of murder; another had fled south with Jefferson Davis after the fall of Richmond and had not been heard from. Rumors from Knoxville indicated that he was under indictment for treason in federal court, and his extensive properties there were either being "destroyed or lawlessly sold." The family's ancestral home lay in ashes, deliberately torched by Union soldiers shortly after Burnside's arrival, and his library, his collection of antiquities, and his unfinished manuscript of the history of Tennessee since statehood had all been destroyed. With forty-two dollars to his name he could not afford to move elsewhere, and so at the age of sixty-eight he started a new life among strangers, renting a run-down farm—which he named "Exile's Retreat"—and resuming the practice of medicine. His new neighborhood, unfortunately, "was exceedingly healthy," and even with his wife and daughter working as tutors, it was hard to put bread on the table. They soon "learned to live on little and that of the plainest kind," as his wife explained to a relative in Knoxville. "True we have no homes and not much enjoyment," Margaret Ramsey observed philosophically, "but thousands are in the same condition."[38]

Although their son Crozier headed for Nashville as soon as he was released from jail, his "great distaste for East Ten." soon gave way to homesickness, and for the next three years he carefully monitored the environment in Knoxville, hoping that he and his parents might soon be reunited there. Old Dr. Ramsey did not share his son's longing.[39] Returning to Knoxville would mean returning to a state where he could not vote, to a region dominated by insufferable Lincolnites, and to a town now inundated with Yankees and still palpably influenced by his old nemesis, Parson Brownlow. Shortly after the war, Ramsey had allowed his son to initiate on his behalf an application for a presidential pardon (the step was necessary if he was ever to recover his property), but in his heart he knew he had done nothing wrong. Expressions of remorse and regret were a staple of such applications—C. W. Charlton, for example, had admitted to "grievous wrongs" for which he was "heartily sorry"—but the doctor could not bring himself to utter such apostasy. "In all I have done since 1861 I know I was honest," he wrote in the personal statement that would accompany his applica- tion. "I believed I was patriotic. . . . If I have erred," he conceded in the closest he could come to an apology, "it was the error of the head & not of the heart I am sure."[40] But he had *not* erred. As he insisted to an old friend after the war, he had fought in a "righteous cause"—a view that he held with undiminished fervor until his dying day. And when historians went through his personal pa- pers long afterward, they found attached to his unpublished autobiography a handwritten sheet with the lyrics for a popular postwar song entitled "O I'm a Good Old Rebel." After rejoicing that the South had killed three hundred thou- sand Yankees—and wishing that it had been three million—the song concluded with a declaration of defiance that Ramsey could have written himself: "And I don't want no pardon / For what I was and am / I won't be reconstructed / And I don't care a dam."[41]

Although their personal attitudes and circumstances varied, Knoxville's Con- federate elite largely followed the example of McAdoo, Wallace, and Ramsey in their aversion to East Tennessee during the war's immediate aftermath. Their diaspora literally covered every point of the compass. Those traveling southward to Georgia included Samuel T. Atkins and William Sneed, who settled for a time in Atlanta; Charles and Frank McClung, who relocated temporarily to Macon; and former congressman William Swan, who journeyed even farther south, to Columbus.[42] C. W. Charlton initially also moved to Georgia, but after he went bankrupt trying to run a cotton plantation he ventured westward to Missouri. William Williams headed in the same direction but stopped when he got to Nashville. Railroad entrepreneur George M. Branner ventured southwest, relo- cating in Mississippi, where his wife held large properties. Others looked north- ward. John H. Crozier, the Parson's archenemy, settled in southwestern Virginia. Robert B. Reynolds moved permanently to Illinois. Merchant Henry Ault re- moved temporarily to Cincinnati, T. J. Powell selected New York City, and physician John M. Boyd opted for Philadelphia. William M. Cocke and the Reverend Joseph Martin turned their eyes eastward, settling in North and South Carolina, respectively. Shortly after his return from exile, Parson Brownlow had exulted that, thanks to "the mercy of God" and the "madness of the Southern Confederacy," the day was fast approaching when "it will require lamps and gas-lights in day-time to find the aristocracy of this town." As was often the case, the Parson had both exaggerated and oversimplified. Not all of the town's wealthy had been Confederates to begin with, and many wealthy Confederates who had supported secession quietly and reluctantly would find it possible to remain at home after the war. This much was unmistakable, however: with the exception of the shamelessly opportunistic Joseph Mabry—who in 1865 took on a Union officer as a business partner and by 1866 was passing himself off as a "Union" man—the town's most prominent "original secessionists" were nowhere to be seen.[43]

THEIR "PUPPETS, TOOLS, and instruments" were returning in full force, however, as a correspondent with the *Whig* noted in mid-May 1865. For weeks after Lee's surrender, small parties of Confederate soldiers regularly trickled into Knoxville—nearly eight hundred during the first two weeks of May alone. Some were local men who had already mustered out and were seeking to return to their homes. Others hailed from surrounding counties and had come to Knoxville in search of Federal authorities to whom they could surrender. All received a less than warm welcome. Decades later, after it had become common to romanticize the reconciliation of North and South, Oliver Temple wrote that the returning Confederate veteran "and his Union neighbor at once became friends as of old." Each had been brave and honorable, Temple explained, and each had respected the other and quickly buried the past. It was a noble vision—and an exercise in creative writing. Such genuine reconciliation did develop eventually, as East Tennesseans later liked to recall, but the process was more gradual and much more arduous than Temple would acknowledge. In the spring and summer of 1865, there was still simply too much passion and too much pain to avoid an ugly conclusion to a terrible war.[44]

Rather then welcome their old neighbors with open arms, many Knoxville Unionists believed that John Bell Brownlow's proscription of secessionist leaders should apply to their followers as well. "It may be better for returning rebels to travel on a little further," an anonymous *Whig* correspondent observed ominously. "They voted separation four years ago. If the doctrine was good then it is good yet." Toward the end of the summer, Laura Maynard noted that such views were widespread. "You know they used to say that the Union men & 'Southern' men could not live here together," she reminded her son. "The former now take them at their word, & send them away rather hurriedly." When he visited Knoxville in the fall, Whitelaw Reid similarly was struck by the "strong conflict between Unionists and their former oppressors." The well-traveled reporter concluded that there was no place in the South where the bitterness engendered by the war was as pronounced.[45]

The most popular target for Unionist retribution was always the returning Rebels in uniform. When one hundred or so Confederate soldiers from upper East Tennessee came into town in late April to take the oath, their appearance "produced considerable excitement," and several men threatened to shoot them. Ten days later a band of Rebel cavalry rode boldly through the streets under a flag of truce, and again an angry crowd gathered. A Federal quartermaster who witnessed the encounter observed that "many of the band were known to citizens of the town, who declare[d] them the veriest rufians [sic] and scape gallowses [sic] among the guerillas of East Tennessee." The officer understood that many in Knoxville had suffered, directly or indirectly, from their depredations, and he concluded that, if given the opportunity, "their hot Southern blood would take vengeance into its own hands."[46]

Opportunity for vengeance abounded in Knoxville during the spring and summer of 1865. In mid-May, the same Union quartermaster recorded in his diary that the air was filled with the fragrance of blooming roses, though the peace and quiet of the community was marred by the "private settlements of difficulties" between Unionists and Rebels. A druggist received "a thorough cowhiding" at the hands of a Union officer, he noted, whereas another Confederate took "a good cudgeling" and was chased through the streets "followed disagreeably close by his cursing assailant, stones, billets, and brickbats." Two days later he described how a "disgraceful mob" of discharged Union soldiers had chased two Confederate veterans "down the street pell mell shouting rebels! rebels! and hurling after them . . . whatever missiles came to hand." The following month a Confederate widow reported the latest atrocities to her teenage son, then away at boarding school. "A great many southern men have been severely used by the soldiers," she related. One had been "terribly cowhided," a second had "had his skull broken," a third had been "beaten all most to death." Father Abram Ryan, a staunchly Confederate priest assigned to the Knoxville parish at the close of the war, admired the town's matchless scenery but was disgusted by the "bigotry" of its inhabitants. "Scarcely a day passes," he informed friends in Nashville, "that is not signalized by some murder or other crimes." Around the same time Ellen House returned from exile in southwestern Georgia, where she had eventually settled after her banishment from Knoxville. She loathed the fact that the place was filled with Yankees—"the vilest race that ever disgraced humanity"—but her greatest concern was for the safety of her brothers. In her diary she recorded almost daily assaults of Rebels by Unionists. "There certainly is a dreadful state of things," she lamented. "No mans [sic] life is safe."[47]

Not all the battles on the streets of Knoxville were between Rebels and white Unionists, however. In mid-July, House gladly reported that there had been a fight on the street "between Yanks and negro soldiers." There had been black soldiers off and on in Knoxville since January of the previous year, when Burnside's successor, General John Foster, had begun recruiting blacks for a new artillery regiment. Within a month, nearly five hundred black men had enlisted in what would become the First Regiment Heavy Artillery, U.S. Colored Troops; by the beginning of the summer the number had increased to eleven hundred, and by January 1865 the unit had its full complement of eighteen hundred men, all encamped, for the moment, right outside of town.[48] Although the townspeople complained from the start about the "insolence" of the black soldiers, there were relatively few incidents until white Union veterans began to pour into town once the war was over. In late summer, for example, the town's streets were crowded with the veterans of the Eighth, Ninth, and Thirteenth regiments of Tennessee Cavalry, all of whom had been ordered to Knoxville to be paid and then mustered out of the service. The only troops on active duty at the time in Knoxville were black—the First Colored Artillery—and it became their responsibility to police the behavior of a couple of thousand exuberant white veterans with money in their pockets and a fondness for the town's innumerable saloons. The wonder was not that violence ensued, but rather that a race war of monumental proportions did not erupt.[49]

In late August, the *Whig* paused to catalog the most recent alleged incidents of black aggression on innocent whites. In an article titled "Colored Men Shooting White Men," the newspaper listed three assaults in the space of a week. Various black soldiers had shot one white man in the leg, fired shots at another, and bayoneted to death a third on Gay Street in broad daylight. In a masterful understatement, the *Whig* reported that the killing had "produced intense feeling among the Tennessee troops." The white provost marshal of the Knoxville garrison responded with a letter to the editor in which he chronicled a separate list of abuses—assaults by white veterans against black soldiers—that somehow failed to get into the newspaper. The tragedy on Gay Street, for example, had begun with an unprovoked attack on a black soldier by a drunken veteran. Similarly, only days before, a band of whites had jumped a solitary guard at the pontoon bridge over the Holston and beaten him within an inch of his life. Then there was the black soldier who mysteriously ended up drowned in the river with a musket tied to his back—only days after the white veterans of the Eight Tennessee had vowed "to kill every negro soldier in the street."[50]

Everyone had a theory as to how to bring peace to the streets of Knoxville. White Unionists were certain that racial conflict would end the moment that the black troops were transferred elsewhere. Governor Brownlow suggested to President Johnson that they be ordered to the Cotton States, "where the spirit of the Rebellion is kept up." Loyal East Tennessee could take care of itself, he assured the president. Knoxville attorney Sam Rodgers seconded the Parson's sentiments, informing Johnson that "the negro soldiers are committing depredations" and declaring that "if they could be removed, we would have peace and good order at once." Johnson was sympathetic to such pleas, and in early September he began to pressure the Union commander in Nashville, General George H. Thomas, to order the removal of all black troops from East Tennessee. The black soldiers were "perfectly lawless," Johnson explained to Thomas, and could not be controlled "in the event of an insurrection."[51]

The general expressed a willingness to comply but informed the president that he had no white troops with which to replace them and reminded him of the almost daily difficulties in the region "between the returned rebels and loyal citizens." Thomas then telegraphed the Union commander in East Tennessee, General George Stoneman, and directed him to order the black regiment at Knoxville to Chattanooga, "unless it is in a good state of discipline." Stoneman, whose headquarters were in Knoxville, cabled back that the reports the president had received about the black troops at Knoxville were untrue. In Stoneman's opinion, the First Colored Artillery was "as well behaved a regiment as there is in the service." Thomas reiterated the opinion in a second report to President Johnson, assuring him that "the negro soldiers are under good discipline" and sharing the opinion that the majority of collisions between white and black soldiers could be traced to efforts to "bully the negro." In the end, the black troops stayed, much to the chagrin of Knoxville whites. As a partial compromise, General Stoneman ordered that they be restricted to camp unless actually on duty; one soldier per company per day would also be granted leave to come into town, but only then with a written pass and in the company of a noncommissioned officer.[52]

Stoneman's order did nothing to address the frequent combat between Confederates and white Unionists, however. All agreed that Union veterans were typically the instigators of the clashes, but Rebels and loyalists disagreed about what—or who—was prompting their aggression. Confederates believed that the perpetrators were limited to the "lower grade" of Union men and blamed the *Knoxville Whig* for whipping such "worthless" men into frenzy. The *Whig* "excites the people to murder and pillage," Elisa Bolli lamented. It was solely responsible for "the increasing hostility towards the returning Confederates," a Rebel veteran complained to conservative Unionist Thomas Nelson. "The rabble have it as their guide and textbook." Father Ryan agreed. All the "decent people" were leaving, which merely served to intensify the bigotry and violent party spirit of the remainder. "No one can live here safe & secure that does not swear by Brownlow," he reported. "He is their prophet."[53]

Though understandable, Confederates' emphasis on Parson Brownlow as the primary cause of all their troubles was simplistic and self-serving. Brownlow's prominence as a journalist had always stemmed, at least in part, from his uncanny grasp of political currents, meaning that in the spring of 1865 the *Whig* was probably reflecting popular attitudes as much as shaping them. Certainly Whitelaw Reid thought so. After reading the *Whig and Ventilator* and visiting extensively with the locals, Reid concluded that the newspaper was a "pretty good index . . . to the temper of the people among whom it is a favorite." By focusing on the Parson's vindictiveness, Confederates diverted attention from the ways in which their own behavior during and after the war had contributed to Unionists' animosity. Reid, for example, found it less than remarkable that men who had been "driven from their homes" should deal roughly with the enemies whom they held responsible. David Deaderick similarly pointed to the link between wartime behavior and postwar violence. Although the reluctant secessionist deplored the disposition of local Unionists "to take revenge and gratify their malice," he conceded that they primarily targeted those who had "made themselves busy and forward as rebels" during the period of Confederate ascendancy, leaving the mass of the remainder unmolested.[54]

The attitude of many returning Confederate soldiers at the close of the war may have also exacerbated tensions and invited conflict. In May, Horace Maynard informed Andrew Johnson that the rebels returning to Knoxville were immediately "desiring their constitutional rights." A correspondent of the *Whig* elaborated on this point, claiming that the Confederate veterans had returned "with spirits unconquered and with hate unsatisfied," demanding their possessions, their rights, and their traditional political power. If true, such openly unrepentant attitudes begged for a violent reaction. In sum, if Confederate veteran William Vestal got bashed over the head with a rock after getting drunk and screaming in the middle of the street that he was not finished fighting "damned Yankees," Parson Brownlow was not necessarily to blame.[55]

At the same time, it is also true that neither the current nor the former editor of the *Whig* did anything to discourage the postwar epidemic of violence. When a Unionist named Isham Alley clubbed a recently returned Confederate over the head in broad daylight, John Brownlow reported the incident under the heading "Just Retribution." His account of the episode stressed that the victim was "an original, vindictive, and bloody rebel" who had caused Alley's arrest early in the war. "So far as we are concerned," the junior editor concluded, "we approve of Mr. Alley's course." Similarly, two weeks later the *Whig* matter-of-factly recounted a brawl in which a discharged Union captain from Knox County had assaulted "an old citizen of this place," breaking several of his ribs. Their private encounter was both predictable and just, the story implied, inasmuch as the old Rebel allegedly had called for the assailant's execution when he had been in prison in Knoxville during the period of Confederate occupation. When northerners newly arrived in Knoxville claimed to be appalled at the violence between Unionists and Rebels, young Brownlow suggested that they could always live elsewhere. Knoxville loyalists welcomed northern men among them, he explained, unless they were of that class of northern "Copperheads" who commiserated with southern Rebels.[56]

The elder Brownlow was similarly unsympathetic when a number of loyal East Tennesseans—including several from Knoxville—petitioned their governor in May to issue a proclamation condemning the outbreak of personal violence.

Nearly ninety prominent East Tennessee loyalists from a half dozen counties endorsed the petition, which deplored the numerous attacks on returning Rebel soldiers and their civilian supporters and submitted that the only proper course for the redress of grievances was "by legal process through the civil courts." The Parson immediately smelled a trap, viewing the petition as a politically motivated overture calculated to embarrass him. He was probably right. The Knoxville signatories were top-heavy with McClellan Democrats such as John Williams, Frederick Heiskell, and Thomas Nelson. The governor replied promptly nonetheless, issuing an official proclamation in which he urged "all aggrieved citizens to apply for redress of their wrongs . . . to the civil courts." There was a huge caveat, however. "Should the guilty be shielded by the corruption of civil or judicial officers," Brownlow cautioned, transparently referring to Judge Connally Trigg, "it will then be impossible to prevent the injured and oppressed from taking their remedies into their own hands." Virtually thumbing his nose at the petitioners, the governor concluded his proclamation by addressing those Confederates who had driven Union men from their homes early in the war, advising them that they "would act wisely to quietly and forever withdraw from the country." This was far from what the petitioners had in mind, and the Parson knew it. "I think you will agree with me," he gloated in a letter to Oliver Temple on the day that he issued the proclamation, "the *tricksters* who got up the petition . . . have not made much by the operation."[57]

THE EPISODES OF BLOODY retribution in the spring and summer of 1865 were as short-lived as they were intense. By autumn they were declining noticeably, and by early 1866 both Unionists and Confederates agreed that things in Knoxville were pretty quiet.[58] Both sides also agreed that the gateway to this more genuine peace lay in one final instance of cathartic, collective violence against a Confederate veteran. No one knows for sure why twenty-two-year-old Abner Baker left his home out on the Kingston pike and rode into town on a Monday morning in early September 1865. The pistol that the discharged Rebel cavalryman carried in his coat pocket suggests that he knew the excursion could be risky. Baker had already been charged with treason in federal court, and he was aware that well-known Rebels who ventured on the streets of Knoxville could expect taunts and jeers, if not worse. Perhaps Baker had urgent business in town that required his presence—pertaining to his impending trial, for example—or perhaps he was just looking for trouble. He certainly had motive enough for the latter: Union soldiers had killed his father back in June 1863.[59]

One of Knoxville's wealthiest citizens, Harvey Baker had also been a prominent Confederate sympathizer, and when word reached him that Union cavalry under Colonel William Sanders were galloping up the road from Lenoir City, the fifty-two-year-old doctor had grabbed his gun and set out for Knoxville to aid in its defense. While he was still in his front yard, however, Confederate

skirmishers positioned behind his house had fired on a squad of Federal cavalrymen nearby. Dr. Baker *may* have joined in the attack immediately or, as his family
later insisted, may have only fired at the Yankees after they began to shoot at
him, mistaking him for one of the Rebel sharpshooters. At any rate, Federal
soldiers followed him when he retreated into the house and killed him in his own
home. The pro-Confederate *Knoxville Register* published an inflammatory account of the incident, claiming that the Yankees had shot the doctor repeatedly,
bayoneted him at least once, and then bashed his skull with a rifle butt, all while
his wife and children watched in horror. Six months later, after Burnside's occupation of Knoxville, an investigation by the Union provost marshal ruled that
the killing of Dr. Baker "was justified by the laws of war." Many local Confederates—likely including his son Abner—viewed it as cold-blooded murder.[60]

Whether he was looking for it or just prepared for it, the young Confederate veteran soon found trouble on this Monday morning. His path took him to
the Knox County courthouse, where almost immediately he encountered Will
Hall, a twenty-five-year-old veteran of the Second Tennessee Cavalry (U.S.A.)
and the deputy clerk of the circuit court. Afterward, the townspeople agreed only
on the most basic details: within a matter of minutes, Hall lay dead with a bullet in his brain, and Abner Baker was on his way to jail. The *Whig* reported that
Baker had accosted Hall, evidently still nursing an "old grudge" dating to the
beginning of the war. According to the account, Baker drew his revolver without provocation, prompting Hall, who was unarmed, to defend himself with a
small rattan cane. When the cane broke, Hall tried to flee and Baker shot him
from behind. As Hall's twin sister lamented, her brother had been "murdered,
so cruelly murdered."[61]

Confederates saw things differently. David Deaderick, who had an office in
the courthouse, maintained that Hall had been the aggressor. Deaderick had not
actually witnessed the crime, but he had come running when he heard a shot ring
out and talked with those who did. He learned that Hall, "a large man over the
common size," had assaulted the much smaller Baker for no apparent reason
"other than that Baker was a *rebel*." Baker pulled his pistol only after being attacked, according to Deaderick's informants, killing his assailant in self-defense.
Ellen House, who was nowhere near the courthouse at the time, claimed to be
privy to other pertinent information. Hall had been drinking heavily that morning, she recorded in her diary, and had boasted in a barroom that he would knock
down the next "damned Rebel" he lay eyes on. That turned out to be Baker, "a
good, quiet, noble little fellow" who had defended himself manfully and who had
only killed Hall when the drunken bully gave him no choice.[62]

For all the stark differences in their versions of the slaying, Unionists and
Confederates could agree about one final detail: that night a large body of Federal soldiers from East Tennessee took Abner Baker out of the jail and hanged
him. Unionists insisted that with his last breath Baker had boasted of the Yan-

kees he had killed. The *Whig* expressed regret that Baker had been hanged "in violation of the law" but implied that such episodes were inevitable as long as Rebels were "parading the streets loaded down to the guards with revolvers, swearing they have been overpowered, but not convinced!" Confederates recounted his end differently, claiming that Baker "never flinched" when presented with the noose but coolly informed the lynch mob, "I will show you how a brave man can die." They proclaimed Baker a "martyr" and erected a monument to his memory in the cemetery of the First Presbyterian Church. The young soldier's death was "an honor to himself," the inscription declared, "but an everlasting disgrace to his enemies."[63]

In the short run, the primary result of the murder of Abner Baker was to convince numerous Confederate veterans to get out of town. The frequent assaults of that spring and summer had prompted many Rebels to leave long before, but others had resolved to stick it out, hoping to mind their own business and stay out of trouble. Baker's lynching changed the minds of many. The death of the "innocent" youth at the hands of a mob was bad enough, but even more chilling to local Rebels was the utter indifference of the authorities. David Deaderick surely exaggerated when he claimed that "all the returned rebel soldiers" headed south "in consequence of this lawless act," but there is no question that the lynching initiated a major exodus. Laura Maynard listed nine who left for safer parts the very next day and noted reports that "others are going as soon as they can settle their affairs." Among the latter were Deaderick's sons Oakley and Chalmers, who headed for Macon, Georgia, and Ellen House's brother Johnnie, who left for Nashville within three days of Baker's death. Others scattered as far away as New York and Texas.[64]

In an odd way, however, Baker's murder surely contributed to a reduction of violence thereafter. The wholesale departure of Confederates meant that Unionists and Rebels bumped into one another much less frequently, significantly reducing the potential for dangerous confrontation. Beyond this, the Confederates who stayed behind had more reason than ever to keep their mouths shut, while even local Unionists may have been more likely to think twice before picking fights. In November, a prominent Confederate refugee whose family was still in Knoxville shared his opinion with William McAdoo that the shooting of Hall and hanging of Baker had had "an effect to discourage the assassination of Southerners by Brownlow's cutthroats." His assessment may not have been entirely fair, but the incidence of violence had definitely begun to diminish markedly. By the following spring, J. C. Ramsey's informants reported that things were quiet in Knoxville, and when the former Confederate district attorney visited his old home, he was struck by how "cordially" he was received. Even Brownlow's "McClellanite" critics conceded as much. Whereas the previous spring they had petitioned the governor to condemn the widespread and "reprehensible disturbance of the public peace," twelve months later they deemed it "a matter of sincere congratulation that so much quiet and peace prevail, and a commendable observance of the laws obtains so generally."[65]

The restoration of peace and order also paved the way, ultimately, for the gradual return of Rebel refugees. Admittedly, many never came back. In 1870 the federal census taker in Knoxville could find scarcely three-tenths of the town's original Confederate male population, compared with almost one-half of male Unionists.[66] As glaring as the disparity was, it would have been greater had a census been taken at the close of 1865, for by the following spring Confederate veterans were already beginning to slip back into town. Robert and Inslee Deaderick were among the first, returning in May 1866 after a year of self-imposed exile in Texas. Others waited years. The Deadericks' brother Chalmers remained in Virginia until 1871, for example, while Jim Luttrell and Charles Ducloux both worked in New York for at least five years before returning. More significantly, many of the town's most prominent original secessionists were also finding it safe to come home. William Sneed moved back to town sometime in 1867, regained his property, was readmitted to the bar, and practiced law in Knoxville until his premature death two years later. John H. Crozier, C. W. Charlton, William Williams, Robert B. Reynolds, and Samuel T. Atkins were all back in town by 1870. Even the supremely embittered J. G. M. Ramsey eventually came back, returning to Knoxville for good in 1872.[67]

This partial return of "the chivalry" considerably blurred the long-term social consequences of Union victory. In truth, society in Knoxville had been in a state of upheaval ever since Ambrose Burnside had "liberated" the town. While many of the "best" families were leaving, a multitude of poor white refugees and former slaves had been flooding in to take their place, along with a veritable "deluge" of Yankees. Abram Ryan likened the latter to a "plague of locusts" and descried the ubiquitous presence of "Yankee ministers—Yankee schoolmasters and schoolmams—Yankee merchants—Yankee doctors and lawyers—and Yankees of every calling imaginable." In contrast, the Massachusetts-born Laura Maynard found their presence encouraging and was of the opinion that "some of the new families that have come in are very nice, cultivated, refined people— far exceeding in common sense & intelligence, some of those we have lost." Even so, the wife of one of Knoxville's most outspoken "Radicals" was far from confident in contemplating the town's future. "Society is completely revolutionized," she declared to an absent relative only a year after Appomattox, and the "Knoxville of old" was no more. "Indeed, I hardly know of what 'society' is composed right now," she admitted. Only time would tell, but she was increasingly skeptical of Parson Brownlow's boast that the town's Rebel "aristocracy" had been a casualty of the war. "I fear," she confessed gloomily, that "the monied power is settling upon the rebel side."[68]

Maynard was perhaps overly pessimistic, but her instincts were sound, as an examination of the town's wealthiest residents before and after the war reveals.

A look at the fate of the town's *prewar* elite—the richest tenth of white house-holds in 1860—shows that wealthy Confederates had been scattered by the war far more than had wealthy Unionists. Even five years after the war, after many prominent Rebels had returned, barely half of Confederates who survived the decade were still living in Knoxville, as opposed to more than four-fifths of the Unionists.[69] In assessing the war's overall impact on the community, however, the more crucial question concerns the makeup of the *postwar* elite. As Laura Maynard understood, the real issue was not about which individuals had left and which had remained, but about where the "monied power" would ultimately settle.

Here an examination of the richest tenth of white households in 1870 is re-vealing. In an absolute sense, the 115 men and women who headed these house-holds were not as wealthy as their prewar counterparts, owning on average little more than half the value of real and personal property as the 1860 elite. The war had been hard on nearly everyone, however, and despite their more modest hold-ings, in 1870 the top 10 percent of wealth holders still commanded nearly three-quarters of the total property in Knoxville, while the bottom half of white households controlled less than 1 percent. So much for the war's leveling influence. Approximately one in ten of the town's propertied elite were north-ern-born individuals who had arrived since the war began, indicating that the "deluge" of Yankees was affecting even the wealthiest ranks of society. Seven-eighths of the postwar elite were still southern-born, however, and more than two-thirds had roots in Knoxville dating to before the war.[70]

Of the seventy-eight individuals in the latter group, it is possible to catego-rize sixty-five with some confidence—thirty had been Unionists, thirty-five had been Confederates. Such an even division between Confederates and Unionists does not fully sustain Maynard's fear that wealth was "settling upon the rebel side." Indeed, given that three-quarters of the prewar elite had eventually sup-ported the Confederacy, the postwar elite was considerably less top-heavy with Rebels than it once had been. Even so, Parson Brownlow had been badly mis-taken in his earlier prediction: by 1870 there was no shortage of wealthy former Confederates walking the streets of Knoxville, and it did not require a gaslight in daytime to spy them. For all the anger and resentment that it aroused, the war had not engendered the degree of sustained class antagonism necessary to topple the Confederate "chivalry" more thoroughly, nor had Parson Brownlow been able to manufacture it. This reflected, in part, the propertied conservatism of the town's Unionist leadership, most of whom had never desired such an outcome in the first place. But what of the rank and file, the kind of men who had joined with a thousand others to affirm the lynching of the son of one of Knoxville's wealthiest Confederates?

A clue can be found in the fact that some of the same men also gathered five months after the lynching of Abner Baker to watch a black Union soldier twist at the end of a rope. When Whitelaw Reid arrived in Knoxville toward the end of 1865, the journalist was well aware of the recent conflict between returning Rebels and white Unionists, but he noticed that "the prevailing tendency to violence was now turned in a new direction." In February 1866 the Union men of Knoxville pointedly confirmed Reid's judgment. The gruesome incident began behind a government warehouse in north Knoxville, where the chief quartermaster for the District of East Tennessee was holding a public auction of surplus military stores. The quartermaster, a Captain Wainwright, had stationed a member of the First Regiment U.S. Colored Artillery at the rear entrance of the warehouse while he conducted the public sale out front. Concerned about theft, the white officer had instructed the black private that no civilian should be allowed to enter without first presenting a written receipt for goods purchased. The orders were reasonable enough, but in a community that was deeply ambivalent about emancipation—not to mention the arming of former slaves—they put in place all the necessary ingredients for tragedy.[71]

Within hours a white man named Calvin Dyer lay dead near the warehouse's rear entrance.[72] Although from an adjacent county, Dyer was highly respected in Knoxville. Lieutenant colonel of the First Tennessee Cavalry (U.S.A.) until his discharge, he had served during the war with Parson Brownlow's son James, was a good friend of John Brownlow, and was generally well known among Knoxville's Union veterans. Sometime before midday, having bought surplus stores from Wainwright, Dyer had walked around to the rear of the warehouse to pick up his purchase. What happened next is a matter of some conjecture. Only two brief accounts of the killing have been found, and although both agree that the guard shot Dyer, they differ with regard to his motive. In the *Whig*, John Brownlow proclaimed that his friend had been "cruelly, foully murdered . . . without the shade of the shadow of a provocation." According to Brownlow, when the sentry ordered Dyer to halt, the latter had produced the necessary bill of sale and then entered the warehouse as he was entitled, only to be shot down from behind by the "vicious, insulting negro." An anonymous correspondent to the *New York Times* recounted the episode with a slight but crucial difference. According to "D. M.," the guard had discharged his weapon when Dyer reached into his pocket for the bill of sale—not well after he had produced it—suggesting that the sentry may have feared that Dyer was drawing a gun. This bespoke a criminal recklessness but seemed to absolve the guard of the cold-blooded premeditation that John Brownlow had described.

Whatever had transpired behind the warehouse, the guard's life was now in great peril, and it is small wonder that he took the opportunity to flee when the black soldiers charged with escorting him to jail were less than vigilant in their duty. Word soon spread of his escape, along with swirling rumors that either his company commander or the local agent of the Freedmen's Bureau would try to spirit him out of town. Outraged that the murderer might evade justice, a mob of perhaps a hundred Union veterans quickly materialized and began to search among the "negro shanties" between the warehouse and the railroad depot. Around two o'clock in the afternoon they found the terrified soldier hiding in the government corral, put a noose around his neck, and dragged him nearly the full length of Gay Street to the headquarters of the Freedmen's Bureau. Their attempt to hang him in that symbolic spot failed when the victim struggled so mightily that the rope snapped. Undaunted, they took their prisoner back up Gay Street to the office of the chief quartermaster, now ensconced in the residence once owned by John H. Crozier. There they procured a stronger rope and, in their second attempt, successfully lynched the "murderous sentinel." To prolong his agony they left his hands free, allowing the poor soldier to pull up on the rope until his strength gave out and he slowly strangled. The process took two hours, during which time the mob, now swollen to several hundred, "stood around the dangling form of the atrocious murderer." When his struggling finally ceased, they pinned a placard to his breast to explain their deed: "Hung to show nigger officers and the Freedmen's Bureau what it takes to make a true Tennessean, and whether they will be run over or not."

It was a grisly epitaph but pregnant with meaning: a "true Tennessean," the mob had declared, was loyal not only to the Union but also to his race. If they disagreed with their Confederate neighbors on the former point, they spoke with them as one on the latter. By discouraging further individual acts of revenge, the hanging of Abner Baker had effectively ended the frequent violent clashes among whites. By both promoting and symbolizing white solidarity, the hanging of this black Union soldier now foreshadowed the basis for their genuine reconciliation.

AFTERWORD

THEY GATHERED EAST of downtown, not far from the remains of the battlefield where they had met twenty-seven years earlier. The community had been proud to sponsor a commemoration of the siege of Knoxville, and prouder still that the event would involve one of the first joint reunions of Confederate and Union veterans ever held in the United States. Noting that Knoxville had sent "many of her noblest sons" into both armies, the *Knoxville Daily Tribune* boasted that "no more appropriate place in all the Union could have been selected." To confirm the claim, the now-bustling city of forty thousand had rolled out the red carpet. Merchants bedecked storefronts and streetcars with bunting and flags, while the city fathers planned a succession of concerts, receptions, fireworks displays, and parades. Responding to the warm invitation, more than eight thousand blue and gray survivors had converged on Knoxville, and now, on a sun-drenched autumn afternoon in 1890, they crowded in and around a large tent erected within sight of Fort Sanders to receive an official welcome from their hosts.

There were many dignitaries on the speakers' platform—old General Longstreet himself was there—but the official greeting came from Knoxville's Joshua Caldwell, an up-and-coming young jurist who had been five years old when the first shots were fired at Fort Sumter. "What does this occasion signify?" Caldwell asked his audience. "We have met to remember and to forget," he explained to the old soldiers, "to remember the heroic deeds and the mighty works of the past . . . and to forget all else." At bottom, this translated into the conclusion that both Unionists and Confederates had been honorable during the "late unpleasantness," as the *Knoxville Daily Tribune* was now calling the war, and both were now worthy of "equal reverence." Banished from Caldwell's selective retelling were the causes of the war, the issues raised by the war, the war's brutal ugliness and bitter passions. All that remained were the comforting truths that "courage, chivalry and genius" had belonged to both sides, and that only the politicians—never the soldiers—had ever truly been angry. "After all," Caldwell proclaimed, "we were never enemies. We were of one race. We were one in history and in hope."[1]

SUCH PRONOUNCEMENTS WERE COMMON across America by 1890. A generation removed from Lee's surrender at Appomattox, both North and South were well on their way to romanticizing a war that had claimed 620,000 lives, choosing to remember the bloody conflict as a family quarrel in which both sides had been noble and their respective values almost indistinguishable. Practicing the "politics of forgetting," both regions had begun to minimize the ideological issues that contributed to the collapse of the Union and to locate the war's lasting significance solely in the conflict itself, focusing on the bravery of the soldiers and their eventual reconciliation. Historians generally characterize this as an "invented" past, a politically useful "memory" that both sides consciously promoted to facilitate the goal of sectional reconciliation.[2] As applied to the overall sectional conflict, their critique is persuasive. And yet, as applied not to the great Civil War between North and South but to the local civil war in Knoxville, Judge Caldwell's remarks contained more than a modicum of truth—there was a measure of trenchant recollection to go along with the self-serving forgetfulness. The contention that Lincolnites and Rebels "were never enemies" was utterly absurd, of course, and Parson Brownlow surely turned over in his grave when the young orator delivered such a preposterous pronouncement. At the same time, Caldwell's claim that the two groups had much in common accurately captured an important dimension of the town's civil war.

It took me some time to understand this. When I first studied that evocative pencil sketch of Knoxville in the spring of 1861, the artist's portrayal of simultaneous Union and Confederate rallies at opposite ends of Gay Street suggested to me an already starkly divided community, an impression that only increased during the initial stages of my research. Out of necessity, I began my investigation with published primary sources that were readily obtainable: Parson Brownlow's *Sketches of Secession*, J. G. M. Ramsey's autobiography, Ellen House's diary. In the process I made the acquaintance of some wonderfully colorful personalities with passionate convictions, but I now see that while these individuals were reinforcing my fascination they were also deceiving me, tempting me to conclude that the line between Lincolnites and Rebels was vivid and clear. Only later did I discover that the Parson had purged from his wartime narrative every hint of ambiguity or personal compromise, declining to inform northern audiences of his promise to stand with the South against Republican aggression or his support of neutrality in the aftermath of Fort Sumter. Similarly, I did not immediately appreciate how few Knoxville Confederates shared Dr. Ramsey's fervent support of secession, nor did I understand right away that "very violent Rebels" like Ellen House were no more prevalent in Knoxville than "quiet and peaceable" ones.[3]

What now impresses me most is the vast range of common ground that initially united the town's free population, even as the community was splitting apart under the strain of the larger sectional conflict. Despite later claims to the contrary, "unconditional Unionists" were nonexistent during the secession crisis, and ardent secessionists—those favoring dissolution "in spite of the world, the flesh, and the devil"—were not much more common.[4] Eschewing extremes, future Confederates and Unionists agreed on a great deal. Most conspicuously, they shared an unquestioning commitment to the preservation of slavery and white supremacy. Beyond this, both groups agreed that southern rights had been violated in the past. Both deplored the election of Abraham Lincoln but saw evidence of irresponsible extremism and political opportunism in both North and South. Neither group tended to assert a constitutional right of secession. Both recognized the natural right of revolution if southern interests could not be protected otherwise. Above all, both groups hoped to keep war from their homes.

And yet "the war came," as Abraham Lincoln famously observed in his second inaugural, and when it did, the townspeople were ultimately forced to take sides in a conflict not of their own making. The battle at Fort Sumter and Lincoln's call for troops electrified the town, and Knoxville voters split almost literally down the middle in the secession referendum that followed. The factors that influenced how they cast their ballots are even now something of a mystery. A partial list would include partisan affiliation, church and family ties, and class and racial identity, as well as overlapping commitments to East Tennessee, to the state as a whole, to the South, and to the entire country. Whatever the reasons for their final decisions, many of the townspeople chose sides begrudgingly and more or less privately, keeping their sympathies to themselves and hoping to pursue business as usual, "without reference to politics," for as long as possible.[5] If a handful of young men rushed off to enlist in the summer of 1861, a far larger number stayed at home, and for several months thereafter Lincolnites and Rebels coexisted in an uneasy truce that allowed them to think of the war as a distant abstraction—not wholly irrelevant to their lives, and yet comfortably remote.

This all changed between November 1861 and April 1862, as events occurring outside Knoxville dramatically altered the community's internal conflict. First, the bridge burnings of late 1861 angered and frightened hitherto tolerant Rebels and prompted Confederate authorities to suppress all public expressions of disloyalty. Second, the passage of the Confederate Conscription Act the following spring deeply offended Unionists by promising to require active support of the Confederacy from all military-age white males. The cumulative result was a hardening of attitudes on both sides, especially among white men not old enough, wealthy enough, or well connected enough to avoid the draft. Confederates frequently came to support a military crackdown on "traitors" within the community; Unionists typically went even further, eventually favoring emancipation as the ultimate act of retribution against the "rebels" within their midst. Neighbors had become enemies.

This reminds us that if the *onset* of war can reveal a society's most deeply held values, the *dynamic* of war can also transform them. This is precisely what happened in Knoxville—but only up to a point. Even as the momentum of events carried the majority of Unionists to ever more radical positions concerning slavery, a small but influential faction of conservative loyalists balked at the demise of the institution. Connected to the local Confederate leadership by ties of kinship and commerce, they sought to minimize the war's permanent impact on patterns of power and wealth. The rank and file of loyalists spurned their example, but they, too, had their limits. If the Unionist coalition survived to the war's end, it was in large part because the collapse of slavery did not immediately threaten the framework of white supremacy with which it was intimately related.

Postwar developments would underscore the fragility of that coalition. Ever since the onset of the sectional crisis, Knoxville secessionists had appealed to racial solidarity to shame their opponents. A vote for separation, they had declared after Lincoln's election, was a vote against the "infamous doctrine of negro equality." Continued support for the Union, they had proclaimed in the wake of the Emancipation Proclamation, represented cowardly submission to the "abolition fiends who would . . . make us the slaves of slaves." Unionists had successfully withstood this onslaught, at first by denying that slavery was in danger, then, after 1863, by denying that emancipation would jeopardize white supremacy. By the end of 1865, however, the latter was becoming more and more difficult to believe. The town's black population had mushroomed (it would triple during the 1860s), and every street corner, in the view of anxious whites, seemed to teem with "idle, unemployed, and loafing" freedmen. What is worse, they were seemingly encouraged in their indolence by the agents of the Freedmen's Bureau and protected from chastisement by assertive black troops more than willing to "level their muskets at white men."[6]

Most distressing of all were the initiatives coming from the state capital. As the war was coming to a close, Parson Brownlow had insisted that emancipation would punish disloyal slaveholders without socially elevating the former slaves. He had also endorsed colonization, predicting that blacks would otherwise "gradually disappear as did the Indian," succumbing to starvation, idleness, and disease.[7] Within months of his inauguration, however, the new Republican governor felt pressure to endorse a bill that would allow blacks to testify in court, possibly in the belief that such a measure was necessary to secure acceptance in Washington of the state's newly elected congressional delegation. Well before 1865 was out, he had also begun to suggest that it might be necessary to give the ballot to the former slaves in order for Unionists to retain control of the state government. And so it was. Early in 1867 the Republican majority in the General Assembly would pass a black enfranchisement measure, and that fall Brownlow would use the Tennessee State Guard to protect black voters who, for their part, would help the governor to secure a second term in office.[8]

In sum, the costs of maintaining political power were high—ultimately too high for many Knoxville Unionists. By 1866 East Tennessee's fledging Republican Party was already learning an expensive lesson: despite the region's overwhelming opposition to secession throughout the recent war, area whites would go over to the Democrats—the party of disunion—before they would support a political party that apparently pandered to black voters.[9] J. C. Ramsey discovered as much during his first postwar visit to East Tennessee. After his release from jail at the close of the war, the former Confederate district attorney had initially stayed far away from Knoxville, repulsed by reports of the "outrageous scenes . . . constantly transpiring" there. As late as September 1865 he had denounced the treatment of Rebels in Knoxville as "disgraceful to humanity." Yet scarcely a half year later—only weeks after the lynching of the black Union sentinel—Ramsey felt safe in returning to Knoxville to initiate legal proceedings to reclaim the family's property. "East Ten. is to day as conservative as any section of the South," he informed his father in March 1866. "Prominent Union men . . . speak their sentiments freely and say that when they were for the Union, they had no idea that the condition of things would be as they are now." The bottom line, Ramsey exulted, was that "the radical party . . . is completely buried in East Ten."[10]

If the die-hard Democrat exaggerated the case, it is nonetheless true that local Republicans came to see support of racial equality as politically suicidal, and they would spend much of Reconstruction trying to distance themselves from the national party's stance on black civil rights. By 1874 even Parson Brownlow was taking this tack. Brownlow, who had won election to the U.S. Senate in 1869, publicly blasted a federal civil rights bill initiated by Massachusetts Republican Charles Sumner that would have required the integration of public schools. Gravely ill and lacking further political ambition, Senator Brownlow denounced the bill as "the quintessence of abominations" and acknowledged "that under no conceivable circumstances will East Tennessee Republicans support any man for any office who favors mixed schools." When Knoxville Republicans went down in defeat in a series of local elections that fall, John Bell Brownlow blamed "the excitement over the Civil Rights Bill" and acknowledged that the measure had produced a "fearful demoralization" among the party faithful. They would not even field a candidate for mayor in 1875, effectively forcing the elder Brownlow to do the unthinkable: cast his ballot for a Democrat and former Confederate.[11]

Although the vote did not kill him, the Parson was not long for this world. He died in early 1877, not long after the so-called Compromise of 1877, the informal agreement between national Republican and Democratic leaders that secured the withdrawal of the last Federal troops from the South and marked, at least symbolically, the end of Reconstruction. The political party Brownlow had helped to create in East Tennessee did not die, however. It survived and even flourished again, but only by turning away from the divisive questions of the past generation and focusing on local issues pertaining to education and economic development. The same kind of intentional forgetfulness came to characterize the people of Knoxville more generally. Aging Unionists and Confederates both formed local veterans' organizations during the 1880s, each of which pledged to avoid "everything which partakes of partisanship" and repudiate all efforts "to prolong the animosities engendered by the war." Each group also understood that true reconciliation would require a fair amount of amnesia on both sides. Thus by 1890 both organizations could gladly endorse the plan for a joint reunion of Lincolnites and Rebels. Both could applaud the three-day-long "love-feast of patriotism and peace" that resulted, and both—with the aid of a properly selective memory—could echo the gathering's central theme: "We were never enemies. We were of one race. . . ."[12]

Identifying Individual Unionists and Confederates

EW SOUTHERN COMMUNITIES have left as rich a historical record from the Civil War as Knoxville. Given the small size of the town, there is a surprisingly large number of surviving primary sources that afford glimpses into the personal beliefs of individual citizens. Most prominently among these are the four book-length histories or memoirs written by prominent players in the town's civil war: William Brownlow, Oliver Temple, Thomas Humes, and J. G. M. Ramsey. Beyond these, there are also fifteen or so detailed diaries or collections of extensive correspondence (and a dozen or more smaller collections besides), numerous pardon applications from Knoxville Confederates to President Andrew Johnson, and the town's two major newspapers, both of which, albeit imperfectly, gave voice to widely held popular convictions. Collectively, these sources yield rich insights into the values, motivations, and personal struggles of a few dozen individuals. I have relied on them extensively throughout *Lincolnites and Rebels* to integrate "flesh and blood" into the narrative.

Most of Knoxville's inhabitants did not leave such detailed paper trails, of course. The scant evidence that the average household left behind brings to mind Thomas Gray's famous meditation on "the short and simple annals of the poor." Abraham Lincoln once quoted from the poet's "Elegy Written in a Country Churchyard" to discourage an effort to chronicle his own humble upbringing. "That's my life," he informed a reporter for the *Chicago Tribune*, "and that's all you or any one else can make of it."[1] Even with the comparative richness of Knoxville's historical record, in other words, it remains impossible to penetrate the private thoughts of the vast majority of the townspeople, making it foolhardy to generalize dogmatically about the "determinants" of loyalty. Yet if they do not regularly reveal individual *motives*, a number of sources have survived that yield information concerning the *sympathies* of individual townspeople or, more precisely, how those sympathies were perceived by contemporaries.

A variety of civil and military records are helpful in this regard. The minutes of both the Knox County Circuit Court and the Federal District Court for East Tennessee list individuals charged with giving "aid and comfort" to the enemies of the United States. The military service records of Confederate and Union soldiers help to identify men mustered into either army, although the frequent absence of information on age and place of residence can make positive identification difficult. Copious military records generated in the Union provost marshal general's office during the Federal occupation of Knoxville between September 1863 and the end of the war offer insight into the sympathies and behavior of civilians. For example, the provost marshal faithfully recorded the names of all civilians who came forward to take President Lincoln's amnesty oath during the winter of 1863–64. Equally revealing are records of the claims of townspeople seeking reimbursement from the U.S. government for food and forage confiscated by Ambrose Burnside's Army of the Ohio during that same winter. In response to widespread complaints, the Union general created a claims board consisting of one staff officer and three prominent Knoxville Unionists whose loyalty was considered unassailable—initially merchants Perez Dickinson and John Williams and banker Sam Morrow, the latter of whom also served in the Fifth Tennessee Cavalry (U.S.A.). Known popularly as the "Burnside Commission," the board was charged with taking testimony concerning both the confiscation of property and, significantly, the loyalty of claimants.[2]

A number of postwar governmental records are also illuminating. In 1868, the Republican-controlled Tennessee General Assembly established a short-lived statewide claims commission to procure testimony not only concerning unpaid claims by Unionists against the federal government but also with regard to damages inflicted by Confederate military and civil authorities. Applying the model of the Burnside Commission to the state as a whole, the enabling act called for the creation of civilian boards in each county of the state. It then charged these bodies with compiling evidence concerning the taking of property and the "ironclad" loyalty of claimants. No action was ever taken on these claims, as the authority of the Tennessee General Claims Commission, as it was known, was revoked in 1869 after the Republican Party lost its tenuous control of the legislature.[3] Knoxville residents continued to press their claims for reimbursement, however, filing applications in substantial numbers before the Southern Claims

Commission in the early 1870s and before the U.S. Court of Claims from the 1880s until early in the next century.[4]

Cumulatively, these sources provide information concerning the loyalties of 483 Knoxville adults (444 males) residing in some 323 households (not including hotels and boardinghouses), or just over one of every two white households in town on the eve of the war. I have excluded from consideration a handful of wives who were not household heads, a small number of males on whom pertinent information from the census is missing (concerning nativity, wealth, etc.), as well as some thirty-eight white males who entered the Confederate army after the passage of the Confederate Conscription Act in April 1862. In one sense, the Conscription Act made it easier to identify individuals loyal to the Union, inasmuch as it forced countless Unionist sympathizers who were keeping a low profile to adopt an openly pro-Union stance. At the same time, the act makes it extremely difficult to gauge the sympathies of men who entered the Confederate army after its passage. Some of those who either joined or were conscripted after the spring of 1862 were surely sincere supporters of the Confederacy, but as relatively poor men, often with families to feed, they had heretofore felt obliged to stay at home. Far from a reflection of "Unionism," such instances reflected a commitment to family above either national or regional attachments. Others who enlisted after the passage of conscription were undoubtedly opponents of the Confederacy who feared for their families should they not answer the Confederacy's call; postwar records repeatedly identify particular Confederate draftees as "Unionists." Such ambiguity renders this group far too difficult to categorize. Technically speaking, the remaining 422 individuals do not constitute a random sample of the town's population in any statistically verifiable sense. As is so often the case with historical evidence, the wealthy and articulate—slaveholders and white-collar professionals, in particular—are overrepresented. Nevertheless, if used cautiously and with these limitations in mind, the surviving record offers an extraordinary glimpse into the patterns of wartime sympathies. In particular, the records of the various claims commissions are uniquely valuable in that they divulge who leading Unionists at the time considered to be loyal among their neighbors. Rather than having to establish some abstract standard of "authentic" Unionist behavior and then determine which individuals measured up to it, it becomes possible instead to make a list of those deemed loyal and then investigate how they behaved. Because of the variety of the sources, it is often not possible to pinpoint the moment at which Confederates embraced the cause of the South; hence I have used voting statistics to estimate the proportion of the townspeople who supported the Confederacy at the time of the statewide secession referenda in February and June 1861, and the records outlined here to estimate patterns of sympathy as of the summer of 1863, just before the "liberation" of the town by Federal forces.

TABLE 1.

Characteristics of Confederate Soldiers Enlisting
before and after the Passage of the Confederate Conscription Act

	Soldiers Enlisting prior to March 1862	Soldiers Enlisting after February 1862
Age (median)	24	25.5
Married (%)	33.3	44.7
"White collar" (%)	54.1	16.2
Slave owning household (%)	20.2	2.6
Household wealth (median)	$1,200	$75
Number	109	38

TABLE 2.

Characteristics of Unionists and Confederates[a]

	Unionists	Confederates
Northern-born (%)	12.3	4.0
Foreign-born (%)	9.0	9.0
Slave owning household (%)	17.2	24.7
"White collar" (%)	39.2	63.1
Household wealth (median)	$2,200	$3,250
Number	122	300

[a] Statistics are based on 1860 census data for all adult males plus female heads of households for whom information on sympathies could be obtained.

NOTES

INTRODUCTION

1 Quoted in C. Vann Woodward, *Origins of the New South, 1877–1913* (Baton Rouge: Louisiana State University Press, 1951), p. viii.
2 David M. Potter, *The South and the Sectional Conflict* (Baton Rouge: Louisiana State University Press, 1968), p. v.
3 Mark E. Neely Jr., *Southern Rights: Political Prisoners and the Myth of Confederate Constitutionalism* (Charlottesville: University Press of Virginia, 1999), p. 99.
4 Major works focusing on the Civil War in some portion of southern Appalachia include Martin Crawford, *Ashe County's Civil War: Community and Society in the Appalachian South* (Charlottesville: University Press of Virginia, 2001); Durwood Dunn, *Cades Cove: The Life and Death of a Southern Appalachian Community, 1818–1937* (Knoxville: University of Tennessee Press, 1988); Noel C. Fisher, *War at Every Door: Partisan Politics and Guerilla Violence in East Tennessee, 1860–1869* (Chapel Hill: University of North Carolina Press, 1997); John Derrick Fowler, *Mountaineers in Gray: The Story of the Nineteenth Tennessee Volunteer Infantry Regiment, C.S.A.* (Knoxville: University of Tennessee Press, 2004); W. Todd Groce, *Mountain Rebels: East Tennessee Confederates and the Civil War, 1860–1870* (Knoxville: University of Tennessee Press, 1999); John C. Inscoe and Gordon B. McKinney, *The Heart of Confederate Appalachia: Western North Carolina in the Civil War* (Chapel Hill: University of North Carolina Press, 2000); Kenneth W. Noe, *Southwest Virginia's Railroad: Modernization and the Sectional Crisis* (Urbana: University of Illinois Press, 1994); Kenneth W. Noe and Shannon H. Wilson, eds., *The Civil War in Appalachia: Collected Essays* (Knoxville: University of Tennessee Press, 1997); John W. Shaffer, *Clash of Loyalties: A Border County in the Civil War* (Morgantown: West Virginia University Press, 2003); David Williams, *Rich Man's War: Class, Caste, and Confederate Defeat in the Lower Chattahoochie Valley* (Athens: University of Georgia Press, 1998).
5 Emory M. Thomas, *The Confederate Nation: 1861–1865* (New York: Harper and Row, 1979), pp. 87, 94; George C. Rable, *The Confederate Republic: A Revolution against Politics* (Chapel Hill: University of North Carolina Press, 1994), pp. 114, 145; Paul Escott, *After Secession: Jefferson Davis and the Failure of Confederate Nationalism* (Baton Rouge: Louisiana State University Press, 1978), pp. 96, 185, 194; William W. Freehling, *The South vs. the South: How Anti-Confederate Southerners Shaped the Course of the Civil War* (New York: Oxford University Press, 2001), pp. 60–61.
6 Digby Gordon Seymour, *Divided Loyalties: Fort Sanders and the Civil War in East Tennessee*, rev. ed. (Knoxville: East Tennessee Historical Society, 1982), p. 2.
7 *Daily National Intelligencer* [Washington, DC], 10 September 1863; Roy P. Basler, ed., *The Collected Works of Abraham Lincoln*, 8 vols. (New Brunswick, NJ: Rutgers University Press, 1953–55), vol. 7, p. 35.
8 William B. Hesseltine, ed., *Dr. J. G. M. Ramsey: Autobiography and Letters* (Nashville: Tennessee Historical Commission, 1954), pp. 40–41; Daniel E. Sutherland, ed., *A Very Violent Rebel:*

The Civil War Diary of Ellen Renshaw House (Knoxville: University of Tennessee Press, 1996), p. 108.

9 *Knoxville Whig*, 27 April, 3 August 1861.

10 See Appendix, "Identifying Individual Unionists and Confederates."

CHAPTER ONE

1 *Jonesborough Whig and Independent Journal*, 5 and 12 February 1849. On "gold fever" in Tennessee, see Walter T. Durham, *Volunteer Forty-niners: Tennesseans and the California Gold Rush* (Nashville: Vanderbilt University Press, 1997).

2 *Jonesborough Whig and Independent Journal*, 5 February 1849. For an assessment of Brownlow's motives by a former Knoxville journalist, see Frederick S. Heiskell to John Bell, 18 April 1849, Frederick S. Heiskell Papers, Archives of Appalachia, East Tennessee State University.

3 On the Second Party System in Tennessee, see Jonathan M. Atkins, *Parties, Politics, and the Sectional Conflict in Tennessee, 1832–1861* (Knoxville: University of Tennessee Press, 1997); Paul H. Bergeron, *Antebellum Politics in Tennessee* (Lexington: University Press of Kentucky, 1982); and Mark E. Neely Jr., *Southern Rights: Political Prisoners and the Myth of Confederate Constitutionalism* (Charlottesville: University Press of Virginia, 1999), especially chap. 6. Quotations are from Atkins, *Parties, Politics, and the Sectional Conflict*, pp. 3, 81.

4 Samuel Mayes Arnell, "The Southern Unionist," unpublished manuscript, Samuel Mayes Arnell Papers, Special Collections, University of Tennessee Libraries, p. 40; *Chicago Tribune*, 11 April 1862; E. Merton Coulter, *William G. Brownlow: Fighting Parson of the Southern Highlands* (Chapel Hill: University of North Carolina Press, 1937), pp. 4–6, 17.

5 Steve Humphrey, *"That D----d Brownlow": Being a Saucy and Malicious Description of Fighting Parson William Gannaway Brownlow* (Boone, NC: Appalachian Consortium Press, 1978), pp. 13–14; R. N. Price, "William G. Brownlow and His Times," chap. 14 of *Holston Methodism: From Its Origin to the Present Time* (Nashville and Dallas: Publishing House of the Methodist Episcopal Church, 1908), vol. 3, p. 340; William G. Brownlow, *The Great Iron Wheel; or, Its False Spokes Extracted, and an Exhibition of Elder Graves, Its Builder* (Nashville: published for the author, 1856), pp. 23, 131 (italics in the original); William G. Brownlow, *Helps to the Study of Presbyterianism* (Knoxville: F. S. Heiskell, 1834), pp. 253, 292.

6 Humphrey, *"That D----d Brownlow,"* p. 9; *Jonesborough Whig and Independent Journal*, 13 December 1843, 16 June 1845.

7 E. G. Caren to William G. Brownlow, 14 July 1860, James Clift to William G. Brownlow, 10 January 1860, both in folder 416, E. E. Patton Collection, McClung Historical Collection, Knox County Public Library; Royal Forrest Conklin, "The Public Speaking Career of William Gannaway (Parson) Brownlow" (Ph.D. diss., Ohio University, 1967), pp. 31–33, 50–51, 94.

8 U.S. Census Bureau, Seventh Census [1850], *Statistics of Population* (Washington, DC: Government Printing Office, 1853), p. 574; J. B. Killebrew, *Introduction to the Resources of Tennessee* (Nashville: Tavel, Eastman and Howell, 1874), p. 423.

9 At the time of the Civil War the stretch of river forming the southern boundary of Knoxville was known as the Holston. The Holston and the French Broad, which rise in Virginia and North Carolina, respectively, flow to the south and west until they merge a few miles east of Knoxville. Today we think of their confluence as forming the Tennessee River, although until 1874 locals thought in terms of the French Broad emptying into the Holston, rather than speaking of the two rivers as joining to form a third. They viewed the Tennessee River as being formed by the junction of the Holston and the Little Tennessee, twenty-five miles or so farther downstream. See Mary U. Rothrock, ed., *French Broad–Holston Country: A History of Knox County, Tennessee* (Knoxville: East Tennessee Historical Society, 1946), pp. 19–26.

10   Robert E. Corlew, *Tennessee: A Short History*, 2nd ed. (Knoxville: University of Tennessee Press, 1981), pp. 43–51; William Rule, ed., *Standard History of Knoxville, Tennessee* (Chicago: Lewis Publishing, 1900), pp. 37–41, 46–63, 275; Rothrock, *French Broad-Holston Country*, pp. 19–26; Betsey Beeler Creekmore, *Knoxville*, 3rd ed. (Knoxville: University of Tennessee Press, 1976), pp. 45–50; *A Sketch of Knoxville from 1792, with Portraits of Thirty Representative Men Who Have Occupied the City's Executive Chair* (Knoxville: n.p., 189?), p. 3; *History of Tennessee from the Earliest Time to the Present, Together with an Historical and a Biographical Sketch of the County of Knox and the City of Knoxville* (Chicago: Goodspeed Publishing, 1887), pp. 841, 817.

11   *Jonesborough Whig and Independent Journal*, 8 December 1841; John C. Inscoe, "Mountain Unionism, Secession, and Regional Self-Image: The Contrasting Cases of Western North Carolina and East Tennessee," in Winfred B. Moore Jr. and Joseph F. Tripp, eds., *Looking South: Chapters in the Story of an American Region* (New York: Greenwood Press, 1989), p. 125. The situation was actually more complicated, as the bill to move the capital passed with the support of several legislators from upper East Tennessee (north of Knoxville), who for political reasons had allied themselves on the issues with congressmen from Middle Tennessee. See Eric Russell Lacy, *Vanquished Volunteers: East Tennessee Sectionalism from Statehood to Secession* (Johnson City: East Tennessee State University Press, 1965), pp. 47–50.

12   Rule, *Standard History of Knoxville*, p. 91; Stanley J. Folmsbee, "Sectionalism and Internal Improvements in Tennessee, 1796–1845" (Ph.D. diss., University of Pennsylvania, 1939), p. 8; Lacy, *Vanquished Volunteers*, p. 31; Corlew, *Tennessee: A Short History*, pp. 3–5, 228–29; Eugene W. Hilgard, *Report on Cotton Production in the United States* (Washington, DC: Government Printing Office, 1884), p. 383; Killebrew, *Introduction to the Resources of Tennessee*, pp. 619–24, 1014–22.

13   Rothrock, *French Broad-Holston Country*, pp. 12–17.

14   Folmsbee, "Sectionalism and Internal Improvements," pp. 10–14; Killebrew, *Introduction to the Resources of Tennessee*, pp. 277–83; James T. Lloyd, *Lloyd's Steamboat Directory* (Cincinnati, OH: James T. Lloyd, 1856), p. 47; Donald L. Winters, *Tennessee Farming, Tennessee Farmers: Antebellum Agriculture in the Upper South* (Knoxville: University of Tennessee Press, 1994), p. 83; Edmond Cody Burnett, "Hog Raising and Hog Driving in the Region of the French Broad River," *Agricultural History* 20 (1946): 86–88. See also David C. Hsiung, *Two Worlds in the Tennessee Mountains: Exploring the Origins of Appalachian Stereotypes* (Lexington: University Press of Kentucky, 1997), pp. 74–92.

15   Hilgard, *Report on Cotton Production*, pp. 409–11. In 1860 the average wealth per free family was $6,640 in Middle Tennessee, $7,130 in West Tennessee, but only $2,830 in East Tennessee. While there is sometimes a tendency to romanticize the lives of rural households in areas remote from the market economy, whatever its intangible benefits, "self-sufficiency" was synonymous with rural poverty. My analysis of more than a thousand farm operators in upper East Tennessee in 1860 revealed that farmers who produced primarily for market exchange earned per capita incomes three to four times higher than those who were oriented toward household subsistence. See Robert Tracy McKenzie, "Wealth and Income: The Preindustrial Structure of East Tennessee in 1860," *Appalachian Journal* 21 (1994): 272–79.

16   William B. Hesseltine, ed., *Dr. J. G. M. Ramsey: Autobiography and Letters* (Nashville: Tennessee Historical Commission, 1954), p. 17; David Deaderick Diary, McClung Historical Collection, Knox County Public Library, entry for 1829.

17   Hermann Bokum, *The Tennessee Handbook and Immigrants' Guide* (Philadelphia: Lippincott, 1868), p. 8; Horace Maynard to Ephraim Maynard, 6 February 1849, Horace Maynard Papers, Special Collections, University of Tennessee Libraries; *Relief for East Tennessee: Address of Honorable N. G. Taylor, March 10, 1864* (New York: Wm. C. Bryant, 1864), p. 10; Hesseltine, *Ramsey Autobiography*, p. 17; J. G. M. Ramsey to Crozier Ramsey, 4 August 1850, J. G. M. Ramsey Papers, Special Collections, University of Tennessee Libraries; Deaderick Diary, entry for 1826; Hsiung, *Two Worlds in the Tennessee Mountains*, p. 101.

18   Lacy, *Vanquished Volunteers*, pp. 111, 114, 121; Folmsbee, "Sectionalism and Internal Improvements," pp. 177–215; Hesseltine, *Ramsey Autobiography*, p. 19; J. G. M. Ramsey to Crozier Ramsey,
29 July 1850, Ramsey Papers.

19   Lacy, *Vanquished Volunteers*, pp. 114–27; Ezekiel Birdseye to Gerrit Smith, 14 December 1841,
in Durwood Dunn, *An Abolitionist in the Appalachian South: Ezekiel Birdseye on Slavery, Capitalism, and Separate Statehood in East Tennessee, 1841–1846* (Knoxville: University of Tennessee Press, 1997), p. 202; *Jonesborough Whig and Independent Journal*, 8 December, 15 December,
1841.

20   Lacy, *Vanquished Volunteers*, pp. 125–26, 143–44, 152, 163; Dunn, *Abolitionist in the Appalachian
South*, p. 251; Rothrock, *French Broad–Holston Country*, pp. 105–7; James W. Holland, "The East
Tennessee and Georgia Railroad, 1836–1860," *East Tennessee Historical Society's Publications* 3
(1931): 89–107; David Hunter Strother, "A Winter in the South," pt. 5, *Harper's New Monthly
Magazine* 16 (1858): 733.

21   *Knoxville Whig*, 17 April 1858; George W. Featherstonhaugh, *Excursion through the Slave States,
from Washington on the Potomac to the Frontier of Mexico; with Sketches of Popular Manners and
Geological Notices* (New York: Harper and Row, 1844), p. 45.

22   *Knoxville Whig*, 23 June 1849.

23   Seventh United States Census [1850], schedule V, Productions of Industry, Knox County, Tennessee; *Appleton's Illustrated Hand-Book of American Travel* (New York: D. Appleton, 1857),
pt. 2, pp. 316–17.

24   Rothrock, *French Broad–Holston Country*, p. 75; *History of Tennessee from the Earliest Time to the
Present*, p. 843; Knox County Merchants' Licenses, Tennessee State Library and Archives [here-
after TSLA].

25   Stanley J. Folmsbee, "East Tennessee University: Pre-war Years, 1840–1861," *East Tennessee
Historical Society's Publications* 22 (1950): 60–93; Laura Elizabeth Luttrell, comp., *U.S. Census,
1850, for Knox County, Tennessee* (Knoxville: East Tennessee Historical Society, 1949), p. iv;
History of Tennessee from the Earliest Time to the Present, p. 846; *Jonesborough Whig and Independent Journal*, 17 January 1849.

26   Rule, *Standard History of Knoxville*, p. 527; William G. Brownlow to Thomas A. R. Nelson,
31 August, 9 September 1854, E. E. Patton Collection, McClung Historical Collection, Knox
County Public Library; Humphrey, *"That D----d Brownlow,"* pp. 183–84.

27   Rule, *Standard History of Knoxville*, pp. 96–97, 101–4, 197, 413; *History of Tennessee from the Earliest Time to the Present*, p. 812; *Knoxville Whig*, 17 November 1860; Rebecca Hunt Moulder, *May
the Sod Rest Lightly* (Tucson, AZ: Skyline Printing, 1977), p. 19; Lowell L. Giffin, *A History of
Second Presbyterian Church* (Knoxville: n.p., 1994), pp. 20–23.

28   Holland, "East Tennessee and Georgia Railroad," quotation on p. 104; Rothrock, *French Broad–
Holston Country*, pp. 106–7; Stock Reports, East Tennessee and Georgia Railroad, Record Group
[hereafter RG] 5, Internal Improvements: Railroads, TSLA; *Appleton's Illustrated Hand-Book
of American Travel*, p. 315. For a map of the southeastern railroad network, see Ulrich Bonnell
Phillips, *A History of Transportation in the Eastern Cotton Belt to 1860* (New York: Columbia
University Press, 1908).

29   James W. Holland, "The Building of the East Tennessee and Virginia Railroad," *East Tennessee Historical Society's Publications* 4 (1932): 83–101; Rothrock, *French Broad–Holston Country*,
pp. 110–11; *Knoxville Whig*, 23 June 1855, 17 April 1858.

30   *Knoxville Whig*, 29 December 1855, 18 April 1858; Donald W. Buckwalter, "Effects of Early Nineteenth Century Transportation Disadvantage on the Agriculture of Eastern Tennessee," *Southeastern Geographer* 27 (1987): 18–37; Winters, *Tennessee Farming, Tennessee Farmers*, pp. 62, 181;
Rothrock, *French Broad–Holston Country*, p. 76. The average value of farm land per acre increased
from $5.83 in 1850 to $13.67 ten years later.

31 Knox County Merchants' Licenses; Knox County Credit Reports, Tennessee Vol. 12, p. 27, R. G. Dun & Co. Collection, Baker Library, Harvard University Graduate School of Business Administration.
32 *Williams' Knoxville Directory, City Guide, and Business Mirror*, vol. 1 (Knoxville: C. S. Williams, 1859), pp. 83–87.
33 *Knoxville Whig*, 23 June 1856, 12 June 1858; Rule, *Standard History of Knoxville*, p. 110.
34 Rule, *Standard History of Knoxville*, p. 440; William G. Brownlow, *Americanism Contrasted with Foreignism, Romanism, and Bogus Democracy, in the Light of Reason, History, and Holy Scripture; in Which Certain Demagogues in Tennessee, and Elsewhere, Are Shown Up in Their True Colors* (Nashville: published for the author, 1856), p. 66.
35 *Knoxville Whig*, 14 September 1861; Moulder, *May the Sod Rest Lightly*, p. 22. On the distribution of wealth in antebellum cities, see Edward Pessen, *Riches, Class, and Power before the Civil War* (Lexington, MA: D. C. Heath, 1973), pp. 34, 39.
36 *Knoxville Whig*, 4 February, 9 June, 7 July 1860.
37 *Knoxville Whig*, 28 January, 28 April, 14 and 28 July, 8 September 1860.
38 *Knoxville Whig*, 21 and 28 April, 16 June, 25 August, 1860; entries for 23 and 25 February 1860, William G. McAdoo Diary, Floyd-McAdoo Family Diaries and Letterbooks, Library of Congress; *New York Times*, 8 March 1860.

CHAPTER TWO

1 For overviews of the Second Party System in Tennessee, see Jonathan M. Atkins, *Parties, Politics, and the Sectional Conflict in Tennessee, 1832–1861* (Knoxville: University of Tennessee Press, 1997); and Paul H. Bergeron, *Antebellum Politics in Tennessee* (Lexington: University Press of Kentucky, 1982).
2 Yancey's appearance in Knoxville is recounted in three primary sources, only one of which was recorded at the time, however, and none of which offers a secessionist perspective. Brownlow's contemporary account can be found in the *Knoxville Whig*, 22 September 1860. See also Samuel Mayes Arnell, "The Southern Unionist," unpublished manuscript, Samuel Mayes Arnell Papers, Special Collections, University of Tennessee Libraries, pp. 174–79; Thomas William Humes, *The Loyal Mountaineers of Tennessee* (Knoxville: Ogden Brothers, 1888), pp. 81–85. The following four paragraphs draw from all three accounts but rely primarily on Brownlow's description, which, though hardly unbiased, has the advantage of proximity in time to the event it describes.
3 George C. Rable, *The Confederate Republic: A Revolution against Politics* (Chapel Hill: University of North Carolina Press, 1994), p. 6.
4 *Knoxville Whig*, 22 September 1860.
5 James M. McPherson, *Battle Cry of Freedom: The Civil War Era* (New York: Oxford University Press, 1988), pp. 196, 243. See also J. D. B. DeBow, "The Non-slaveholders of the South: Their Interest in the Present Sectional Controversy Identical with That of the Slaveholders," *DeBow's Review* 30 (1861): 67–77.
6 *Knoxville Whig*, 22 September 1860. The quotations come from Brownlow's summary of Yancey's remarks.
7 Ibid. Yancey had asked Brownlow whether he would support Federal troops marching into the South to coerce the secessionists. The Parson had answered by declaring his resolve to aid Federal troops defending the national capital from secessionist forces marching northward. Writing decades after the fact, Brownlow's political ally Samuel Arnell retold the story differently. According to Arnell, the editor declared himself "in favor of coercing them [states that might secede] back into the Union at the point of a bayonet." If so, Brownlow was reluctant to put such sentiments in print. See Arnell, "Southern Unionist," p. 177.

8   *Knoxville Whig*, 22 September 1860 (italics in the original); *New York Times*, 29 September 1860 (quoting the *Knoxville Register* of unspecified date); Humes, *Loyal Mountaineers of Tennessee*, p. 84.

9   Humes, *Loyal Mountaineers of Tennessee*, p. 84; *Knoxville Whig*, 22 September 1860.

10 *Ought American Slavery to Be Perpetuated? A Debate between Rev. W. G. Brownlow and Rev. A. Pryne* (Philadelphia: Lippincott, 1858), p. 263.

11 *Knoxville Whig*, 20 October, 16 June 1860.

12 *Knoxville Whig*, 6, 13 October 1860, 19 January 1861.

13 *Knoxville Whig*, 29 September, 27 October 1860. On the efforts of *Register* shareholders to drive Brownlow out of business, see marginal notation of John Bell Brownlow, *Knoxville Whig*, May 19, 1849; W. G. Brownlow to "Dear Sir" [probably Thomas A. R. Nelson], 9 August, 15 October, 8 November, 17 December 1849, E. E. Patton Collection, McClung Historical Collection, Knox County Public Library; Frederick S. Heiskell to John Bell, 31 December 1849, Frederick S. Heiskell Papers, Archives of Appalachia, East Tennessee State University; and Oliver P. Temple, *Notable Men of Tennessee from 1833 to 1875: Their Times and Their Contemporaries* (New York: Cosmopolitan Press, 1912), pp. 274–76.

14 Humes, *Loyal Mountaineers of Tennessee*, p. 31; Oliver P. Temple, *East Tennessee and the Civil War* (Cincinnati: Robert Clarke, 1899), p. 557. See also William Rule, *The Loyalists of Tennessee in the Late War* (Cincinnati: H. C. Sherick, 1887). Noel Fisher critically assesses the works by Temple and Humes in "Definitions of Loyalty: Unionist Histories of the Civil War in East Tennessee," *Journal of East Tennessee History* 67 (1995): 58–88.

15 *Knoxville Register*, 27 September 1860, 5 June 1861.

16 Temple, *East Tennessee and the Civil War*, pp. 85–105, 111–20; Richard B. Drake, "Slavery and Antislavery in Appalachia," *Appalachian Heritage* 14 (1986): 29–30. See also Asa Earl Martin, "The Anti-slavery Societies of Tennessee," *Tennessee Historical Magazine* 1 (1915): 261–81; John C. Inscoe, "Olmstead in Appalachia: A Connecticut Yankee Encounters Slavery and Racism in the Southern Highlands," *Slavery and Abolition* 9 (1988): 171–82; John C. Inscoe, "Race and Racism in Nineteenth-Century Southern Appalachia," in Mary Beth Pudup, Dwight B. Billings, and Altina L. Waller, eds., *Appalachia in the Making: The Mountain South in the Nineteenth Century* (Chapel Hill: University of North Carolina Press, 1995), pp. 103–31; Durwood Dunn, *An Abolitionist in the Appalachian South: Ezekiel Birdseye on Slavery, Capitalism, and Separate Statehood in East Tennessee, 1841–1846* (Knoxville: University of Tennessee Press, 1997). There were two petitions from Knox County, signed by a total of 120 men. See petititions 37-1834 and 22-1834, Legislative Petitions, TSLA.

17 Horace Maynard, "To the Slaveholders of Tennessee," box 2, f. 28, Horace Maynard Papers, Special Collections, University of Tennessee Libraries; Merton L. Dillon, "Three Southern Antislavery Editors: The Myth of the Southern Antislavery Movement," *East Tennessee Historical Society's Publications* 42 (1970): 55; petitions 39-1834, 25-1834, 40-1834, 32-1834, Legislative Petitions, TSLA.

18 Dillon, "Three Southern Antislavery Editors"; testimony of Clinton B. Fisk in U.S. Congress, *Report of the Joint Committee on Reconstruction*, House Report No. 30, 39th Cong., 1st sess. (Washington, DC: Government Printing Office, 1866), pt. 1, p. 122; petition 23-1834, Legislative Petitions, TSLA.

19 Entries for 1826, David Deaderick Diary, McClung Historical Collection, Knox County Public Library; Horace Maynard to Ephraim Maynard, 23 January 1839, Maynard Papers; petition 38-1834, Legislative Petitions, TSLA. My thanks to Professor Durwood Dunn for alerting me to Brownlow's signature on the Jefferson County petition.

20 Dunn, *Abolitionist in the Appalachian South*, pp. 8–9; Temple, *East Tennessee and the Civil War*, p. 120; Homer Sears to Rev. Bro. Hill, 12 June 1846, Records of the First Baptist Church, Knoxville, Tennessee, TSLA.

21 *Knoxville Whig*, 16 June 1849, 19 June 1852. Humes, however, had allowed at least one of his slaves to purchase his freedom. See testimony of Anthony Humes, claim 2,494, Records of the General Accounting Office, RG 217, National Archives and Records Administration [hereafter NARA].

22 William B. Hesseltine, ed., *Dr. J. G. M. Ramsey: Autobiography and Letters* (Nashville: Tennessee Historical Commission, 1954), pp. 91–93; A. Woodward, *A Review of Uncle Tom's Cabin; or, an Essay on Slavery* (Cincinnati: Applegate, 1853), pp. 106–7; *Knoxville Whig*, 16 June 1849, 19 June 1852.

23 Hesseltine, *Ramsey Autobiography*, pp. 83–97, quotations on pp. 87, 91, 96. Ramsey's correspondent in these pages is L. W. Spratt, editor of the *Charleston Mercury* and a major advocate of the reopening of the transatlantic slave trade. See Vicki Vaughn Johnson, *The Men and the Vision of the Southern Commercial Conventions, 1845–1871* (Columbia: University of Missouri Press, 1992), p. 134.

24 Dorothy K. Riggs, "Horace Maynard: Some Facts and Stories Collected for His Descendants," p. 4, Maynard Papers; Horace Maynard to Ephraim Maynard, 23 January 1839, 20 July 1841, Maynard Papers.

25 Horace Maynard to Ephraim Maynard, 3 February 1844, 24 October 1845, Maynard Papers.

26 Horace Maynard to Ephraim Maynard, 15 August 1850, Maynard Papers.

27 Horace Maynard to Ephraim Maynard, 7 December 1850, 7 March 1851, Maynard Papers; Riggs, "Horace Maynard," p. 8; John C. Rives, ed., *Appendix to the Congressional Globe*, vol. 30, pt. 2 (Washington, DC: Congressional Globe Office, 1861), p. 165.

28 Temple, *East Tennessee and the Civil War*, pp. 119–20.

29 The question of whether Brownlow ever succeeded in acquiring slaves is open to dispute. In 1862 Brownlow told northern audiences that he had been a slaveholder, though never a large one, and claimed that a unit of Alabama troops had stolen a valuable "boy" from his home the preceding year. Neither census reports nor local deed records indicate that Brownlow owned slaves on the eve of the war, however, and Brownlow's best friend, Oliver Temple, flatly declared that Brownlow was "not a slave owner." See *Boston Daily Evening Transcript*, 24 May 1862; Temple, *Notable Men of Tennessee*, p. 289. Steve Humphrey asserts that the evidence that Brownlow owned two household slaves is "conclusive," citing the recollection of descendants who recalled long afterward that there had been slaves in the Brownlow household. The 1860 population census, however, lists two free black servants in the household in 1860, which could explain an understandable but erroneous perception on the part of the descendants. See Steve Humphrey, *"That D----d Brownlow": Being a Saucy and Malicious Description of Fighting Parson William Gannaway Brownlow* (Boone, NC: Appalachian Consortium Press), pp. 264, 276n.

30 William G. Brownlow, *Helps to the Study of Presbyterianism* (Knoxville: F. S. Heiskell, 1834), p. 110; *Knoxville Whig*, 30 April 1845.

31 Mitchell Snay, *Gospel of Disunion: Religion and Separatism in the Antebellum South* (Chapel Hill: University of North Carolina Press, 1993), chaps. 1–2; Donald G. Mathews, *Religion in the Old South* (Chicago: University of Chicago Press, 1977), chap. 4.

32 Brownlow, *Helps to the Study of Presbyterianism*, p. 110; *Jonesborough Whig and Independent Journal*, 12 June 1844, 6 May, 4 June 1845; *Knoxville Whig*, 6 August 1853. See also William G. Brownlow, *A Sermon on Slavery; A Vindication of the Methodist Church, South: Her Position Stated* (Knoxville: Kinsloe and Rice, 1857).

33 *Ought American Slavery to Be Perpetuated?* p. 21. See also J. Jeffery Auer, ed., *Antislavery and Disunion, 1858–1861: Studies in the Rhetoric of Compromise and Conflict* (New York: Harper and Row, 1963), pp. 1–10.

34 *Ought American Slavery to Be Perpetuated?* pp. 43, 98, 252, 270, 263, 217–18. For coverage of the debate, see *National Era* [Washington, DC], 23 September 1858; *New York Times*, 10, 13 September 1858.

35 *Knoxville Whig*, 22 September 1860.

36 Occupational statistics are derived from a systematic assessment of the manuscript census of free population for Knox County. In categorizing occupations, I have adopted the subdivisions that Stephen Thernstrom lays out in *The Other Bostonians: Poverty and Progress in the American Metropolis* (Cambridge, MA: Harvard University Press, 1973), appendix B.

37 See my article "Rediscovering the 'Farmless' Farm Population: The Nineteenth-Century Census and the Postbellum Reorganization of Agriculture in the U.S. South, 1860–1900," *Histoire Sociale* 28 (1995): 501–20.

38 Gustavus W. Dyer and John Trotwood, comps., *The Tennessee Civil War Veterans Questionnaires* (Easley, SC: Southern Historical Press, 1985), vol. 2, pp. 541–42; vol. 4, p. 1670; Robert Tracy McKenzie, "Wealth and Income: The Preindustrial Structure of East Tennessee in 1860," *Appalachian Journal* 21 (1994): 265–69. By comparison, the proportion of farm households without land in 1860 was 19 percent in the Alabama Black Belt, 24 percent in the Alabama Uplands, 25 percent in the Mississippi Delta, 33 percent in Mississippi's northeastern hill country, 24 percent in the Georgia Black Belt, 37 percent in the Georgia Piedmont, 26 percent for East Texas, and 25 percent in the plantation districts of southwestern Tennessee. See Frederick A. Bode and Donald L. Ginter, *Farm Tenancy and the Census in Antebellum Georgia* (Athens: University of Georgia Press, 1986), appendix D; and Randolph B. Campbell and Richard G. Lowe, *Wealth and Power in Antebellum Texas* (College Station: Texas A & M University Press, 1977), pp. 108–11.

39 Temple, *East Tennessee and the Civil War*, pp. 80–81; William G. Brownlow, *Sketches of the Rise, Progress, and Decline of Secession* (Philadelphia: George W. Childs, 1862), p. 211. Modern historians have sometimes characterized southern Appalachia in general in much the same way. See, for example, Ronald Eller, *Miners, Millhands, and Mountaineers: Industrialization of the Appalachian South, 1880–1930* (Knoxville: University of Tennessee Press, 1982). In recent years social scientists trained in a wide variety of disciplines have begun to develop a considerably different profile of preindustrial Appalachia's social and economic structure. For a careful review of the most recent literature, see Ronald L. Lewis, "Beyond Isolation and Homogeneity: Diversity and the History of Appalachia," in Dwight B. Billings, Gurney Norman, and Katherine Ledford, eds., *Confronting Appalachian Stereotypes: Back Talk from an American Region* (Lexington: University Press of Kentucky, 1999), pp. 21–43.

40 This can be demonstrated by comparing the Gini coefficient of concentration for rural Knox County with coefficients scholars have calculated for other rural areas in 1860. The Gini coefficient is a standardized measurement of wealth concentration that ranges from 0.0, when each household owns an equivalent share of locally owned wealth, to 1.0, when one household owns 100 percent and all others are propertyless. I calculate a coefficient of 0.75 for rural Knox County free households for 1860. By comparison, Campbell and Lowe compute a Gini coefficient of total wealth concentration for eastern Texas of 0.74, whereas in an earlier study I calculated a coefficient of 0.70 for southwestern Tennessee (farm households only). Although Jonathan Wiener does not include Gini coefficients in his study of landholding in the Alabama Black Belt, one can calculate from his published decile table a coefficient of 0.68. Finally, Jeremy Atack and Fred Bateman calculate coefficients of 0.63 and 0.62, respectively, for the rural Northeast and Midwest. See Campbell and Lowe, *Wealth and Power in Antebellum Texas*, p. 46; Robert Tracy McKenzie, *One South or Many? Plantation Belt and Upcountry in Civil War–Era Tennessee* (New York: Cambridge University Press, 1994), p. 60; Jonathan Wiener, *Social Origins of the New South: Alabama, 1860–1885* (Baton Rouge: Louisiana State University Press, 1978), p. 15; Jeremy Atack and Fred Bateman, "The 'Egalitarian Ideal' and the Distribution of Wealth in the Northern Agricultural Community: A Backward Look," *Review of Economics and Statistics* 63 (1981): 125.

41 The exact proportion of total wealth commanded by the top 5 percent of Knoxville households in 1860 was 64 percent. By comparison, in New York City in 1845, the top 4 percent of house-

holds owned 66 percent of total noncorporate wealth; in 1848 the richest 4 percent of Boston households controlled 64 percent of noncorporate wealth. See Edward Pessen, *Riches, Class, and Power before the Civil War* (Lexington, MA: D. C. Heath, 1973), pp. 34, 39.

42 According to Michael P. Johnson, the richest 5 percent of households in Charleston in 1860 owned 60.1 percent of the city's total wealth, whereas the poorest 70 percent owned but 1.6 percent of the total. Johnson calculates a Gini coefficient of 0.89 for Charleston; the comparable coefficient for Knoxville is 0.83. See Johnson, "Wealth and Class in Charleston in 1860," in Walter J. Fraser Jr. and Winfred B. Moore Jr., eds., *From the Old South to the New: Essays on the Transitional South* (Westport, CT: Greenwood Press, 1981), p. 67.

43 I have been able to ascertain the educational background of only thirteen of the thirty-three individuals who headed the richest 5 percent of Knoxville's free households. Nine of the thirteen were college graduates; of these, six had attended East Tennessee College. See Mary U. Rothrock, ed., *French Broad–Holston Country: A History of Knox County, Tennessee* (Knoxville: East Tennessee Historical Society, 1946), pp. 363–508; *History of Tennessee from the Earliest Time to the Present, Together with an Historical and a Biographical Sketch of the County of Knox and the City of Knoxville* (Chicago: Goodspeed, 1887), p. 1023.

44 John and Rhoda Campbell Williams Papers, McClung Historical Collection, Knox County Public Library; *History of Tennessee from the Earliest Time to the Present*, p. 878; *Williams' Knoxville Directory, City Guide, and Business Mirror*, vol. 1 (Knoxville: C. S. Williams, 1859), pp. 24–30.

45 Daniel Read Larned to "Henry," 28 September 1863, Daniel Read Larned Papers, Library of Congress; W. G. Brownlow to Thomas A. R. Nelson, 26 April 1852, E. E. Patton Collection; *Knoxville Whig*, 25 June 1853; William G. McAdoo Diary, vol. 29, Floyd-McAdoo Family Diaries and Letterbooks, Library of Congress; Madeleine B. Stern, *Purple Passage: The Life of Mrs. Frank Leslie* (Norman: University of Oklahoma Press, 1953), pp. 23–24.

46 *Knoxville Whig*, 22 September, 13 October 1860.

47 See, for example, *Knoxville Whig*, 19 June 1852, 2 June 1855.

48 *Knoxville Whig*, 2 June 1849, 29 July 1849, 12 January 1850, 19 June 1852, 25 June 1853, 29 June 1850. In his biography of Brownlow, E. Merton Coulter makes the indefensible claim that "the most that the Parson had to say about aristocrats was to make some good-natured fun at their expense." See *William G. Brownlow: Fighting Parson of the Southern Highlands* (Chapel Hill: University of North Carolina Press, 1937), p. 92.

49 See, for example, Brownlow's criticism of East Tennessean Andrew Johnson for his support of the "white basis" for the apportionment of legislative seats in the Tennessee General Assembly in *Knoxville Whig*, 5, 12 May, 30 June, 7 July 1855; and in W. G. Brownlow, *Americanism Contrasted with Foreignism, Romanism, and Bogus Democracy, in the Light of Reason, History, and Holy Scripture; in Which Certain Demagogues in Tennessee, and Elsewhere, Are Shown Up in Their True Colors* (Nashville: published for the author, 1856), pp. 22–23, 70.

50 *Knoxville Whig*, 29 September 1860.

51 On this point, see William J. Cooper Jr., *The South and the Politics of Slavery, 1828–1856* (Baton Rouge: Louisiana State University Press, 1978), p. xiii; Michael F. Holt, *The Political Crisis of the 1850s* (New York: Wiley, 1978), p. 38; Harry L. Watson, *Jacksonian Politics and Community Conflict: The Emergence of the Second Party System in Cumberland County, North Carolina* (Baton Rouge: Louisiana State University Press, 1981), pp. 323–24; Daniel W. Crofts, *Reluctant Confederates: Upper South Unionists in the Secession Crisis* (Chapel Hill: University of North Carolina Press, 1989), pp. 49–54.

52 Joseph Howard Parks, "John Bell and Secession," *East Tennessee Historical Society's Publications* 16 (1944): 34–35.

53 *Knoxville Register*, 27 September 1860; Oliver Temple to W. G. Brownlow, 1 August 1865, William Gannaway Brownlow Letters, Special Collections, University of Tennessee Libraries; *Knoxville Whig*, 22 September 1860. During the debates over the Compromise of 1850, Bell had argued

that Congress did have the right to abolish slavery in the District of Columbia, and had even expressed his willingness to support such a measure if he thought it would bring an end to abolitionist agitation. In the end, however, he voted with eighteen other southern senators against the proposed measure to abolish the slave trade in the district. Bell had not openly denounced the *Dred Scott* decision of 1857, but he had contended that the Court's ruling had not settled the question of the power of Congress with regard to slavery in the territories. See Joseph Howard Parks, *John Bell of Tennessee* (Baton Rouge: Louisiana State University Press, 1950), pp. 260–61, 327–28.

54   *Knoxville Whig*, 27 October 1860.

55   Ibid.

56   *Knoxville Whig*, 10 March, 23 June, 21 July, 8 September, 17 November 1860.

57   *Knoxville Whig*, 27 October 1860. For earlier accusations against Crozier and Swan, see Brownlow, *Americanism Contrasted with Foreignism*, pp. 186–87.

58   *Knoxville Whig*, 28 July, 8 September, 20 October 1860.

59   C. W. Charlton to Andrew Johnson, 15 March 1860, John Crozier Ramsey to Andrew Johnson, 30 March 1860, in Leroy P. Graf, Ralph W. Haskins, and Paul H. Bergeron, eds., *The Papers of Andrew Johnson* [hereafter cited as *Johnson Papers*], 16 vols. (Knoxville: University of Tennessee Press, 1967–2000), vol. 3, pp. 468–69, 504–5; *Knoxville Register*, 27 September 1860; Marguerite Bartlett Hamer, "The Presidential Campaign of 1860 in Tennessee," *East Tennessee Historical Society's Publications* 3 (1931): 17; Oliver P. Temple to W. G. Brownlow, 1 August 1865, Brownlow Letters.

60   Roy P. Basler, ed., *Abraham Lincoln: His Speeches and Writings* (Cleveland: World, 1946), p. 209 (italics in the original). See also James L. Huston, "Southerners against Secession: The Arguments of the Constitutional Unionists in 1850–1851," *Civil War History* 46 (2000): 293.

61   James L. Roark, *Masters without Slaves: Southern Planters in the Civil War and Reconstruction* (New York: Norton, 1977), pp. 10–13; McPherson, *Battle Cry of Freedom*, pp. 239–41.

62   *The Official and Political Manual of the State of Tennessee* (Nashville: Marshall and Bruce, 1890), pp. 81, 84.

63   *Knoxville Whig*, 16 June 1860.

64   *Knoxville Whig*, 20 October 1860.

65   *Knoxville Whig*, 6 August 1859, 10 November 1860; Eric Russell Lacy, *Vanquished Volunteers: East Tennessee Sectionalism from Statehood to Secession* (Johnson City: East Tennessee State University Press, 1965), pp. 163–70.

66   David M. Potter, *The Impending Crisis: 1848–1861* (New York: Harper and Row, 1976), p. 444.

CHAPTER THREE

1   Oliver P. Temple, *East Tennessee and the Civil War* (Cincinnati: Robert Clarke, 1899), pp. 135–36.

2   William G. McAdoo Diary, vol. 29, Floyd-McAdoo Family Diaries and Letterbooks, Library of Congress, entry for 8 November 1860.

3   Ibid.; W. G. McAdoo to W. S. Patton, 8 November 1860, unprocessed document in Special Collections, University of Tennessee Libraries.

4   Ibid.

5   Steven A. Channing, *Crisis of Fear: Secession in South Carolina* (New York: Norton, 1974), pp. 249–51; McAdoo Diary, entry for 30 November 1860; David M. Potter, *The Impending Crisis: 1848–1861* (New York: Harper and Row, 1976), pp. 491–92.

6   McAdoo Diary, entries for 12 and 13 December 1860.

7   Temple, *East Tennessee and the Civil War*, pp. 135–36.

8   See, for example, *Knoxville Whig*, 9 February 1861; McAdoo Diary, entry for 30 November 1860.
9   Although they may not have known it, this was also the view of Abraham Lincoln, who main-
    tained that revolution without a "morally justifiable cause" was "no right, but simply a wicked
    exercise of physical power." See James M. McPherson, *Battle Cry of Freedom: The Civil War
    Era* (New York: Oxford University Press, 1988), p. 248.
10 *Knoxville Whig*, 24 November 1860.
11 The phrase "masterly inactivity" was used widely in both North and South during the secession
    crisis, but I employ it here as quoted by William McAdoo. See McAdoo Diary, entry for
    30 November 1860. See also Daniel W. Crofts, *Reluctant Confederates: Upper South Unionists in
    the Secession Crisis* (Chapel Hill: University of North Carolina Press, 1989), p. 260; Mary E. R.
    Campbell, "The Significance of the Unionist Victory in the Election of February 9, 1861 in
    Tennessee," *East Tennessee Historical Society's Papers* 14 (1942): 12–13.
12 Henry Melville Doak Memoirs (typescript), p. 7, TSLA; *Knoxville Register*, 6 December 1860;
    Blackston McDannel to Andrew Johnson, 16 February 1861, *Johnson Papers*, vol. 4, p. 295. See
    also Thomas W. Humes, *The Loyal Mountaineers of Tennessee* (Knoxville: Ogden Brothers,
    1888), p. 121.
13 Mary U. Rothrock, ed., *The French Broad–Holston Country: A History of Knox County, Tennessee*
    (Knoxville: East Tennessee Historical Society, 1946), pp. 403–4; Robert M. McBride, ed., *Bio-
    graphical Directory of the Tennessee General Assembly* (Nashville: Tennessee Historical Commis-
    sion, 1975), vol. 1, p. 179; McAdoo Diary, entry for 30 November 1860.
14 Temple, *East Tennessee and the Civil War*, p. 413; Rothrock, *French Broad–Holston Country*,
    pp. 493–95.
15 Eighth Census [1860], manuscript population schedule for Knox County, Tennessee; *Williams'
    Knoxville Directory, City Guide, and Business Mirror* (Knoxville: C. S. Williams, 1859), pp. 25–
    27; Knox County Credit Reports, Tennessee Vol. 18, p. 34, R. G. Dun & Co. Collection, Baker
    Library, Harvard University Graduate School of Business Administration.
16 Rothrock, *French Broad–Holston Country*, pp. 394–96; R. N. Price, *Holston Methodism: From Its
    Origin to the Present Time* (Nashville: Publishing House of the Methodist Episcopal Church,
    1908), vol. 4, pp. 101–9; Joseph C. S. McDannel to Andrew Johnson, 29 December 1860, *Johnson
    Papers*, vol. 4, p. 102; *Knoxville Whig*, 2 March 1861. Johnson had made a strong antisecession
    speech in the U.S. Senate on 18 and 19 December; the complete text is reprinted in *Johnson Papers*,
    vol. 4, pp. 3–46.
17 William B. Hesseltine, ed., *Dr. J. G. M. Ramsey: Autobiography and Letters* (Nashville: Tennes-
    see Historical Commission, 1954), pp. 40–41, 47, 99–100.
18 Ibid., pp. 93–96.
19 *Knoxville Whig*, 17 and 24 November 1860, 5 January 1861; Temple, *East Tennessee and the Civil
    War*, pp. 131–33.
20 Application of Nathan Gammon, Case Files of Applications from Former Confederates for
    Presidential Pardons, 1865–1867 [hereafter cited as Amnesty Papers], in Records of the Adju-
    tant General's Office, RG 94, NARA, microcopy 1003, roll 49; McAdoo Diary, entry for
    12 December 1860; *Knoxville Whig*, 2 February 1861.
21 McAdoo Diary, entry for 30 November 1860; Temple, *East Tennessee and the Civil War*, pp. 153–
    54.
22 Frederick S. Heiskell to John Bell, 17 November 1860 and W. J. Baker to F. S. Heiskell,
    23 November 1860, Frederick S. Heiskell Papers, Archives of Appalachia, East Tennessee State
    University; McAdoo Diary, entries for 30 November, 12 December 1860 (italics in the original).
23 Temple, *East Tennessee and the Civil War*, pp. 148–54; *Knoxville Whig*, 24 November, 15 Decem-
    ber 1860. Temple, one of Brownlow's closest friends, stated that the unsigned editorial supporting
    a southern convention was authored by Baxter, whom Brownlow respected. There is no other

direct evidence for Baxter's authorship, but I am firmly convinced that Brownlow himself was not the author, and among local politicians who endorsed the idea, Brownlow was politically most closely aligned with Baxter.

24   McAdoo Diary, entries for 30 November, 12 December 1860; Temple, *East Tennessee and the Civil War*, pp. 148–61; *Knoxville Whig*, 15 December 1860.

25   McAdoo Diary, entry for 5 July 1862; *Knoxville Whig*, 24 November 1860; McPherson, *Battle Cry of Freedom*, pp. 235–37. The "cooperationist" position was widely repudiated across the upper South. Daniel Crofts persuasively concludes that "many lower South 'cooperationists' would have been considered secessionists in the upper South." See Crofts, *Reluctant Confederates*, pp. 136, 379. In Knoxville the identification of the convention movement with the cause of secession was further cemented on 17 December when a much smaller public meeting, confined almost entirely to overt secessionists, passed a series of resolutions endorsing a southern convention, opposing Federal coercion of any seceded state, and proclaiming support for the Deep South. See *Knoxville Register*, 20 December 1860.

26   John Randolph Neal, *Disunion and Restoration in Tennessee* (New York: Knickerbocker Press, 1899), pp. 2–6.

27   Ibid., p. 6; Temple, *East Tennessee and the Civil War*, pp. 167–72; *Knoxville Whig*, 26 January 1861.

28   Sneed's circular, dated 23 January 1861, appeared in the *Knoxville Whig* on 2 February 1861 and is the basis of the synopsis in the following three paragraphs. The best overview of the secession crisis in the upper South is in Crofts, *Reluctant Confederates*.

29   On this point see also *Knoxville Register*, 7 February 1861, for editor Bradfield's assertion that "Lincoln repudiates all distinction on account of color. . . . According to his doctrine the *Negro* is as good as the White man."

30   The statewide tally was 69,387 against secession and 57,798 in favor. See Paul H. Bergeron, Stephen V. Ash, and Jeanette Keith, *Tennesseans and Their History* (Knoxville: University of Tennessee Press, 1999), pp. 134–35; Campbell, "Significance of the Unionist Victory," pp. 25–27. The vote in favor of the convention greatly exceeded the support for immediate secession per se, since nearly half of those who approved of the proposed convention also voted for Unionist delegates. Unlike the vote on the proposed convention, the returns for individual delegates were never officially compiled, although county-level results were typically submitted to Nashville. Daniel Crofts has painstakingly analyzed the archival record to reconstruct the statewide vote. He estimates the vote in favor of Unionist delegates at 99,150 to 30,586. See Crofts, *Reluctant Confederates*, p. 411 n. 2.

31   *Knoxville Whig*, 9 and 16 February, 15 June 1861. The vote in Knoxville against the convention was 735 to 216, but the three Unionist candidates were named on between 834 and 842 ballots, indicating that around 100 supporters of the proposed state convention preferred to be represented by avowed Unionists. See *Knoxville Whig*, 15 June 1861. On the comparatively greater support for secession in the towns and villages, see Sam Milligan to Andrew Johnson, 8 January 1861, *Johnson Papers*, vol. 4, p. 148; Oliver Temple and William G. Brownlow to Hon. T. A. R. Nelson, 12 January 1861, Thomas A. R. Nelson Papers, McClung Historical Collection, Knox County Public Library; Temple, *East Tennessee and the Civil War*, pp. 187–88, 200; deposition of Felix A. Reeve in Case 357, Perez Dickinson vs. the United States, Congressional Jurisdiction Files, entry 22, RG 123, Records of the U.S. Court of Claims [hereafter cited as U.S. Court of Claims], NARA; see also W. Todd Groce, *Mountain Rebels: East Tennessee Confederates and the Civil War, 1860–1870* (Knoxville: University of Tennessee Press, 1999), p. 39.

32   My thoughts on the multiple dimensions of southern Unionism have been stimulated enormously by David Potter's provocative essay "The Historian's Use of Nationalism and Vice Versa," in his *The South and the Sectional Conflict* (Baton Rouge: Louisiana State University Press, 1968), pp. 34–83. The discussion that follows draws heavily on its ideas, albeit with substantial modifications.

33 *Portrait and Biography of Parson Brownlow, the Tennessee Patriot* (Indianapolis: Asher, 1862), p. 30; Hermann Bokum, *Wanderings North and South* (Philadelphia: King and Baird, 1864), pp. 13, 18.

34 "Message of the President of the United States Transmitting an Address of the 'East Tennessee Relief Association,'" Senate Exec. Doc. No. 40, 38th Cong., 1st sess. (Washington, DC: Government Printing Office, 1864), p. 2; Humes, *Loyal Mountaineers of Tennessee*, p. 11. See also William Rule, *The Loyalists of Tennessee in the Late War* (Cincinnati: H. C. Sherick, 1887); Will A. McTeer, *Among Loyal Mountaineers* (Maryville, TN: n.p., n.d); Temple, *East Tennessee and the Civil War*, p. 218. The description of Humes's book is from Henry D. Shapiro, *Appalachia on Our Mind: The Southern Mountains and Mountaineers in the American Consciousness, 1870–1920* (Chapel Hill: University of North Carolina Press, 1978), p. 88.

35 *Knoxville Register*, 12 March 1862, 23 October 1861.

36 *Nashville Banner* quoted in *Knoxville Register*, 12 February 1862; *Southern Republic* [Camden, AL] quoted in *Knoxville Whig*, 30 March 1861; Edward A. Pollard, *Southern History of the War: The First Year of the War*, reprinted from the Richmond corrected edition (New York: C. B. Richardson, 1863), p. 197. See also Robert Reid Howison, "History of the War, chapter VI," *Southern Literary Messenger* 34, no. 12 (December 1862): 603.

37 Richard Nelson Current, *Lincoln's Loyalists: Union Soldiers from the Confederacy* (Boston: Northeastern University Press, 1992), p. 215.

38 James C. Kelley, "William Gannaway Brownlow," *Tennessee Historical Quarterly* 43 (1984): 30; Price, *Holston Methodism*, p. 320; O. P. Temple, *Notable Men of Tennessee from 1833 to 1875: Their Times and Their Contemporaries* (New York: Cosmopolitan Press, 1912), pp. 272, 277; Samuel Mayes Arnell, "The Southern Unionist," unpublished manuscript, Samuel Mayes Arnell Papers, Special Collections, University of Tennessee Libraries, p. 57.

39 Bird G. Manard to Thomas A. R. Nelson, 28 June 1865, Nelson Papers; "Southron" in *Knoxville Register*, 23 October 1861; *Knoxville Whig*, 13 October 1860; 2 March, 11 May, 1 June, 10 August 1861.

40 For examples of patriotic rhetoric after Lincoln's election, see *Knoxville Whig*, 17 November 1860; 2, 16, 23 February 1861.

41 Alexander B. Small to Andrew Johnson, 18 February 1861, *Johnson Papers*, vol. 4, p. 312; *Knoxville Whig*, 19 January, 23 February, 18 May 1861. See also issues for 24 November 1860; 26 January, 23 March 1861.

42 *Knoxville Whig*, 26 January, 9 March, 23 March 1861. See also "Speech of Hon. H. Maynard, of Tennessee, in the House of Representatives, February 6, 1861," John C. Rives, ed., *Appendix to the Congressional Globe*, 36th Cong., 2nd sess. (Washington, DC: Congressional Globe Office, 1861), pp. 164–67. In private, Maynard was less sanguine about the likelihood of a satisfactory compromise. See Maynard to Col. Oliver Temple, 8 January 1861, box 3, folder 3, Oliver Perry Temple Papers, Special Collections, University of Tennessee Libraries. In contrast, Thomas A. R. Nelson, another East Tennessee congressman and Brownlow's longtime political ally, was optimistic that Congress would soon restore the Missouri Compromise line. Combined with the *Dred Scott* decision, Nelson believed that the step should "satisfy all Union loving men and Democrats willing to be satisfied." See T. A. R. Nelson to William G. Brownlow, 30 January 1861, E. E. Patton Collection, McClung Historical Collection, Knox County Public Library.

43 Rothrock, *French Broad-Holston Country*, pp. 449–50; *Knoxville Whig*, 9 February, 9 March 1861.

44 *Knoxville Whig*, 15 December 1860 (quote). See also 9 February, 9 and 23 March, 18 May, 1 June, 20 July 1861. For a similar argument from other upper South unionists, see Temple, *East Tennessee and the Civil War*, pp. 119–20; Horace Maynard, "How, by Whom, and for What Was the War Begun? Speech of Hon. Horace Maynard Delivered in the City of Nashville, March 20, 1862," n.p., n.d., Special Collections, University of Tennessee Libraries; Crofts, *Reluctant Confederates*, pp. 109–11; Jon L. Wakelyn, ed., *Southern Unionist Pamphlets and the Civil War*

(Columbia: University of Missouri Press, 1999), pp. 61–63, 84; John C. Inscoe and Gordon B. McKinney, *The Heart of Confederate Appalachia: Western North Carolina in the Civil War* (Chapel Hill: University of North Carolina Press, 2000), p. 89.

45 *Knoxville Whig*, 5 January, 2 March 1861.

46 *Knoxville Whig*, 4 May 1861.

47 Edward Everett, *Account of the Fund for the Relief of East Tennessee; with a Complete List of the Contributors* (Boston: Little, Brown, 1864), p. 17.

48 *Jonesborough Whig and Independent Journal*, 13 December 1843; Joseph C. S. McDannel to Andrew Johnson, 29 December 1860, *Johnson Papers*, vol. 4, pp. 102–3; *Knoxville Whig*, 12 January 1861. The complete text of Johnson's Senate speech of 18–19 December is given in *Johnson Papers*, vol. 4, pp. 3–46.

49 James M. McPherson, *Ordeal by Fire: The Civil War and Reconstruction*, 2nd ed. (New York: McGraw-Hill, 1992), p. 124.

50 Blackston McDannel to Andrew Johnson, 16 February 1861, *Johnson Papers*, vol. 4, p. 295.

51 In the early 1890s, Oliver Temple and John B. Brownlow conducted an extensive correspondence as the former was gathering evidence for his history of the Civil War in East Tennessee, and even three decades after the secession crisis both were adamant about this point. A central theme of Temple's history is the centrality of the Whig Party to East Tennessee Unionism. See Brownlow to Temple, 9 March and 22 August 1891, Temple Papers; and Temple, *East Tennessee and the Civil War*, especially chap. 25.

52 John C. McGaughey to Andrew Johnson, *Johnson Papers*, vol. 4, pp. 437–38; *Knoxville Whig*, 6 April 1861.

53 George C. Rable, *The Confederate Republic: A Revolution against Politics* (Chapel Hill: University of North Carolina Press, 1994); *Knoxville Whig*, 10 March 1860.

54 *Knoxville Whig*, 23 February, 23 March 1861 (quotes). See also the issues for 21 and 28 July, 25 August, 8 September, 17 November 1860; 30 March, 4 May, 29 June 1861. In his excellent overview of upper South Unionists during the secession crisis, Daniel Crofts asserts that Tennessee Unionists "displayed unprecedented bipartisanship" in the aftermath of the February 1861 referendum. Although I suspect that he overstates the strength of this trend, my goal is not primarily to dispute his assertion; the extent of bipartisanship was indeed much greater than had traditionally existed across the state. Rather, I wish to call attention to the persistent importance of traditional partisan allegiances and rhetoric that often lay just beneath the surface of ostensibly bipartisan behavior. I do take issue with the explanation Crofts offers for Brownlow's criticism of Johnson's patronage recommendations in March and April. He contends that Brownlow's resentment of Johnson's influence in the Unionist movement rested primarily on his suspicion that Johnson would support a West Tennessee Whig, Emerson Etheridge, for governor, thus frustrating Brownlow's own aspirations for the office. This conjecture is consistent with Crofts's larger point that Tennessee Unionists were so confident that they had permanently thwarted secession on 9 February that they soon felt free to "jostle for leadership" of the new Union Party. Even though Brownlow briefly advanced himself as a gubernatorial candidate in March 1861, he never seriously campaigned for the Union Party's nomination, and there is no evidence that he ever believed he had the slightest chance of receiving it. Perceptions of self-interest surely influenced Brownlow's course, but Brownlow had fought the Democratic Party for a quarter of a century, and Crofts too easily dismisses Brownlow's objections as a simple case of self-promotion. At any rate, by focusing almost exclusively on political elites and the national stage, Crofts loses sight of the persistent partisanship among the rank and file that made the appointment of a postmaster a source of significant contention. See Crofts, *Reluctant Confederates*, pp. 265, 327 (quotes), 445–46 n. 57.

55 *Knoxville Whig*, 26 January, 20 and 27 April 1861. Regarding other similar proposals for a "Middle

Confederacy," see Crofts, *Reluctant Confederates*, p. 109; John C. Inscoe, *Mountain Masters: Slavery and the Sectional Crisis in Western North Carolina* (Knoxville: University of Tennessee Press, 1989), pp. 234–35; Thomas B. Alexander, *Thomas A. R. Nelson of East Tennessee* (Nashville: Tennessee Historical Commission, 1956), p. 70.

56 *Knoxville Whig*, 2 March, 26 January 1861; 22 December 1860.

57 *Knoxville Whig*, 29 September 1860; 26 January 1861.

58 *Knoxville Whig*, 22 and 29 September, 13 October 1860; 30 March 1861.

59 *Knoxville Whig*, 20 April 1861; Roy P. Basler, ed., *The Collected Works of Abraham Lincoln*, 8 vols. (New Brunswick, NJ: Rutgers University Press, 1953–55), vol. 4, pp. 331–32; Humes, *Loyal Mountaineers of Tennessee*, p. 98.

60 McPherson, *Battle Cry of Freedom*, p. 276; Temple, *East Tennessee and the Civil War*, pp. 205–11; J. Milton Henry, "The Revolution in Tennessee, February, 1861, to June, 1861," *Tennessee Historical Quarterly* 18 (1959): 99–119; Orville J. Victor, *Incidents and Anecdotes of the War Together with Life Sketches of Eminent Leaders* (New York: James D. Torrey, 1862), pp. 252–55. Technically, on 8 June voters were to address two questions. These were "separation," that is, whether the declaration of independence should be approved, and "representation," that is, whether the state should ratify the Confederate constitution and assume formal membership in the Confederacy.

61 Neal, *Disunion and Restoration in Tennessee*, p. 7; Temple, *East Tennessee and the Civil War*, pp. 135–36; *Knoxville Whig*, 2 February 1861.

62 J. G. M. Ramsey to A. Porter, Esq., 16 April 1861, and J. G. M. Ramsey to J. K. Tefft, Esq., 16 April 1861, in J. G. M. Ramsey Papers, Special Collections, University of Tennessee Libraries; J. G. M. Ramsey "To my friends everywhere in the Southern Confederacy," 16 April 1861, originally published in *Atlanta Intelligencer* and reprinted in *Knoxville Whig*, 27 April 1861; pardon application of John A. McAffrey, Amnesty Papers, microcopy 1003, roll 50. In his autobiography written a decade or so later, J. G. M. Ramsey mistakenly recalled that his son Robert had left Knoxville in March. See Hesseltine, *Ramsey Autobiography*, p. 128.

63 W. G. McAdoo to Hon. John Bell, 18 April 1861, William G. McAdoo Papers, Library of Congress; Minutes, Knoxville Mayor and Board of Aldermen, Knox County Archives, 26 April 1861.

64 The standoff is described, with slight variation of detail, in Humes, *Loyal Mountaineers of Tennessee*, p. 100; Temple, *East Tennessee and the Civil War*, pp. 184–86; and *Knoxville Whig*, 4 May 1861.

65 Oliver Temple to Hon. T. A. R. Nelson, 18 April 1861, Nelson Papers; *Knoxville Whig*, 6 April 1861.

66 W. J. Baker to Hon. T. A. R. Nelson, 4 January 1861, Nelson Papers; David Deaderick Diary, McClung Historical Collection, Knox County Public Library, p. 53 (italics in the original); Hu. L. McClung to Thos. A. R. Nelson, 7 October 1862, Nelson Papers.

67 Martha Hall to Carrie Stakely, 1 July 1861, Hall-Stakely Papers, McClung Historical Collection, Knox County Public Library. On the position of Martha Hall's husband, Edmund, see *Knoxville Whig*, 30 March 1861.

68 Temple, *East Tennessee and the Civil War*, pp. 153, 156; *Knoxville Whig*, 9 June and 15 December 1860, 2 February and 6 April 1861; service record of John J. Reese, Compiled Service Records of Confederate Soldiers Who Served in Organizations from the State of Tennessee, microcopy 268, roll 127, RG 109, War Department Collection of Confederate Records, NARA; *Tennesseans in the Civil War: A Military History of Confederate and Union Units with Available Rosters of Personnel* (Nashville: Civil War Centennial Commission, 1964), pt. 1, pp. 178–79.

69 Pardon application of William M. Cocke, Amnesty Papers, roll 48.

70 Willene B. Clark, ed., *Valleys of the Shadow: The Memoir of Confederate Captain Reuben G. Clark, Company I, 59th Tennessee Mounted Infantry* (Knoxville: University of Tennessee Press, 1994), pp. xx–xxiii, 9–10; pardon application of Reuben G. Clark, Amnesty Papers, roll 48.

71 W. G. McAdoo to Hon. John Bell, 18 April 1861, McAdoo Papers; *Knoxville Whig*, 20 April 1861.

72 *Knoxville Whig*, 20 and 27 April 1861.

73 *Knoxville Whig*, 27 April 1861.

74 *Knoxville Whig*, 20 and 27 April 1861.

75 *Knoxville Whig*, 27 April, 11 May 1861.

76 Temple, *East Tennessee and the Civil War*, pp. 205–11; Henry, "Revolution in Tennessee," p. 117; Victor, *Incidents and Anecdotes of the War*, pp. 252–55; *Goodspeed History of Tennessee* (Nashville: Goodspeed, 1887), pt. 1, pp. 519–28.

77 *Knoxville Whig*, 11 May 1861; Temple, *East Tennessee and the Civil War*, p. 212; Humes, *Loyal Mountaineers of Tennessee*, pp. 104–5.

78 *Knoxville Whig*, 11, 18, 25 June 1861.

79 Neal, *Disunion and Restoration in Tennessee*, p. 10; Rule, *Loyalists of Tennessee in the Late War*, p. 6; *Knoxville Whig*, 18 May, 15 June 1865; Humes, *Loyal Mountaineers of Tennessee*, pp. 104–5; Victor, *Incidents and Anecdotes of the War*, pp. 252–56.

80 *Knoxville Whig*, 8 June 1861.

81 *Goodspeed History of Tennessee*, pt. 1, p. 530; *Tennesseans in the Civil War*, p. 9; *Knoxville Whig*, 18 May 1861.

82 W. M. Churchwell to Hon. L. P. Walker, 15 May 1861, in Letters Received by the Confederate Secretary of War, RG 109, War Department Collection of Confederate Records, NARA; *Tennesseans in the Civil War*, pp. 246–47. After being mustered into the Confederate service, Churchwell's regiment became the Thirty-fourth Tennessee Infantry (C.S.A.). Prior to returning to Tennessee, Churchwell was a partner in the New York City law firm of Ward and Churchwell. See *Knoxville Register*, 28 February 1861, 20 August 1862.

83 These were Company E, Nineteenth Tennessee Infantry (also known as the "Knoxville Guards"); and Company C of Churchwell's Fourth Infantry Regiment, later detached as Captain Burroughs's light artillery company (also known as the "Rhett Artillery"). A handful of Knoxville men had also enrolled in the Third Tennessee Infantry. See *Tennesseans in the Civil War*, pp. 127–28, 178–79, 214–15; Stewart Sifakis, *Compendium of the Confederate Armies: Tennessee* (New York: Facts on File, 1992), p. 30; and W. J. Worsham, *The Old Nineteenth Tennessee Regiment, C.S.A.* (Knoxville: Paragon Printing, 1902).

84 J. G. M. Ramsey to Robert Ramsey, 17 May 1861, Ramsey Papers; *Knoxville Whig*, 11 and 25 May 1861; Humes, *Loyal Mountaineers of Tennessee*, pp. 101–2; William G. Brownlow, *Sketches of the Rise, Progress, and Decline of Secession* (Philadelphia: George W. Childs, 1862), pp. 278–79.

85 W. M. Churchwell to Hon. L. P. Walker, 25 May 1861, Letters Received by the Confederate Secretary of War; Isham Harris to Genl. W. G. McAdoo, 10 June 1861, McAdoo Papers; J. G. M. Ramsey to Gov. Isham Harris, 24 April 1861, William Rule Papers, McClung Historical Collection, Knox County Public Library.

86 The letters that have survived from the exchange between Lawrence and Charlton (in the guise of Johnson) are reprinted in *Johnson Papers*, vol. 4, pp. 476–84. See also Brownlow, *Sketches of Secession*, pp. 121–33; Barry Crouch, "The Merchant and the Senator: An Attempt to Save East Tennessee for the Union," *East Tennessee Historical Society's Publications* 46 (1974): 53–75.

87 *Knoxville Register*, 5 June 1861.

88 "Proceedings of the East Tennessee Convention, Held at Knoxville, May 30 and 31, 1861," reprinted in *War of the Rebellion: A Compilation of the Official Records of the Union and Confederate Armies* [hereafter cited as *OR*] (Washington, DC: Government Printing Office, 1880–1901), ser. 1, vol. 52, pt. 1, pp. 148–56. See also *Knoxville Whig*, 8 June 1861; Temple, *East Tennessee and the Civil War*, pp. 340–43; Humes, *Loyal Mountaineers of Tennessee*, p. 106ff.

89 Resolution 4, "Proceedings of the East Tennessee Convention, Held at Knoxville."

90 Mary E. R. Campbell, *The Attitude of Tennesseans toward the Union, 1847–1861* (New York: Vantage Press, 1961), pp. 291–94; Minutes, Knoxville Mayor and Board of Aldermen, 5 June 1861.

91 For the published returns, see *Knoxville Register*, 11 June 1865; for figures on ballots cast by non-resident soldiers, see statement of Knox County sheriff William P. Crippen in RG 87, Tennessee Election Returns, mf. roll 1861–62, TSLA. Under the military act of 6 May, Tennesseans serving in the state forces were authorized to vote in camp, but in most of the state their ballots were reported separately, rather than as part of the official return of the county in which the camp was located.

92 Eleanor Wilson White Diary, entries for 8 and 12 June 1861, McClung Historical Collection, Knox County Public Library; Martha Hall to Carrie Stakely, 12 August 1861, Hall-Stakely Papers; Wm. G. McAdoo to Dear Mother, 7 June 1861, McAdoo Papers.

93 B. Frazier to Hon. T. R. Nelson, 15 June 1861, Nelson Papers.

94 "Proceedings of the East Tennessee Convention, Held at Greeneville," *OR*, ser. 1, vol. 52, pt. 1, pp. 168–79, quotations on p. 175; see also Temple, *East Tennessee and the Civil War*, pp. 347–48; Charles F. Bryan Jr., "A Gathering of Tories: The East Tennessee Convention of 1861," *Tennessee Historical Quarterly* 39 (1980): 27–48.

95 "Proceedings of the East Tennessee Convention, Held at Greeneville," p. 178; Temple, *East Tennessee and the Civil War*, p. 357; *Knoxville Whig*, 29 June 1861.

96 Bryan, "Gathering of Tories," p. 45.

CHAPTER FOUR

1 Thomas W. Humes, *The Loyal Mountaineers of Tennessee* (Knoxville: Ogden Brothers, 1888), p. 152.

2 *Knoxville Register*, 1 August 1862.

3 James M. McPherson, *Ordeal by Fire: The Civil War and Reconstruction*, 2nd ed. (New York: McGraw-Hill, 1992), p. 187; Allan Nevins, *The War for the Union: The Improvised War, 1861–1862* (New York: Scribner's, 1959), p. 75; M. B. C. Ramsey to Robert Ramsey, 10 July 1861, J. G. M. Ramsey Papers, Special Collections, University of Tennessee Libraries; William J. Cooper Jr., *Jefferson Davis, American* (New York: Knopf, 2000), p. 342.

4 Oliver P. Temple, *East Tennessee and the Civil War* (Cincinnati: Robert Clarke, 1899), p. 368; Edward Maynard to Hon. Horace Maynard, 1 September 1861, Horace Maynard Papers, Special Collections, University of Tennessee Libraries.

5 The rough estimate of fifteen hundred East Tennessee volunteers is based on the number of companies that had been formed by the end of September, according to *Tennesseans in the Civil War: A Military History of Confederate and Union Units with Available Rosters of Personnel*, pt. 1 (Nashville: Civil War Centennial Commission, 1964). It is impossible to calculate precisely the number of white East Tennesseans who served in the Union army. There were thirty-three officially designated Tennessee units—eight regiments each of infantry and mounted infantry, twelve cavalry regiments, and five batteries of light artillery—and estimates of the number of Tennesseans serving in regiments from other states run as high as seven thousand. Richard Current has estimated that Tennessee sent forty-two thousand men into the Union army, counting African American troops. Based on East Tennessee's share of the Unionist vote in June 1861, a conservative estimate of the number of white East Tennesseans who served would be thirty thousand. See *Report of the Adjutant General of the State of Tennessee of the Military Forces of the State from 1861 to 1866* (Nashville: S. C. Mercer, 1866), pp. 8–9; Richard Nelson Current, *Lincoln's Loyalists: Union Soldiers from the Confederacy* (Boston: Northeastern University Press, 1992), p. 215.

6 Here I differ in emphasis significantly from Noel C. Fisher, who views the incidence of violence in the summer and fall of 1861 as already considerable, if not nearly as great as it would become. In a book-length study that focuses on guerrilla warfare, he argues that "violence flared

throughout East Tennessee" prior to the bridge burnings of November 1861, basing his conclusion on a few occurrences of "bushwhacking" that resulted in a handful of fatalities. Given the sizable population of the region (more than fifty thousand white males ultimately served in either the Confederate or the Union army) and the depth of partisan rancor, I find the extent of violent conflict surprisingly minimal. See *War at Every Door: Partisan Politics and Guerrilla Violence in East Tennessee, 1860–1869* (Chapel Hill: University of North Carolina Press, 1997), especially pp. 42–43.

7   Charles F. Bryan Jr., "A Gathering of Tories: The East Tennessee Convention of 1861," *Tennessee Historical Quarterly* 39 (1980): 40.

8   *Knoxville Register*, 11 June, 11 July 1861; Martha Hall to Carrie Stakely, 18 June 1861, 1 July 1861, Hall-Stakely Papers, McClung Historical Collection, Knoxville Public Library; *Knoxville Whig*, 14 September 1861; McPherson, *Ordeal by Fire*, pp. 288–89; W. B. Wood to J. P. Benjamin, 4 November 1861, *OR*, ser. 2, vol. 1, pp. 836–37; James A. Caldwell to Carrie Stakely, 10 June 1862, Hall-Stakely Papers.

9   *Knoxville Register*, 8 April, 26 August 1863.

10 Charles F. Bryan Jr., "'Tories' amidst Rebels: Confederate Occupation of East Tennessee, 1861–1863," *East Tennessee Historical Society's Publications* 60 (1988): 3–22; *Knoxville Whig*, 27 July (quote), 14 September 1861. In his private correspondence, Brownlow was more assertive than in the pages of the *Whig*. Shortly after the Greeneville Convention, for instance, he shared with a correspondent his conviction that, with sufficient arms and the right leader, the people would "over turn this Secession movement." See W. G. Brownlow to W. R. Hurley, 28 June 1861, Robert Todd Lincoln Collection of the Papers of Abraham Lincoln, Library of Congress.

11 Isham Harris to Genl. W. G. McAdoo, 10 June 1861, William G. McAdoo Papers, Library of Congress; entry for 25 July 1862, William G. McAdoo Diary, Floyd-McAdoo Family Diaries and Letterbooks, Library of Congress; Fisher, *War at Every Door*, p. 120.

12 This view of East Tennessee's military importance is nicely summarized in "Are We to Be Defended?" *Knoxville Register*, 27 July 1862.

13 J. G. M. Ramsey to L. P. Walker, 5 July 1861, Letters Received by the Confederate Secretary of War, RG 109, War Department Collection of Confederate Records, NARA; *New York Times*, 22 June 1861. East Tennesseans were also aware of the *Times* article. See Landon C. Haynes to Hon. L. P. Walker, 6 July 1861, *OR*, ser. 1, vol. 4, pp. 364–65. On the importance northerners attached to East Tennessee in the summer of 1861, see also Johnston H. Jordan to Andrew Johnson, 15 July 1861, *Johnson Papers*, vol. 4, pp. 583–84.

14 Roy P. Basler, ed., *The Collected Works of Abraham Lincoln*, 8 vols. (New Brunswick, NJ: Rutgers University Press, 1953–55), vol. 4, pp. 457–58; Jesse Burt, "East Tennessee, Lincoln, and Sherman," pt. 1, *East Tennessee Historical Society's Publications* 34 (1962): 10.

15 See, for example, J. G. M. Ramsey to L. P. Walker, 5 July 1861, Letters Received by the Confederate Secretary of War; William G. Swan to Jefferson Davis, 11 July 1861, *OR*, ser. 1, vol. 4, pp. 366–67; C. Wallace to Isham G. Harris, *OR*, ser. 2, vol. 1, pp. 835–36.

16 W. Y. C. Humes to Oliver Temple, 2 December 1865, Oliver Perry Temple Papers, Special Collections, University of Tennessee Libraries. See also Robertson Topp to Robert Josselyn, 26 October 1861, *OR*, ser. 2, vol. 1, p. 834.

17 *Knoxville Whig*, 27 July 1861; William B. Hesseltine, ed., *Dr. J. G. M. Ramsey: Autobiography and Letters* (Nashville: Tennessee Historical Commission, 1954), p. 103; W. M. Churchwell, "To the Disaffected People of East Tennessee," *OR*, ser. 2, vol. 1, pp. 887–88; Temple, *East Tennessee and the Civil War*, pp. 412–13; Charles F. Bryan Jr., "The Civil War in East Tennessee: A Social, Political, and Economic Study" (Ph.D. diss., University of Tennessee, 1978), chap. 3.

18 William G. Brownlow, *Americanism Contrasted with Foreignism, Romanism, and Bogus Democracy, in the Light of Reason, History, and Holy Scripture, in Which Certain Demagogues in Tennessee, and Elsewhere, Are Shown Up in Their True Colors* (Nashville: published for the author, 1856),

pp. 186–87; *Knoxville Whig*, 7 and 28 January, 13 October 1860; Steve Humphrey, *"That D----d Brownlow": Being a Saucy and Malicious Description of Fighting Parson William Gannaway Brownlow* (Boone, NC: Appalachian Consortium Press, 1978), pp. 143–46.

19 *Knoxville Whig*, 13 July 1861; see also issues for 22 June, 27 July, 28 September, and 26 October, 1861.

20 W. G. Brownlow, *Sketches of the Rise, Progress, and Decline of Secession* (Philadelphia: George W. Childs, 1862), p. 290; *Knoxville Whig*, 5 May 1860, 2 March 1861, 27 July 1861 (quote).

21 Robertson Topp to Robert Josselyn, 26 October 1861, *OR*, ser. 2, vol. 1, p. 834.

22 Isham G. Harris to W. G. McAdoo, 10 June 1861, McAdoo Papers; Bryan, "'Tories' amidst Rebels," p. 5.

23 Fisher, *War at Every Door*, pp. 44–45; Samuel Cooper to Gen. F. K. Zollicoffer, 31 July 1861, *OR*, ser. 2, vol. 1, pp. 829–830; James W. McKee Jr., "Felix K. Zollicoffer: Confederate Defender of East Tennessee," pt. 1, *East Tennessee Historical Society's Publications* 43 (1971): 34–58.

24 *Knoxville Whig*, 13 July, 10 August 1861; Bryan, "Civil War in East Tennessee," pp. 69–71. Earlier in the spring, William Brownlow had actually announced himself as a candidate for the "Union" nomination for governor, but he did nothing to campaign for the nomination, and it is difficult to determine how serious he was about the possibility. In private, he encouraged Middle Tennessee Whig William B. Campbell to declare his candidacy and vowed to support him. When Campbell ultimately declined the nomination, Brownlow shifted his support to Knoxville lawyer Connally Trigg, who also bowed out after it was determined that he had not lived in Tennessee long enough to be eligible. See *Knoxville Whig*, 23 and 30 March, 13 and 20 July 1861; W. G. Brownlow to William B. Campbell, 6 May 1861, David Campbell Papers, Duke University.

25 *Knoxville Register*, 11 June 1861; *Knoxville Whig*, 10 August 1861.

26 Isham G. Harris to Hon. L. P. Walker, 3 August 1861; Harris to Walker, 16 August 1861; Walker to Harris, 20 August 1861, all in *OR*, ser. 2, vol. 1, pp. 830–32; Samuel Cooper to General F. K. Zollicoffer, 13 August 1861, *OR*, ser. 1, vol. 4, p. 387.

27 F. K. Zollicoffer to Adjt. Gen. S. Cooper, 6 August 1861, *OR*, ser. 1, vol. 4, pp. 381–82. At about the same time, Knoxville banker J. J. Craig traveled through the region and reported that, although East Tennesseans supported the Union by more than two to one, "they do not wish to resist the State authorities." See *New York Times*, 21 August 1861, quoting *Louisville Democrat*, 16 August 1861.

28 F. K. Zollicoffer to Adjutant-General Cooper, 9 September 1861; Zollicoffer to Lieutenant-Colonel Mackall, 24 September 1861, in *OR*, ser. 1, vol. 4, pp. 424–25; McKee, "Felix K. Zollicoffer," pp. 46–49.

29 *Knoxville Whig*, 10 August 1861; Fisher, *War at Every Door*, p. 45; Brig. Gen. F. K. Zollicoffer, General Orders no. 3, *OR*, ser. 2, vol. 1, p. 831. James McKee cites Zollicoffer's proclamation "To the People of East Tennessee" as evidence of the general's early commitment to conciliation of Unionists, then argues that the outcome of the gubernatorial and congressional elections prompted him to move toward a more severe policy. Zollicoffer's proclamation was made on 7 August, six days *after* the gubernatorial and congressional elections. See McKee, "Felix K. Zollicoffer," pp. 44–45.

30 Bryan, "'Tories' amidst Rebels," p. 7; W. Todd Groce, *Mountain Rebels: East Tennessee Confederates and the Civil War, 1860–1870* (Knoxville: University of Tennessee Press, 1999), p. 78. See also Humes, *Loyal Mountaineers of Tennessee*, pp. 304–5.

31 Claim 20,096, Records of the General Accounting Office, RG 217, NARA; claims 15,191 and 18,738, Records of the U.S. House of Representatives, RG 233, NARA.

32 *Knoxville Whig*, 14 September 1861; *Knoxville Register*, 26 February, 13 March 1862; James D. Richardson, ed., *The Messages and Papers of Jefferson Davis and the Confederacy*, vol. 1 (New York: Chelsea House–Robert Hector, 1966), p. 225. On the close relationship between declarations of martial law and prohibition in the Confederacy, see Mark E. Neely Jr., *Southern*

Rights: Political Prisoners and the Myth of Confederate Constitutionalism (Charlottesville: University Press of Virginia, 1999), pp. 29–42.

33 W. B. Wood to F. K. Zollicoffer, 28 October 1861, *OR*, ser. 1, vol. 4, pp. 482–83; claim 15,189, RG 233, Records of the U.S. House of Representatives, NARA; Minutes, Knoxville Mayor and Board of Aldermen, Knox County Archives, 6 November 1861; Humes, *Loyal Mountaineers of Tennessee*, pp. 131–32.

34 *OR*, ser. 2, vol. 2, pp. 1368–70; Neely, *Southern Rights*, pp. 146–47; William M. Robinson Jr., *Justice in Grey: A History of the Judicial System of the Confederate States of America* (Cambridge, MA: Harvard University Press, 1941), p. 385. Interpretation hinged on the question of whether citizens of the Confederate states had automatically become citizens of the Confederacy when their states seceded, or whether they retained the right to choose to remain subject to the United States or go with their states into the new Confederacy. If the latter, then basically anyone not submitting to Confederate authority might be viewed as an "alien enemy" under the act. If the former, then "alien enemies" would be limited essentially to the "foreign-born," that is, to individuals born outside the Confederate states who had recently immigrated. Jefferson Davis emphatically denied that citizens of the Confederate states could elect to become citizens of a foreign nation. As he told the Confederate Congress in 1863, "This directly repudiates State sovereignty and admits that a citizen's allegiance to his State may be renounced while resident therein." See Richardson, *Messages and Papers of Jefferson Davis and the Confederacy*, p. 324.

35 *OR*, ser. 4, vol. 1, pp. 586–93; Richard Franklin Bensel, *Yankee Leviathan: The Origins of Central State Authority in America, 1859–1877* (New York: Cambridge University Press, 1990), pp. 156–58; E. Merton Coulter, *William G. Brownlow: Fighting Parson of the Southern Highlands* (Chapel Hill: University of North Carolina Press, 1937), p. 39.

36 Minute Book, pp. 1–27, Confederate States of America, Eastern District of Tennessee, District Court, Knoxville, 1861–1863, NARA—Southeast Regional Branch; Robinson, *Justice in Grey*, pp. 288–89.

37 Confederate District Court Minute Book, p. 4; Hinton Rowan Helper, *The Impending Crisis of the South: How to Meet It* (New York: Burdick Brothers, 1857); *Knoxville Whig*, 14 January 1860, 20 April, 14 September 1861; Humes, *Loyal Mountaineers of Tennessee*, pp. 123–24; McAdoo Diary, entry for 5 July 1862.

38 Humphreys eventually abrogated the bond entirely. See Mary U. Rothrock, ed., *French Broad–Holston Country: A History of Knox County, Tennessee* (Knoxville: East Tennessee Historical Society, 1946), pp. 411–12; Confederate District Court Minute Book, pp. 15, 20; *Knoxville Whig*, 21 September 1861; Kermit L. Hall, "West H. Humphreys and the Crisis of the Union," *Tennessee Historical Quarterly* 34 (1975): 58; *Knoxville Whig*, 21 September 1861.

39 McAdoo Diary, entry for 16 August 1861 (italics in the original); J. G. M. Ramsey to Judah P. Benjamin, 29 November 1861, *OR*, ser. 1, vol. 7, pp. 721–22.

40 *Knoxville Whig*, 14 September 1861; Robertson Topp to Robert Josselyn, Esq., 26 October 1861, *OR*, ser. 2, vol. 1, p. 834; McAdoo Diary, entry for 12 October 1861; Humes, *Loyal Mountaineers of East Tennessee*, p. 152.

41 *Knoxville Whig*, 17 and 31 August, 7 and 21 September 1861.

42 *Knoxville Register*, 30 May 1862; R. N. Price, "William G. Brownlow and His Times," chap. 14 of *Holston Methodism: From Its Origin to the Present Time* (Nashville and Dallas: Publishing House of the Methodist Episcopal Church, 1908), vol. 3, pp. 323–24; Humphrey, *"That D----d Brownlow,"* pp. 225–27. The accusation that Brownlow was primed to declare his allegiance to the Confederacy was repeated after the war by two individuals who, by that time, were among Brownlow's bitterest enemies: George D. Prentice and John Baxter. It is telling that the neo-Confederate historian E. Merton Coulter, who wrote with great condescension not only about Brownlow but with regard to southern Unionists generally, gave considerable credence to their charges. Because of Brownlow's "erratic temperament," Coulter concluded that "it would do no

violence to his character" to say that he might very well have cast his support to the Confederacy. See *William G. Brownlow*, p. 152.

43 W. G. Brownlow to W. R. Hurley, 28 June 1861, Robert Todd Lincoln Collection; *Knoxville Whig*, 27 July, 3 August 1861; Thomas B. Alexander, *Thomas A. R. Nelson of East Tennessee* (Nashville: Tennessee Historical Commission, 1956), pp. 88–93; Oliver P. Temple, *Notable Men of Tennessee from 1833 to 1875: Their Times and Their Contemporaries* (New York: Cosmopolitan Press, 1912), pp. 303–8; Joseph Wade Needham, "Oliver Perry Temple: Entrepreneur, Agrarian, and Politician" (Ph.D. diss., University of Tennessee, 1990), pp. 51–52; *Johnson Papers*, vol. 5, p. 73; *New York Times*, 26 December 1861.

44 *Knoxville Whig*, 17 August, 14 September 1861; Felix K. Zollicoffer, General Orders no. 3, 18 August 1861, *OR*, ser. 2, vol. 1, p. 831; F. K. Zollicoffer to Col. W. B. Wood, 30 October 1861, *OR*, ser. 1, vol. 4, p. 487. For the hypothesis that Brownlow was trying to isolate the local Democratic leadership, see Humphrey, *"That D----d Brownlow,"* pp. 222–26.

45 *Knoxville Whig*, 7 September 1861; L. P. Walker to Isham Harris, 20 August 1861, *OR*, ser. 2, vol. 1, pp. 831–32.

46 *Knoxville Whig*, 21 September, 12 October 1861.

47 *Knoxville Whig*, 12 October 1861.

48 J. G. M. Ramsey to Jefferson Davis, 4 November 1861, *OR*, ser. 1, vol. 4, pp. 511–12; *Chattanooga Gazette and Advertiser*, 4 January 1862, quoted in Groce, *Mountain Rebels*, p. 81.

49 An analysis of the 1860 population census reveals 947 white males between the ages of seventeen and forty-five within the area presumed to correspond to the boundaries of the town. The list of Confederate soldiers from units in Tennessee may be found in *Tennesseans in the Civil War: A Military History of Confederate and Union Units with Available Rosters of Personnel*, pt. 2 (Nashville: Civil War Centennial Commission, 1964). I have calculated the estimate by comparing a list of adult white males in the census for Knoxville with the statewide list of Confederate volunteers given in *Tennesseans in the Civil War*. To ensure that the estimate is an upper bound, I have included all possible matches and also multiplied the number of potential matches by a factor of 1.1 to account for individuals who may have enlisted in units from other states.

50 Brownlow, *Sketches of Secession*, p. 333; Dorothy K. Riggs, "Horace Maynard: Some Facts and Stories Collected for His Descendants," p. 13, Maynard Papers; *Knoxville Register*, 5 and 29 October 1861, 2 October 1862; Confederate Papers Relating to Citizens or Business Firms, RG 109, War Department Collection of Confederate Records, NARA.

51 Temple, *Notable Men of Tennessee*, p. 305; *Knoxville Whig*, 26 October 1861; R. H. Hodson to Oliver Temple, 23 October 1861, Temple Papers; J. C. Ramsey to Jefferson Davis, 7 December 1861, *OR*, ser. 1, vol. 7, p. 744. The *New York Times* published his farewell statement in its entirety and proclaimed, "No man in the country has shown more true courage in his adhesion to the Constitution during this rebellion, than Parson Brownlow." See *New York Times*, 8 November 1861.

52 On the bridge burnings, see especially David Madden, "Unionist Resistance to Confederate Occupation: The Bridge Burners of East Tennessee," *East Tennessee Historical Society's Publications* 52–53 (1980–81): 22–39; Burt, "East Tennessee, Lincoln, and Sherman," pt. 1, pp. 3–25; Temple, *East Tennessee and the Civil War*, pp. 375–85.

53 Isham G. Harris to Jefferson Davis, 12 November 1861; J. P. Benjamin to John R. Branner, 13 November 1861; Benjamin to Col. W. B. Wood, 25 November 1861; F. K. Zollicoffer to Col. W. B. Wood, 12 November 1861; Zollicoffer to Lt. Col. Mackall, 20 November 1861, all in *OR*, ser. 2, vol. 1, p. 841, 842–43, 847, 848.

54 F. K. Zollicoffer to Lt. Col. Mackall, 20 November 1861, *OR*, ser. 2, vol. 1, p. 847; H. C. Young to Hon. D. M. Currin, 19 December 1861, *OR*, ser. 1, vol. 7, pp. 777–79.

55 William Rule, *The Loyalists of Tennessee in the Late War* (Cincinnati: H. C. Sherick, 1887), p. 9;

Isham Harris to Jefferson Davis, 12 November 1861, W. B. Wood to General S. Cooper, 11 November 1861, *OR*, ser. 2, vol. 1, pp. 840, 841; General Wm. H. Carroll to J. P. Benjamin, 11 December 1861, *OR*, ser. 1, vol. 7, pp. 759–60.

56   Madden, "Unionist Resistance to Confederate Occupation," pp. 30–34; Bryan, "'Tories' amidst Rebels," pp. 8–11; W. B. Wood to Adjutant-General Cooper, 11 November 1861; John R. Branner to J. P. Benjamin, 13 November 1861, *OR*, ser. 2, vol. 1, pp. 840, 843. For a view that gives maximum credence to the nervous reports of widespread revolt, see Fisher, *War at Every Door*, pp. 54–58.

57   At least two townsmen were ultimately sent to the Confederate prison in Tuscaloosa after 8 November, although not for participating directly in the attacks. The records of the Tuscaloosa prison have not survived, but the diary of one of the prisoners held there indicates that both John Kinsloe, a foreman printer for the *Knoxville Whig*, and William Homer, a brick mason and merchant, were incarcerated there for at least a time. See Alice Hunt Lynn Howell, ed., *Adventures of a Nineteenth-Century Medic* (Franklin, TN: Hillsboro Press, 1998), p. 45.

58   Fisher, *War at Every Door*, p. 56; W. B. Wood to Adjutant-General Cooper, 11 November 1861, *OR*, ser. 2, vol. 1, p. 840; Wm. H. Carroll to Maj. Gen. G. B. Crittenden, 9 December 1861; Carroll to J. P. Benjamin, 13 December 1861, *OR*, ser. 1, vol. 7, pp. 749–52, 764–66.

59   W. B. Wood to Adjutant-General Cooper, 11 November 1861, *OR*, ser. 2, vol. 1, pp. 840–41; Martha Hall to Carrie Stakely, 13 November 1861, Hall-Stakely Papers; Humes, *Loyal Mountaineers of Tennessee*, pp. 152–53; Confederate District Court Minute Book, p. 31; Case 10,468, Hyram Hackney and Frederick S. Heiskell vs. the United States, U.S. Court of Claims, NARA.

60   Fisher, *War at Every Door*, p. 58; Bryan, "Civil War in East Tennessee," pp. 88–93; Howell, *Adventures of a Nineteenth-Century Medic*, pp. 41–42; Hall, "West H. Humphreys and the Crisis of the Union," p. 60; Rothrock, *French Broad–Holston Country*, p. 132; *OR*, ser. 1, vol. 7, p. 760.

61   H. C. Young to Hon. D. M. Currin, 19 December 1861, *OR*, ser. 1, vol. 7, pp. 777–79; J. P. Benjamin to the Members of the Tennessee Delegation in the Congress, 24 February 1862, *OR*, ser. 2, vol. 1, pp. 879–80. See also Wm. H. Carroll to Hon. J. P. Benjamin, 11 December 1861, *OR*, ser. 1, vol. 7, pp. 759–60.

62   Madden, "Unionist Resistance to Confederate Occupation," p. 37; Humes, *Loyal Mountaineers of Tennessee*, p. 151; Hermann Bokum, *Wanderings North and South* (Philadelphia: King and Baird, 1864), p. 8.

63   Temple, *Notable Men of Tennessee*, pp. 309–10; W. G. Brownlow to Wm. H. Carroll, 22 November 1861, *OR*, ser. 2, vol. 1, pp. 902–3.

64   W. G. Brownlow to General W. H. Carroll, 22 November 1861; Carroll to J. P. Benjamin, 26 November 1861; Carroll to Brownlow, 28 November 1861, *OR*, ser. 2, vol. 1, pp. 902–4.

65   John Baxter to J. P. Benjamin, 30 November 1861, *OR*, ser. 1, vol. 7, pp. 725–26; Brownlow, *Sketches of Secession*, pp. 293–94. According to Steve Humphrey, Crittenden knew when he invited Brownlow to turn himself in that the civil authorities in Knoxville intended to arrest Brownlow upon his return, but I have found no conclusive evidence to support that. If J. C. Ramsey can be believed, the commissioner of the court, Robert B. Reynolds, checked with Crittenden before issuing the warrant to make sure that the army would not interfere, but the exact moment that he did so cannot be determined. See Humphrey, *"That D----d Brownlow,"* pp. 237–38; and J. C. Ramsey to J. P. Benjamin, 7 December 1861, *OR*, ser. 1, vol. 7, pp. 744–45.

66   J. C. Ramsey to J. P. Benjamin, 6 December 1861; Ramsey to Benjamin, 7 December 1861; W. G. Brownlow to Benjamin, 16 December 1861, *OR*, ser. 2, vol. 1, pp. 905, 907–8; *New York Times*, 6 December 1861; Basler, *Collected Works of Abraham Lincoln*, vol. 5, pp. 59–60. Rumors about Brownlow's military exploits circulated widely. See *New York Herald*, 7 December 1861; *Saturday Evening Post*, 14 December 1861; *Scientific American*, 21 December 1861; J. T. Boyle to Brig. Gen. George H. Thomas, 19 December 1861, *OR*, ser. 1, vol. 7, p. 508.

67   W. G. Brownlow to Benjamin, 16 December 1861, *OR*, ser. 2, vol. 1, p. 910; *Knoxville Register*, 7 and 13 December 1861.

68   C. Wallace to J. P. Benjamin, 13 December 1861, *OR*, ser. 1, vol. 7, p. 768; Wm. G. Swan to Jefferson Davis, 7 December 1861; J. G. M. Ramsey and Wm. H. Tibbs to Davis, 7 December 1861; J. C. Ramsey to Davis, 7 December 1861, *OR*, ser. 2, vol. 1, pp. 905–8.

69   John Baxter to J. P. Benjamin, 28 December 1861; J. J. Craig to J. P. Benjamin, 3 January 1862; W. G. Brownlow to Jefferson Davis, n.d., *OR*, ser. 2, vol. 1, p. 918, 919–21, 923–24.

70   J. P. Benjamin to J. C. Ramsey, 22 December 1861, *OR*, ser. 2, vol. 1, pp. 916–17; Humes, *Loyal Mountaineers of Tennessee*, pp. 156–58; *Knoxville Register*, 9 February, 7 March 1862.

71   *Knoxville Register*, 13 March 1862.

72   Bokum, *Wanderings North and South*, p. 7; Temple, *Notable Men of Tennessee*, pp. 114–17.

73   James M. McPherson, *Battle Cry of Freedom: The Civil War Era* (New York: Oxford University Press, 1988), pp. 305, 395–403.

CHAPTER FIVE

1   William G. Brownlow, *Sketches of the Rise, Progress, and Decline of Secession* (Philadelphia: George W. Childs, 1862), p. 407.

2   *National Anti-Slavery Standard*, 24 May 1862.

3   Numerous lecture invitations can be found in folder 437, E. E. Patton Collection, McClung Historical Collection, Knox County Public Library. For newspaper coverage of Brownlow's speaking engagements, see *Chicago Tribune*, 11 April 1862; *New York Times*, 1 and 3 April, 14 and 22 May 1862; *New York Daily Tribune*, 16 and 20 May 1862; *National Anti-Slavery Standard* [New York], 24 May 1862; *Public Ledger* [Philadelphia], 19 April, 14 June 1862; *Boston Daily Evening Transcript*, 24 May 1862; *Christian Recorder*, 31 May, 21 June 1862; *Saturday Evening Post*, 26 April 1862. See also *Ladies Repository*, vol. 22, no. 7 (July 1862): 388; *Sketch of Parson Brownlow and His Speeches at the Academy of Music and Cooper Institute* (New York: E. D. Barker, 1862); as well as E. Merton Coulter, *William G. Brownlow: Fighting Parson of the Southern Highlands* (Chapel Hill: University of North Carolina Press, 1937), chap. 10. For Brownlow's personal perspective on his northern tour, see Brownlow to George Childs, 26 June, 15 September, 10 November 1862, William Gannaway Brownlow Letters, Special Collections, University of Tennessee Libraries; Brownlow to George Childs, 7 August 1862, Brownlow to Dr. Sprague, 2 October 1862, William Gannaway Brownlow Papers, Library of Congress; Brownlow to Miss C. M. Melville, 28 June 1862, Crosby Noyes Autograph Collection, Library of Congress.

4   Brownlow, *Sketches of Secession*, p. 401. At least one other poem was composed in his honor. One small collection of Brownlow's correspondence includes the text of a poem sent to Brownlow by a Samuel Eckel in June 1862. The poem, titled simply "To W. G. Brownlow," consisted of five verses, the first of which will give an accurate sense of the tenor of the remainder: "Thou noble champion of the West, knight errant of the free, / Each patriot heart must ever yield, its homage unto thee; / As granite rock withstands the shock, of Ocean's raging wave, / So thou against Secession's flood, defiant stood, and brave." See folder 444, E. E. Patton Collection.

5   Brownlow, *Sketches of Secession*, pp. 426–29; *Chicago Tribune*, 11 April 1862; *New York Times*, 16 May 1862; *National Anti-Slavery Standard*, 24 May 1862.

6   *New York Times*, 22 May 1862; George W. Childs to Rev. W. G. Brownlow, 17 March 1862, Brownlow Letters; *Saturday Evening Post*, 5 July 1862. For contemporary reviews, see the following monthly periodicals for July 1862: *Historical Magazine*, *Continental Monthly*, *Arthur's Home Magazine*, and *American Publisher's Circular and Literary Gazette*. For a deftly edited and condensed edition of Brownlow's memoir, see Stephen V. Ash, ed., *Secessionists and Other*

Scoundrels: Selections from Parson Brownlow's Book (Baton Rouge: Louisiana State University Press, 1999). A good critical overview of the book may be found in Noel C. Fisher, "Definitions of Loyalty: Unionist Histories of the Civil War in East Tennessee," *Journal of East Tennessee History* 67 (1995): 58–88.

7   *Brownlow, the Patriot and Martyr, Showing His Faith and Works, as Reported by Himself* (Philadelphia: R. Weir, 1862); *Portrait and Biography of Parson Brownlow, the Tennessee Patriot* (Indianapolis: Asher, 1862); Major W. D. Reynolds, *Miss Martha Brownlow; or the Heroine of Tennessee* (Philadelphia: Barclay, n.d.); *Parson Brownlow's Farewell Address, in View of His Imprisonment by the Rebels* (Philadelphia: Thomas W. Hartley, 1862); *Parson Brownlow and the Unionists of East Tennessee* (New York: Beadle, 1862); *Vanity Fair*, vol. 5, nos. 127, 129, 130 (1862); *New York Daily Tribune*, 15 May 1862; Coulter, *William G. Brownlow*, p. 242; *Saturday Evening Post*, 2 August 1862; *Christian Recorder*, 21 June 1861. The stationery bearing Brownlow's likeness can be found in portfolio 157, folder 20a, Printed Ephemera Collection, Rare Book and Special Collections Division, Library of Congress. Other sources that attest to Brownlow's popularity in the wartime North include Orville J. Victor, ed., *Incidents and Anecdotes of the War together with Life Sketches of Eminent Leaders* (New York: James D. Torrey, 1862), pp. 252–76; George Ripley and Charles A. Dana, eds., *The New American Cyclopaedia* (New York: D. Appleton, 1859–63), pp. 689–90; John C. S. Abbott, *The History of the Civil War in America* (New York: H. Bill, 1864–66), p. 348; James R. Gilmore, *Down in Tennessee and Back by Way of Richmond*, by Edmund Kirke [pseud.] (New York: Carleton, 1864), pp. 104–5. For a Pennsylvania housewife's reading of the Parson's book, see James C. Mohr and Richard E. Winslow, eds., *Cormany Diaries: A Northern Family in the Civil War* (Pittsburgh: University of Pittsburgh Press, 1982), p. 500.

8   *Chicago Tribune*, 11 April 1862; *New York Times*, 3 April, 14 and 23 May 1862; Brownlow, *Sketches of Secession*, pp. 397, 417.

9   *New York Times*, 1 April 1862. On the progress of the war in the spring of 1862, see James M. McPherson, *Battle Cry of Freedom: The Civil War Era* (New York: Oxford University Press, 1988), p. 454.

10   Roy P. Basler, ed., *Abraham Lincoln: His Speeches and Writings* (Cleveland: World, 1946), p. 606.

11   Brownlow, *Sketches of Secession*, pp. 333–34, 446–47; *Sketch of Parson Brownlow and His Speeches*, p. 31. On Lincoln's persistent belief in the strength of southern Unionism, see, for example, Allen C. Guelzo, *Abraham Lincoln: Redeemer President* (Grand Rapids, MI: Eerdman's, 1999).

12   Brownlow, *Sketches of Secession*, p. 407. See also *Parson Brownlow and the Unionists of East Tennessee*, p. 32.

13   Brownlow, *Sketches of Secession*, p. 5; *Chicago Tribune*, 11 April 1862. See also *Public Ledger*, 19 April 1862; *New York Daily Tribune*, 14 May 1862.

14   Fisher, "Definitions of Loyalty," p. 86.

15   Capt. James A. Caldwell to Callie Stakely, 10 June 1862, Martha Hall to Carrie Stakely, 8 May 1862, Hall-Stakely Papers, McClung Historical Collection, Knox County Public Library; entry for 19 August 1862, Eleanor Wilson White Diary, McClung Historical Collection, Knox County Public Library; Henry Elliott to William G. McAdoo, 8 July 1862, William G. McAdoo Papers, Library of Congress; McPherson, *Battle Cry of Freedom*, pp. 517–22; entry for 1 November 1862, William G. McAdoo Diary, Floyd-McAdoo Family Diaries and Letterbooks, Library of Congress; Henry Elliott to W. G. McAdoo, 28 October 1862, McAdoo Papers; *Knoxville Register*, 11 September 1862. On the invasion of Kentucky and the Battle of Perryville, see Kenneth W. Noe, *Perryville: This Grand Havoc of Battle* (Lexington: University Press of Kentucky, 2001).

16   William G. McAdoo to Dear Mother and Sister Mary, 7 October 1861; H. Douglass to McAdoo, 28 April 1862, McAdoo Papers; Martha Hall to Carrie Stakely, 8 May 1862, Hall-Stakely Papers; *Knoxville Register*, 20 February, 24 and 30 July, 10 December 1862; *Chicago Tribune*, 11 April 1862; entries for 31 October, 10 December 1862, McAdoo Diary.

17 *Knoxville Register*, 19 and 24 January, 4 March 1862; Oliver P. Temple, *East Tennessee and the Civil War* (Cincinnati: Robert Clarke, 1899), p. 449.

18 *Knoxville Register*, 19 and 20 February 1862; entries for 6 and 31 December 1862, McAdoo Diary; Eliza J. McClung to Matthew McClung, 27 August 1862, David Campbell Papers, Duke University; John H. Crozier to my Dear Wife, 7 March 1862, Edith Scott Manuscript Collection, McClung Historical Collection, Knox County Public Library.

19 *Knoxville Register*, 11 July 1861, 19 and 26 February, 9 March, 22 and 31 May 1862.

20 McPherson, *Battle Cry of Freedom*, pp. 430–31, 611–12; *Knoxville Register*, 9 October 1862; Charles F. Bryan Jr., "'Tories' amidst Rebels: Confederate Occupation of East Tennessee, 1861–1863," *East Tennessee Historical Society's Publications* 61 (1988): 12–13; Wilma Dykeman, *The French Broad* (New York: Rinehart, 1955), pp. 79, 90–91; James D. Richardson, ed., *The Messages and Papers of Jefferson Davis and the Confederacy*, vol. 1 (New York: Chelsea House–Robert Hector, 1966), p. 225; Milton P. Jarnagin Memoirs, TSLA.

21 Laura Maynard to Washburn Maynard, 23 April 1863, Horace Maynard Papers, Special Collections, University of Tennessee Libraries; service record of Samuel B. Boyd, Samuel Beckett Boyd Papers, Special Collections, University of Tennessee Libraries.

22 Discharge certificate of Alfred Buffat, Emmanual Bolli to Elisa Bolli, 12 January 1863, Buffat Family Papers, McClung Historical Collection, Knox County Public Library; deposition of Nicholas Lewis, case 6,332, Nicholas Lewis vs. the United States, U.S. Court of Claims, NARA; John R. Branner to George W. Randolph, 5 November 1862, Letters Received by the Confederate Secretary of War, RG 109, War Department Collection of Confederate Records, NARA; *Knoxville Register*, 23 March, 16 July 1862.

23 See Appendix, Table 1.

24 *Knoxville Whig*, 22 December 1860.

25 James M. McPherson, *Ordeal by Fire: The Civil War and Reconstruction*, 2nd ed.(New York: McGraw-Hill, 1992), pp. 264–70; *Knoxville Register*, 9 August 1862.

26 *Knoxville Register*, 14 August; 1, 2, 17 October 1862.

27 *Knoxville Register*, 5 October 1862.

28 *Knoxville Register*, 11 April, 9 October 1862.

29 Of 422 adult male or female heads of household for whom loyalty could be positively determined, 122, or approximately 29 percent, were Unionist as late as the end of Confederate occupation in August 1863. Individuals from blue-collar households are significantly underrepresented among those definitely categorized, however; if we statistically adjust for this difference by assuming that the observed correlation between occupational category and sympathies held throughout the free population, we would estimate that about 34 percent of the total free population remained Unionist. See Appendix, "Identifying Individual Unionists and Confederates."

30 Temple, *East Tennessee and the Civil War*, p. 422.

31 Thomas W. Humes, *The Loyal Mountaineers of Tennessee* (Knoxville: Ogden Brothers, 1888), pp. 357–58; E. Kirby Smith to T. A. Washington, 26 April 1862, *OR*, ser. 1, vol. 10, pt., 2, pp. 453–54. To further discourage "stampeding," Smith allowed his newly appointed provost marshal—none other than bankrupt Knoxville financier William Churchwell—to threaten retribution against those Tories unwilling to accept his magnanimity. In a proclamation in late April, Churchwell announced that those who had fled beyond the enemy's lines must return to take care of their wives and children, and that those who failed to do so "will have them sent to their care in Kentucky or beyond the Confederate lines at their own expense." Given the number of families potentially involved, the edict was never remotely enforceable, and Churchwell actually applied it in only two instances, ordering the wives and children of William Brownlow and Horace Maynard beyond the Confederate lines on 25 April 1862. See "To the Disaffected People of East Tennessee," 23 April 1862, *OR*, ser. 2, vol. 1, p. 884; Henry Elliott, to William G. McAdoo, 25 April 1862, McAdoo Papers; Brownlow, *Sketches of Secession*, pp. 446–56; *Knoxville Register*, 22 April 1862. For an overview of

General Smith's handling of East Tennessee Unionists, see Noel C. Fisher, *War at Every Door: Partisan Politics and Guerilla Violence in East Tennessee, 1860–1869* (Chapel Hill: University of North Carolina Press, 1997), pp. 107–10; W. Todd Groce, *Mountain Rebels: East Tennessee Confederates and the Civil War, 1860–1870* (Knoxville: University of Tennessee Press, 1999), pp. 83–87.

32 *Knoxville Register*, 16 October 1862, 13 and 28 February 1863; entries for 31 October and 8 December 1862, McAdoo Diary (italics in the original).

33 W. G. Brownlow to Abraham Lincoln, 25 December 1862, Robert Todd Lincoln Collection of the Papers of Abraham Lincoln, Library of Congress.

34 *Brownlow's Knoxville Whig and Rebel Ventilator* [hereafter cited as *Knoxville Whig*], 6 February 1864; Horace Maynard, "To the Slaveholders of Tennessee," Maynard Papers; W. G. Brownlow to Abraham Lincoln, 27 March 1863, and Andrew Johnson, Horace Maynard, and Allen A. Hall to Abraham Lincoln, 27 March 1863, Robert Todd Lincoln Collection. James M. McPherson employs the phrase "practical abolitionists" with regard to Union soldiers in *What They Fought For, 1861–1865* (Baton Rouge: Louisiana State University Press, 1994), p. 59.

35 See, for example, James B. Campbell, "East Tennessee during Federal Occupation, 1863–1865," *East Tennessee Historical Society's Publications* 19 (1947): 65.

36 *Knoxville Register*, 23 October 1861; Temple, *East Tennessee and the Civil War*, pp. 536, 540; John B. Brownlow to Oliver Temple, 22 August 1891, Oliver Perry Temple Papers, Special Collections, University of Tennessee Libraries.

37 See Appendix, Table 2.

38 Humes, *Loyal Mountaineers of Tennessee*, pp. 124–25; Temple, *East Tennessee and the Civil War*, p. 113.

39 Humes, *Loyal Mountaineers of Tennessee*, p. 91. For works that investigate the socioeconomic correlates of Unionist and Confederate sympathies in East Tennessee, see Walter Lynn Bates, "Southern Unionists: A Socio-economic Examination of the Third East Tennessee Volunteer Infantry Regiment, U.S.A., 1862–1865," *Tennessee Historical Quarterly* 50 (1991): 226–39; Peter Wallenstein, "'Helping to Save the Union': The Social Origins, Wartime Experiences, and Military Impact of White Union Troops from East Tennessee," in Kenneth W. Noe and Shannon H. Wilson, eds., *The Civil War in Appalachia: Collected Essays* (Knoxville: University of Tennessee Press, 1997), pp. 1–29; and Groce, *Mountain Rebels*, chap. 3.

40 *Knoxville Register*, 5 June 1861; *Knoxville Whig*, 2 June 1849, 13 October 1860.

41 Here I am particularly influenced by the arguments of Todd Groce and John Inscoe. See Groce, *Mountain Rebels*, pp. 50–53; John C. Inscoe, "Mountain Unionism, Secession, and Regional Self-Image: The Contrasting Cases of Western North Carolina and East Tennessee," in Winfred B. Moore Jr. and Joseph F. Tripp, eds., *Looking South: Chapters in the Story of an American Region* (New York: Greenwood Press, 1989), pp. 115–29.

42 Works that reach similar conclusions about the relative paucity of class conflict in southern communities during the war include Daniel Sutherland, *Seasons of War: The Ordeal of a Confederate Community* (New York: Free Press, 1995); John C. Inscoe and Gordon B. McKinney, *The Heart of Confederate Appalachia: Western North Carolina in the Civil War* (Chapel Hill: University of North Carolina Press, 2000); Martin Crawford, *Ashe County's Civil War: Community and Society in the Appalachian South* (Charlottesville: University Press of Virginia, 2001); and John W. Shaffer, *Clash of Loyalties: A Border County in the Civil War* (Morgantown: West Virginia University Press, 2003). For a study that arrives at a diametrically opposite conclusion, see Wayne K. Durrill, *War of Another Kind: A Southern Community in the Great Rebellion* (New York: Oxford University Press, 1990).

43 On the theme of divided families, see Catherine Clinton, *Southern Families at War: Loyalty and Conflict in the Civil War South* (New York: Oxford University Press, 2000), p. 6; and John C. Inscoe and Gordon B. McKinney, "Highland Households Divided: Family Deceptions, Diversions, and Divisions in Southern Appalachia's Inner Civil War," in John C. Inscoe and Robert

C. Kenzer, eds., *Enemies of the Country: New Perspectives on Unionists in the Civil War South* (Athens: University of Georgia Press, 2001), pp. 54–72.

44 Martha Luttrell Mitchell Memoir, TSLA; Amnesty Papers, microcopy 1003, roll 50, NARA; Mary U. Rothrock, ed., *The French Broad–Holston Country: A History of Knox County, Tennessee* (Knoxville: East Tennessee Historical Society, 1946), pp. 440–41; entries for 16 and 23 August 1861, McAdoo Diary; *Tennesseans in the Civil War: A Military History of Confederate and Union Units with Available Rosters of Personnel* (Nashville: Civil War Centennial Commission, 1965), vol. 2, p. 545. Of course, there were almost certainly other sets of divided brothers who had already formed their own households and are thus impossible to identify in the absence of detailed genealogical information.

45 *Knoxville Register*, 17 May 1863; Humes, *Loyal Mountaineers of Tennessee*, p. 181; William Rule, *Standard History of Knoxville, Tennessee* (Chicago: Lewis, 1900), p. 440; Martha Hall to Carrie Stakely, 12 August 1861, Hall-Stakely Papers; entries for 9, 13, 16 June 1861, White Diary; Records of St. John's Episcopal Church, Knoxville, Tennessee, vol. 1, 1844–1887, TSLA.

46 Records of the First Presbyterian Church, Knoxville, Tennessee, vol. 4, TSLA; Records of the Second Presbyterian Church, Knoxville, Tennessee, vols. 1–2, TSLA; Brownlow, *Sketches of Secession*, pp. 333–34, 446–47; *Sketch of Parson Brownlow and His Speeches*, p. 31; Dorothy K. Riggs, "Horace Maynard: Some Facts and Stories Collected for His Descendants," p. 13, Maynard Papers; David Sullins, *Recollections of an Old Man: Seventy Years in Dixie, 1827–1897* (Bristol, TN: King Printing Company, 1910), p. 252.

47 Richard Nelson Current, *Lincoln's Loyalists: Union Soldiers from the Confederacy* (Boston: Northeastern University Press, 1992), p. 133.

48 As governor of Tennessee in 1865, Brownlow employed the phrase "they have not been hurt with loyalty" to criticize several self-described Unionists who were endorsing the amnesty application of an East Tennessee Confederate named James M. Mauk. This form of skepticism, albeit in different words, recurs repeatedly in his written remarks on Tennessee applications. See Amnesty Papers, roll 50.

49 The federal government's Southern Claims Commission, established in 1871, assumed that all citizens of insurrectionary states had been disloyal and placed the burden on claimants to prove otherwise. The standards of loyalty that the commission imposed, according to a careful study of its operations, literally "demanded a life of treason to the Confederacy." See Frank W. Klingberg, *The Southern Claims Commission* (Berkeley: University of California Press, 1959), p. 17. Evidence of persecution was not officially required to establish loyalty, but the standard questionnaire used by the commission asked claimants whether they had been abused or molested on account of their Union sentiments or otherwise victimized by "Confederate depredations." Claimants regularly appealed to such persecution as prima facie evidence of loyalty.

50 Temple, *East Tennessee and the Civil War*, pp. 428–29; Oliver P. Temple, *Notable Men of Tennessee from 1833 to 1875: Their Times and Their Contemporaries* (New York: Cosmopolitan Press, 1912), p. 114; Humes, *Loyal Mountaineers of Tennessee*, pp. 184, 188, 191, 196. See also Fisher, "Definitions of Loyalty," pp. 75, 86. Fisher argues that both Temple and Humes consciously purged their histories of references to guerrilla warfare in East Tennessee, although he admits that most documented instances of such irregular conflict occurred far from Knoxville. In reality, although both Temple and Humes claimed to be writing histories of the larger region, both relied heavily on personal experience, and for the period after Tennessee's secession, both concentrated disproportionately on Knoxville alone.

51 Entry for 9 June 1862, McAdoo Diary; deposition of Jonathan K. Newman in case 3931, John R. Branner (estate) vs. the United States, U.S. Court of Claims; deposition of S. P. Carter, case 357, Perez Dickinson vs. the United States, U.S. Court of Claims. Confederate attorney Henry Elliott similarly maintained that the "Tory" element was "struck dumb" in the presence of large numbers of Rebel soldiers. See Henry Elliott to W. G. McAdoo, 28 October 1862, McAdoo Papers.

52   Temple, *East Tennessee and the Civil War*, p. 427; Temple, *Notable Men of Tennessee*, pp. 115–17; deposition of George W. Mabry, case 13,222, G. W. Mabry vs. the United States, U.S. Court of Claims; Bryan, "'Tories' amidst Rebels," p. 12; *Knoxville Register*, 3 March 1863.

53   Endorsements Sent by the Provost Marshal General, District of East Tennessee, Sept. 1863–July 1864, pp. 23, 25, 47, 97, in entry 2759, RG 393, U.S. Army Continental Commands, NARA; Groce, *Mountain Rebels*, p. 118.

54   Pardon application of Robert J. McKinney, Amnesty Papers, roll 50.

55   Ibid.; *Knoxville Register*, 24 January 1862; entries for 18 November 1862 and 9 June 1863, McAdoo Diary; Henry Elliott to William G. McAdoo, 14 May 1862, McAdoo Papers; Edward Maynard to Washburn Maynard, 17 November 1863, Laura Maynard to Washburn Maynard, 19 January 1864, Maynard Papers; *Knoxville Whig*, 8 March 1865. Decades later, a laudatory obituary described McKinney as opposing the war but "retaining his allegiance to his State." See W. A. Henderson, *Life and Character of Judge McKinney* (Nashville: Albert B. Tavel, 1884), p. 11.

56   Deposition of George W. Mabry, case 13,222, G. W. Mabry vs. the United States, U.S. Court of Claims; roll 611, Confederate Papers Relating to Citizens or Business Firms, RG 109, microcopy 346, War Department Collection of Confederate Records, NARA.

57   Deposition of Nicholas Lewis, case 6332, Nicholas Lewis vs. the United States, U.S. Court of Claims; John R. Branner to George W. Randolph, 5 November 1862, RG 109, Letters Received by the Confederate Secretary of War, microcopy 437, roll 36; *Knoxville Register*, 23 March 1862; defendant's brief on loyalty, case 3931, John R. Branner (estate) vs. the United States, U.S. Court of Claims; John R. Branner to J. P. Benjamin, 2 December 1861, *OR*, ser. 1, vol. 7, p. 733; John B. Brownlow to Oliver P. Temple, 27 November 1892, Temple Papers.

58   Pardon application of William C. Baley, Amnesty Papers, roll 48; County Court Minutes, Knox County, vol. 22, p. 421, TSLA; entry for 10 January 1862, Minutes, Knoxville Mayor and Board of Aldermen, Knox County Archives. Parson Brownlow made a point of identifying his old ally Luttrell as a Unionist, despite his continuing to hold office under Confederate rule. See Brownlow, *Sketches of Secession*, p. 439. Brownlow boasted that the "Union ticket" had carried by more than two to one in every ward in the 1862 election, but it seems likely that he misstated the case. The moderate Unionist Luttrell did win the race for mayor handily over original secessionist C. W. Charlton, but four of the six aldermen whose loyalties can be established were moderate Confederates, not Unionists. The key in Brownlow's mind, I think, was that the original secessionist faction whom he despised so heartily had been thoroughly repudiated at the polls.

59   Entry for 9 June 1862, McAdoo Diary; *Knoxville Register*, 25 November, 1 August 1862. Temple took the oath in January 1862 when required to do so in order to practice in the local Confederate district court. See Minute Book, p. 46, Confederate States of America, Eastern District of Tennessee, District Court, Knoxville, 1861–1863, NARA—Southeast Regional Branch.

60   "The United States versus James Nuckels," in Register of Cases Tried by General Courts-Martial and Military Commissions, Department of the Ohio, Sept. 29, 1862–Jan. 17, 1865, entry 3533, RG 393, U.S. Army Continental Commands, NARA. Michael Fellman coins the term "survival lying" in *Inside War: The Guerilla Conflict in Missouri during the American Civil War* (New York: Oxford University Press, 1989), p. 49.

61   *Knoxville Register*, 9 August 1862.

62   Temple, *Notable Men of Tennessee*, p. 69; *Knoxville Register*, 28 February 1862.

63   *Knoxville Whig*, 21, 28 September 1861; *Knoxville Register*, 28 February 1862; Temple, *Notable Men of Tennessee*, pp. 70–72; John Bell Brownlow to Oliver Temple, 28 November 1892, Temple Papers.

64   Temple, *Notable Men of Tennessee*, pp. 70–71; Brownlow, *Sketches of Secession*, p. 294; *Knoxville Whig*, 21 and 28 September 1861; Brownlow to Robertson Topp, 1 October 1861, Robertson Topp Papers, TSLA.

65 Landon Carter Haynes to Jefferson Davis, 19 April 1862, Letters Received by the Confederate Secretary of War; Henry Elliott to W. G. McAdoo, 17 September 1862, McAdoo Papers; *Knoxville Register*, 5 October 1861.

66 Major General E. Kirby Smith to Gen. A. S. Johnston, 25 March 1862, Smith to Samuel Morrow, 13 April 1862, in District of East Tennessee, Letters and Telegrams Sent, chap. 2, vol. 51, RG 109, NARA; *Knoxville Register*, 28 February 1862. On Baxter's shift toward neutrality, see McAdoo Diary, 9 June 1862. Pro-Confederate Knoxville attorney Henry Elliott described Baxter in September 1862 as "one of the most notorious of the Tories." See Elliott to McAdoo, 15 September 1862, McAdoo Papers.

67 *Knoxville Register*, 9 October 1863; *Knoxville Whig*, 13 February 1864; entries for 13 February, 22 June 1864 in Register of Letters Received, Department of Ohio, entry 3513, RG 393, U.S. Army Continental Commands, NARA; Temple, *Notable Men of Tennessee*, pp. 53, 73 (quotation on p. 73); Humes, *Loyal Mountaineers of Tennessee*, pp. 108ff., 245–46. On the postwar rivalry between Brownlow and Baxter, see W. G. Brownlow, *To Whom It May Concern* (Washington, DC: n.p., 1871), in Samuel Mayes Arnell Papers, Special Collections, University of Tennessee Libraries; John Baxter, *The Harmon Case: Reply of Colonel John Baxter to the Speech of Senator W. G. Brownlow* (Knoxville: Chronicle Job Printing Office, 1871); and Steve Humphrey, *"That D----d Brownlow": Being a Saucy and Malicious Description of Fighting Parson William Gannaway Brownlow* (Boone, NC: Appalachian Consortium Press, 1978), pp. 351–56.

68 *Knoxville Whig*, 6 July 1861; *Knoxville Register*, 12 January, 13 March, 16 April, 24 July, 1 October, 10 December 1862, 2 February, 5 and 15 May 1863. See also papers pertaining to the business operations of S. T. Atkins, Joseph A. Mabry, A. L. Maxwell, James C. Moses, and Columbus Powell, microfilm rolls 27, 426, 611, 719, and 816, Microcopy 346, Confederate Papers Relating to Citizens or Business Firms, RG 109, NARA; entry 56, payroll nos. 6462, 12536, 12697, RG 109, NARA.

69 Rothrock, *French Broad–Holston Country*, pp. 499–500; *Knoxville Register*, 10 December 1862; Confederate Papers Relating to Citizens or Business Firms; Knox County Credit Reports, Tennessee Vol. 18, p. 24, R. G. Dun Mercantile Agency, Harvard University School of Business, Baker Library of Business Administration.

70 Daniel E. Sutherland, ed., *A Very Violent Rebel: The Civil War Diary of Ellen Renshaw House* (Knoxville: University of Tennessee Press, 1996), pp. 123–24.

71 Confederate Papers Relating to Citizens or Business Firms; case 10565, Thomas J. Powell vs. the United States, U.S. Court of Claims; depositions of S. P. Carter, T. J. Powell, M. S. Temple, and Felix A. Reeve in case 397, Perez Dickinson vs. the United States, U.S. Court of Claims.

72 Entries for 13 February, 22 June 1864 in Register of Letters Received, Department of Ohio; Knoxville *Register*, 14 March 1862, 10 October 1863.

73 *Knoxville Register*, 10 October 1863; entry 963, Records of Special Claims, RG 92, Records of the Office of the Quartermaster General, NARA.

74 Confederate Papers Relating to Citizens or Business Firms; M. S. Temple to Oliver Temple, 9 September 1862, Temple Papers; McAdoo Diary, 6 December 1862, Floyd-McAdoo Papers. Although McAdoo's claims cannot be verified, surviving Confederate records do indicate that sometime in the fall of 1862 Temple received a passport from the Confederate provost marshal in Knoxville authorizing him to travel to Saltville, Virginia. See passport 10,065 (undated), Passport Book, Department of East Tennessee, ch. IX, vol. 140B-C, RG 109, NARA. For the details of Major Temple's salt contract, see M. S. Temple to Stewart, Buchanan & Co., 19 July 1862, in Letters Received by the Confederate Secretary of War.

75 M. S. Temple to Col. Oliver Temple, 9 April 1864, Temple Papers.

76 *Chicago Tribune*, 11 April 1862.

CHAPTER SIX

1   S. P. Carter, "A Sketch of the Military Services of Sam P. Carter, Brig. Genl. & Brevt. Maj. Genl. of U.S. Vols. during the Rebellion of the Southern States, 1861–1865," pp. 102–3, in Samuel Powhatan Carter Papers, Library of Congress.

2   Daniel E. Sutherland, ed., *A Very Violent Rebel: The Civil War Diary of Ellen Renshaw House* (Knoxville: University of Tennessee Press, 1996), p. 4.

3   Thomas W. Humes, *The Loyal Mountaineers of Tennessee* (Knoxville: Ogden Brothers, 1888), pp. 232–33; William S. Speer, *Sketches of Prominent Tennesseans* (Nashville: Albert B. Tavel, 1888), pp. 497–99; Application of Thomas W. Humes [nephew of Reverend Humes], Amnesty Papers, roll 49; Martha Hall to Carrie Stakely, 12 August 1861, Hall-Stakely Papers, McClung Historical Collection, Knox County Public Library (quote); "List of Communicants," Records of St. John's Episcopal Church, Knoxville, Tennessee, vol. 1, 1844–1887, TSLA.

4   Entries for 9, 13, and 16 June 1861, Eleanor Wilson White Diary, McClung Historical Collection, Knox County Public Library; Humes, *Loyal Mountaineers of Tennessee*, p. 188; Speer, *Sketches of Prominent Tennesseans*, p. 498. Eleanor White was Humes's niece and a devout Confederate.

5   Humes, *Loyal Mountaineers of Tennessee*, pp. 232–33.

6   "List of Communicants," St. John's Episcopal Church; *Williams' Knoxville Directory, City Guide, and Business Mirror* (Knoxville: C. S. Williams, 1859). Ellen House never indicated her address specifically, but the close neighbors that she mentioned most frequently, Mrs. Claib Kain and Mrs. George White, each lived within a block of Thomas Humes to the west and east, respectively, on the north side of Cumberland Street. Horace Maynard was also a nearby neighbor, living on the south side of Cumberland directly across from Thomas Humes.

7   Sutherland, *Very Violent Rebel*, pp. xvii–xx, 7, 70.

8   Ibid., pp. 12, 13, 16, 19.

9   Ibid., pp. 4–13 (quotations on pp. 6, 4).

10 Jesse Burt, "East Tennessee, Lincoln, and Sherman," pt. 2, *East Tennessee Historical Society's Publications* 35 (1963): 54–75 (quotation on p. 64); Horace Maynard to Abraham Lincoln, 14 October 1862, John M. Fleming and Robert Morrow to Abraham Lincoln, 8 August 1863, Robert Todd Lincoln Collection of the Papers of Abraham Lincoln, Library of Congress; Roy P. Basler, ed., *The Collected Works of Abraham Lincoln*, 8 vols. (New Brunswick, NJ: Rutgers University Press, 1953–55), vol. 6, p. 373. For earlier efforts by East Tennessee Unionists to galvanize the Lincoln administration into action, see Andrew Johnson and William B. Carter to Abraham Lincoln, 6 August 1861; Johnson to Lincoln, 26 April 1862; Robert Todd Lincoln Collection; Andrew Johnson and Horace Maynard to General Don Carlos Buell, 10 December 1861; Johnson and Maynard to William H. Seward, 2 January 1862; Horace Maynard to Andrew Johnson, 30 April 1862, *Johnson Papers*, vol. 5, pp. 46, 91, 352–53.

11 *Knoxville Register*, 6 and 19 February, 16 March, 29 April, 13 June, 27 July 1862.

12 *Knoxville Register*, 14 April, 5 and 15 May 1863.

13 *Knoxville Register*, 27 July 1862, 5 May, 18 June 1863.

14 Col. W. P. Sanders to Lieut. Col. Lewis Richmond, 26 July 1862, *OR*, ser. 1, vol. 23, pt. 1, pp. 386–89.

15 Milton A. Haynes to Major Von Sheliha, 21 June 1863, *OR*, ser. 1, vol. 23, pt. 1, pp. 391–93; *Holston Journal*, 9 July 1863; [William Morrow] to W. G. McAdoo, 1 July 1863, William G. McAdoo Papers, Library of Congress; *Knoxville Register*, 23 June 1863; Humes, *Loyal Mountaineers of Tennessee*, pp. 199–207; Ellen McClung to Dear Brother and Sister, 24 June 1863, David Campbell Papers, Duke University.

16 [William Morrow] to W. G. McAdoo, 1 July 1863, McAdoo Papers; William B. Hesseltine, ed., *Dr. J. G. M. Ramsey: Autobiography and Letters* (Nashville: Tennessee Historical Commission, 1954), pp. 106–12; Charles F. Bryan Jr., "'Tories' amidst Rebels: Confederate Occupation of East Ten-

nessee, 1861–1863," *East Tennessee Historical Society's Publications* 60 (1988): 19–20; Oliver P. Temple, *East Tennessee and the Civil War* (Cincinnati: Robert Clarke, 1899), pp. 471–73.

17 See Steve Humphrey, *"That D----d Brownlow": Being a Saucy and Malicious Description of Fighting Parson William Gannaway Brownlow* (Boone, NC: Appalachian Consortium Press, 1978), p. viii.

18 *Chicago Tribune,* 9 September 1863. Only a few weeks earlier, Brownlow had bragged that at least twenty thousand mountaineers would join the Federal armies as soon as East Tennessee was "redeemed." See *Christian Recorder,* 25 July 1863.

19 Organization of the Department of the Ohio, 31 August 1863, *OR,* ser. 1, vol. 30, pt. 2, pp. 552–56; *Tennesseans in the Civil War: A Military History of Confederate and Union Units with Available Rosters of Personnel* (Nashville: Civil War Centennial Commission, 1964), pp. 375–77.

20 William Todd, *The Seventy-ninth Highlanders New York Volunteers in the War of the Rebellion, 1861–1865* (Albany, NY: Brandow, Barton, 1886), p. 331; Irwin Shepard to Parents, 25 September 1863, Irwin W. Shepard Letters and Diaries (typescript), p. 126, Michigan State Historical Society; Joseph W. Wilshire, *A Reminiscence of Burnside's Knoxville Campaign: Paper Read before the Ohio Commandery of the Loyal Legion, April 3rd, 1912* (Cincinnati: The Commandery, 1912) in McClung Historical Collection; Daniel Larned to Sister, 18 October 1863, Daniel Read Larned Papers, Library of Congress; William H. Brearley, *Recollections of the East Tennessee Campaign* (Detroit: Tribune Book and Job Office, 1871), p. 4. See also *History of the Thirty-fifth Regiment Massachusetts Volunteers, 1862–1865* (Boston: Mills, Knight, 1884), p. 166.

21 Robert Jameson to Mother, 3 October 1863, Robert Edwin Jameson Papers, Library of Congress; William Draper to Father, 29 September 1863, William Draper to Wife, 30 September 1863, William Franklin Draper Letters, Library of Congress; Daniel Larned to Sister, 18 October, 29 September 1863, Larned Papers; O. M. Poe to Wife, 10 September, 5 September 1863, Orlando M. Poe Papers, Library of Congress; "The Siege of Knoxville, Tennessee," in Frank Moore, ed., *The Rebellion Record* (New York: D. Van Nostrand, 1865), vol. 8, p. 253.

22 Daniel Larned to Henry, 28 September 1863, Larned Papers; O. M. Poe to Wife, 5 September 1863, Poe Papers; *Boston Evening Transcript,* 1 February 1864.

23 Brearley, *Recollections of the East Tennessee Campaign,* p. 6; Todd, *Seventy-ninth Highlanders,* pp. 334–35; B. F. Thompson, *History of the 112th Regiment of Illinois Volunteer Infantry in the Great War of the Rebellion, 1862–1865* (Toulon, IL: Stark Co. News Office, 1885), pp. 74–75; John Watkins to Sarah, 6 October 1863, John Watkins Collection, Special Collections, University of Tennessee Libraries.

24 Brearley, *Recollections of the East Tennessee Campaign,* pp. 5–6; O. M. Poe to Wife, 5 September 1863, Poe Papers; Daniel Larned to Henry, 28 September 1863, Daniel Larned to Sister, 5 October 1863, Larned Papers. Confederates visiting the region for the first time sometimes responded similarly. See G. Moxley Sorrel, *Recollections of a Confederate Staff Officer* (Jackson, TN: McCowat-Mercer Press, 1958), pp. 210–12.

25 *Chicago Tribune,* 11 September 1863; *Harper's Weekly,* 24 October 1863; O. M. Poe to Wife, 26 August 1863, Poe Papers; William Draper to Wife, 8 October 1863, Draper to Father, 9 October 1863, Draper Papers. See also entry for 3 September 1863, Oliver Lyman Spaulding Diary, Spaulding Family Papers, Library of Congress; Carter, "Sketch of the Military Services of Sam. P. Carter"; P. C. Hayes, "Campaigning in East Tennessee," in Commandery of the State of Illinois, Military Order of the Loyal Legion of the United States, *Military Essays and Recollections,* vol. 4 (Chicago: Cozzens and Beaton, 1907), pp. 320–22; and William Douglas Hamilton, *Recollections of a Cavalryman of the Civil War after Fifty Years, 1861–1865* (Columbus, OH: F. J. Heer, 1915), pp. 64–65.

26 Robert Jameson to Mother, 3 October 1863, Jameson Papers; *Harper's Weekly,* 24 October 1863; O. M. Poe to Wife, 4 September 1863; *New York Herald,* 9 October 1863; Wilshire, *Reminiscence of Burnside's Knoxville Campaign.* See also August V. Kautz, "Reminiscences of the Civil War,"

p. 55, August Valentine Kautz Papers, Library of Congress; Elisa Bolli Buffat, "Some Recollections of My Childhood Days and Incidents of My Life during the Civil War," reprinted in David Babelay, *They Trusted and Were Delivered: The French-Swiss of Knoxville, Tennessee* (Knoxville: Vaud-Tennessee, 1988), vol. 2, p. 449. For newspaper coverage of Burnside's "triumphal entry into Knoxville" emphasizing the "inexpressible joy" of the inhabitants, see *New York Herald*, 14 September, 9 October, 3 December 1863 (quote); *Chicago Tribune*, 11 September 1863 (quote); *Daily National Intelligencer*, 10 September 1863; *Harper's Weekly*, 24 October 1863; *New York Times*, 4, 5, and 9 September 1863; *Boston Evening Transcript*, 6, 9, 10, and 11 September 1863; *Public Ledger*, 11 September 1863.

27   *Knoxville Register*, 15 September, 10 October 1863; Hesseltine, *Ramsey Autobiography*, pp. 115–16, 120 (quote). See also William G. McAdoo to Dear Mother, 13 August 1863, McAdoo Papers.

28   Entries for 1 and 10 September 1863, James McMillan Journal, McClung Historical Collection, Knox County Public Library; Temple, *East Tennessee and the Civil War*, pp. 474–78.

29   *Chicago Tribune*, 11 April 1863; H. W. Halleck to Hon. E. M. Stanton, 15 November 1863, *OR*, ser. 1, vol. 30, pt. 2, pp. 545–46. Only months before, Brownlow had testified before a Federal military commission that a temporary advance of Union troops into East Tennessee could be disastrous for local loyalists. See "Transcript from Phonographic Notes of the Buell Court of Inquiry," 4 April 1863, *OR*, ser. 1, vol. 16, pt. 1, p. 678.

30   On the journey from Cincinnati, Brownlow overtook the Thirty-fifth Massachusetts Infantry near Cumberland Gap as that unit also made its way toward Knoxville. A soldier in the Thirty-fifth recalled how the men cheered at the sight of the "old hero" and the band struck up a patriotic tune as a "triumphal welcome home to the redoubtable patriot." See *History of the Thirty-fifth Regiment Massachusetts Volunteers*, p. 169. On Maynard's determination to move his family back to Knoxville, see Maynard to Andrew Johnson, 28 September 1863, *Johnson Papers*, vol. 6, p. 387.

31   Edwin M. Stanton to W. G. Brownlow, 19 September 1863, *OR*, ser. 1, vol. 30, pt. 3, p. 745; Daniel Larned to Sister, 18 October 1863, Larned Papers; O. M. Poe to Eleanor Poe, 20 October 1863, Poe Papers; Sutherland, *Very Violent Rebel*, pp. 24–25; Kautz, "Reminiscences of the Civil War," p. 56.

32   *Sketch of Parson Brownlow and His Speeches at the Academy of Music and Cooper Institute* (New York: E. D. Barker, 1862), p. 18; William G. Brownlow, *Sketches of the Rise, Progress, and Decline of Secession* (Philadelphia: George W. Childs, 1862), p. 438. See also *Parson Brownlow and the Unionists of East Tennessee* (New York: Beadle, 1862), pp. 44–45; W. G. Brownlow to E. T. Hall, 26 April 1863, Hall-Stakely Papers.

33   Undated newspaper clipping enclosed in Andrew Johnson, Horace Maynard, and Allen A. Hall to Abraham Lincoln, 27 March 1863, Robert Todd Lincoln Collection; *Knoxville Whig*, 14 April 1869. Brownlow himself acknowledged after the war that the federal government had provided him with cash and the use of wagons. The evidence that he received a printing press as well is less certain. In late August 1863, Union troops operating in Middle Tennessee confiscated a printing press and printing supplies, and the Federal commander on the scene reported to his superior that he would turn over the press to Brownlow unless otherwise instructed. His commander's response has not survived. Even so, it is uncertain whether the Union officer intended for Brownlow actually to use the press (Knoxville had not yet been occupied by the Union army), or whether he was conveying the confiscated property to Brownlow in the latter's new capacity as "assistant special agent" of the U.S. Treasury. See Brig. Gen. James G. Spears to Maj. Gen. W. S. Rosecrans, 31 August 1863, *OR*, ser. 1, vol. 30, pt. 3, p. 260.

34   *Knoxville Whig*, 11 and 18 November 1863.

35   Sutherland, *Very Violent Rebel*, pp. 37–39; A. E. Burnside to General Parke, 15 November 1863, *OR*, ser. 1, vol. 31, pt. 3, p. 157; *Knoxville Whig*, 9 January 1869. According to Thomas Humes, other prominent refugees included John Baxter, Oliver Temple, banker Sam Morrow, attorney

John Fleming, and former congressman Thomas A. R. Nelson, who had moved to Knoxville during the war. See Humes, *Loyal Mountaineers of Tennessee*, pp. 245–46.

36 James Longstreet to R. E. Lee, 5 September 1863, *OR*, ser. 1, vol. 29, pt. 2, p. 699; James Longstreet to R. E. Lee, 2 September 1863, *OR*, ser. 1, vol. 29, pt. 2, p. 694. In addition to a broad range of evidence left by participants and observers, my narrative of the Knoxville campaign is informed by the following secondary overviews: H. J. Eckenrode and Bryan Conrad, *James Longstreet: Lee's War Horse* (Chapel Hill: University of North Carolina Press, 1936), pp. 214–68; Harold S. Fink, "The East Tennessee Campaign and the Battle of Knoxville in 1863," *East Tennessee Historical Society's Publications* 29 (1957): 79–117; James F. Davidson, "Michigan and the Defense of Knoxville, Tennessee, 1863," *East Tennessee Historical Society's Publications* 35 (1963): 21–53; Digby Gordon Seymour, *Divided Loyalties: Fort Sanders and the Civil War in East Tennessee*, rev. ed. (Knoxville: University of Tennessee Press, 1982); Maury Klein, "The Knoxville Campaign," *Civil War Times Illustrated* 10 (1971): 5–10, 40–42; William Marvel, *Burnside* (Chapel Hill: University of North Carolina Press, 1991), pp. 295–343; Jeffry D. Wert, *General James Longstreet: The Confederacy's Most Controversial Soldier—A Biography* (New York: Simon and Schuster, 1993), pp. 323–58; Robert K. Krick, "Longstreet versus McLaws—and Everyone Else—about Knoxville," in *The Smoothbore Volley That Doomed the Confederacy: The Death of Stonewall Jackson and Other Chapters in the Army of Northern Virginia* (Baton Rouge: Louisiana State University Press, 2002), pp. 85–116.

37 James Longstreet to R. E. Lee, 5 September 1863, *OR*, ser. 1, vol. 29, pt. 2, p. 699.

38 James M. McPherson, *Battle Cry of Freedom: The Civil War Era* (New York: Oxford University Press, 1988), pp. 670–74.

39 J. Longstreet to Hon. J. A. Seddon, 26 September 1863, *OR*, ser. 1, vol. 30, pt. 4, p. 706; Petition to His Excellency Jefferson Davis, 4 October 1863, *OR*, ser. 1, vol. 30, pt. 2, pp. 65–66.

40 Jefferson Davis to B. Bragg, 29 October 1863, *OR*, ser. 1, vol. 52, pt. 2, p. 554; Braxton Bragg to James Longstreet, 4 November 1863, *OR*, ser. 1, vol. 31, pt. 3, pp. 634–35.

41 Gary W. Gallagher, ed., *Fighting for the Confederacy: The Personal Recollections of General Edward Porter Alexander* (Chapel Hill: University of North Carolina Press, 1989), p. 311; McPherson, *Battle Cry of Freedom*, pp. 675–76; Bruce Catton, *Never Call Retreat* (New York: Doubleday, 1965), pp. 255–60. On the campaign's unjustifiable risks, see Ulysses S. Grant, *Personal Memoirs of U. S. Grant* (New York: Charles L. Webster, 1886), vol. 2, pp. 95–98.

42 James Longstreet, *From Manassas to Appomattox: Memoirs of the Civil War in America* (Philadelphia: Lippincott, 1896), pp. 480–88. Longstreet's chief of artillery, E. Porter Alexander, corroborated this account in *Military Memoirs of a Confederate* (Bloomington: Indiana University Press, 1962), p. 480. Conversely, Confederate general William J. Hardee, who was present at the 3 November meeting with Longstreet and Bragg, wrote five months later that he did not recall Longstreet recommending that Bragg retire to a position behind the Chickamauga. Furthermore, he claimed that Longstreet had agreed in the meeting "that 15,000 men would be a force sufficient to destroy Burnside." See W. J. Hardee to James Longstreet, 8 April 1864, *OR*, ser. 1, vol. 31, pt. 1, p. 474.

43 Alexander, *Military Memoirs*, p. 481; J. Longstreet to B. Bragg, 4 and 5 November 1863, *OR*, ser. 1, vol. 31, pt. 3, pp. 635, 636–37; Longstreet, *From Manassas to Appomattox*, pp. 484–85; Brearley, *Recollections of the East Tennessee Campaign*, p. 46; J. Longstreet to Braxton Bragg, 11 November 1863, *OR*, ser. 1, vol. 31, pt. 3, p. 681. Months later Longstreet continued to complain that Bragg had sent him toward Knoxville short-handed. See James Longstreet to S. Cooper, 1 January 1864, *OR*, ser. 1, vol. 31, pt. 1, pp. 455–66; J. Longstreet to R. E. Lee, 27 February 1864, *OR*, ser. 1, vol. 32, pt. 2, pp. 809–10.

44 C. A. Dana to Hon. E. M. Stanton, 18 November 1863, *OR*, ser. 1, vol. 31, pt. 1, pp. 260–61; Bruce Catton, *Glory Road* (New York: Doubleday, 1952), pp. 17–62.

45 Longstreet, *From Manassas to Appomattox*, pp. 483–87; Gallagher, *Fighting for the Confederacy*, pp. 311–13; Sorrel, *Recollections of a Confederate Staff Officer*, p. 201; "Report of Maj. R. Z. Moses, Commissary of Subsistence," 1 January 1864, *OR*, ser. 1, vol. 31, pt. 1, pp. 476–77. To compound matters, there was an insufficient number of wagons for the foraging parties, these frequently broke down, and they were pulled by mules often so weak they could scarcely pull their own weight. See "Report of Capt. Frank Potts, Assistant Quartermaster," 26 December 1863, *OR*, ser. 1, vol. 31, pt. 1, p. 476.

46 Robert B. Potter to Lewis Richmond, 20 November 1863, *OR*, ser. 1, vol. 31, pt. 1, pp. 335–36; H. S. Burrage, "Retreat from Lenoir's and the Siege of Knoxville," *Atlantic Monthly* 18 (1866): 21; Todd, *Seventy-ninth Highlanders*, pp. 353–54; Longstreet, *From Manassas to Appomattox*, pp. 490–92. See also William F. Draper, *Recollections of a Varied Career* (Boston: Little, Brown, 1909), p. 125; Irwin Shepard to "Most Loved Ones at Home," 5 November 1863, Shepard Letters and Diaries, p. 137.

47 Even after the conclusion of the Knoxville campaign, a soldier in the Ninth Corps remained convinced that Longstreet's force was three times that of Burnside. See Irwin Shepard to Parents, 6 December 1863, Shepard Letters and Diaries, p. 149.

48 C. A. Dana to E. M. Stanton, 13, 14, and 18 November 1863, *OR*, ser. 1, vol. 31, pt. 1, pp. 258–61; Daniel Larned to Dear Sister, 14 November 1863, Larned Papers; James H. Wilson to Grant, 13 November 1863, *OR*, ser. 1, vol. 31, pt. 1, pp. 265–66.

49 A. E. Burnside to Grant, 13 November 1863, *OR*, ser. 1, vol. 31, pt. 3, p. 138; A. E. Burnside to Adjutant-General, U.S. Army, 13 November 1865, *OR*, ser. 1, vol. 31, pt. 1, p. 273; Grant, *Personal Memoirs*, vol. 2, p. 50; U. S. Grant to Ambrose E. Burnside, 14 and 15 November 1863, *OR*, ser. 1, vol. 31, pt. 2, p. 30.

50 A. E. Burnside to Adjutant-General, U.S. Army, 13 November 1865; James Longstreet to S. Cooper, 1 January 1864; Robert B. Potter to Lewis Richmond, 18 November 1863, *OR*, ser. 1, vol. 31, pt. 1, pp. 273–74, 332–35, 457–58.

51 Thompson, *History of the 112th Regiment of Illinois Volunteer Infantry*, p. 138; Todd, *Seventy-ninth Highlanders*, p. 358; Brearley, *Recollections of the East Tennessee Campaign*, p. 25; Sutherland, *Very Violent Rebel*, p. 39; Burrage, "Retreat from Lenoir's," p. 26; John Watkins to Friend John, 15 December 1863, Watkins Collection; Orlando M. Poe, "The Defense of Knoxville," in Robert Underwood Johnson and Clarence Clough Buel, eds., *Battles and Leaders of the Civil War*, vol. 3 (New York: Thomas Yoseloff, 1887–88), pp. 734–35. On heavy rainfall in October, see Daniel Larned to sister, 18 October 1863, Larned Papers; William Draper to wife, 21 October 1863, Draper Letters.

52 O. M. Poe to Nell Poe, 28 November 1863, Poe Papers; "Report of Col. James D. Nance, Third South Carolina Infantry," 6 January 1864, *OR*, ser. 1, vol. 31, pt. 1, pp. 509–12.

53 James Longstreet to S. Cooper, 1 January 1864, *OR*, ser. 1, vol. 31, pt. 1, p. 459; Brearley, *Recollections of the East Tennessee Campaign*, p. 28; Orlando M. Poe to Ambrose E. Burnside, 13 January 1864, *OR*, ser. 1, vol. 31, pt. 1, p. 296.

54 Daniel Larned to Dear Sister, 14 November 1863, Larned Papers; H. H. Thomas, "Personal Reminiscences of the East Tennessee Campaign," in Commandery of the State of Illinois, *Military Essays and Recollections*, vol. 4, p. 293; Sutherland, *Very Violent Rebel*, p. 38; Hesseltine, *Ramsey Autobiography*, p. 149. See also Hamilton, *Recollections of a Cavalryman*, p. 66. For the common view among Longstreet's subordinates, see "Report of Maj. Gen. Lafayette McLaws," 19 April 1864, *OR*, ser. 1, vol. 31, pt. 1, pp. 498–99; Alexander, *Military Memoirs*, p. 484; Sorrel, *Recollections of a Confederate Staff Officer*, p. 203. Long after the war, Lafayette McLaws claimed to have "volunteered to assault the city" while "the works were incomplete." McLaws and Longstreet were bitter enemies, however, and in fairness to the latter, it should be noted that the former may have been guilty of some foot-dragging of his own. At the very least, Longstreet maintained that he had recommended an attack by McLaws's division on the twenty-second

but that McLaws had objected. See McLaws to Marcus J. Wright, 7 June 1882, quoted in Krick, "Longstreet versus McLaws," p. 96; James Longstreet to S. Cooper, 1 January 1864, *OR*, ser. 1, vol. 31, pt. 1, p. 459.

55 Orlando M. Poe to Ambrose E. Burnside, 13 January 1864, *OR*, ser. 1, vol. 31, pt. 1, pp. 296, 302; Poe, "Defense of Knoxville," pp. 738–39. See also O. M. Poe to Wife, 28 November 1863, Poe Papers.

56 J. Longstreet to General Bragg, 20 November 1863, *OR*, ser. 1, vol. 31, pt. 3, p. 721; Longstreet to Bragg, 21 November 1863, ibid., p. 732.

57 Seymour, *Divided Loyalties*, p. 166n; Draper, *Recollections of a Varied Career*, pp. 140–41; entry for 1 December 1863, Shepard Letters and Diaries, p. 142; Shepard to Parents, 6 December 1863, Shepard Letters and Diaries, p. 149. See also O. M. Poe to Wife, 22 October 1863, Poe Papers; John Watkins to Sarah, 8 November 1863, Watkins Collection; Temple, *East Tennessee and the Civil War*, p. 500; Todd, *Seventy-ninth Highlanders*, pp. 373–74; Brearley, *Recollections of the East Tennessee Campaign*, pp. 33–35; *History of the Thirty-fifth Regiment Massachusetts Volunteers*, p. 191; and reports from Burnside to Grant dated 21, 23, and 30 November 1863, *OR*, ser. 1, vol. 31, pt. 1, pp. 269–71.

58 Sutherland, *Very Violent Rebel*, pp. 4–10, 42; Memoirs of Margaret Oswald Klein, McClung Historical Collection, Knox County Public Library (unpaginated); Elizabeth Baker Crozier Journal, Special Collections, University of Tennessee Libraries (unpaginated typescript).

59 Lewis Richmond, A.A.G. to Lt. Col. James M. Ellis, 27 September 1863, Letters Sent, Aug. 1863–Jan. 1865, Department of the Ohio, entry 3504, RG 393, U.S. Army Continental Commands, NARA; entries for 23 and 28 January, 1864, Thomas Doak Edington Diary, Special Collections, University of Tennessee Libraries; Humes, *Loyal Mountaineers of Tennessee*, p. 273; Endorsements Sent by the Provost Marshal General, Sept. 1863–July 1864, District of East Tennessee, entry 2759, pp. 5, 27, RG 393, NARA; entry 3533, "List of Claimants Investigated by a Military Commission, 1864," p. 100, RG 393, NARA; Major General Foster to H. W. Halleck, 14 December 1863, "Letters Sent, Department of the Ohio"; claims 7560, 2494, and 15864, Records of the General Accounting Office, RG 217, NARA.

60 Michael Rule to Dear Uncle, 27 September 1863, Mrs. F. Graham Bartlett Collection, Rule Correspondence, McClung Historical Collection, Knox County Public Library; Daniel Larned to Henry, 28 September 1863, Larned Papers; Hayes, "Campaigning in East Tennessee," pp. 336–37; Sutherland, *Very Violent Rebel*, p. 42; testimony of Titus Robinson in claim 15166, Records of the General Accounting Office, RG 217, NARA, Thomas, "Personal Reminiscences of the East Tennessee Campaign," p. 294. See also Hannibal Armstrong, "How I Hid a Union Spy," *Journal of Negro History* 9 (1924): 38. I am grateful to Thomas Pressly for calling the last source to my attention.

61 David Deaderick Diary, Special Collections, University of Tennessee Libraries, pp. 59–61; Sutherland, *Very Violent Rebel*, pp. 40, 41, 45; entry for 18 November 1863, Burrage, "Retreat from Lenoir's," pp. 27–28; entry for 18 November 1863, Shepard Letters and Diaries, p. 139; John Watkins to John, 15 December 1863, Watkins Collection.

62 Crozier Journal; Humes, *Loyal Mountaineers of Tennessee*, p. 259; "Siege of Knoxville," p. 254; Sutherland, *Very Violent Rebel*, pp. 41–47; entry for 23 November 1863, Shepard Letters and Diaries. See also Burrage, "Retreat from Lenoir's," p. 29; Thompson, *History of the 112th Regiment of Illinois Volunteer Infantry*, p. 151.

63 Longstreet, *From Manassas to Appomattox*, pp. 484–85; Braxton Bragg to Longstreet, 22 November 1863, *OR*, ser. 1, vol. 31, pt. 3, p. 736.

64 Longstreet, *From Manassas to Appomattox*, p. 501; Gallagher, *Fighting for the Confederacy*, pp. 323–34. Alexander later claimed that Longstreet had been ready to attack Fort Sanders on the twenty-sixth but had canceled the assault when Leadbetter arrived and disapproved. Longstreet makes no mention of this, either in his official report after the campaign or in his subsequent memoirs. See James Longstreet to S. Cooper, 1 January 1864, *OR*, ser. 1, vol. 31, pt. 1, pp. 459–60; Longstreet, *From Manassas to Appomattox*, pp. 501–2.

65 Gallagher, *Fighting for the Confederacy*, pp. 324–26; Poe, "Defense of Knoxville," p. 742.

66 Poe, "Defense of Knoxville," pp. 741–42; Burrage, "Retreat from Lenoir's," p. 31; Longstreet, *From Manassas to Appomattox*, p. 503; Alexander, *Military Memoirs*, pp. 485–86. Estimates of the number of Union soldiers actually inside the fort when it was attacked vary widely. I have chosen Poe's, which although on the high end, strikes me as the most judicious.

67 Gallagher, *Fighting for the Confederacy*, pp. 326–28; Todd, *Seventy-ninth Highlanders*, pp. 382–83.

68 Davidson, "Michigan and the Defense of Knoxville," p. 42; John Watkins to John, 15 December 1863, Watkins Collection; Gallagher, *Fighting for the Confederacy*, p. 328.

69 *Harper's Weekly*, 9 January 1864, pp. 24–25.

70 John F. Martin to Dear——, 30 November 1863, reprinted in *New York Herald*, 21 December 1863; Todd, *Seventy-ninth Highlanders*, pp. 383, 389–90. A member of the Twentieth Georgia Infantry claimed that the work of the Confederate sharpshooters was so effective that almost no volleys were fired from within Fort Sanders itself. See Seymour, *Divided Loyalties*, p. 202.

71 Samuel N. Benjamin to Ambrose Burnside, 20 December 1864, *OR*, ser. 1, vol. 31, pt. 1, p. 342; Todd, *Seventy-ninth Highlanders*, p. 391. See also John Watkins to John, 15 December 1863, Watkins Collection; Brearley, *Recollections of the East Tennessee Campaign*, pp. 37–38; and "Report of Maj. General Lafayette McLaws," 19 April 1864, *OR*, ser. 1, vol. 31, pt. 1, p. 490.

72 Brearley, *Recollections of the East Tennessee Campaign*, pp. 37–38; Burrage, "Retreat from Lenoir's," p. 31; Todd, *Seventy-ninth Highlanders*, p. 389; James Longstreet to S. Cooper, 1 January 1864, *OR*, ser. 1, vol. 31, pt. 1, p. 461. See also Davidson, "Michigan and the Defense of Knoxville," p. 45.

73 Fink, "East Tennessee Campaign," p. 109; O. M. Poe to Wife, 30 November 1863, Poe Papers; Davidson, "Michigan and the Defense of Knoxville," pp. 44–45; Seymour, *Divided Loyalties*, p. 273; John Watkins to John, 15 December 1863, Watkins Collection; "Return of Casualties in Longstreet's Corps, November 14–December 4," *OR*, ser. 1. vol. 31, pt. 1, p. 475; Samuel N. Benjamin to Ambrose Burnside, 20 December 1864, *OR*, ser. 1, vol. 31, pt. 1, p. 344. See also Thompson, *History of the 112th Regiment of Illinois Volunteer Infantry*, p. 164.

74 O. M. Poe to Wife, 30 November and 1 December 1863, Poe Papers; A. E. Burnside to Adjutant-General, U.S. Army, 13 November 1865; James Longstreet to S. Cooper, 1 January 1864; "Report of Maj. Gen. Lafayette McLaws," all in *OR*, ser. 1, vol. 31, pt. 1, pp. 278, 462, 498. McLaws was eventually exonerated and returned to duty. See Krick, "Longstreet Versus McLaws."

75 Ulysses Grant to H. W. Halleck, 6 December 1863, *OR*, ser. 1, vol. 31, pt. 3, p. 345; A. Lincoln to U. S. Grant, 25 November 1863, *OR*, ser. 1, vol. 31, pt. 2, p. 25; Grant, *Personal Memoirs*, vol. 2, pp. 98–99; John G. Nicolay and John Hay, *Abraham Lincoln: A History* (New York: Century, 1904), pp. 186–87; Basler, *Collected Works of Abraham Lincoln*, vol. 7, p. 35. See also *New York Herald*, 3 December 1863; *New York Times*, 8 December 1863. For a southern account of the end of the siege, see *Charleston Mercury*, 5 December 1863.

76 Entry for 5 December 1863, Deaderick Diary; Crozier Journal; Sutherland, *Very Violent Rebel*, pp. 57, 75, 77.

CHAPTER SEVEN

1 Elisa Bolli Buffat, "Some Recollections of My Childhood Days and Incidents of My Life during the Civil War," reprinted in David Babelay, *They Trusted and Were Delivered: The French-Swiss of Knoxville, Tennessee* (Knoxville: Vaud-Tennessee, 1988), vol. 2, p. 452.

2 Mrs. John Williams to Rufus Williams, 15 November 1864, John and Rhoda Campbell Williams Papers, McClung Historical Collection, Knox County Public Library.

3 "Message of the President of the United States Transmitting an Address of the 'East Tennes-

see Relief Association,'" Senate Exec. Doc. No. 40, 38th Cong., 1st sess. (Washington, DC: GPO, 1864), pp. 2–3; Edward Everett, *Account of the Fund for the Relief of East Tennessee; with a Complete List of the Contributors* (Boston: Little, Brown, 1864), p. 11; *Harper's Weekly*, 24 October 1863. See also *Report to the Contributors to the Pennsylvania Relief Association for East Tennessee* (Philadelphia: printed for the association, 1864).

4   Joseph W. Wilshire, *A Reminiscence of Burnside's Knoxville Campaign: Paper Read before the Ohio Commandery of the Loyal Legion, April 3rd, 1912* (Cincinnati: The Commandery, 1912).

5   *Daily National Intelligencer*, 10 September 1863.

6   Gerald F. Linderman, *Embattled Courage: The Experience of Combat in the American Civil War* (New York: Free Press, 1987), p. 1; "The Siege of Knoxville, Tennessee," in Frank Moore, ed., *The Rebellion Record* (New York: D. Van Nostrand, 1865), vol. 8, p. 254.

7   Buffat, "Some Recollections of My Childhood Days," p. 456; entry for 5 December 1863, David Deaderick Diary, McClung Historical Collection, Knox County Public Library; Daniel E. Sutherland, ed., *A Very Violent Rebel: The Civil War Diary of Ellen Renshaw House* (Knoxville: University of Tennessee Press, 1996), pp. 57, 72, 92; *Knoxville Whig*, 23 January 1864; E. T. Hall to Martha Hall, 16 and 27 January 1864, Hall-Stakely Papers, McClung Historical Collection, Knox County Public Library. See also entry for 24 January 1864, Thomas Doak Edington Diary, Special Collections, University of Tennessee Libraries; *Boston Evening Transcript*, 1 February 1864; Paul E. Rieger, ed., *Through One Man's Eyes: The Civil War Experiences of a Belmont County Volunteer* (Mt. Vernon, OH: Print Arts Press, 1974), pp. 86–87. See also *Bristol Gazette*, 18 February 1864.

8   Buffat, "Some Recollections of My Childhood Days," p. 456; *Knoxville Whig*, 5 March 1864; Whitelaw Reid, *After the War: A Tour of the Southern States, 1865–1866* (Cincinnati: Moore, Wilstach and Baldwin, 1866), p. 351; "Siege of Knoxville," pp. 255, 253; Edward Maynard to Washburn Maynard, 17 November 1863, Horace Maynard Papers, Special Collections, University of Tennessee Libraries; Endorsements Sent by the Provost Marshal General, District of East Tennessee, Sept. 1863–July 1864, p. 225, entry 2759, RG 393; U.S. Army Continental Commands, NARA; case 2,136, Isabella R. Boyd vs. the United States, U.S. Court of Claims, NARA.

9   *Knoxville Whig*, 5 March 1864; Mrs. John Williams to My Dear Sons, 27 March 1864, Williams Papers; Laura Maynard to Washburn Maynard, 19 January 1864, Maynard Papers; Major General Foster to H. W. Halleck, 14 December 1863, Letters Sent, Aug. 1863–Jan. 1865, Department of the Ohio, entry 3504, RG 393, U.S. Army Continental Commands, NARA; Rieger, *Through One Man's Eyes*, pp. 85, 88; Babelay, *They Trusted and Were Delivered*, vol. 1, p. 12; Cecile Chavannes and Albert Chavannes, *East Tennessee Sketches* (Knoxville: Albert Chavannes, 1900), p. 104; Endorsements Sent by the Provost Marshal General, p. 5; Frederick S. Heiskell to Horace Maynard, 16 March 1874, Frederick S. Heiskell Papers, Archives of Appalachia, East Tennessee State University; Thomas A. R. Nelson to Brig. General S. P. Carter, 26 December 1863, *OR*, ser. 1, vol. 31, pt. 3, p. 508.

10 James Longstreet, *From Manassas to Appomattox: Memoirs of the Civil War in America* (Philadelphia: Lippincott, 1896), pp. 520–21; J. Longstreet to R. E. Lee, 27 February 1864, *OR*, ser. 1, vol. 32, pt. 2, p. 810.

11 *Knoxville Whig*, 14 May, 14 December 1864; Thomas W. Humes, *The Loyal Mountaineers of Tennessee* (Knoxville: Ogden Brothers, 1888), pp. 298–99; Thomas W. Humes, *Report to the East Tennessee Relief Association at Knoxville* (Knoxville: printed for the association, 1865), pp. 7–8, 15; Endorsements Sent by the Provost Marshal General, p. 213.

12 O. M. Poe to wife, 19 September 1863, Orlando M. Poe Papers, Library of Congress; Thomas A. R. Nelson to Brig. General S. P. Carter, 26 December 1863, *OR*, ser. 1, vol. 31, pt. 3, p. 508; "Rations Issued to Destitute Loyal Persons," in District of East Tennessee, Records of the Provost Marshal General, 1863–1865 (7 vols.), vol. 2, entry 2764, RG 393, U.S. Army Continental Commands, NARA.

13 Thomas W. Humes, *Second Report to the East Tennessee Relief Association at Knoxville* (Knoxville: Brownlow, Haws, 1866), p. 10; *Knoxville Whig*, 13 February 1864. See also William C. Harris, "The East Tennessee Relief Movement of 1864–1865," *Tennessee Historical Quarterly* 48 (1989): 86–96.

14 Entry for 2 September 1863, William G. McAdoo Diary, Floyd-McAdoo Family Diaries and Letterbooks, Library of Congress; Sutherland, *Very Violent Rebel*, pp. 123–24; *Knoxville Register*, 5 and 29 October 1861, 9 October 1863; *Knoxville Journal*, 7 May 1894; *Knoxville Whig*, 13 February 1864. See also W. Todd Groce, *Mountain Rebels: East Tennessee Confederates and the Civil War, 1860–1870* (Knoxville: University of Tennessee Press, 1999), p. 109.

15 *Knoxville Register*, 15 September, 10 October 1863; William B. Hesseltine, ed., *Dr. J. G. M. Ramsey: Autobiography and Letters* (Nashville: Tennessee Historical Commission, 1954), pp. 115–16; J. G. M. Ramsey to Sue Ramsey, 21 June 1864, J. G. M. Ramsey Papers, Special Collections, University of Tennessee Libraries; William H. Sneed to J. A. Sneddon, 12 December 1863, Letters Received by the Confederate Secretary of War, RG 109, War Department Collection of Confederate Records, NARA; William G. McAdoo to Dear Mother, 13 August 1863, William McAdoo Papers, Library of Congress; Elizabeth Baker Crozier Journal, Special Collections, University of Tennessee Libraries (unpaginated typescript); M. S. Temple to Col. O. P. Temple, 19 April 1864, Oliver Perry Temple Papers, Special Collections, University of Tennessee Libraries; notations for 23 February and 16 November 1864, in Registers of Letters Received, Department of Ohio, Aug. 1863–Feb. 1865, entry 3513, RG 393, U.S. Army Continental Commands, NARA; Ellen McClung to My Dear Brother, 13 October 1864, David Campbell Papers, Duke University.

16 "Roll of Prisoners in Custody," in Records of the Provost Marshal General, vol. 1 (bound as vol. 17).

17 *Knoxville Whig*, 28 May 1864; Sutherland, *Very Violent Rebel*, pp. 13, 45–46; "Oaths of Allegiance," in District of East Tennessee, Records of the Provost Marshal General, 1863–1865, entry 2764, RG 393, NARA; Deaderick Diary, p. 70; Application of Nathan Gammon, Amnesty Papers, roll 49. See also [C. W. Hall], *Threescore Years and Ten* (Cincinnati: Elm Street Printing Company, 1884), p. 199.

18 *Knoxville Whig*, 9 and 16 January 1864; *Bristol Gazette*, 18 February 1864; Noel C. Fisher, *War at Every Door: Partisan Politics and Guerrilla Violence in East Tennessee, 1860–1869* (Chapel Hill: University of North Carolina Press, 1997), p. 137.

19 Horace Maynard to Andrew Johnson, 28 September 1863, *Johnson Papers*, vol. 6, pp. 386–87; *Knoxville Whig*, 9 and 16 January 1864.

20 *Knoxville Whig*, 30 January, 6 February 1864; Sutherland, *Very Violent Rebel*, pp. 93, 95, 127; "Persons of Disloyal Sentiments Desirous of Being Sent South," in Registers of Letters Received, Department of Ohio, 16 November 1864; Thomas Humes to Maj. Gen. J. G. Foster, 23 January 1864, Registers of Letters Received, Department of Ohio. See also Charles F. Bryan Jr., "The Civil War in East Tennessee: A Social, Political, and Economic Study" (Ph.D. diss., University of Tennessee, 1978), p. 125; Edward to Washington Maynard, 7 February 1864, Maynard Papers.

21 Martha Luttrell Mitchell Memoir, TSLA; Sutherland, *Very Violent Rebel*, pp. 29–32, 54–57 (quotation on p. 54). See also Hesseltine, *Ramsey Autobiography*, chap. 13; Edward Maynard to Washington Maynard, 17 November 1863, Maynard Papers.

22 Hesseltine, *Ramsey Autobiography*, pp. 171, 177–78; Sutherland, *Very Violent Rebel*, pp. 87–88, 112–13, 127, 129; S. P. Carter, "A Sketch of the Military Services of Sam P. Carter, Brig. Genl. & Brevt. Maj. Genl. of U.S. Vols. during the Rebellion of the Southern States, 1861–1865," pp. 104–11, in Samuel Powhatan Carter Papers, Library of Congress.

23 Hesseltine, *Ramsey Autobiography*, pp. 163, 166–68, 176–78. See also Sutherland, *Very Violent Rebel*, p. 18.

24 *Knoxville Whig*, 11 November 1863, 16 and 23 November 1864.
25 *Knoxville Whig*, 9 January, 28 May 1864. See also Horace Maynard, *To the Slaveholders of Tennessee* (n.p., 1863), p. 20.
26 Sutherland, *Very Violent Rebel*, pp. 10, 14, 27; Hesseltine, *Ramsey Autobiography*, p. 176.
27 A. Woodward, *A Review of Uncle Tom's Cabin; or, an Essay on Slavery* (Cincinnati: Applegate, 1853), pp. 106–7; claims of Anthony Humes (2,494), Isaac Gammon (7,560), and Titus Robinson (15,166), Records of the General Accounting Office, RG 217, NARA [hereafter cited as Southern Claims Commission—Allowed Claims].
28 James M. McPherson, *For Cause and Comrades: Why Men Fought in the Civil War* (New York: Oxford University Press, 1997), chapter 9.
29 Mitchell Memoir; Sutherland, *Very Violent Rebel*, p. 22; Daniel Larned to my Dear Sister, 5 October 1863, in Daniel Read Larned Papers, Library of Congress; Edward Maynard to Washburn Maynard, 7 February 1864, Maynard Papers.
30 Mitchell Memoir; Sutherland, *Very Violent Rebel*, pp. 9, 99; Hesseltine, *Ramsey Autobiography*, pp. 170–71; Register of Letters Received by the Provost Marshal, July 1864–Feb. 1865, District of East Tennessee, entry 2761, RG 393, U.S. Army Continental Commands, NARA; William G. Brownlow to W. P. Mellen, 20 May 1864, E. E. Patton Collection, McClung Historical Collection, Knox County Public Library.
31 William W. Freehling, *The South vs. the South: How Anti-Confederate Southerners Shaped the Course of the Civil War* (New York: Oxford University Press, 2001), chaps. 6–8.
32 Endorsements Sent by the Provost Marshal General, p. 172; claim of William Bradley (12,834), Southern Claims Commission—Allowed Claims; Humes, *Loyal Mountaineers of Tennessee*, p. 298; Endorsements Sent by the Provost Marshal General, p. 1; claim of Charles Ballard (11,524), Records of the U.S. House of Representatives, 1871–1880, RG 233, NARA [hereafter cited as Southern Claims Commission—Disallowed Claims]; Sutherland, *Very Violent Rebel*, p. 10.
33 Deposition of Anderson Moffitt, case 8,780, Estate of J. S. Moffitt vs. the United States, Court of Claims, NARA; claims of Isaac Gammon (7,560) and Titus Robinson (15,166), Southern Claims Commission—Allowed Claims; Orlando M. Poe to Ambrose E. Burnside, 13 January 1864, *OR*, ser. 1, vol. 31, pt. 1, pp. 302; Mitchell Memoir.
34 Major J. J. Anderson to George L. Stearns, 17 December 1863, Letters Sent, Department of the Ohio; *Knoxville Whig*, 9 January, 30 April 1864.
35 *Knoxville Whig*, 28 May 1864. The permission granted to Joseph Mabry is in a written statement dated 20 January 1864 and signed by Brigadier General Davis Tillson. The document can be found among the unprocessed archival holdings of the University of Tennessee Special Collections.
36 William G. Brownlow to W. P. Mellen, 20 May 1864, Patton Collection; *New York Daily Tribune*, 30 April 1864; James M. McPherson, *Battle Cry of Freedom: The Civil War Era* (New York: Oxford University Press, 1988), p. 564; *Knoxville Whig*, 30 January 1864.
37 Ira Berlin, Barbara J. Fields, Thavolia Glymph, Joseph P. Reidy, and Leslie S. Rowland, eds., *Freedom: A Documentary History of Emancipation, 1861–1867* (New York: Cambridge University Press, 1985), ser. 1, vol. 1, pp. 320–22.
38 *New York Daily Tribune*, 9 April 1864.
39 Brownlow to W. P. Mellen, 20 May 1864, Patton Collection; Endorsements Sent by the Provost Marshal General, p. 246. Actually, the provost marshal's office was trying to crack down on black prostitution. Soldiers arrested twenty-one black women on charges of prostitution between March and June; twenty-seven white women were charged with the same offense during that period. See "Record of Prostituted Women Confined in Prison at Knoxville," Records of the Provost Marshal, vol. 3; "List of Prostitute Women Confined in Prison at Knoxville, Tenn., June 1–20, 1864," Records of the Provost Marshal, vol. 4.
40 *New York Daily Tribune*, 12 April 1864.
41 *Knoxville Whig*, 12 March, 7 and 28 May 1864.

42 Steve Humphrey, *"That D----d Brownlow": Being a Saucy and Malicious Description of Fighting Parson William Gannaway Brownlow* (Boone, NC: Appalachian Consortium Press, 1978), p. 278; W. G. Brownlow to Abraham Lincoln, 27 March 1863, and Andrew Johnson, Horace Maynard, and Allen A. Hall to Abraham Lincoln, 27 March 1863, Robert Todd Lincoln Collection of the Papers of Abraham Lincoln, Library of Congress; *Knoxville Whig*, 6 February, 30 April 1864.

43 *Knoxville Whig*, 5 March, 2 April 1864.

44 *Knoxville Whig*, 16 and 23 April 1864; *New York Times*, 15 April 1864; *New York Daily Tribune*, 18 April 1864; Roy P. Basler, ed., *The Collected Works of Abraham Lincoln* (Springfield, IL: Abraham Lincoln Association, 1953–55), vol. 7, p. 54; undated draft of a letter to the editor of the *Knoxville Commercial*, Heiskell Papers; Thomas B. Alexander, *Thomas A. R. Nelson of East Tennessee* (Nashville: Tennessee Historical Commission, 1956), p. 115.

45 *Knoxville Whig*, 23 April 1864.

46 Mrs. John Williams to Rufus Williams, 1 May, 22 September, 15 November 1864, Williams Papers; undated memorandum and undated draft of a letter to the editor of the *Knoxville Commercial*, Heiskell Papers (parentheses added for clarity).

47 McPherson, *Battle Cry of Freedom*, pp. 772–76; John B. Brownlow to Oliver P. Temple, 27 November 1892, Temple Papers; William G. Brownlow to Andrew Johnson, 7 September 1864, *Johnson Papers*, vol. 7, p. 139; Mrs. John Williams to Rufus Williams, 22 September 1864, Williams Papers.

48 William G. Brownlow to Andrew Johnson, 18 August 1864, *Johnson Papers*, vol. 7, p. 101; Brownlow to Johnson, 5 May 1864, *Johnson Papers*, vol. 6, p. 689. Writing a half century after the fact, Oliver Temple agreed that most of the Unionist leaders of 1861 supported McClellan in 1864. See Temple, *Notable Men of Tennessee from 1833 to 1875: Their Times and Their Contemporaries* (New York: Cosmopolitan Press, 1912), p. 45.

49 *New York Daily Tribune*, 30 April 1864; "Speech at Knoxville," *Johnson Papers*, vol. 6, pp. 674–75. See also Humphrey, *"That D----d Brownlow,"* pp. 278–79.

50 *Knoxville Whig*, 14 May, 4 June 1864.

51 *Knoxville Whig*, 17 August, 7 May, 21 September 1864.

52 *Knoxville Whig*, 18 June, 5 October 1864. See also *Knoxville Whig*, 7, 14, 21, 28 September and 12 October 1864.

53 *New York Times*, 13 September 1864; Andrew Johnson, "Proclamation re Presidential Election," 30 September 1864, *Johnson Papers*, vol. 7, pp. 203–5. In a bit of a conflict of interest, Johnson was taking measures not only to disfranchise McClellan supporters but also to promote his election as the next vice president. For northern criticism of the test oath, see Daniel E. Sickles to Abraham Lincoln, 13 October 1864, Robert Todd Lincoln Collection.

54 Abraham Lincoln to William B. Campbell and Others, 22 October 1864, in Basler, *Collected Works of Abraham Lincoln*, vol. 7, pp. 62, 64, 72.

55 *Knoxville Whig*, 9 November 1864.

56 Rhoda Williams to Rufus Williams, 15 November 1864, Williams Papers.

57 *Knoxville Whig*, 23 November 1864.

58 Joshua W. Caldwell, *Studies in the Constitutional History of Tennessee*, 2nd ed. (Cincinnati: Robert Clarke, 1907), pp. 282–84. The vote in Knoxville, which undoubtedly included both a large number of recent immigrants and probably some nonresident Tennessee Federal soldiers as well, was 1,078 to 2. See *Knoxville Whig*, 1 March 1865.

CHAPTER EIGHT

1   Laura Maynard to Washburn Maynard, 26 September 1865, Horace Maynard Papers, Special Collections, University of Tennessee Libraries.

2   Oliver P. Temple, *East Tennessee and the Civil War* (Cincinnati: Robert Clarke, 1899), p. 530.
3   *Knoxville Register*, 24 October 1863; Paul W. Prindle, comp., *Ancestry of William Sperry Beinecke* (North Haven, CT: Van Dyck, 1974), pp. 134–36; William B. Hesseltine, ed., *Dr. J. G. M. Ramsey: Autobiography and Letters* (Nashville: Tennessee Historical Commission, 1954), pp. 122–24. Ramsey's status as a noncombatant is not entirely certain. His father, who regularly exaggerated his sons' wartime heroism, insisted that Crozier had joined the staff of Confederate general J. C. Vaughn after being denied reappointment as Confederate district attorney in 1862, a position that he held until captured and paroled at Vicksburg. I have been unable to find Crozier Ramsey's military service record, however, and it may be that his status on Vaughn's staff— if he served at all—was informal and unofficial.
4   Charles F. Bryan Jr., "The Civil War in East Tennessee: A Social, Political, and Economic Study" (Ph.D. diss., University of Tennessee, 1978), pp. 151–54; General Alvin C. Gillem to Governor Andrew Johnson, 15 November 1864, *Johnson Papers*, vol. 7, pp. 290–91; Prindle, *Ancestry of William Sperry Beinecke*, pp. 233–34; E. T. Hall to Martha Hall, 17 November 1864, Hall-Stakely Papers, McClung Historical Collection, Knox County Public Library. The work compiled by Prindle includes as an appendix the transcription of a brief diary of J. A. Sperry.
5   Bryan, "Civil War in East Tennessee," p. 155; Noel C. Fisher, *War at Every Door: Partisan Politics and Guerrilla Violence in East Tennessee, 1860–1869* (Chapel Hill: University of North Carolina Press, 1997), p. 130; Reports of Maj. General George Stoneman, U.S. Army, commanding, Expedition from East Tennessee into Southwest Virginia, 10–29 December 1864, *OR*, ser. 1, vol. 45, pp. 807–15.
6   Crippled with lumbago, Ramsey was soon released to the hospital, but both Fox and Sperry remained in jail, the former until his sudden death from pneumonia in February, the latter until well after the war was over. To what extent the three prisoners were actually forced to perform hard labor with the ball and chain is a matter of dispute. The most direct evidence comes from J. A. Sperry himself. In the brief diary that he began after his capture in Bristol, Sperry noted that on 27 December he and Robert Fox were forced to wear the ball and chain while working for two hours on the fortifications on Temperance Hill, near their jail. Unfortunately, Sperry's diary ends on that date, and there is no reliable evidence concerning how he and Fox were subsequently treated. For their part, Federal military authorities in Knoxville denied that the prisoners had ever been mistreated, insisting that they were made "as comfortable as prisoners can expect to be." Partially corroborating their rejoinder, Crozier Ramsey wrote to his father on 10 January that he was being "kindly treated." See Prindle, *Ancestry of William Sperry Beinecke*, pp. 244–55; Wm. G. Swan to J. G. M. Ramsey, 13 February 1865, Crozier Ramsey to J. G. M. Ramsey, 10 January 1865, J. G. M. Ramsey Papers, Special Collections, University of Tennessee Libraries; R. Ould to Lieut. Col. John E. Mulford, 9 March 1865, *OR*, ser. 2, vol. 8, p. 371; S. P. Carter to Lt. S. F. Shaw, 29 December 1864, Register of Letters Sent by the Provost Marshal, July 1864–August 1865, District of East Tennessee, entry 2758, RG 393, U.S. Army Continental Commands, NARA; Application of J. Austin Sperry, Amnesty Papers, RG 94, roll 51, NARA; C. F. Trigg to S. P. Carter, 10 January 1865, Register of Letters Received by the Provost Marshal, July 1864–February 1865, District of East Tennessee, entry 2761, RG 393, NARA; Hesseltine, *Ramsey Autobiography*, pp. 240–45.
7   John C. Breckinridge to Commanding Officer, U.S. Forces, Knoxville, 12 January 1865, John C. Vaughn to Brig. Gen. L. S. Trowbridge, 20 February 1865, *OR*, ser. 2, vol. 8, pp. 58, 272–74; *Knoxville Whig*, 11 January 1865; W. G. Brownlow to Abraham Lincoln [telegram], 28 December 1864, Robert Todd Lincoln Collection of the Papers of Abraham Lincoln, Library of Congress; Andrew Johnson to Abraham Lincoln, 29 December 1864, *Johnson Papers*, vol. 7, pp. 367–68; Minute Book A, pp. 126, Minute Book B, pp. 99, 197, 248, in U.S. Circuit Court, Eastern District, Tennessee, Knoxville, 1864–1865, NARA—Southeast Regional Branch.
8   *Knoxville Whig*, 9 January 1864, 11 January, 1 March, 17 May 1865.

9   *Knoxville Whig*, 30 January, 14 May 1864.

10 *Knoxville Whig*, 9 January 1864; Papers of William G. "Parson" Brownlow Received from the First Auditor's Office entry 21, RG 366, Records of Civil War Special Agencies of the Treasury Department, NARA; Daniel E. Sutherland, ed., *A Very Violent Rebel: The Civil War Diary of Ellen Renshaw House* (Knoxville: University of Tennessee Press, 1996), p. 82. Documents pertaining to Brownlow's appointment by the Treasury Department may also be found in folder 6, box 1, William G. Brownlow Papers, Special Collections, University of Tennessee Libraries.

11 *Knoxville Whig*, 9 January 1864, 1 March 1865; state supreme court transcript of *William G. Brownlow vs. Robert B. Reynolds, Thomas J. Campbell, John H. Crozier, William H. Sneed, and John C. Ramsey*, included in Thomas A. R. Nelson Papers, McClung Historical Collection, Knox County Public Library; undated draft of a letter to the editor of the *Knoxville Commercial*, Frederick S. Heiskell Papers, Archives of Appalachia, East Tennessee State University. The impending auction of the property was announced by Sheriff Marcus Bearden in the *Whig* of 22 March 1865.

12 *Knoxville Whig*, 16 January 1864; Federal District Court transcript of *J. G. M. Ramsey vs. J. R. Ludlow*, 5 September 1867, Nelson Papers.

13 Minute Book A, 1864–1865, Records of the U.S. Circuit Court, Eastern District, Tennessee, Knoxville, NARA—Southeast Region; Records of the Attorney General's Office, General Records, Letters Received, 1809–1870, entry 9, RG 60, General Records of the Department of Justice, NARA; Knox County Circuit Court Minutes, vol. 15B, pp. 81–257; Application of Reuben G. Clark, Amnesty Papers, roll 48; E. T. Hall to A. J. Fletcher, 10 June 1865, Records of the Secretary of State of Tennessee, RG 30, TSLA; W. C. Kain, J. R. McCann, and Reuben Roddie to Hon. W. B. Campbell, 15 January 1866, David Campbell Papers, Duke University. The list of individuals charged with treason in the federal court does not contain sufficient information to positively identify Knoxville residents in all instances. The number of townspeople so charged may have approached one hundred.

14 J. C. Ramsey to J. G. M. Ramsey, 15 March 1867, Ramsey Papers; Willene B. Clark, ed., *Valleys of the Shadow: The Memoir of Confederate Captain Reuben G. Clark, Company I, 59th Tennessee Mounted Infantry* (Knoxville: University of Tennessee Press, 1994), pp. 70–75; *Knoxville Whig*, 17 May 1865 (marginal notation by John Bell Brownlow), 27 June 1866; Bryan, "Civil War in East Tennessee," p. 170.

15 Bryan, "Civil War in East Tennessee," p. 126; Steve Humphrey, *"That D----d Brownlow": Being a Saucy and Malicious Description of Fighting Parson William Gannaway Brownlow* (Boone, NC: Appalachian Consortium Press, 1978), pp. 347–48; John W. Green, *Bench and Bar of Knox County, Tennessee* (Knoxville: Archer and Smith, 1947), pp. 33–35; W. G. Brownlow to Childs, 15 September 1862, William Gannaway Brownlow Papers, Special Collections, University of Tennessee Libraries; W. G. Brownlow to Editors, *New York Weekly*, 28 June 1862, William Gannaway Brownlow Papers, Library of Congress; John B. Brownlow to Oliver Temple, 28 November 1892, Oliver P. Temple Papers, Special Collections, University of Tennessee Libraries; *Knoxville Whig*, 7 December 1864; William G. Brownlow to Andrew Johnson, 30 November 1864, *Johnson Papers*, vol. 7, p. 323; *Opinion of the Hon. Connally F. Trigg on the Constitutionality of the Act of Congress Prescribing an Oath on the Admission of Attorneys* (Memphis: Whitmore Brothers, 1865).

16 Clark, *Valleys of the Shadow*, p. 59; William G. Brownlow to Andrew Johnson, 5 November 1864, *Johnson Papers*, vol. 7, p. 267; *Knoxville Whig*, 10 August 1864; 11 January, 1 February 1865. See also *Knoxville Whig*, 31 August 1864; James R. Hood to Andrew Johnson, 24 August 1864, *Johnson Papers*, vol. 7, pp. 114–15 n. 4.

17 Endorsements Sent by the Provost Marshal General, District of East Tennessee, September 1863–July 1864, entry 2759, RG 393, U.S. Army Continental Commands, NARA, pp. 74, 170, 179, 181, 212; Knox County Circuit Court Minutes, vol. 16, pp. 235, 346; List of Claimants Investigated by a Military Commission, 1864, entry 3533, RG 393, U.S. Army Continental Commands,

NARA; William G. Brownlow to Andrew Johnson, 21 November 1864, *Johnson Papers*, vol. 7, pp. 307–9; John R. Branner to J. P. Benjamin, 2 December 1861, *OR*, ser. 1, vol. 7, p. 733.

18 Minute Book A, pp. 186, 253, 259, 261, 319, 355, Minute Book B, pp. 99, 197, 200, in Records of the U.S. Circuit Court, Eastern District, Tennessee, Knoxville, 1864–1870, NARA—Southeast Regional Branch; Knox County Circuit Court Minutes, vol. 16, p. 235; S.R.W. to Judge Trigg, 27 May 1865, Heiskell Papers. For pardon applications, see among many those of Robert A. Armstrong, Abner Baker, John E. Blackwell, James W. Bowman, William M. Cocke, W. W. Giddins, James Kennedy, J. C. Luttrell Jr., John A. McAffry, Hugh L. McClung, Robert J. McKinney, Frank A. Moses, J. A. Sperry, and William P. Vestal in Amnesty Papers, rolls 48–51. The statement praising Judge Trigg may be found in the records of the federal court and was signed by twenty-eight of the thirty-five men originally called to serve in either the grand or petit juries, including foreman Perez Dickinson, Frederick Heiskell, Abner Jackson, and John Williams. It is possible that Heiskell was the author of the resolution. A copy of the statement (written on the back of an envelope) may be found in series 1, box 2, folder 7, Heiskell Papers.

19 *Goodspeed's History of Tennessee* (Nashville: Goodspeed, 1887), p. 411; *Knoxville Whig*, 11 January, 1 March, 21 June 1865.

20 Clark, *Valleys of the Shadow*, p. 59; "Trip to Washington in 1861," undated memorandum in series 3, box 8, folder 3, Temple Papers; Sutherland, *Very Violent Rebel*, pp. 7, 26, 45, 135, 210, 222; Hugh Brown Heiskell Diary, TSLA; John Baxter, *The Harmon Case: Reply of Colonel John Baxter to the Speech of Senator W. G. Brownlow* (Knoxville: Chronicle Job Printing Office, 1871), p. 2; Green, *Bench and Bar of Knox County*, pp. 67–68.

21 *Knoxville Whig*, 31 August 1864.

22 "Message of the President of the United States transmitting an Address of the 'East Tennessee Relief Association,'" Senate Exec. Doc. No. 40, 38th Cong., 1st sess. (Washington, DC: Government Printing Office, 1864), p. 2; *New York Daily Tribune*, 12 April 1864. The charter members of the association are listed in *Knoxville Whig*, 13 February 1864. Each of the individuals mentioned in this and the following paragraph was a member of the organization. The two dozen Knoxville men in the association constituted more than half of its original membership.

23 *Knoxville Register*, 25 November, 10 December 1862, 20 February 1863; Oliver P. Temple, *Notable Men of Tennessee from 1833 to 1875: Their Times and Their Contemporaries* (New York: Cosmopolitan Press, 1912), pp. 66–74; Confederate Papers Relating to Citizens or Business Firms, RG 109, War Department Collection of Confederate Records, NARA; M. S. Temple to O. P. Temple, 9 September 1862, Temple Papers; M. S. Temple to Stewart, Buchanan & Co., 19 July 1862, Letters Received by the Confederate Secretary of War, RG 109, War Department Collection of Confederate Records, NARA; Register of Letters Sent by the Provost Marshal, p. 711, depositions of S. P. Carter, T. J. Powell, and Felix A. Reeve, case 397, Perez Dickinson vs. the United States, U.S. Court of Claims, NARA; Temple, *East Tennessee and the Civil War*, pp. 430–31.

24 Humphrey, *"That D----d Brownlow,"* p. 269; *Knoxville Whig*, 5 October, 16 November 1864, 1 February, 21 June 1865; William G. Brownlow to Andrew Johnson, 21 November 1864, *Johnson Papers*, vol. 7, p. 309.

25 All wealth statistics for 1860 and 1870 are based on information from the manuscript population schedules of the eight and ninth federal censuses for Knox County.

26 Bryan, "Civil War in East Tennessee," pp. 157–58; *Knoxville Whig*, 5 and 12 April 1865; entry for 3 April 1865, Lyman Potter Spencer Diary, Library of Congress; John Willard Hill Diary, entry for 6 April 1865, Special Collections, University of Tennessee Libraries.

27 Temple, *Notable Men of Tennessee*, p. 319; Humphrey, *"That D----d Brownlow,"* pp. 282–85; *Knoxville Whig*, 29 March, 19 April 1865.

28 See especially Fisher, *War at Every Door*, chaps. 6 and 7.

29 Eric L. McKitrick, *Andrew Johnson and Reconstruction* (Chicago: University of Chicago Press, 1960), pp. 20, 87; James M. McPherson, *Ordeal by Fire: The Civil War and Reconstruction*, 2nd

ed. (New York: McGraw-Hill, 1992), pp. 493–94; *Knoxville Whig*, 19 April 1865; Application of Nathan Gammon, Amnesty Papers, roll 49; application of Frank A. Moses, Amnesty Papers, roll 50.

30 Whitelaw Reid, *After the War: A Tour of the Southern States, 1865–66* (Cincinnati: Moore, Wilstach and Baldwin, 1866), p. 353. Behind the scenes, Brownlow did try to moderate Johnson's pardoning policy. Typically, applications for presidential pardons from Tennesseans first went to the governor's office, and Brownlow had the prerogative of attaching a personal recommendation before forwarding them to Washington. Of the fifty-two applications to President Johnson originating from Knox County, for example, Brownlow endorsed twenty-three, recommended rejection of ten, and offered no comment on the remaining nineteen. See Amnesty Papers, rolls 49–51.

31 *Knoxville Whig*, 19 April 1865; James Welch Patton, *Unionism and Reconstruction in Tennessee* (Chapel Hill: University of North Carolina Press, 1934), pp. 91–93; Thomas B. Alexander, *Political Reconstruction in Tennessee* (Nashville: Vanderbilt University Press, 1950), pp. 71–75.

32 Alexander, *Political Reconstruction in Tennessee*, p. 74; Humphrey, "*That D----d Brownlow*," pp. 284–91; John B. Brownlow to Col. O. P. Temple, 9 September 1864, Temple Papers (italics in the original).

33 Humphrey, "*That D----d Brownlow*," p. 285; *Knoxville Whig*, 3 and 10 May 1865.

34 J. C. Ramsey to Elizabeth Breck, 4 August 1865, Ramsey Papers; application of William G. McAdoo, Amnesty Papers, roll 21.

35 J. G. Whitson to William G. McAdoo, 20 September 1865, William G. McAdoo to Dear Mother, 11 June 1866, William G. McAdoo Papers, Library of Congress; entry for 11 November 1865, William G. McAdoo Diary, Floyd-McAdoo Family Diaries and Letterbooks, Library of Congress.

36 *Knoxville Whig*, 31 May 1865; W. G. Brownlow, *Sketches of the Rise, Progress, and Decline of Secession* (Philadelphia: George W. Childs, 1862), pp. 333–34, 446–47.

37 Campbell Wallace to Andrew Johnson, 5 July 1865, *Johnson Papers*, vol. 8, pp. 357–60; C. Wallace to J. P. Benjamin, 13 December 1861, *OR*, ser. 1, vol. 7, p. 768.

38 Hesseltine, *Ramsey Autobiography*, pp. 122–24, 140, 164–65, 193–94; 197, 213–15, 217–32; J. G. M. Ramsey to Sue Ramsey, 21 June 1864; J. G. M. Ramsey to Margaret Ramsey, 16 August 1864; Christian and Rebecca Kline to M. B. Ramsey, 3 June 1866; Margaret Ramsey to Elizabeth Breck, 9 September 1866; Margaret Ramsey to Elizabeth Breck, 21 December 1866, all in Ramsey Papers.

39 J. C. Ramsey to Elizabeth Breck, 4 August 1865; Margaret Ramsey to Elizabeth Breck, 9 September 1866; J. C. Ramsey to J. G. M. Ramsey, 19 January 1867; J. G. M. Ramsey to J. C. Ramsey, 21 October 1867; J. C. Ramsey to J. G. M. Ramsey, 28 November 1868, all in Ramsey Papers.

40 Applications of J. G. M. Ramsey and C. W. Charlton, Amnesty Papers, rolls 50, 17. J. C. Ramsey, who was also applying for a presidential pardon, left nothing to doubt. He first solicited the assistance of "his particular friend," David T. Patterson, President Johnson's son-in-law, and then traveled to Washington himself, where the president "received [him] cordially." Johnson granted a pardon to the two fellow Democrats in early November 1865. See J. C. Ramsey to Elizabeth Breck, 4 August 1865; J. C. Ramsey to J. G. M. Ramsey, 7 October 1865; J. C. Ramsey to J. G. M. Ramsey, 16 November 1865, all in Ramsey Papers.

41 Hesseltine, *Ramsey Autobiography*, pp. 248n, 258; Richard Crawford, comp., *The Civil War Songbook* (New York: Dover, 1977), pp. 70–72.

42 Knox County Credit Reports, Tennessee Vol. 18, p. 22, R. G. Dun & Co. Collection, Baker Library, Harvard University Graduate School of Business Administration; state supreme court transcript of *William G. Brownlow vs. Robert B. Reynolds et al*, in Nelson Papers; David Deaderick

Diary, McClung Historical Collection, Knox County Public Library, p. 74; entry for 21 November 1865, McAdoo Diary; application of William G. Swan, Amnesty Papers, roll 51.

43 Agreement between C. W. Charlton and P. L. Rogers, Mitchell County, Georgia, 22 January 1866; American Sunday School commission for C. W. Charlton, 23 March 1867; C. W. Charlton to Jos. A. Mabry, 11 December 1867, all in Mabry-Charlton Papers, McClung Historical Collection, Knox County Public Library; Knox County Credit Reports, Tennessee Vol. 18, pp. 12, 26, 51, R. G. Dun & Co. Collection; *Knoxville Whig*, 20 February 1864, 18 October 1865; applications of Robert B. Reynolds, John M. Boyd, William M. Cocke, and Joseph H. Martin, Amnesty Papers, rolls 48, 50; Richard Pryor to Thomas Nelson, 23 August 1866, Nelson Papers; Hesseltine, *Ramsey Autobiography*, p. 261.

44 *Knoxville Whig*, 17 May 1865; Mrs. E. C. Caswell to William Caswell, 19 June 1865, William Richard Caswell Papers, McClung Historical Collection, Knox County Public Library; Fisher, *War at Every Door*, pp. 156–59; W. Todd Groce, *Mountain Rebels: East Tennessee Confederates and the Civil War, 1860–1870* (Knoxville: University of Tennessee Press, 1999), pp. 133–35; Temple, *East Tennessee and the Civil War*, p. 531.

45 *Knoxville Whig*, 17 May 1865; Laura Maynard to Washburn Maynard, 26 September 1865, Maynard Papers; Reid, *After the War*, pp. 351–52. See also [C. W. Hall], *Threescore Years and Ten* (Cincinnati: Elm Street Printing, 1884), pp. 201–2.

46 Martha Hall to Carrie Stakely, 21 April 1865, Hall-Stakely Papers; entry for 1 May 1865, Spencer Diary.

47 Entries for 16 and 18 May 1865, Spencer Diary; Mrs. E. C. Caswell to William Caswell, 19 June 1865, Caswell Papers; Abram Ryan to Mr. and Mrs. Curry [?], 12 September 1865, Father Abram Joseph Ryan Correspondence, TSLA; Sutherland, *Very Violent Rebel*, pp. 172–81. See also Felix A. Reeves to Mssrs. Temple and Rodgers, 28 August 1865, Temple Papers; W. W. Wallace to T. A. R. Nelson, 26 August 1865, Nelson Papers.

48 Sutherland, *Very Violent Rebel*, p. 176; *Knoxville Whig*, 16 January 1864; L. Thomas to E. M. Stanton, 15 February 1864, 15 June 1864, 18 January 1865, *OR*, ser. 3, vol. 4, pp. 101, 433–34, 1058; William G. Brownlow to Andrew Johnson, 14 November 1864, *Johnson Papers*, vol. 7, p. 286.

49 *Knoxville Whig*, 30 January 1864; William G. Brownlow to Andrew Johnson, 31 August 1865, *Johnson Papers*, vol. 8, p. 686.

50 *Knoxville Whig*, 30 August, 27 September 1865; Sutherland, *Very Violent Rebel*, pp. 183–84.

51 William G. Brownlow to Andrew Johnson, 31 August 1865, *Johnson Papers*, vol. 8, p. 686; Samuel R. Rodgers to Andrew Johnson, 22 November 1865, *Johnson Papers*, vol. 9, pp. 417–18; Andrew Johnson to W. G. Brownlow, 6 September 1865, George H. Thomas to George Stoneman, 7 September 1865, Johnson to Thomas, 8 September 1865, all in *OR*, ser. 1, vol. 49, pp. 1109–11.

52 George H. Thomas to Andrew Johnson, 7 September 1865; Thomas to George Stoneman, 7 September 1865; Stoneman to Thomas, 8 September 1865; Thomas to Johnson, 9 September 1865, all in *OR*, ser. 1, vol. 49, pp. 1110–12.

53 Elisa Bolli Buffat, "Some Recollections of My Childhood Days and Incidents of My Life during the Civil War," reprinted in David Babelay, *They Trusted and Were Delivered: The French-Swiss of Knoxville, Tennessee* (Knoxville: Vaud-Tennessee, 1988), vol. 2, p. 466; Bird G. Manard to Thomas Nelson, 28 June 1865, Nelson Papers; Abram Ryan to Mr. and Mrs. Curry, 12 September 1865, Ryan Correspondence. See also J. C. Ramsey to Elizabeth Breck, 4 August 1865, Ramsey Papers; Sam Milligan to Andrew Johnson, 1 September 1865, *Johnson Papers*, vol. 9, pp. 10–11.

54 Reid, *After the War*, p. 353; Deaderick Diary, pp. 72–73.

55 Horace Maynard to Andrew Johnson, 16 May 1865, *Johnson Papers*, vol. 8, p. 78; *Knoxville Whig*, 17 May, 20 September 1865.

56 *Knoxville Whig*, 10 and 24 May, 13 September 1864.

57   East Tennessee Unionists to Governor William G. Brownlow, 18 May 1865, Governor William
      G. Brownlow Papers, TSLA; *Knoxville Whig*, 7 June 1865; Bryan, "Civil War in East Tennes-
      see," p. 180. See also William G. Brownlow to Andrew Johnson, 10 November 1865, *Johnson
      Papers*, vol. 9, p. 367.

58   William G. Brownlow to Andrew Johnson, 10 November 1865; Samuel Milligan to Andrew
      Johnson, 16 January 1866, *Johnson Papers*, vol. 9, pp. 367, 602–3; J. C. Ramsey to J. G. M. Ramsey,
      26 April 1866, Ramsey Papers.

59   Ellen House claimed that Abner and one sister had been staying with their uncle, William J.
      Baker, in town. I have found no evidence to corroborate this, and the remainder of her discus-
      sion of the tragedy surrounding Abner Baker is highly unreliable. See Sutherland, *Very Violent
      Rebel*, pp. 184–85.

60   Elizabeth Baker Crozier Journal, Special Collections, University of Tennessee Libraries; *Knox-
      ville Register*, 23 June 1863; Endorsements Sent by the Provost Marshal General, p. 107.

61   *Knoxville Whig*, 6 September 1865; Mattie Hall to Martha Hall, 20 September 1865, Hall-Stakely
      Papers. See also Laura Maynard to Washburn Maynard, 26 September 1865, Maynard Papers.

62   Deaderick Diary, p. 73; Sutherland, *Very Violent Rebel*, p. 184; *Knoxville Whig*, 6 September 1865.
      See also J. H. Gibbs to General J. J. Dana, 25 June 1881, in case 17045, Heirs of Harvey Baker vs.
      the United States, U.S. Court of Claims.

63   *Knoxville Whig*, 6 September 1865; Sutherland, *Very Violent Rebel*, p. 184.

64   Deaderick Diary, pp. 73–74; Laura Maynard to Washburn Maynard, 26 September 1865, Maynard
      Papers; Sutherland, *Very Violent Rebel*, p. 185. The evidence on emigrating Confederates is ex-
      tensive. See, among many sources, William M. Stakely to Martha Hall, 18 July 1865 (back of
      envelope), Hall-Stakely Papers; J. C. Ramsey to Elizabeth Breck, 4 August and 15 September
      1865, Ramsey Papers; W. Y. C. Humes to Oliver Temple, 3 December 1865, Temple Papers;
      entry for 31 December 1865, William Rule Diary, William Rule Papers, McClung Historical
      Collection, Knox County Public Library; Mrs. D. A. Plant, "Recollections of War as a Child,
      1861–1865," *Confederate Veteran* 36 (1928); 129–30; and Clement A. Evans, ed., *Confederate Mili-
      tary History: A Library of Confederate States History* (Atlanta: Confederate Pub. Co., 1899),
      vol. 10, pp. 399, 457, 491–92, 592–93.

65   Entry for 21 November 1865, McAdoo Diary; J. C. Ramsey to J. G. M. Ramsey, 7 March and
      2 April 1866, Ramsey Papers; Minute Book B, p. 200, Records of the U.S. Circuit Court, East-
      ern District, Tennessee. The quotation from McClellan Democrats celebrating the peace and
      order in Knoxville is from a resolution entered into the minutes of the May 1866 term of the
      federal district court. Prominent signatories included Frederick Heiskell, Abner Jackson, and
      John Williams.

66   The precise "persistence rate" was 30.2 percent for Confederates and 49.2 percent for Unionists.

67   Deaderick Diary, pp. 74–78; Evans, *Confederate Military History*, pp. 442–43, 457; J. C. Ramsey
      to J. G. M. Ramsey, 19 January 1867, Ramsey Papers; Minute Book B, pp. 309, 471, Records of
      the U.S. Circuit Court, Eastern District, Tennessee; manuscript federal census of population
      for Knox County, 1870; Hesseltine, *Ramsey Autobiography*, p. 267.

68   Abram Ryan to My very Dear Mrs. Curry [?], 16 September 1866, Ryan Correspondence; Laura
      Maynard to Edward Maynard, 27 April 1866, Maynard Papers. See also Hesseltine, *Ramsey
      Autobiography*, pp. 253–54.

69   Excluding those who died during the 1860s, eighteen of thirty-four wealthy Confederates were
      living in Knoxville in 1870 (53 percent) compared with ten of twelve wealthy Unionists (83
      percent).

70   Of the 115 individuals heading households in the top 10 percent in 1870, 78 (67.8 percent) had
      been living in Knoxville in 1860, 99 (86.1 percent) had been born in the South, and 11 (9.6 per-
      cent) were northern-born individuals who had arrived in Knoxville since the war began.

71   Reid, *After the War*, p. 352; *Knoxville Whig*, 14 February 1866.

72   The next two paragraphs are based on the accounts in *Knoxville Whig*, 14 and 21 February 1866; and *New York Times*, 25 February 1866.

AFTERWORD

1   The reunion is described with minor variations in *Knoxville Daily Tribune*, 7 and 9 October 1890; *Knoxville Journal*, 8 and 10 October, 1890.
2   Among many, see Nina Silber, *The Romance of Reunion: Northerners and the South, 1865–1900* (Chapel Hill: University of North Carolina Press, 1993); David W. Blight, "A Quarrel Forgotten or a Revolution Remembered? Reunion and Race in the Memory of the Civil War, 1875–1913," in *Beyond the Battlefield: Race, Memory, and the American Civil War* (Amherst: University of Massachusetts Press, 2002), pp. 120–52; Eric Foner, "Ken Burns and the Romance of Reunion," in *Who Owns History? Rethinking the Past in a Changing World* (New York: Hill and Wang, 2002), pp. 189–204.
3   Daniel E. Sutherland, ed., *A Very Violent Rebel: The Civil War Diary of Ellen Renshaw House* (Knoxville: University of Tennessee Press, 1996); Endorsements Sent by the Provost Marshal General, Sept. 1863–July 1864, District of East Tennessee, p. 97, in entry 2759, RG 393, U.S. Army Continental Commands, NARA.
4   William G. McAdoo Diary, vol. 29, Floyd-McAdoo Family Diaries and Letterbooks, Library of Congress, entry for 30 November 1860.
5   Deposition of M. S. Temple in case 397, Perez Dickinson vs. the United States, Court of Claims, NARA.
6   *Knoxville Whig*, 23 February 1861, 12 July 1865; *Knoxville Daily Register*, 1 October 1862.
7   *Knoxville Whig*, 23 and 30 August 1865. See also *Knoxville Whig*, 19 April, 28 June, 2 August 1865.
8   *Knoxville Whig*, 11 October, 8 November, 13 December 1865; Andrew J. Fletcher to Andrew Johnson, 20 November 1865, *Johnson Papers*, vol. 9, pp. 411–12; Verton M. Queener, "The Origin of the Republican Party in East Tennessee," *East Tennessee Historical Society's Publications* 13 (1941): 88. On the racial policies of the Brownlow administration, see William Gillespie McBride, "Blacks and the Race Issue in Tennessee Politics, 1865–1876" (Ph.D. diss., Vanderbilt University, 1989); and Ben H. Severance, *Tennessee's Radical Army: The State Guard and Its Role in Reconstruction, 1867–1869* (Knoxville: University of Tennessee Press, 2005).
9   On this point with regard to southern Appalachia generally, see Gordon B. McKinney, *Southern Mountain Republicans, 1865–1900* (Chapel Hill: University of North Carolina Press, 1978), chap. 3.
10   J. Crozier Ramsey to Dear Sister, 15 September 1865, J. Crozier Ramsey to J. G. M. Ramsey, 7 March 1866, J. G. M. Ramsey Papers, Special Collections, University of Tennessee Libraries.
11   Verton M. Queener, "A Decade of East Tennessee Republicanism, 1867–1876," *East Tennessee Historical Society's Publications* 14 (1942): 83–84.
12   McKinney, *Southern Mountain Republicans*, pp. 30–41, 76–86; *History of Tennessee from the Earliest Time to the Present, Together with an Historical and a Biographical Sketch of the County of Knox and the City of Knoxville* (Chicago: Goodspeed, 1887), pp. 869–70; *Knoxville Journal*, 10 October 1890.

APPENDIX

1   The quotation is from stanza 8 of Thomas Gray's "Elegy Written in a Country Churchyard." Lincoln's allusion to the poem is quoted in David Herbert Donald, *Lincoln* (New York: Random House, 1995), p. 19.

2   The commission was referred to in official documents as either the "Knoxville Board" or the "Burnside Commission." The complete records of the commission have not survived intact, but summaries with regard to the action taken on each claim may be found in RG 393, entry 2759, District of East Tennessee, Endorsements Sent by the Provost Marshal General, Sept. 1863–July 1864, NARA.

3   A listing of every claim—giving the name and residence of claimant, the type and amount of claim, and the recommendation of the local civilian board—can be found in RG 247, Records of the Tennessee General Claims Commission, 1868, TSLA. When the Democratic Party gained control of the state legislature, the Democratic majority almost immediately passed an act disbanding the commission and ordering the Tennessee secretary of state to return the original records of each board to the clerks of the county courts, who were in turn authorized to release affidavits and other documents to claimants who wished to pursue their claims through other channels. The original records for Knox County, at least, do not seem to have been preserved locally, but some of the original affidavits and claim forms may be found interspersed among various other kinds of Civil War claims in RG 92, Records of the Office of the Quartermaster General, entry 963, "Miscellaneous Claims—Knoxville Board," NARA. These claims are indexed, although incorrectly identified, in RG 92, entry 948, "Index to Papers in Possession of the Commissioner of Claims Relating to Tennessee Claims for Quartermaster and Commissary Stores, and Chiefly Accounts and Exhibits Presented to the Knoxville Board appointed by Major General Burnside, 1875," NARA.

4   The Southern Claims Commission, which was established by Congress in 1871 to review and act on the claims of southern Unionists, operated for six years. Depending on whether the claim was approved or rejected, the applications and supporting materials can be found in either RG 217, Records of the General Accounting Office, NARA (paid claims), or RG 233, Records of the U.S. House of Representatives, 1871–1880, NARA (unpaid claims). Records of the Court of Claims are in entry 22, of the U.S. Court of Claims.

BIBLIOGRAPHY

Unpublished Primary Sources

Samuel Mayes Arnell Papers, Special Collections, University of Tennessee Libraries
Mrs. F. Graham Bartlett Collection, McClung Historical Collection, Knox County Public Library
Samuel Beckett Boyd Papers, Special Collections, University of Tennessee Libraries
Governor William G. Brownlow Papers, Tennessee State Library and Archives
William Gannaway Brownlow Papers, Special Collections, University of Tennessee Libraries
William Gannaway Brownlow Papers, Library of Congress
Buffat Family Papers, McClung Historical Collection, Knox County Public Library
David Campbell Papers, Duke University
Samuel Powhatan Carter Papers, Library of Congress
Case Files of Applications from Former Confederates for Presidential Pardons, 1865–1867, Record Group
    94, Records of the Adjutant General's Office, National Archives and Records Administration
William Richard Caswell Papers, McClung Historical Collection, Knox County Public Library
Compiled Service Records of Confederate Soldiers Who Served in Organizations from the State of
    Tennessee, Record Group 109, War Department Collection of Confederate Records, National
    Archives and Records Administration
Confederate Papers Relating to Citizens or Business Firms, Record Group 109, War Department
    Collection of Confederate Records, National Archives and Records Administration
Congressional Jurisdiction Files, Record Group 123, Records of the U.S. Court of Claims, National
    Archives and Records Administration
County Court Minutes, Knox County, Tennessee State Library and Archives
Elizabeth Baker Crozier Journal, Special Collections, University of Tennessee Libraries
David Deaderick Diary, McClung Historical Collection, Knox County Public Library
District of East Tennessee, Letters and Telegrams Sent, chap. 2, vol. 51, Record Group 109, War
    Department Collection of Confederate Records, National Archives and Records Administration
District of East Tennessee, Records of the Provost Marshal General, 1863–1865, entry 2764, Record
    Group 393, U.S. Army Continental Commands, National Archives and Records Administration
Henry Melville Doak Memoirs, Tennessee State Library and Archives
Thomas Doak Edington Diary, Special Collections, University of Tennessee Libraries
William Franklin Draper Letters, Library of Congress
Endorsements Sent by the Provost Marshal General, District of East Tennessee, Sept. 1863–July
    1864, entry 2759, Record Group 393, U.S. Army Continental Commands, National Archives and
    Records Administration
Hall-Stakely Papers, McClung Historical Collection, Knox County Public Library
Frederick S. Heiskell Papers, Archives of Appalachia, East Tennessee State University
Hugh Brown Heiskell diary, Tennessee State Library and Archives
John Willard Hill Diary, Special Collections, University of Tennessee Libraries
Robert Edwin Jameson Papers, Library of Congress

Milton P. Jarnagin Memoirs, Tennessee State Library and Archives

August Valentine Kautz Papers, Library of Congress

Memoirs of Margaret Oswald Klein, McClung Historical Collection, Knox County Public Library

Knox County Circuit Court Minutes, Tennessee State Library and Archives

Knox County Credit Reports, Tennessee Vols. 12, 18, R. G. Dun & Co. Collection, Baker Library,
    Harvard University Graduate School of Business Administration

Knox County Merchants Licenses, Tennessee State Library and Archives

Daniel Read Larned Papers, Library of Congress

Legislative Petitions, Tennessee State Library and Archives

Letters Received by the Confederate Secretary of War, Record Group 109, War Department
    Collection of Confederate Records, National Archives and Records Administration

Letters Sent, Aug. 1863–Jan. 1865, Department of the Ohio, entry 3504, Record Group 393, U.S. Army
    Continental Commands, National Archives and Records Administration

Robert Todd Lincoln Collection of the Papers of Abraham Lincoln, Library of Congress

List of Claimants Investigated by a Military Commission, 1864, entry 3533, Record Group 393, U.S.
    Army Continental Commands, National Archives and Records Administration

Mabry-Charlton Papers, McClung Historical Collection, Knox County Public Library

Horace Maynard Papers, Special Collections, University of Tennessee Libraries

William G. McAdoo Diary, Floyd-McAdoo Family Diaries and Letterbooks, Library of Congress

William G. McAdoo Papers, Library of Congress

James McMillan Journal, McClung Historical Collection, Knox County Public Library

Minute Book, Confederate States of America, Eastern District of Tennessee, District Court,
    Knoxville, 1861–1863, National Archives and Records Administration—Southeast Regional
    Branch

Minute Books, 1864–1870, Records of the U.S. Circuit Court, Eastern District, Tennessee, Knoxville,
    National Archives and Records Administration—Southeast Regional Branch

Minutes, Knoxville Mayor and Board of Aldermen, Knox County Archives

Martha Luttrell Mitchell Memoir, Tennessee State Library and Archives

Thomas A. R. Nelson Papers, McClung Historical Collection, Knox County Public Library

Crosby Noyes Autograph Collection, Library of Congress

Papers of William G. "Parson" Brownlow Received from the First Auditor's Office, entry 21, Record
    Group 366, Records of Civil War Special Agencies of the Treasury Department, National
    Archives and Records Administration

Passport Book, Department of East Tennessee, chap. 9, volume 140B-C, Record Group 109, War
    Department Collection of Confederate Records, National Archives and Records Administration

E. E. Patton Collection, McClung Historical Collection, Knox County Public Library

Orlando M. Poe Papers, Library of Congress

Printed Ephemera Collection, Rare Book and Special Collections Division, Library of Congress

J. G. M. Ramsey Papers, Special Collections, University of Tennessee Libraries

Records of Special Claims, entry 963, Record Group 92, Records of the Office of the Quartermaster
    General, National Archives and Records Administration

Records of St. John's Episcopal Church, Knoxville, Tennessee, Tennessee State Library and Archives

Records of the Attorney General's Office, General Records, Letters Received, 1809–1870, entry 9,
    Record Group 60, General Records of the Department of Justice, National Archives and Records
    Administration

Records of the First Baptist Church, Knoxville, Tennessee, Tennessee State Library and Archives

Records of the First Presbyterian Church, Knoxville, Tennessee, Tennessee State Library and
    Archives

Records of the General Accounting Office, Record Group 217, National Archives and Records
    Administration

Records of the Second Presbyterian Church, Knoxville, Tennessee, Tennessee State Library and Archives

Records of the Secretary of State of Tennessee, Record Group 30, Tennessee State Library and Archives

Records of the U.S. House of Representatives, Record Group 233, National Archives and Records Administration

Register of Cases Tried by General Courts-Martial and Military Commissions, Department of the Ohio, Sept. 29, 1862–Jan. 17, 1865, entry 3533, Record Group 393, U.S. Army Continental Commands, National Archives and Records Administration

Register of Letters Received, Department of Ohio, entry 3513, Record Group 393, U.S. Army Continental Commands, National Archives and Records Administration

Register of Letters Received by the Provost Marshal, July 1864–February 1865, District of East Tennessee, entry 2761, Record Group 393, U.S. Army Continental Commands, National Archives and Records Administration

Register of Letters Sent by the Provost Marshal, July 1864–August 1865, District of East Tennessee, entry 2758, Record Group 393, U.S. Army Continental Commands, National Archives and Records Administration

William Rule Papers, McClung Historical Collection, Knox County Public Library

Father Abram Joseph Ryan Correspondence, Tennessee State Library and Archives

Edith Scott Manuscript Collection, McClung Historical Collection, Knox County Public Library

Irwin W. Shepard Letters and Diaries, Michigan State Historical Society

Oliver Lyman Spaulding Diary, Spaulding Family Papers, Library of Congress

Lyman Potter Spencer Diary, Library of Congress

Stock Reports, East Tennessee and Georgia Railroad, Record Group 5, Internal Improvements: Railroads, Tennessee State Library and Archives

Oliver Perry Temple Papers, Special Collections, University of Tennessee Libraries

Tennessee Election Returns, Record Group 87, Tennessee State Library and Archives

Tennessee General Claims Commission Records, Record Group 247, Tennessee State Library and Archives

Robertson Topp Papers, Tennessee State Library and Archives

John Watkins Collection, Special Collections, University of Tennessee Libraries

Eleanor Wilson White Diary, McClung Historical Collection, Knox County Public Library

John and Rhoda Campbell Williams Papers, McClung Historical Collection, Knox County Public Library

Newspapers and Magazines

Boston Daily Evening Transcript
Bristol Gazette
Charleston Mercury
Chicago Tribune
Christian Recorder
Daily National Intelligencer [Washington, DC]
DeBow's Review
Harper's New Monthly Magazine
Harper's Weekly
Holston Journal
Jonesborough Whig and Independent Journal
Knoxville Journal

Knoxville Register
Knoxville Whig
Ladies Repository
National Anti-Slavery Standard [New York]
National Era [Washington, DC]
New York Daily Tribune
New York Herald
New York Times
Public Ledger [Philadelphia]
Saturday Evening Post
Scientific American
Southern Literary Messenger
Vanity Fair

Other Published Primary Sources

Abbott, John C. S. *The History of the Civil War in America.* 2 vols. New York: H. Bill, 1864–66.

Alexander, E. Porter. *Military Memoirs of a Confederate.* Bloomington: Indiana University Press, 1962.

Appleton's Illustrated Hand-Book of American Travel. New York: D. Appleton, 1857.

Armstrong, Hannibal. "How I Hid a Union Spy." *Journal of Negro History* 9 (1924): 34–40.

Ash, Stephen V., ed. *Secessionists and Other Scoundrels: Selections from Parson Brownlow's Book.* Baton Rouge: Louisiana State University Press, 1999.

Basler, Roy P., ed. *The Collected Works of Abraham Lincoln.* 8 vols. New Brunswick, NJ: Rutgers University Press, 1953–55.

Baxter, John. *The Harmon Case: Reply of Colonel John Baxter to the Speech of Senator W. G. Brownlow.* Knoxville: Chronicle Job Printing Office, 1871.

Bokum, Hermann. *The Tennessee Handbook and Immigrants' Guide.* Philadelphia: Lippincott, 1868.

———. *Wanderings North and South.* Philadelphia: King and Baird, 1864.

Brearley, William H. *Recollections of the East Tennessee Campaign.* Detroit: Tribune Book and Job Office, 1871.

Brownlow, the Patriot and Martyr, Showing His Faith and Works, as Reported by Himself. Philadelphia: R. Weir, 1862.

Brownlow, William G. *Americanism Contrasted with Foreignism, Romanism, and Bogus Democracy, in the Light of Reason, History, and Holy Scripture; in which Certain Demagogues in Tennessee, and Elsewhere, Are Shown Up in Their True Colors.* Nashville: Published for the author, 1856.

———. *The Great Iron Wheel; or, Its False Spokes Extracted, and an Exhibition of Elder Graves, Its Builder.* Nashville: published for the author, 1856.

———. *Helps to the Study of Presbyterianism.* Knoxville: F. S. Heiskell, 1834.

———. *A Sermon on Slavery; A Vindication of the Methodist Church, South: Her Position Stated.* Knoxville: Kinsloe and Rice, 1857.

———. *Sketches of the Rise, Progress, and Decline of Secession.* Philadelphia: George W. Childs, 1862.

———. *To Whom It May Concern.* Washington, DC: n.p., 1871.

Buffat, Elisa Bolli. "Some Recollections of My Childhood Days and Incidents of My Life during the Civil War." Reprinted in David Babelay, *They Trusted and Were Delivered: The French-Swiss of Knoxville, Tennessee.* 2 vols. Knoxville: Vaud-Tennessee Publisher, 1988.

Burrage, H. S. "Retreat from Lenoir's and the Siege of Knoxville." *Atlantic Monthly* 18 (1866): 21–32.

Chavannes, Cecile, and Albert Chavannes. *East Tennessee Sketches.* Knoxville: Albert Chavannes, 1900.

Clark, Willene B., ed. *Valleys of the Shadow: The Memoir of Confederate Captain Reuben G. Clark, Company I, 59th Tennessee Mounted Infantry.* Knoxville: University of Tennessee Press, 1994.

Crawford, Richard, comp. *The Civil War Songbook*. New York: Dover, 1977.

Draper, William F. *Recollections of a Varied Career*. Boston: Little, Brown, 1909.

Dyer, Gustavus W., and John Trotwood, comps. *The Tennessee Civil War Veterans Questionnaires*. Easley, SC: Southern Historical Press, 1985.

Evans, Clement A., ed. *Confederate Military History: A Library of Confederate States History*. 12 vols. Atlanta: Confederate, 1899.

Everett, Edward. *Account of the Fund for the Relief of East Tennessee; with a Complete List of the Contributors*. Boston: Little, Brown, 1864.

Featherstonhaugh, George W. *Excursion through the Slave States, from Washington on the Potomac to the Frontier of Mexico; with Sketches of Popular Manners and Geological Notices*. New York: Harper and Row, 1844.

Gallagher, Gary W., ed. *Fighting for the Confederacy: The Personal Recollections of General Edward Porter Alexander*. Chapel Hill: University of North Carolina Press, 1989.

Gilmore, James R. *Down in Tennessee and Back by Way of Richmond*, by Edmund Kirke [pseud.]. New York: Carleton, 1864.

Graf, Leroy P., Ralph W. Haskins, and Paul H. Bergeron, eds. *The Papers of Andrew Johnson*. 16 vols. Knoxville: University of Tennessee Press, 1967–2000.

Grant, Ulysses S. *Personal Memoirs of U. S. Grant*. New York: Charles L. Webster, 1886.

[Hall, C. W.] *Threescore Years and Ten*. Cincinnati: Elm Street Printing Company, 1884.

Hamilton, William Douglas. *Recollections of a Cavalryman of the Civil War after Fifty Years, 1861–1865*. Columbus, OH: F. J. Heer Printing Company, 1915.

Hayes, P. C. "Campaigning in East Tennessee." Commandery of the State of Illinois, Military Order of the Loyal Legion of the United States. *Military Essays and Recollections*. Vol. 4, pp. 320–22. Chicago: Cozzens and Beaton, 1907.

Henderson, W. A. *Life and Character of Judge McKinney*. Nashville: Albert B. Tavel, 1884.

Hesseltine, William B., ed. *Dr. J. G. M. Ramsey: Autobiography and Letters*. Nashville: Tennessee Historical Commission, 1954.

Hilgard, Eugene W. *Report on Cotton Production in the United States*. Washington, DC: Government Printing Office, 1884.

History of the Thirty-fifth Regiment Massachusetts Volunteers, 1862–1865. Boston: Mills, Knight, 1884.

Howell, Alice Hunt Lynn, ed. *Adventures of a Nineteenth-Century Medic*. Franklin, TN: Hillsboro Press, 1998.

Humes, Thomas W. *The Loyal Mountaineers of Tennessee*. Knoxville: Ogden Brothers, 1888.

———. *Report to the East Tennessee Relief Association at Knoxville*. Knoxville: Printed for the Association, 1865.

———. *Second Report to the East Tennessee Relief Association at Knoxville*. Knoxville: Brownlow, Haws, 1866.

Johnson, Robert Underwood, and Clarence Clough Buel, eds. *Battles and Leaders of the Civil War*. 4 vols. New York: Thomas Yoseloff, 1884–88.

Killebrew, J. B. *Introduction to the Resources of Tennessee*. Nashville: Tavel, Eastman and Howell, 1874.

Lloyd, James T. *Lloyd's Steamboat Directory*. James T. Lloyd, 1856.

Longstreet, James. *From Manassas to Appomattox: Memoirs of the Civil War in America*. Philadelphia: Lippincott, 1896.

Luttrell, Laura Elizabeth, comp. *U.S. Census, 1850, for Knox County, Tennessee*. Knoxville: East Tennessee Historical Society, 1949.

Maynard, Horace. *How, by Whom, and for What Was the War Begun? Speech of Hon. Horace Maynard Delivered in the City of Nashville, March 20, 1862*. N.p., n.d. Special Collections, University of Tennessee Libraries.

———. *To the Slaveholders of Tennessee*. N.p., 1863. Special Collections, University of Tennessee Libraries.

"Message of the President of the United States Transmitting an Address of the 'East Tennessee Relief Association.'" Senate Exec. Doc. No. 40, 38th Cong., 1st sess. Washington, DC: GPO, 1864.

Moore, Frank, ed. *The Rebellion Record.* New York: D. Van Nostrand, 1865.

Nicolay, John G., and John Hay. *Abraham Lincoln: A History.* New York: Century, 1904.

Opinion of the Hon. Connally F. Trigg on the Constitutionality of the Act of Congress Prescribing an Oath on the Admission of Attorneys. Memphis: Whitmore Brothers, 1865.

Ought American Slavery to Be Perpetuated? A Debate between Rev. W. G. Brownlow and Rev. A. Pryne. Philadelphia: Lippincott, 1858.

Parson Brownlow and the Unionists of East Tennessee. New York: Beadle, 1862.

Parson Brownlow's Farewell Address, in View of His Imprisonment by the Rebels. Philadelphia: Thomas W. Hartley, 1862.

Plant, Mrs. D. A. "Recollections of War as a Child, 1861–1865." *Confederate Veteran* 36 (1928): 129–30.

Pollard, Edward A. *Southern History of the War: The First Year of the War.* New York: C. B. Richardson, 1863.

Portrait and Biography of Parson Brownlow, the Tennessee Patriot. Indianapolis: Asher, 1862.

Reid, Whitelaw. *After the War: A Tour of the Southern States, 1865–1866.* Cincinnati: Moore, Wilstach and Baldwin, 1866.

Relief for East Tennessee: Address of Honorable N. G. Taylor, March 10, 1864. New York: Wm. C. Bryant, 1864.

Report of the Adjutant General of the State of Tennessee of the Military Forces of the State from 1861 to 1866. Nashville: S. C. Mercer, 1866.

Report to the Contributors to the Pennsylvania Relief Association for East Tennessee. Philadelphia: Printed for the Association, 1864.

Reynolds, Major W. D. *Miss Martha Brownlow; or the Heroine of Tennessee.* Philadelphia: Barclay, n.d.

Richardson, James D., ed. *The Messages and Papers of Jefferson Davis and the Confederacy.* 2 vols. New York: Chelsea House–Robert Hector, 1966.

Rieger, Paul E., ed. *Through One Man's Eyes: The Civil War Experiences of a Belmont County Volunteer.* Mt. Vernon, OH: Print Arts Press, 1974.

Ripley, George, and Charles A. Dana, eds. *The New American Cyclopaedia.* New York: D. Appleton, 1859–63.

Rives, John C., ed. *Appendix to the Congressional Globe.* Vol. 30, pt. 2. 36th Cong., 2nd sess. Washington, DC: Congressional Globe Office, 1861.

Rule, William. *The Loyalists of Tennessee in the Late War.* Cincinnati: H. C. Sherick, 1887.

Sketch of Parson Brownlow and His Speeches at the Academy of Music and Cooper Institute. New York: E. D. Barker, 1862.

Sorrel, G. Moxley. *Recollections of a Confederate Staff Officer.* Jackson, TN: McCowat-Mercer Press, 1958.

Strother, David Hunter. "A Winter in the South," pt. 5. *Harper's New Monthly Magazine* 16 (1858): 721–36.

Sullins, David. *Recollections of an Old Man: Seventy Years in Dixie, 1827–1897.* Bristol, TN: King Printing, 1910.

Sutherland, Daniel E., ed. *A Very Violent Rebel: The Civil War Diary of Ellen Renshaw House.* Knoxville: University of Tennessee Press, 1996.

Temple, Oliver P. *East Tennessee and the Civil War.* Cincinnati: Robert Clarke, 1899.

———. *Notable Men of Tennessee from 1833 to 1875: Their Times and Their Contemporaries.* New York: Cosmopolitan Press, 1912.

The Official and Political Manual of the State of Tennessee. Nashville: Marshall and Bruce, 1890.

Thomas, H. H. "Personal Reminiscences of the East Tennessee Campaign." Commandery of the State of Illinois. *Military Essays and Recollections.* Vol. 4, pp. 284–300. Chicago: Cozzens and Beaton, 1907.

Thompson, B. F. *History of the 112th Regiment of Illinois Volunteer Infantry in the Great War of the Rebellion, 1862–1865.* Toulon, IL: Stark Co. News Office, 1885.

Todd, William. *The Seventy-ninth Highlanders New York Volunteers in the War of the Rebellion, 1861–1865.* Albany, NY: Brandow, Barton, 1886.

U.S. Census Bureau, Seventh Census [1850], *Statistics of Population.* Washington, DC: Government Printing Office, 1853.

U.S. Congress, *Report of the Joint Committee on Reconstruction.* House Report No. 30, 39th Cong., 1st sess. Washington, DC: Government Printing Office, 1866.

Victor, Orville J. *Incidents and Anecdotes of the War together with Life Sketches of Eminent Leaders.* New York: James D. Torrey, 1862.

War of the Rebellion: A Compilation of the Official Records of the Union and Confederate Armies. Washington, DC: Government Printing Office, 1880–1901.

Williams' Knoxville Directory, City Guide, and Business Mirror. Vol. 1. Knoxville: C. S. Williams, 1859.

Wilshire, Joseph W. *A Reminiscence of Burnside's Knoxville Campaign: Paper Read before the Ohio Commandery of the Loyal Legion, April 3rd, 1912.* Cincinnati: The Commandery, 1912.

Woodward, A. *A Review of Uncle Tom's Cabin; or, an Essay on Slavery.* Cincinnati: Applegate, 1853.

Worsham, W. J. *The Old Nineteenth Tennessee Regiment, C.S.A.* Knoxville: Paragon Printing, 1902.

Secondary Books, Articles, and Dissertations

Alexander, Thomas B. *Political Reconstruction in Tennessee.* Nashville: Vanderbilt University Press, 1950.

———. *Thomas A. R. Nelson of East Tennessee.* Nashville: Tennessee Historical Commission, 1956.

Atkins, Jonathan M. *Parties, Politics, and the Sectional Conflict in Tennessee, 1832–1861.* Knoxville: University of Tennessee Press, 1997.

Auer, J. Jeffery, ed. *Antislavery and Disunion, 1858–1861: Studies in the Rhetoric of Compromise and Conflict.* New York: Harper and Row, 1963.

Bates, Walter Lynn. "Southern Unionists: A Socio-economic Examination of the Third East Tennessee Volunteer Infantry Regiment, U.S.A., 1862–1865." *Tennessee Historical Quarterly* 50 (1991): 226–39.

Bensel, Richard Franklin. *Yankee Leviathan: The Origins of Central State Authority in America, 1859–1877.* New York: Cambridge University Press, 1990.

Bergeron, Paul H. *Antebellum Politics in Tennessee.* Lexington: University Press of Kentucky, 1982.

Bergeron, Paul H., Stephen V. Ash, and Jeanette Keith. *Tennesseans and Their History.* Knoxville: University of Tennessee Press, 1999.

Berlin, Ira, Barbara J. Fields, Thavolia Glymph, Joseph P. Reidy, and Leslie S. Rowland, eds. *Freedom: A Documentary History of Emancipation, 1861–1867.* New York: Cambridge University Press, 1985.

Billings, Dwight B., Gurney Norman, and Katherine Ledford, eds. *Confronting Appalachian Stereotypes: Back Talk from an American Region.* Lexington: University Press of Kentucky, 1999.

Blight, David W. "A Quarrel Forgotten or a Revolution Remembered? Reunion and Race in the Memory of the Civil War, 1875–1913." In *Beyond the Battlefield: Race, Memory, and the American Civil War,* pp. 120–52. Amherst: University of Massachusetts Press, 2002.

Bode, Frederick A., and Donald L. Ginter. *Farm Tenancy and the Census in Antebellum Georgia.* Athens: University of Georgia Press, 1986.

Bryan, Charles F., Jr. "The Civil War in East Tennessee: A Social, Political, and Economic Study." Ph.D. diss., University of Tennessee, 1978.

———. "A Gathering of Tories: The East Tennessee Convention of 1861." *Tennessee Historical Quarterly* 39 (1980): 27–48.

———. "'Tories' amidst Rebels: Confederate Occupation of East Tennessee, 1861–1863." *East Tennessee Historical Society's Publications* 60 (1988): 3–22.

Buckwalter, Donald W. "Effects of Early Nineteenth Century Transportation Disadvantage on the Agriculture of Eastern Tennessee." *Southeastern Geographer* 27 (1987): 18–37.

Burnett, Edmond Cody. "Hog Raising and Hog Driving in the Region of the French Broad River." *Agricultural History* 20 (1946): 86–103.

Burt, Jesse. "East Tennessee, Lincoln, and Sherman," pt. 1. *East Tennessee Historical Society's Publications* 34 (1962): 3–25.

———. "East Tennessee, Lincoln, and Sherman," pt. 2. *East Tennessee Historical Society's Publications* 35 (1963): 54–75.

Caldwell, Joshua W. *Studies in the Constitutional History of Tennessee.* 2nd ed. Cincinnati: Robert Clark, 1907.

Campbell, James B. "East Tennessee during Federal Occupation, 1863–1865." *East Tennessee Historical Society's Publications* 19 (1947): 64–80.

Campbell, Mary E. R. *The Attitude of Tennesseans toward the Union, 1847–1861.* New York: Vantage Press, 1961.

———. "The Significance of the Unionist Victory in the Election of February 9, 1861 in Tennessee." *East Tennessee Historical Society's Papers* 14 (1942): 11–30.

Campbell, Randolph B., and Richard G. Lowe. *Wealth and Power in Antebellum Texas.* College Station: Texas A & M University Press, 1977.

Catton, Bruce. *Glory Road.* New York: Doubleday, 1952.

———. *Never Call Retreat.* New York: Doubleday, 1965.

Channing, Steven A. *Crisis of Fear: Secession in South Carolina.* New York: Norton, 1974.

Clinton, Catherine. *Southern Families at War: Loyalty and Conflict in the Civil War South.* New York: Oxford University Press, 2000.

Conklin, Royal Forrest. "The Public Speaking Career of William Gannaway (Parson) Brownlow." Ph.D. diss., Ohio University, 1967.

Cooper, William J., Jr. *Jefferson Davis, American.* New York: Knopf, 2000.

———. *The South and the Politics of Slavery, 1828–1856.* Baton Rouge: Louisiana State University Press, 1978.

Corlew, Robert E. *Tennessee: A Short History.* 2nd ed. Knoxville: University of Tennessee Press, 1981.

Coulter, E. Merton. *William G. Brownlow: Fighting Parson of the Southern Highlands.* Chapel Hill: University of North Carolina Press, 1937.

Crawford, Martin. *Ashe County's Civil War: Community and Society in the Appalachian South.* Charlottesville: University Press of Virginia, 2001.

Creekmore, Betsey Beeler. *Knoxville.* 3rd ed. Knoxville: University of Tennessee Press, 1976.

Crofts, Daniel W. *Reluctant Confederates: Upper South Unionists in the Secession Crisis.* Chapel Hill: University of North Carolina Press, 1989.

Crouch, Barry. "The Merchant and the Senator: An Attempt to Save East Tennessee for the Union." *East Tennessee Historical Society's Publications* 46 (1974): 53–75.

Current, Richard Nelson. *Lincoln's Loyalists: Union Soldiers from the Confederacy.* Boston: Northeastern University Press, 1992.

Davidson, James F. "Michigan and the Defense of Knoxville, Tennessee, 1863." *East Tennessee Historical Society's Publications* 35 (1963): 21–53.

Dillon, Merton L. "Three Southern Antislavery Editors: The Myth of the Southern Antislavery Movement." *East Tennessee Historical Society's Publications* 42 (1970): 47–56.

Drake, Richard B. "Slavery and Antislavery in Appalachia." *Appalachian Heritage* 14 (1986): 25–33.

Dunn, Durwood. *An Abolitionist in the Appalachian South: Ezekiel Birdseye on Slavery, Capitalism, and Separate Statehood in East Tennessee, 1841–1846*. Knoxville: University of Tennessee Press, 1997.

———. *Cades Cove: The Life and Death of a Southern Appalachian Community, 1818–1937*. Knoxville: University of Tennessee Press, 1988.

Durham, Walter T. *Volunteer Forty-niners: Tennesseans and the California Gold Rush*. Nashville: Vanderbilt University Press, 1997.

Durrill, Wayne K. *War of Another Kind: A Southern Community in the Great Rebellion*. New York: Oxford University Press, 1990.

Dykeman, Wilma. *The French Broad*. New York: Rinehart, 1955.

Eckenrode, H. J., and Bryan Conrad. *James Longstreet: Lee's War Horse*. Chapel Hill: University of North Carolina Press, 1936.

Eller, Ronald. *Miners, Millhands, and Mountaineers: Industrialization of the Appalachian South, 1880–1930*. Knoxville: University of Tennessee Press, 1982.

Fellman, Michael. *Inside War: The Guerilla Conflict in Missouri during the American Civil War*. New York: Oxford University Press, 1989.

Fink, Harold S. "The East Tennessee Campaign and the Battle of Knoxville in 1863." *East Tennessee Historical Society's Publications* 29 (1957): 79–117.

Fisher, Noel C. "Definitions of Loyalty: Unionist Histories of the Civil War in East Tennessee." *Journal of East Tennessee History* 67 (1995): 58–88.

———. *War at Every Door: Partisan Politics and Guerrilla Violence in East Tennessee, 1860–1869*. Chapel Hill: University of North Carolina Press, 1997.

Folmsbee, Stanley J. "East Tennessee University: Pre-war Years, 1840–1861." *East Tennessee Historical Society's Publications* 22 (1950): 60–93.

———. "Sectionalism and Internal Improvements in Tennessee, 1796–1845." Ph.D. diss., University of Pennsylvania, 1939.

Foner, Eric. "Ken Burns and the Romance of Reunion." In *Who Owns History? Rethinking the Past in a Changing World*. New York: Hill and Wang, 2002, pp. 189–204.

Fowler, John Derrick. *Mountaineers in Gray: The Story of the Nineteenth Tennessee Volunteer Infantry Regiment, C.S.A*. Knoxville: University of Tennessee Press, 2004.

Freehling, William W. *The South vs. the South: How Anti-Confederate Southerners Shaped the Course of the Civil War*. New York: Oxford University Press, 2001.

Giffin, Lowell L. *A History of Second Presbyterian Church*. Knoxville: n.p., 1994.

Green, John W. *Bench and Bar of Knox County, Tennessee*. Knoxville: Archer and Smith, 1947.

Groce, W. Todd. *Mountain Rebels: East Tennessee Confederates and the Civil War, 1860–1870*. Knoxville: University of Tennessee Press, 1999.

Guelzo, Allen C. *Abraham Lincoln: Redeemer President*. Grand Rapids, MI: Eerdman's, 1999.

Hall, Kermit L. "West H. Humphreys and the Crisis of the Union." *Tennessee Historical Quarterly* 34 (1975): 48–69.

Hamer, Marguerite Bartlett. "The Presidential Campaign of 1860 in Tennessee." *East Tennessee Historical Society's Publications* 3 (1931): 3–22.

Harris, William C. "The East Tennessee Relief Movement of 1864–1865." *Tennessee Historical Quarterly* 48 (1989): 86–96.

Henry, J. Milton. "The Revolution in Tennessee, February, 1861, to June, 1861." *Tennessee Historical Quarterly* 18 (1959): 99–119.

History of Tennessee from the Earliest Time to the Present, Together with an Historical and a Biographical Sketch of the County of Knox and the City of Knoxville. Chicago: Goodspeed Publishing Company, 1887.

Holland, James W. "The Building of the East Tennessee and Virginia Railroad." *East Tennessee Historical Society's Publications* 4 (1932): 83–101.

———. "The East Tennessee and Georgia Railroad, 1836–1860." *East Tennessee Historical Society's Publications* 3 (1931): 89–107.

Holt, Michael F. *The Political Crisis of the 1850s.* New York: Wiley, 1978.

Hsiung, David C. *Two Worlds in the Tennessee Mountains: Exploring the Origins of Appalachian Stereotypes.* Lexington: University Press of Kentucky, 1997.

Humphrey, Steve. *"That D——d Brownlow": Being a Saucy and Malicious Description of Fighting Parson William Gannaway Brownlow.* Boone, NC: Appalachian Consortium Press, 1978.

Huston, James L. "Southerners against Secession: The Arguments of the Constitutional Unionists in 1850–1851." *Civil War History* 46 (2000): 280–99.

Inscoe, John C. *Mountain Masters: Slavery and the Sectional Crisis in Western North Carolina.* Knoxville: University of Tennessee Press, 1989.

———. "Mountain Unionism, Secession, and Regional Self-Image: The Contrasting Cases of Western North Carolina and East Tennessee." In Winfred B. Moore Jr. and Joseph F. Tripp, eds., *Looking South: Chapters in the Story of an American Region.* New York: Greenwood Press, 1989, pp. 115–29.

———. "Olmstead in Appalachia: A Connecticut Yankee Encounters Slavery and Racism in the Southern Highlands." *Slavery and Abolition* 9 (1988): 171–82.

———. "Race and Racism in Nineteenth-Century Southern Appalachia." In Mary Beth Pudup, Dwight B. Billings, and Altina L. Waller, eds., *Appalachia in the Making: The Mountain South in the Nineteenth Century.* Chapel Hill: University of North Carolina Press, 1995, pp. 103–31.

Inscoe, John C., and Robert C. Kenzer, eds. *Enemies of the Country: New Perspectives on Unionists in the Civil War South.* Athens: University of Georgia Press, 2001.

Inscoe, John C., and Gordon B. McKinney. *The Heart of Confederate Appalachia: Western North Carolina in the Civil War.* Chapel Hill: University of North Carolina Press, 2000.

Johnson, Vicki Vaughn. *The Men and the Vision of the Southern Commercial Conventions, 1845–1871.* Columbia: University of Missouri Press, 1992.

Kelley, James C. "William Gannaway Brownlow." *Tennessee Historical Quarterly* 43 (1984): 25–43, 155–72.

Klein, Maury. "The Knoxville Campaign." *Civil War Times Illustrated* 10 (1971): 5–10, 40–42.

Klingberg, Frank W. *The Southern Claims Commission.* Berkeley: University of California Press, 1959.

Krick, Robert K. *The Smoothbore Volley That Doomed the Confederacy: The Death of Stonewall Jackson and Other Chapters in the Army of Northern Virginia.* Baton Rouge: Louisiana State University Press, 2002.

Lacy, Eric Russell. *Vanquished Volunteers: East Tennessee Sectionalism from Statehood to Secession.* Johnson City: East Tennessee State University Press, 1965.

Linderman, Gerald F. *Embattled Courage: The Experience of Combat in the American Civil War.* New York: Free Press, 1987.

Madden, David. "Unionist Resistance to Confederate Occupation: The Bridge Burners of East Tennessee." *East Tennessee Historical Society's Publications* 52–53 (1980–81): 22–39.

Martin, Asa Earl. "The Anti-slavery Societies of Tennessee." *Tennessee Historical Magazine* 1 (1915): 261–81.

Marvel, William. *Burnside.* Chapel Hill: University of North Carolina Press, 1991.

Mathews, Donald G. *Religion in the Old South.* Chicago: University of Chicago Press, 1977.

McBride, Robert M., ed. *Biographical Directory of the Tennessee General Assembly.* Nashville: Tennessee Historical Commission, 1975.

McBride, William Gillespie. "Blacks and the Race Issue in Tennessee Politics, 1865–1876." Ph.D. diss., Vanderbilt University, 1989.

McKee, James W., Jr. "Felix K. Zollicoffer: Confederate Defender of East Tennessee," pt. 1. *East Tennessee Historical Society's Publications* 43 (1971): 34–58.

McKenzie, Robert Tracy. *One South or Many? Plantation Belt and Upcountry in Civil War–Era Tennessee.* New York: Cambridge University Press, 1994.

———. "Rediscovering the 'Farmless' Farm Population: The Nineteenth-Century Census and the Postbellum Reorganization of Agriculture in the U.S. South, 1860–1900." *Histoire Sociale* 28 (1995): 501–20.

———. "Wealth and Income: The Preindustrial Structure of East Tennessee in 1860." *Appalachian Journal* 21 (1994): 260–79.

McKinney, Gordon B. *Southern Mountain Republicans, 1865–1900.* Chapel Hill: University of North Carolina Press, 1978.

McKitrick, Eric L. *Andrew Johnson and Reconstruction.* Chicago: University of Chicago Press, 1960.

McPherson, James M. *Battle Cry of Freedom: The Civil War Era.* New York: Oxford University Press, 1988.

———. *For Cause and Comrades: Why Men Fought in the Civil War.* New York: Oxford University Press, 1997.

———. *Ordeal by Fire: The Civil War and Reconstruction.* 2nd ed. New York: McGraw-Hill, 1992.

———. *What They Fought For, 1861–1865.* Baton Rouge: Louisiana State University Press, 1994.

Moulder, Rebecca Hunt. *May the Sod Rest Lightly.* Tucson, AZ: Skyline Printing Company, 1977.

Neal, John Randolph. *Disunion and Restoration in Tennessee.* New York: Knickerbocker Press, 1899.

Needham, Joseph Wade. "Oliver Perry Temple: Entrepreneur, Agrarian, and Politician." Ph.D. diss., University of Tennessee, 1990.

Neely, Mark E., Jr. *Southern Rights: Political Prisoners and the Myth of Confederate Constitutionalism.* Charlottesville: University Press of Virginia, 1999.

Nevins, Allan. *The War for the Union: The Improvised War, 1861–1862.* New York: Scribner's, 1959.

Noe, Kenneth W. *Perryville: This Grand Havoc of Battle.* Lexington: University Press of Kentucky, 2001.

———. *Southwest Virginia's Railroad: Modernization and the Sectional Crisis.* Urbana: University of Illinois Press, 1994.

Noe, Kenneth W., and Shannon H. Wilson, eds. *The Civil War in Appalachia: Collected Essays.* Knoxville: University of Tennessee Press, 1997.

Parks, Joseph Howard. "John Bell and Secession." *East Tennessee Historical Society's Publications* 16 (1944): 30–47.

———. *John Bell of Tennessee.* Baton Rouge: Louisiana State University Press, 1950.

Patton, James Welch. *Unionism and Reconstruction in Tennessee.* Chapel Hill: University of North Carolina Press, 1934.

Pessen, Edward. *Riches, Class, and Power before the Civil War.* Lexington, MA: D. C. Heath, 1973.

Phillips, Ulrich Bonnell. *A History of Transportation in the Eastern Cotton Belt to 1860.* New York: Columbia University Press, 1908.

Potter, David M. *The Impending Crisis: 1848–1861.* New York: Harper and Row, 1976.

———. *The South and the Sectional Conflict.* Baton Rouge: Louisiana State University Press, 1968.

Price, R. N. "William G. Brownlow and His Times." Chap. 14 of *Holston Methodism: From Its Origin to the Present Time.* Nashville and Dallas: Publishing House of the Methodist Episcopal Church, 1908.

Prindle, Paul W., comp. *Ancestry of William Sperry Beinecke.* North Haven, CT: Van Dyck Printing, 1974.

Queener, Verton M. "The Origin of the Republican Party in East Tennessee." *East Tennessee Historical Society's Publications* 13 (1941): 66–90.

———. "A Decade of East Tennessee Republicanism, 1867–1876." *East Tennessee Historical Society's Publications* 14 (1942): 58–85.

Rable, George C. *The Confederate Republic: A Revolution against Politics.* Chapel Hill: University of North Carolina Press, 1994.

Roark, James L. *Masters without Slaves: Southern Planters in the Civil War and Reconstruction*. New York: Norton, 1977.

Robinson, William M., Jr. *Justice in Grey: A History of the Judicial System of the Confederate States of America*. Cambridge, MA: Harvard University Press, 1941.

Rothrock, Mary U., ed. *French Broad–Holston Country: A History of Knox County, Tennessee*. Knoxville: East Tennessee Historical Society, 1946.

Rule, William, ed. *Standard History of Knoxville, Tennessee*. Chicago: Lewis Publishing Company, 1900.

Severance, Ben H. *Tennessee's Radical Army: The State Guard and Its Role in Reconstruction, 1867–1869*. Knoxville: University of Tennessee Press, 2005.

Seymour, Digby Gordon. *Divided Loyalties: Fort Sanders and the Civil War in East Tennessee*. Rev. ed. Knoxville: East Tennessee Historical Society, 1982.

Shaffer, John W. *Clash of Loyalties: A Border County in the Civil War*. Morgantown: West Virginia University Press, 2003.

Shapiro, Henry D. *Appalachia on Our Mind: The Southern Mountains and Mountaineers in the American Consciousness, 1870–1920*. Chapel Hill: University of North Carolina Press, 1978.

Sifakis, Stewart. *Compendium of the Confederate Armies: Tennessee*. New York: Facts on File, 1992.

Silber, Nina. *The Romance of Reunion: Northerners and the South, 1865–1900*. Chapel Hill: University of North Carolina Press, 1993.

Snay, Mitchell. *Gospel of Disunion: Religion and Separatism in the Antebellum South*. Chapel Hill: University of North Carolina Press, 1993.

Speer, William S. *Sketches of Prominent Tennesseans*. Nashville: Albert B. Tavel, 1888.

Stern, Madeleine B. *Purple Passage: The Life of Mrs. Frank Leslie*. Norman: University of Oklahoma Press, 1953.

Sutherland, Daniel. *Seasons of War: The Ordeal of a Confederate Community*. New York: Free Press, 1995.

Tennesseans in the Civil War: A Military History of Confederate and Union Units with Available Rosters of Personnel. 2 parts. Nashville: Civil War Centennial Commission, 1964.

Wakelyn, Jon L., ed. *Southern Unionist Pamphlets and the Civil War*. Columbia: University of Missouri Press, 1999.

Watson, Harry L. *Jacksonian Politics and Community Conflict: The Emergence of the Second Party System in Cumberland County, North Carolina*. Baton Rouge: Louisiana State University Press, 1981.

Wert, Jeffry D. *General James Longstreet: The Confederacy's Most Controversial Soldier—A Biography*. New York: Simon and Schuster, 1993.

Williams, David. *Rich Man's War: Class, Caste, and Confederate Defeat in the Lower Chattahoochie Valley*. Athens: University of Georgia Press, 1998.

Winters, Donald L. *Tennessee Farming, Tennessee Farmers: Antebellum Agriculture in the Upper South*. Knoxville: University of Tennessee Press, 1994.

Woodward, C. Vann. *Origins of the New South, 1877–1913*. Baton Rouge: Louisiana State University Press, 1951.

INDEX

Abingdon, Virginia, 182
Alexander, Porter, 166, 168, 171, 269 n. 64
Alien Enemies Act, 93, 94
Alley, Isham, 216
American Colonization Society, 34
Appalachia, 4, 5
Armstrong, Robert, 168
Army of Northern Virginia, 154
Army of Tennessee, 152, 154, 156, 170
Army of the Cumberland, 123, 145, 152, 154–55, 189
Army of the Ohio: advance on Knoxville, 147–50; arrival of in Knoxville, 7, 142, 150, 196; food shortages in, 162; impact of on slavery, 185–86, 198; and Knoxville civilians, 176–78; leadership of, 156–57
Army of the Potomac, 155, 157
Arnell, Samuel, 239 n. 7
Atkins, Samuel T., 211, 220
Ault, Henry, 211

Baker, Abner, 217–19, 221, 223
Baker, Harvey, 217–18
Baker, William J., 56, 73
Bank of East Tennessee, 25, 88
Baxter, John: ambivalent behavior of during Confederate occupation of Knoxville, 135–37, 191; and arrival of Federal troops, 178; as candidate for Confederate congress, 98,

136; condemnation of by William McAdoo, 95; on emancipation, 191; and first statewide secession referendum, 58; and letter to General Zollicoffer, 96; as McClellan Democrat, 192; as moderate delegate to East Tennessee Union Convention, 82; publication of *East Tennessean* by, 136; role of in securing Parson Brownlow's release, 106, 108; and second statewide referendum, 80; support of "cooperationist" strategy by, 56, 57; and support of local Confederates' applications for pardon, 203; wealth of, 206
Bell, John, 27, 32, 44, 45, 50
Bell House Hotel, 85, 103
Benjamin, Judah, 101, 106, 107, 108
Benjamin, Samuel, 169–70
Blair, A. A., 117
Bokum, Hermann, 61
Bolli, Elisa, 173, 175–76, 215
Bolli, Emmanuel, 118
Boyd, Isabella, 176
Boyd, John M., 211
Boyd, Sam B., 118
Bradfield, George, 53
Bradley, William, 185
Bragg, Braxton, 115, 145, 147, 154–57
Branner, George M., 211
Branner, John R., 119, 134, 202